Symposium on

LAND ECONOMICS RESEARCH

Symposium on

LAND ECONOMICS
RESEARCH, *Lincoln, Neb., 1961.*

Papers presented at a symposium held
at Lincoln, Nebraska, June 16-23, 1961, under
the joint sponsorship of

FARM FOUNDATION
RESOURCES FOR THE FUTURE, INC.

Edited by

Joseph Ackerman, Marion Clawson, and Marshall Harris

RESOURCES FOR THE FUTURE, INC.
1775 Massachusetts Avenue, N. W., Washington 6, D. C.

Distributed by
The Johns Hopkins Press, Baltimore 18, Md.

RESOURCES FOR THE FUTURE, INC.

1775 MASSACHUSETTS AVENUE, N.W., WASHINGTON 6, D. C.

Resources for the Future is a nonprofit corporation for research and education in the development, conservation, and use of natural resources. It was established in 1952 with the co-operation of The Ford Foundation and its activities since then have been financed by grants from that Foundation. Part of the work of Resources for the Future is carried out by its resident staff; part supported by grants to universities and other nonprofit organizations. Unless otherwise stated, interpretations and conclusions in RFF publications are those of the authors; the organization takes responsibility for the selection of significant subjects for study, the competence of the researchers, and their freedom of inquiry.

Preface

The purpose of this book, and the symposium which preceded it, is to present ideas, theories, and suggestions for research in land economics. It is hoped thereby to advance professional thinking in this general field and to stimulate and guide land economics research for the next decade or two in dealing more effectively with significant land problems.

The scope is intentionally broad. All physical types of land, all major uses of land, all land tenure situations, and all types of professional inquiry in or closely related to economics are included. Most of those participating have had a major part of their professional experience in agricultural study, and this book originated from agricultural beginnings. In spite of our best efforts, our origins and earlier interests may still weigh too heavily in the final product. Land problems have perhaps been studied more intensively by agricultural economists than by any other single professional group, and certainly many land problems lie in or close to agriculture. Nevertheless, the participants in this project have done their best to make the approach as broad and as eclectic as possible.

The audience for which this book has been written is primarily a professional one, and an American one. The authors are talking to their fellow economists in universities and in government. But they hope they also have something to say to sociologists, political scientists, lawyers, urban and regional planners, and other professional workers in universities, in government, and in quasi-public and private corporations who are concerned with land use and land institutions. Possibly the most important audience of all will be students.

While these papers are directed primarily to the American scene and an American audience, they may also have some value to students and others in foreign countries, providing ideas for research and an understanding of the American scene. Many American land problems are peculiar to our country, and research regarding them must necessarily have its special characteristics. Other problems are highly similar in various countries, and research methods, in general, have a high degree of universality.

History of This Project

The project which resulted in this book had its origin in the work of the regional land tenure research committees of the land-grant colleges, the U.S. Department of Agriculture, and the Farm Foundation. The four regional committees in the Southeast, Southwest, Great Plains, and North Central regions, formed an Interregional Committee, which sponsored six workshops on research methods between 1945 and 1956. In 1955 a report, Agricultural

Land Tenure Research, Scope and Nature: Reappraisal, 1955 was prepared and released. These committees have necessarily been concerned
primarily with agricultural problems, although these when interpreted
broadly have included other land uses as well.

By 1959, the Interregional Committee felt the need for a re-examination of land economics research. Much work considered by the Regional
Committees, or in this general field, was somewhat broader in interest
than land tenure alone. Moreover, the problems of land for uses other
than agriculture loomed large in the Committee's thinking. In addition,
it seemed desirable to bring in some scholars not closely identified with
the agricultural colleges, and perhaps at the same time not to include all
agricultural colleges simply because of the size of the group thus required,
and the fact that incisive symposia discussions usually fare better in
smaller groups.

Accordingly, in early 1960 the Farm Foundation and Resources for
the Future jointly agreed to sponsor a symposium on land economics
research and to publish the papers presented. The earlier work of the
Interregional Committee was taken as a starting point. A committee con-
sisting of Marshall Harris (Agricultural Research Service), Joseph
Ackerman (Farm Foundation), and Marion Clawson (Resources for the
Future), with the help of several others at different times, developed an
outline for the symposium, invited participants, and generally organized
the project. Invitations were issued in the spring of 1960, and commit-
ments for most papers were made then. On August 10, 1960, most of the
participants met at Ames, Iowa, in a pre-symposium conference. For
that meeting, most had prepared simple preliminary outlines, and all had
considered in a preliminary way what their paper might include. Time
permitted only a limited discussion of each topic, but this conference did
help greatly in the later preparation of the various papers.

From June 16 to 23, 1961, inclusive, a symposium of the authors of
papers and a few others was held at the University of Nebraska. Those in
attendance included Joseph Ackerman, Herman G. Berkman, Marion
Clawson, Mason Gaffney, W. L. Gibson, Jr., Marshall Harris, Roy E.
Huffman, Glenn L. Johnson, Maurice M. Kelso, Charles William Loomer,
Walter G. Miller, Howard W. Ottoson, Harry A. Steele, John F. Timmons,
Louis B. Wetmore, Aaron Wildavsky, Gene Wunderlich, and James G.
Yoho. Members of the staff of the University of Nebraska also participated
in some of the discussions. Invited to the symposium, but unable to attend,
were Carl M. Bogholt, L. I. Hewes, Jr., B. H. Kristjanson, John C.
O'Byrne, Kenneth H. Parsons, Rainer Schickele, and Coleman Woodbury.
Preliminary drafts of papers were circulated in advance of the symposium.
Each of the fifteen papers included herein was the subject of a half-day discussion. In general, the discussions helped to make the final papers
clearer and stronger.

Each paper in this book is the work of one or (in a few cases) two men.
He or they alone decided what to include and what to exclude, and what emphasis to give. The sponsors of the project sought to outline a series of
papers which, taken together, would have a certain logical order and coverage and which would mutually reinforce and supplement each other. Authors
were urged to strive for clarity, but agreement was not insisted upon -- on
the contrary, authors were urged to make clear their differences in viewpoint. Correspondence between authors and the discussions at the symposium have resulted in modifications of papers from those originally con-

ceived; the need for inclusion of additional material or ideas, for restatements in the interests of clarity, and other reasons have underlain these revisions. The participants as a group have gained enormously from the opportunity of trying out their ideas on their colleagues. But, in the end, each chapter is exactly as its signed author decided it should be.

Land

Since the focus of this book is on land economics research, it might appear obvious to begin by defining land. However, this is neither easy nor, perhaps, necessary. Many definitions of land are possible; none is invariably right, and others wrong; each has value in certain contexts or for certain purposes. At the minimum, land is space, or earth's surface, including such almost immutable qualities as climate, geology, and relationship in space to other land resources. This definition may well be expanded to include water, which is naturally associated with land. Soil fertility may be included for some purposes, excluded for others; and so also for minerals, air above the surface, and for such biological superstructure as forests and grasses which occur without regard to or in spite of man's efforts. A researcher, dealing with a particular problem, may wish to include some but not all of these elements; so may the public official or politician. A study of suburban land development might ignore minerals, if available information indicates no valuable minerals exist, for instance; or a study of grazing land tenure might well ignore air pollution and utilization problems. As long as the definition is clear, explicitly or implicitly, there is no need to insist upon a single "right" definition. In this book, each author has been allowed to define land as he chose, either in explicit terms or implicitly by the scope of his discussion.

The authors of this book, like any scholars studying the use of natural resources, are impressed with the interrelationships between Man and his environment -- what may inclusively be termed "Nature". Man operates within physical and economic limits imposed by Nature, yet he also affects Nature, and on an increasing scale. He uses the various aspects of his environment in ways conditioned or limited by his own technology, to his own ends; and in the process he changes that environment, sometimes substantially. By fire, plow, and other devices man has changed his environment in past centuries, and today has at his command tools of infinitely greater effectiveness. Over the centuries Man has eliminated all the larger animals that do not serve his needs, and he wages constant warfare with much of the insect world. He has materially modified the vegetative cover of the earth, through his cutting of forests, grazing of animals, and cultivation of cropland. Erosion has substantially changed some soils and affected soil-water relationships. Man has changed his biological and other environment materially in some areas, often in ways widely considered as unfavorable to his own future; in still larger ways he has discovered or invented new methods of using other parts of his environment to his own greater advantage. The vastly larger numbers and longer average life span of Man is ample biological evidence that his environment plus technology has improved, not worsened, on balance over the past perhaps three centuries. Nevertheless, Man in the United States as elsewhere must be constantly aware of the condition and trend of his environment, in total and in major parts. The United States is one of those few highly fortunate nations in which no serious resource shortage seriously restricts us today or threatens to do so in the foreseeable future. We have built a society and economy in which a particular resource base serves to support an ever larger superstructure of goods and services aimed at our welfare and comfort. Our total economy has a smaller and smaller resource content, relatively speaking, as we add more and more fabrication and refinement to the goods and services we develop from it; and yet resources are as basic, perhaps more so, to the total output as they ever were in this country or as they are today in less developed economies.

One last general remark should be made about land and its uses. In this book and in writings generally, reference is often made to land uses in a way that may lead some readers to infer that each use of land is a separate matter. In fact, the uses of land are often highly interrelated, sometimes actually on the same tract of land, or potentially so, sometimes as between separate tracts which are used in a complex pattern of production or consumption to supplement each other. Land uses often have physical, economic, and institutional interrelationships. For convenience sake, we may refer to each use separately or in turn, but this should not lead us astray as to the possibility of interrelationship in usage.

Philosophy and Viewpoint[1]

The viewpoint and philosophy of a writer or a group of writers is more significantly expressed in the material included, the omissions, the emphasis, the organization of material, the unconscious (and possibly unknown) assumptions, and many other aspects of writing than in statements regarding viewpoint and philosophy. Writings are more revealing than discussions about writings. Nevertheless, it seems useful at this point to give the reader some intimation of what the authors had in mind. As a group of scholars with different backgrounds and interests, the contributors to this book naturally hold different views on many matters and choose different means of expressing their views. The summary here is only a general statement, not completely binding upon each author, and distinctly subordinate to ideas expressed later in the separate chapters.

The American culture has been and is a pragmatic one, in the sense that it has proven highly adaptable to meet significant problems as they arose, without too much inhibition from previous philosophic and theoretical viewpoints. Currently, for instance, in the United States there is great insistance of the importance, not to say dominance, of the free private enterprise system of economy. Yet the nation as a whole, and often those individuals most vociferous in support of free private enterprise, have turned to social and governmental action to solve problems difficult or impossible for individuals or groups to solve unaided. The result is that in fact we have a highly diverse and mixed society and economy, with large room for the individual to exercise his talents and to reap his rewards, but with major activities by the larger society. Examples of this intermixture of private and group action are numerous in the agricultural and resource field, and need not be recited in detail to readers of this book. The authors of this book regard this flexibility and pragmatism of the American culture as a great advantage and strength; but, even if they disapproved of it, its existence would have to be recognized.

---

[1]In particular, see Chapter 3, "Objectives of Land Economics Research," by John F. Timmons.

But underlying this flexibility and pragmatism are certain broad goals and values, widely and strongly held, and usually governing as to the form of specific action. Ours is a society that places great value upon the freedom and worth of the individual and his rights and opportunities. It is to a large degree, an open society, with opportunity for personal and material achievement open to all. We lay stress upon personal competence and personal achievement, and not upon inherited position and rights. As with any system of values and aspirations, the reality is less than the ideal, and in some instances we have fallen far short of what we sought.

In the area of land ownership and control, we have rejected the idea of a landed aristocracy and have glorified the owner-cultivator tilling his own farm. Yet in point of fact we have had, at least at times and in localities, something closely akin to a landed aristocracy. Local government and local social institutions have often been, and sometimes yet are, in the effective control of local major landowners. Basic factors in the operation of our land system were the free public lands in earlier decades and the opportunities for urban employment in later decades. One dissatisfied with the local land situation was not tied irrevocably to it; while movement was often costly in financial as well as in human terms, escape was not only possible but relatively easy.

The American genius for evolution, compromise, adjustment, and invention has perhaps been nowhere better expressed than in the history of our land and resource policies and programs, and in the institutions for carrying out programs in these fields. This is no place for a history of American experience, but a few examples may be helpful. In the Colonial period, we strove mightily to secure fee simple title for land, abolishing primogeniture, entails, and all the other restrictions of European land-ownership of that and earlier periods. While to a large extent we borrowed our ideas from other countries, we pushed them to a degree and at a rate not elsewhere experienced at that time. Students of land use may argue that, in the reaction against earlier restrictions, we went too far in giving the individual complete control over his land; and in fact in recent decades we have reimposed social restrictions on land use, although of a wholly different kind than existed earlier. At a somewhat later period, we freed the corporation of its detailed governmental restrictions, making possible the timeless, impersonal, ubiquitous instrument of economic activity which we know today.

A major expression of inventiveness and innovation in the political field was the evolution of the federal system of government. Jealous of their rights, the individual states after independence were unwilling to surrender all such rights to any central government; yet the need for something more than a loose federation was evident. At the same time, difficulties of transportation and communication made it necessary to solve as much of total governmental problems at the local level as possible. The result was a federal government with certain major powers, state governments with other powers and responsibilities, and various city, county, and township governments to deal with local problems. The relationships between government at these different levels has changed greatly over the decades as the country has grown and the responsibilities of government have changed; a great virtue of our system of government has been that major changes in methods of operation could occur within the framework of the basic constitutional and other documents. The federal government in recent decades has entered into activities of a kind and scale undreamt

of by the founding fathers, yet possible within the framework they established.

As far as land tenure research is concerned, the states generally play
a far more influential role than does the federal government. State and
local rather than federal legislation deals with real estate taxes, tenancy,
land use regulations, local districts, and the like.

Unique American institutions of direct importance in the land field
have been the system of free public education and that of the land-grant
colleges. In many states, it was ownership of public land, often secured
by grant from higher levels of government, which made possible the first
free public schools. The land-grant college system has embodied research, resident teaching, and extension; much of the funds have come
from actual land grants, and much more by federal grants-in-aid. The
result has been a highly flexible system, operative at federal, state, and
local levels, to develop new knowledge and to disseminate that which
existed. No small part of the recent and current agricultural revolution
stems from this institution.

In the past several decades, we have innovated a number of direct
land programs. On the one hand, there has been the development of
permanent public landownership in the national forests, national parks,
wildlife refuges, and other federal areas, as well as in state and sometimes county counterparts, until today over a third of our total land area
is thus owned. Another direction has been federal financial and other
support of resource programs, especially in water development and use,
and in soil conservation. Still another direction has been the rise of the
local district, as a unit of local government operating under delegated
powers, for irrigation, drainage, soil conservation, or other land programs. Publicly-sponsored agricultural credit, electric power through
public help, and other governmental programs have influenced land use.

In these and other ways the American society and economy have shown
considerable flexibility, adaptability, and inventiveness to meet new problems in the fields of land and other resource use. Concurrently, and
sometimes to a more powerful degree, technological change, often
induced by expenditures of public funds, has greatly affected land and the
institutions concerned with it. The agricultural revolution has been mentioned. Other changes are apparent. We have been in a continuous process of change, of adaptability to new techniques; no single innovation
ran its full course because new technological innovation arose before adjustment was complete. Changes in transportation methods, times, and
costs have added their share to the economic and social revolution, especially in recent decades. As a result, the location factor inherent in land
has perhaps become less important, as regards more distant land and
people. And on top of all these changes within the American economy and
society, the last generation has seen a complete reversal of American
relationship to the larger world, from one of isolation and pride in our
ability to stay out of foreign entanglements, to one of free world leadership.

Throughout these many changes, only imperfectly hinted at here, the
institutional framework of the United States in general and as related to
land in particular, has changed as new situations have developed. Change
has sometimes been slow, perhaps not as rational as one would desire,
but nevertheless change has occurred. There is no reason to think
changes will not occur in the future, as the need arises. The authors of

these papers therefore take as basic to their thinking the idea of change --
change consciously directed to serve man's ends. We do not accept any
present institution as irrevocably fixed; although some can be changed more
easily than others. We do not advocate change merely for the sake of
change, but change to meet present and prospective problems. Present
institutions and arrangements are the starting point from which changes
for the future must be measured. We study the past and present to obtain knowledge and ideas that will help to solve present and future problems. But we always have in mind that invention is possible and may be
desirable in institutional and social arrangements no less than in physical
and technological ones.

Perhaps another way of making the same general point is to emphasize
that the authors have a strong belief in the applicability of knowledge to the
solution of man's problems, belief that man has at least some degree of
control over his destiny, and belief in the possibility of rational choice.
We assume that facts and their interrelationships are significant, discover-
able, and useful. Choices are often made without full knowledge of all
ascertainable facts and possibilities; and under any circumstances there
are many imponderables relating to the future which no one can know. But
we believe that in our modern society choice is not blind and may be better
informed and more rational than it often is.

Land Economics Research

Just as "land" may properly be defined variously, depending upon the
purpose at hand, so may land economics research be defined in different
ways, and in fact that has been done in this book. Some may focus upon
the approaches, the theory, or the tools by which such research is advanced; others may focus upon the problems at which the research is aimed.
In some cases, the primary purpose of research is simply knowledge for
its own sake -- knowing for the sake of knowing. Over the past, land
economics research has changed its focus, as the second chapter will
bring out. Yet a fairly basic core of concerns, approaches, and methods
is apparent throughout; it is the specific problems which have changed from
one period to another. For example, in the early 1930's, tax delinquency
was a problem of widespread occurrence about which much concern was
expressed, and as a consequence much research was directed toward it.
Today, this is not a serious problem in any large area, and as a consequence, little research is concerned with it.

The authors of this book consider it possible to study, and even to define, land problems in many different ways. This is true of strictly
"economic" problems, and even more so of problems which recognize none
of the neat but artificial boundaries man has used to divide his knowledge.
The same general situation may be approached by one or more of several
avenues. None of these avenues may be "best" in the sense that it alone
will produce a satisfactory answer, or even demonstrably better answer.
The really difficult problems may require an approach from more than one
direction for their adequate solution. These problems usually lie at the
crossroads of two or more formal disciplines, not neatly within any single
one. This may be true even within economics. This is one reason why
separate essays in this book approach land problems from different theoretical backgrounds.

Many problems affecting land require study from directions other than economics, as that is usually defined. Sociology, political science, law, and other disciplines may have much to contribute, and may be necessary to arrive at a workable practical program. Studies of the more important, stubborn, and difficult problems may need to be taken from several viewpoints. This may be done by single scholars with broad viewpoints, by several scholars working separately with varying degrees of co-ordination, or by a "team approach." The mechanics of bringing different scholars together on a single major problem are important; some consideration is given to them in this book. Of perhaps greater importance, however, is the attitude implicit in the foregoing sentences. What is needed is not mere tolerance for other disciplines, but a positive recognition of the virtues of work that one may not fully understand.

The United States in a Larger World

The authors of this book are mindful of the fact that the United States exists, and always has existed, as part of a larger world.[2] This country inherited a great deal of its culture from Europe, and to a lesser extent from other continents. We have drawn on those other cultures, accepting part and rejecting part. Our concepts of land tenure, in particular, drew heavily upon emerging British ideas of the same general period, while at the same time our forefathers rejected many existing British land arrangements. There has been a continuous interaction between ideas and practices in this country and those in the older countries from which most of our settlers originally came; often the extent and nature of this interaction has not been fully realized in this country.

The possibilities of learning from experience elsewhere are not all in the past; in the future we may learn much from a study of conditions in other countries. A relatively open country, much unsettled in earlier periods and yet used at a comparatively low intensity, has been a major feature of American history. Many older countries, especially some in western Europe, with generally similar institutions and cultural values, have long since had to face a degree of crowding upon the land that we are just now contemplating for the decades ahead. We might well study how they have met the serious problems that intensive settlement brings, not only the physical and land use arrangements they have evolved, but the institutional arrangements also.

The United States may well contribute to solution of vexing land problems in other countries, but our contribution will generally not take the form of trying to encourage the unchanged transfer of our experience and our institutions. Other countries may gain more from a knowledge of our use of scientific method in the study of our problems, and from application of our philosophy of adaptability of institutions to meet needs and desires. We may offer help, but we can hardly expect to guide and determine.

As pointed out earlier, this book is aimed primarily at an American audience. But it is hoped that it will reflect an awareness of the fact we live in a larger world, from which we may learn and to which we may offer help.

---

[2]One specific expression of this is Chapter 6, "Land Economics Research for World Agricultural Development," by Rainer Schickele.

The Symposium in Retrospect

A symposium such as this is not the final word on a subject, but only one step in the development of ideas and concepts. What follows here is not a full-scale evaluation of the symposium, but rather some comments that may be valuable to the readers of this book and to others who may want to carry further the type of discussions undertaken here.

The discussions were stimulating and provocative. The men who prepared these papers are mature scholars, who have ideas and viewpoints developed and matured over years of study and independent research. Such men do not easily give up old, tested ideas, nor do they quickly adopt new and attractive suggestions. They came with viewpoints and left with most of them intact. Yet it is also true that men of this type are constantly on the alert to test their old ideas and to acquire new ones. While no direct measurement is possible, it seems probable that no one left the symposium exactly as he entered it. By exposing his ideas to the scrutiny of his peers, and by in turn examining their ideas with care, he certainly had the opportunity to test, refine, and adapt his thinking. Unfortunately, the spirit and the scope of these discussions can be captured only imperfectly for those not present. The essays in this book reflect, to some degree, the discussions. Only brief, topical notes were taken at the symposium, and these are unsuitable for reproduction to a wider audience. Complete transcripts would have been unusable also, largely because of the informality and unorganized nature of the discussions. The results of the symposium, beyond this book, will thus perhaps show up primarily in the future research and writings of the symposium participants.

The symposium revealed that some subjects had been omitted or underemphasized in the program. Some parts of economic theory were not included, specifically: welfare theory, monetary theory, transportation theory, and some parts of the theory relating to distribution of economic benefits. Some disciplines closely allied to economics were not represented, or were under-represented: sociology, political economy, law, geography, perhaps others. The personnel problems of land economics research were considered only incidentally. The need for research workers, how to train the young men who wish to work in this field, how to develop further the mature research workers -- these important subjects were hardly considered at all. There was no explicit consideration of the data problem for land economics research. It had originally been planned to include this in the symposium, but it had not proven practical to get such a paper prepared. Advanced, imaginative research requires data for its success; and the researcher has an obligation to outline his needs to the data gatherer. Some aspects of land were considered hardly at all -- minerals, air, and to a lesser degree water, received little attention.

In thus outlining some of the possible omissions from the symposium, it is not meant that all these matters should have been included. After all, there is a very real limit to what can be, or should be, covered in a single symposium. As it was, the symposium took more than a week of concentrated intellectual effort by a diverse group of busy people. Had it included more subject matter or a wider range of participation, it might well have been nearly unmanageable.

As pointed out earlier, this symposium had an agricultural origin. Some authors of essays were chosen to broaden this base. In addition persons of generally different backgrounds were invited to participate in the symposium itself. Those present benefited greatly from such people; but, unfortunately, all those invited were not able to attend, and the symposium was still heavily agricultural economics. Urban planners, urban land economists, recreation specialists, forest economists, and transportation specialists were either absent or underrepresented, as were specialists in other disciplines noted above. It should not be inferred that all groups should be fully represented in roughly equal numbers. This might well make too large and too unwieldy a group. It is possible, however, that a somewhat different representation would be desirable in future symposia, if any are held.

Even within the group participating at the symposium, it was clear that more than one way exists for fruitful research on many land economics problems. It is altogether possible that there is no one best way to attack all such problems, or perhaps even to attack any single problem. In many cases, a combination of methods of inquiry has much to recommend it. The use of more and different methods obviously imposes greater burdens on the research man or team, but it may also help avoid partial or incomplete findings. Anyone who participated in the symposium could not help but realize anew the dangers of overconfidence in his own research, in the assumption that he had final and complete answers to what are usually difficult and complex problems. Again and again it was brought out that knowledge is relative to time, place, and past knowledge. The definition that a fact "is an opinion not now in dispute" perhaps summarizes a healthy attitude of the researcher toward his own and other research.

The symposium demonstrated forcefully the need for research that deals with the problems of the future. There was general agreement among the symposium participants that the future will differ from the past in many significant ways, technological, social, and economic. There was a consensus that researchers should not study only what has happened in the past or what exists today. Several of those present emphasized that the researcher must face the new situations of the future and that he must be inventive, not merely analytical of what he finds in the world about him. The agricultural land economist in particular must re-examine his role as a researcher. The problems of agriculture are changing greatly; perhaps more significantly, land problems associated with urban, recreation, forestry, and other land uses are looming larger, relative to agricultural land use, than they have in the past. These new problems have many points of similarity with agricultural land problems of the past, but they also have important differences. The problems include not only land use, but also land tenure, as far as these other uses are concerned. There will be many challenging land problems outside agriculture on which the skills of the agricultural land economist can be particularly effective.

If this symposium and book are but way stations on the road of progress, where do we go from here? A larger and more nearly inclusive intellectual exchange on land economic problems and research has much to recommend itself. In the dynamic and rapidly changing U. S. economy and society, the use of land and the most suitable land tenures are surely important subjects for study. Land problems are no longer as nearly agricultural as they once were. Several disciplines or groups are attacking land problems from various viewpoints; the present symposium demonstrated clearly that such groups are not in effective intellectual contact with each other. Few problems can be solved in isolation, and few techniques are sufficient unto themselves, yet effective collaboration is often far from easy.

The experience reported here suggests that a future symposium should include a considerably broader range of subject matter. The theoretical and general discussions at this symposium were mostly in broad terms, applicable to any land use; but the illustrations tended to be drawn largely from agriculture. The problems of the city, suburb, and metropolis should perhaps be faced more explicitly; so, perhaps, should the use of land for recreation. Forestry and grazing have their own problems which, though amenable to the same basic analysis, yet have special aspects. It is relatively easy to say that the subject matter should be "broader"; but precisely what should be included, and what omitted? It is impossible to try to treat everything in one symposium; the result would almost surely be a hodgepodge. How to attain breadth and yet retain focus?

The experience at this symposium also suggests that future symposia on land problems should include a wider circle of professional interest groups. The focus here was on economists, although a few others were included. If the concern is on land problems, rather than upon a particular discipline, then a good case can be made for including a wide range of professional talents. But this, too presents its problems. Diversity may lead to a more inclusive final view, but it may also make communication during the process more difficult and time-consuming. If an effort is made to include every group, there is grave danger that the symposium will be too large for effective work, or that diversity will overwhelm achievement. Selectivity is certainly necessary, but who selects the selectors?

The symposium here reported was concerned with land economics research. It was not a place to report research findings nor to consider specific land problems, although each of these entered to some extent. It was rather a consideration of research philosophy, theory, research technique or organization, and program for research. We offer no apologies for this orientation, for we think it was useful. However, another symposium might well be organized on a different basis. For one thing, discussions of research in the abstract tend to become stale, even with specialized researchers; many prefer to deal with more specific situations. The wider the range of diversity in subject matter or in interest of participants, the harder it would be to consider research in the abstract. An alternative might be to focus upon a problem, or a group of problems, of considerable diversity and complexity, on which theory, research methodology, data needs, utilization of results, research organization, and other aspects could all be focused. For instance, in the zone between the city core and a radius 50 miles out are to be found many complex and interrelated problems of urban, suburban, agricultural, transportation, recreation, and forestry land use, and all the tenure problems associated with each. Almost every professional group is working on one aspect or another of these problems; the matter of interrelationships would be near a maximum here. A symposium on this general area might easily bring in all the aspects of land economics research, but focus on a particular situation so as to be more readily understood by men of different backgrounds and interests. Other approaches are possible, of course.

Joseph Ackerman
Marion Clawson
Marshall Harris

Contents

PART III. PROCEDURAL FRAMEWORK

PART IV. PROGRAM AND ORGANIZATION

PART I. SCOPE, PROBLEMS, AND OBJECTIVES

1

Future Land Use and
Tenure Problems Requiring Research

by Marion Clawson*

Research, particularly social science research, is oriented toward the future. Man studies problems with an eye to their solution and, given the time required to do research and to translate it into action, this inevitably means that the problems research can cope with will be those of the future rather than those of the present. In coping with a problem, Man brings to bear on it more than the results of past organized research -- past informal experience, folk lore and tradition, his own personal predilections and hunches, and a vast array of other tools. Yet in the long run he is more dependent upon past research than often he realizes; and as our economy and culture grow more complicated, so must the tools of analysis grow more formal and more sophisticated.

It is true that many scholars study the past, and even the present, insisting they are interested in knowledge for its sake alone, without thought of its direct applicability to current or future "practical" problems. Yet even such scholars seek knowledge of past events and past processes so as to understand better what has happened, and from this to understand better what is happening and may happen in the same or closely related fields. More commonly, research in the social sciences as applied to land and other resource problems is rather directly concerned with applicability to current real life problems. Whether "problem" oriented or organized around particular resources, areas, or methods of research, it often has a high utilitarian content.

Social science research in agricultural and other land problems has mostly been concerned with processes and changes under way but as yet

*MARION CLAWSON has been Director of Land Use and Management Program, Resources for the Future, Inc., Washington, D. C., since 1955. He was born in Elko, Nevada, in 1905; took his undergraduate training at the University of Nevada, holds a Ph. D. in economics from Harvard. He was in the Bureau of Agricultural Economics, United States Department of Agriculture, for 17 years; in the Bureau of Land Management of the Department of the Interior for 6 years, the last 5 as its director. He served as a member of an economic advisory staff to the Government of Israel for two years; he is the author or co-author of several books and many articles in professional journals on various economic subjects.

incomplete. The study of landlord-tenant relationships in a particular
area, for instance, deals with a situation in which there are both landlords and tenants with contractual arrangements between them which are
or may be in process of change to different sets of arrangements.
Research on land matters has typically consisted of studying what is and
how it arose, often carrying the analysis forward into what may be or
what should be in the future. Most such research is pragmatic and utilitarian in method and in purpose; both the individual researcher and the
society which supports him financially want "results" that seem usable.

To emphasize the forward-looking and utilitarian aspects of land research does not argue against theoretical and abstract studies. Sometimes, especially in this relatively advanced society in which we live, the
"roundabout" production process is as productive in social science research as it is in factory production processes. Simple problems may
yield to simple tools, but they hardly deserve the attention of our best
researchers; more complicated problems are likely to demand more
sophisticated approaches, and the basic job of the advanced researcher
may be to fashion concepts and tools which he or others may later apply
to a more direct solution of significant current problems.

With these thoughts in mind, this paper seeks to give some idea of
the land use and tenure problems that research in land economics may be
called upon to solve, or to help solve, over the next decade or two. The
discussion is intended to list some of the main problems, without necessarily including all of them. It certainly cannot give a standard of judgment as to the urgency of research needs in each field and subfield.

DEMAND FACTORS FOR LAND

The economist usually finds it convenient to group social and economic changes under the two broad headings of "demand" and "supply,"
recognizing at the same time that each affects the other to a substantial
degree. We shall employ this usual grouping. Among the many demand
forces affecting land use and tenure, we shall briefly describe four:
population changes, income changes, leisure, and transportation. Others
might be mentioned, but their influence has been either less or similar to
the effect of these four. It is unnecessary for our present purpose to
attempt a quantitative measure of the relative importance of each; we
may suppose that it differs, according to the particular use of land.

The combined effect of these four factors in the past has been a
greatly increased demand for the products or uses of land. The prospects
for the future are that the same factors will further increase the demand
for these same products and uses. This does not necessarily mean an
increase in demand for land as a productive factor. The products and
uses of land are produced not only by land, but also by labor, capital, and
management combined with land. As we shall see in the following section,
supply relationships may change so much as not to increase the demand
for land, although the demand for the products and uses of land is increasing rapidly. Changes in the demand and supply situation are almost sure
to lead to changes in the most desirable land tenure relationships.

Throughout our history, the economy and society of the United States
have been dynamic, subject to change and growth. This dynamism can be

expressed quantitatively in such matters as numbers of the total population, gross national product, and the like; but, perhaps more importantly,
it also finds expression in attitudes toward change and toward life in
general. For the purposes of this book, we need not make precise estimates of future economic and social factors -- to do so might lead us
astray, in focusing on the details and the precise figures of such projections. Instead, we can perhaps better focus on the broad changes under
way, with only some idea of the general magnitudes involved and then
consider what these may mean to researchers. For some types of
research, of course, specific projections or forecasts are basic, and
should be made as carefully as possible.

A major social and economic trend of the past, virtually certain to
continue into the future, has been steady and rather rapid growth in total
population. From less than 4 million at the first Census in 1790, we have
increased to almost 180 million in 1960; two major intermediate landmark
dates and figures are 76 million in 1900 and 151 million in 1950. Between
1950 and 1960 we added almost as many people as were found in the nation
at the time of the Civil War. The drama of immigration from the Old
World to the New and the settlement of the frontier have thrilled both the
serious student and the television fan, but must reluctantly be passed over
here. What is often overlooked is that the rate of population growth
declined steadily and to a major extent from early decades, when it was
about 3 per cent annually, to the decade of the 1930's, when it was not
much over .05 per cent annually. The rate of population growth has since
increased, but not to new highs, as much popular literature states or
suggests, but rather to figures comparable to the period from 1910 to
1930, or about 1.7 per cent annually. The source of growth has largely
shifted from immigration to domestic births; declining death rates and
resulting longevity have been major factors also. The really unusual
aspect of American demographic experience has been the major reversal
in trend of birth rates; downward for a century or more, the rate has
turned upward and possibly stabilized at a new and higher level in the past
20 years.

Barring catastrophic war, total population in the United States will
almost certainly continue to increase for the next generation or longer.
The unpredictable variable will continue to be birth rates. Population
projection has a woeful list of failures to record for the past 30 years or
so.[1] For our present purpose it is not necessary to make a precise projection or forecast for any future date. Estimates of 300 to 325 million
people in the year 2000 have been made and can be logically defended;
estimates for intermediate dates, consistent with these long-run estimates, can also be made. If population growth has some relationship to
the base population at any given date -- as the historical record for
humans in the United States and as experience for other animals seem to
suggest -- then we may expect the annual increase in numbers of persons
to be larger and larger as the years go by, although the annual percentage
increase might remain constant or even decline.

All other factors equal, more people demand more products and uses
from land than do fewer people. The increases in demand may be either

---

[1] For a detailed discussion of this point, and for references to literature, by Marion Clawson,
R. Burnell Held, and Charles H. Stoddard, Land for the Future (Baltimore: Johns Hopkins Press,
1960), Appendix A, pp. 481-94.

more or less than proportionate to the changes in total numbers of people, and they may vary from one product or use to another. All other factors have not remained constant in the past and are unlikely to do so in the future; the effect of other factors may either enhance or moderate the effect of population change upon demand. But population changes of the magnitude we have experienced and of the magnitude that seem imminent for the next generation, must have a major effect upon the demand for the products and uses of land. Moreover, such increases in demand -- such comparative "crowding" -- cannot but have major effect upon land institutions also.

Growth in total numbers of persons is accompanied by a vast geographic redistribution. The westward shift is well known. The weighted center of U.S. population, which in 1790 was 28 miles due east of Baltimore, has moved almost exactly due west along the 39th degree of latitude at an average rate of nearly 40 miles per decade, until in 1960 it was about the center of Illinois. A further westward shift is highly probable; California may shortly become the most populous state. A shift to the southwest and to the southeast is also evident, and probably will continue. On the other hand, relatively large other regions or areas have lost population in the past, and some areas or regions will either lose or gain but little in the future. Population growth rates are highly diverse within our country, and will fall with greatly different impact upon land in different regions.

Accompanying these major regional shifts has been a profound shift from country to city. From a rural nation, we have become an urban one. In 1790, only 5 per cent of the people were urban on the basis of today's definitions; as late as 1910, we were half urban and half rural; today we are two-thirds urban, and by 2000 we will be over 80 per cent urban. These shifts from country to city not only measure a change in the occupational structure of our country, but a profound change in the mode of life. Many of today's urban adults are rural in upbringing, but the younger generation has no such rural background. Many of our social values and much of our governmental structure are based upon this rural origin and dominance and have not yet made the adjustments to our new population pattern. Our land institutions have lagged behind social changes. Future shifts in population will also have heavy differential effects upon demand for land and land use. New institutional arrangements for land and water seem essential to meet the greater urbanization of the future.

Other population changes, such as the rise in numbers of old persons, the changing age distribution generally, and the rise in amount of education, may in specific circumstances affect land use and the institutions governing land use; but an attempt merely to catalogue them here would involve more detail than is necessary.

Another basic economic trend over the past has been the rise in real income per capita. This trend has been less regular than that in total population; depressions and booms have led to widely varying rates of growth, and price fluctuations have concealed or at least partly obscured the changes in real income that have taken place. Nevertheless, over the past 100 years or so the average rate of annual increase in real income per capita seems to have been rather steady, at slightly less than 2 per cent. Since 1850 or thereabouts, when our first reasonably reliable data begin, there has certainly been a profound change in average annual

family income and all that this implies in terms of daily life. A century
ago, most of our people lived on the land, with most of their income going
into the basic necessities of life -- food, shelter, and clothing -- in a
manner not too different from the situation in moderately undeveloped
countries elsewhere in the world today. Perhaps we do not yet have a
fully affluent society, but certainly the lot of the average man in the
United States today represents a near-utopia in the perspective of world
history.

The trend toward higher real incomes per capita will surely continue,
barring catastrophic war. The only real argument will relate to the rate
of growth -- whether it shall be 1 per cent, or 2 per cent, or more annually. These differences in annual growth rate amount to very great
differences in total in a generation, of course. A per capita income in
2000 of roughly double today's level has been estimated by many scholars
in this field. It is not necessary to estimate a rate precisely, for our
purpose, nor to indicate the basis upon which the rate rests.

As average per capita incomes have risen and promise to rise further, it appears that the disparity in incomes among individuals has
narrowed somewhat and may do so further -- at the least, the disparity
in incomes among individuals has not grown greater. As average incomes
have risen, a larger proportion of the average income has been available
for discretionary spending, because the requirements for the basic necessities of life have not increased proportionately.

Past and prospective increases in real income per capita have magni-
fied the demand effects of increased total population. People with more
income to spend demand more products and services from land, not
equally for all land. The income elasticity for the various products and
services of land varies, but for few does it appear negative. As average
per capita incomes rise, we may demand less wheat and a few other
agricultural commodities; but we are likely to demand more beef and
other products capable of being produced on the same land. We shall
almost certainly require much more recreation with high incomes than
low ones. The urban dwellers of the future may demand relatively large
areas of land for both daily living and for recreation, in large part
because they can afford it. The kinds of institutions people will support,
demand, or participate in may also depend in part upon their income
situation.

Among the many other aspects of the total society and economy of the
future, perhaps only two need brief mention at this point. One is the rise
in leisure. Average work week of the working population has decreased
from 70 hours in 1850 to less than 40 hours today; we have cut the work
week from 6 or even 7 days to 5 or fewer days, reduced the typical work-
day from 10 or 12 hours to 8 or fewer hours, and instituted the paid
vacation as a typical privilege of all workers, while at the same time
lengthening its average duration. These trends are likely to continue.
We have estimated total leisure in the year 2000 at more than double what
it was in 1950. The real question is how much future leisure will take the
form of fewer workdays per week, fewer work hours per day, or longer
paid vacations; the consequences for land use, especially for recreation,
are great. There has also been a rise in the numbers and percentage of
persons not in the labor force today, but who would have been there a
generation ago.

The other major trend has been the improvement in means of transportation, the lowering of the real costs of moving persons and goods, and the consequent enormous increase in movement of persons and to a lesser extent of goods, over the past several decades. Not only have costs of transportation declined relative to the average person's ability to pay them, but the speed of transportation has increased greatly, thus making possible major savings in time and opening up activities previously impossible for lack of time. Modern transportation methods are also much more flexible than earlier ones, not requiring such close adherence to established routes of travel. These general changes can be expressed in statistical terms. From roughly 500 miles total travel per capita before the first World War, we have moved upward to roughly 6,000 miles today. The prospect is for further increases in travel in the future.

These changes in cost, ease, and flexibility of travel have had enormous effects upon the demand for land in the past, and will have further effects in the future. (They have also had large effects upon the supply of land, which we will consider in the following section.) Land is peculiarly fixed in location, as every student of land matters realizes. When transportation is costly, slow, and inconvenient, the demand for land is necessarily restricted to locations relatively near at hand; or, the demand for a specific tract depends almost entirely upon economic conditions relatively nearby. Institutions to govern or regulate land use need cope only with such a local demand; landowners and land users are likely to be personally known to one another, and both to live in the same political subdivision. When transportation improves dramatically, as it has in the past 50 years, this situation changes greatly. Now, land at a much greater distance is available to meet demands arising in a particular location; and each tract of land is likely to be exposed to demand from a much wider circle of users. The problems of user and owner meeting and dealing with one another are much more complicated; they are less likely now to live in the same political subdivision. As transportation facilities improve and real costs of transportation decrease, land loses some of its locational rigidity and we come closer to regional and national markets for land.

SUPPLY FACTORS FOR LAND

The area of land is, for practical purposes, fixed; but the supply of products and uses from land is variable, and is subject to economic and social forces. First of all, at any given time, the amount of labor, capital, and management combined with a given area of land may be changed in order to produce a greater output of products and services. Secondly, over a period of time, technology may change so as to produce a larger output of products and services from a fixed area of land, with little or no major change in the other inputs combined with land. Lastly, improved transportation may increase greatly the effective supply of land available to a particular consumer or group of consumers. We shall not consider further the first of these relationships; it involves the production functions well-known to agricultural economists.

Not the least dynamic aspect of the American culture and economy is our use of science and technology. A major part of the massive rise in per capita incomes and a factor basic to the population increase and redistribution has been the application of science and technology to the everyday problems of life and work. The American genius is better adapted, apparently, to the application of science than to pioneering on its purer and more abstract frontiers. We have borrowed heavily from other countries, particularly European ones, not only ideas but also major personalities. In the application of ideas, however, we have been well in the advance. The atomic bomb, for instance, was less a triumph of American science -- for we imported many of the ideas and many of the scientists -- than it was of engineering which permitted theoretical ideas to be translated into operation.

Our very large market, arising in part out of our large territorial expanse with few internal barriers, and in part out of the high incomes of our common people, has lent great encouragement to the application of science and technology through mass production for a mass market.

Science and technology have been applied to agriculture no less than to industry, transportation, business, and other fields. The Land Grant College system and the USDA, each with its threefold program of research, resident teaching, and extension, have been basic and major factors in this agricultural revolution. In more recent decades, commercial producers of insecticides, fertilizers, seeds, and other products, as well as marketers of agricultural products, have also contributed greatly. The results of the application of science and technology to agriculture have been a virtual agricultural revolution; in the past 50 years or so, agricultural output has doubled, from a slightly smaller area of cropland, with a substantially smaller total labor force, and with roughly the same amount (but different kinds) of capital. The agricultural revolution has benefited from industrial developments -- better steel for better farm machinery may be basic to more productive farm machines, for instance. But it has also contributed mightily to general economic growth in its provision of ample food and fiber at generally reasonable prices.

In the past generation or two, science and technology have led to major developments, economic and social, which at an earlier time might have been dreamed of but have seemed unattainable. The radio, the airplane, the private auto, television, atomic energy -- all these today are accepted by the younger generation as "natural," as part of the basic facts of life. Yet each represents a long-held dream of mankind, translated in a few years from dream to common everyday reality. To these major changes apparent to the average citizen must be added scores more, less dramatic and less evident but perhaps equally important. It is not necessary to consider these great inventions and discoveries in detail here. We introduce them only to emphasize the dynamic and changing character of the American economy and culture; changes outside of land may nevertheless affect land use and land institutions in a major way.

At any given time, some technological and scientific changes are under way but have not yet run their full course. Between 1920 and 1950, this was perhaps true for farm mechanization and for the spread of hybrid corn, to use but two examples. During such a period, the innovation is known but not fully tested. Differences of opinion may exist as to its ultimate scope and as to its rate of spread, but within some limits an innovation in process of adoption is predictable both as to timing and as to ultimate effect. On the other hand, changes or innovations that are at a much earlier stage–not yet out of the test tube or onto the drawing board–are unpredictable in any significant sense. In 1900, for instance, the Wright Brothers wanted to fly and were seeking the means to do so;

but they had not yet succeeded in a single flight, let alone a flight of practical utility. The same might have been said of electricity 50 years earlier, or of other major developments even later. Such potential innovations are mere gleams in their promoter's eyes; they may or may not develop on a significant scale.

It seems most probable that at the present date there are both well-started and completely unpredictable technological changes ahead for agriculture. Common farm practice lags behind the best farm practice, and the latter often lags behind the best experiment station ideas, for instance. But beyond these there may well be even more basic changes, now too indefinite for even the ablest specialist to evaluate. Many possibilities have been suggested for some remote future time: substantial weather control or modification, ample and vastly cheaper power from fission, vast modifications of the biological inheritance of our major farm crops and livestock, ready conversion of saline waters, and many others.

Although technological change is perhaps easiest to describe for agricultural land use, it is by no means restricted to it. Major changes have taken place in forestry; the use of Southern pines as a source for pulp, current research into the use of low-grade hardwoods for the same purpose, and many others may be mentioned. Forest genetics is in its infancy, yet holds great promise. Major changes have occurred in grazing use of land -- livestock numbers have substantially increased, yet ranges are in better shape today than a generation ago. Building of dams for flood control, hydro-power production, and other purposes has opened up great new recreational possibilities. Technological change has made available boats, water skis, skin-diving apparatus, and other equipment which has revolutionized water sports. The list of technological change affecting land use is long indeed. As uses have changed, so there has grown pressure for changes in institutions affecting land use.

At this seminar, which is concerned with research methods, philosophy, purposes, and the like, it is not necessary that we attempt to estimate either the form or the consequences of further technological and scientific development. We can assert that major changes will occur, basing this on analogy with the past and perhaps on pure faith as well. Just what the changes will be, where they will be most effective, what their consequences will be, are questions we need not answer here. But it is important to emphasize again that the researcher on land problems does not live in a static world, that he must look beyond the land to ascertain the major forces affecting land use and its institutions.

The effect of improved transportation upon demand for land has been mentioned; it has an equal effect upon the supply of land effectively available. Given the primitive transportation conditions of the pre-railroad era, land lying well away from a stream hardly existed at all in an economic sense, because most of its products could not be transported far to market. The building of the transcontinental railroads opened up vast areas of grain-growing land, thus adding to the effective supply of such land. In more modern times, the development of improved refrigerated transport has opened up fruit and vegetable areas all over the nation, to supply the distant metropolitan centers. A typical city resident now lives in the suburbs, where he finds life more enjoyable, and from which he can commute to and from work by improved transport. The supply of urban land has increased. He can go to relatively distant recreation spots for a day's outing -- areas to which his grandfather could have gone only by trips requiring several days, much cost, and considerable discomfort. The effective supply of recreation areas has thus increased. Location factors are still important in land use, but the effective supply of land has been enormously increased in recent decades; and further major changes in the same direction seem highly probable. There are comparatively few "sheltered" areas in the United States today, and there will be still fewer of them in the future.

PROBABLE FUTURE LAND USE SHIFTS[2]

Given the foregoing general estimate of the shape of the future economy and society in the United States, what is this likely to mean for specific land uses? Most of the general changes will mean increased demand for the products and services of land, yet the total area of all land is fixed. Output of goods and services depends not only on the basic qualities of the land itself but also labor, capital, management, and other current inputs. Most of the increase in demand for products and services from land will be met by more intensive use of land, not by shifts in use, which could meet the demand for any one good or service but obviously not all. Shifts toward greater intensity will, therefore, in general be more important than shifts from one use to another. The great conversions from forest or prairie to cropland which characterized the nineteenth century cannot be repeated, for instance. Yet there will be some shifts from one use to another. Such shifts as do occur in the future are likely to be accompanied by greater stresses and strains than land use shifts in the past; as the competition for land grows keener and various uses become more entrenched on their particular areas, change will be harder to bring about.

One shift, which seems perhaps the most certain of all and on a relative scale a large one, will be the expansion of urban use of land.[3] The area actually used for urban purposes today is apparently less than 10 million acres, although our data are so poor that the margin of error is very wide; the area which urban usage withdraws from other use is much larger -- we estimated it at 17 million acres in 1950. The city typically idles a great deal of land in the form of scattered vacant lots, leapfrogged or engulfed areas, and peripheral areas whose value or price has been bid so high as to make their use for other purposes uneconomic. This idled land is hopefully "ripening" for active urban use, but throughout our history the area of such idled land has been excessive, judged by the actual rate of development.

A rough doubling in total population by 2000 would mean a rough doubling in urban area, however that be measured. At the same time, prospective increases in real income per capita are likely to lead to an even higher demand for urban residential land. Improved transportation technology and shortened workweeks will also stimulate suburban living, with its emphasis on comparatively generous use of land. On the other hand, time and discomfort in commuting conceivably could lead some commuters back into revitalized cities. If total national population grows

---

[2]This section briefly summarizes the main conclusions of Land for the Future, op. cit.

[3]For further discussion of this point, see Chapter 4, "Land Economics Research for Urban and Regional Planning" by Coleman Woodbury.

in anything like the fashion now generally expected by all social scientists, and if most of the net growth is in cities or other urban area, then both the area used and the area withdrawn for urban use will expand. Our estimate is that 30 million acres will be withdrawn from other uses by 1980 and 41 million acres by 2000. These estimates are based upon an assumption of city form and type much like that at present, with only modest changes that seem clearly evident from past trends. It would be entirely possible to achieve the necessary expansion of city population on a very much smaller area of land, if rational planning and the necessary effectuating institutions were available; this would accomplish truly major savings in capital and operating costs, as well as in land. However, the prospects of achieving such economies do not appear bright.

The expansion of urban areas has attracted a good deal of attention since the war. Where such conversion takes place, it is about as complete and dramatic a change in land use as any that this nation experiences; it is also a permanent one, so far as present generations are concerned. Many persons have expressed concern at the loss of good agricultural land to such urban expansion. Not all of the added urban areas have been on cropland; some have been on forest, grazing, or idle land. Total urban area today is roughly 1 per cent of total land area, and even by 2000 will be roughly 2 per cent. The consequences of urban expansion are far greater and more indirect than the mere conversion of crop and other land to urban use. The total population growth that has made possible the growth in cities has at the same time created a total demand for agricultural products which has both kept in production much present farm land and has at the same time brought in much additional farm land. Had total population in the United States remained at the 1910 level while the agricultural revolution was taking place, there would be at least 100 million acres less in crops today, as well as an agricultural depression of unprecedented size. American agriculture is market oriented, and the expansion in total market which has accompanied the growth in cities has dominated agricultural land use to a vastly greater extent than has the shift of specific tracts of land from crops to urban use.

If total population is to continue to grow in the United States, then by all odds the most efficient place to put the added people is in cities, if saving of land is the objective. A given population will require for site purposes a great deal more land in open country than in cities; and more land in small cities than in large ones.

One major consequence of the economic and social changes discussed earlier in this chapter has been and will be a greatly increased demand for land for outdoor recreation. More income per person and more leisure, as well as more people and better travel facilities, in the past have greatly increased the demand for recreation. At the same time, the supply of publicly-owned recreation areas has increased, as new parks have been added or old ones enlarged. Total annual attendance at public park and recreation areas has been growing at close to 10 per cent annually for many years, with no clear signs of a slowing down in the rate of growth. Although we lack comprehensive data on recreation costs, there is no evidence that costs per visit have declined to the recreationist. His steadily mounting volume of usage at presumably constant costs or price per visit are clear evidence of steadily shifting demand curves. Since the causal factors will continue upward, we expect the demand for outdoor recreation to shift upward to a major degree.

The total land area of public recreation areas (excluding parks within cities) has increased from 5 million acres in 1900 to 46 million acres in 1950. In addition, recreation has become an increasingly important use on larger areas used primarily for other purposes -- forests, for instance. Virtually no data are available on the area of privately owned land used primarily for recreation. The decision to use land primarily for public recreation is more a political than an economic one. It requires support by interested groups of the public and approval by various governmental bodies; only rarely have calculations of comparative economic costs and returns been influential in such decisions. But considerations of cost, demand, and effect upon local business could be influential in such decisions, were such data available.

Data on past recreation usage are so poor, and our understanding of present recreation usage of resources is so limited, that attempts to estimate future demand (in the economist's sense of a demand curve) are fraught with unusual hazard for error. But it seems clear that future demand will be much above present demand -- the real question is how much greater. We have used an over-all estimate in 2000 of 10 times the total demand as in 1956; this involves a lower rate of increase for the future than experienced in the past. If any such increase in recreation demand occurs, it will be virtually impossible to accommodate it by a corresponding increase in area of land used primarily for public recreation. An attempt to estimate the latter involves political as well as economic factors. We have estimated that an adequate public recreational area in 2000 would embrace 135 million acres, compared with 55 million acres of land and water used primarily for this purpose today; but we have also estimated that area probably used for public recreation in 2000 would be slightly less than 100 million acres. Estimates for intermediate dates assume expansion from present levels, possibly at a faster than average rate in the next few decades and at a slower rate later.

Whatever may be the area actually used primarily for public recreation at future dates, there seems good reason to expect major pressures for expansion of the park and other recreation area, and for substantial actual land shifts in this direction.

Demand for agricultural commodities in the future will expand almost exactly in proportion to increases in total population. The income elasticity for food and fiber crops at the farm is so low that higher average real incomes will affect demand at the farm level very little. On the supply side, agricultural output is determined primarily by the rate of adoption of new technology. The economics of the individual farm are such that no farmer can afford not to adopt new technology which promises to lower costs or to enable him to increase output at a lower marginal cost. Thus, output may expand even though the marginal returns to the agricultural industry are very low or even negative. New technology for agriculture is constantly being developed both by public agencies and private organizations, and the rate of innovation is more likely to increase than to decrease in the future. For these reasons, a continuation of ample or over-ample supplies of agricultural commodities seems probable for the next two decades, and perhaps for much longer.

A reduction in area of cropland is possible today, given the agricultural surplus situation; and an area of cropland somewhat smaller than the present acreage could produce an ample supply of agricultural commodities for many years ahead. However, there are serious reasons to doubt

that the maximum possible reduction in acreage, or even the economic
level assuming fluidity of resources, will be achieved. Low returns have
been relatively ineffective in forcing shifts out of areas or employments
in the past, not only in agriculture but in other activities as well.[4] Moreover, massive governmental assistance to agriculture seems to have
become an accepted part of the American society, and its effects to date
have probably not been to facilitate withdrawal of land from agriculture.
A projection of probable agricultural land use is therefore partly political.
Balancing these various tangible and intangible factors as best we could,
we estimate that the area in crops in 1980 will be about 20 million acres
less than the area in 1950; much of this reduction has already taken
place.

Land use and other projections of the future by any workers
naturally employ the best estimates such workers can make. However,
the choice and publication of a single figure, or even a range of
figures, does not give the reader the benefit of the author's estimates of
the firmness or reliability of such estimates. For example, we can be
very sure of an increase in urban area in future decades, fairly sure of
an increase in public recreation area, but at the best no student can be
very sure of his projections of agricultural area. There are too many
imponderables in the latter; the balance between increase in demand due
to growth in total population (which is so highly dependent upon the uncertain and imperfectly understood variations in birth rate), and the
increase in supply due to the adoption of technological innovation (a
process which we understand most imperfectly) is so close and uncertain
that logically defensible minor changes in either will lead to a widely
different conclusion some years hence. On the other hand, should our
estimate of future cropland requirements prove in error, there are
many ways of adjusting either supply or demand -- certainly no serious
scarcity of agricultural commodities seems likely for several decades,
if ever.

The demand for forest products (in the economist's sense of a
demand curve) seems likely to increase in the future.[5] The physical
possibilities of a substantial increase in forest products output also
exist. However, there are serious reasons to doubt if output will rise to
meet increased demand. A major part of the total commercial forest area
(25 per cent) is in holdings of less than 100 acres each and another part
(20 per cent) is in holdings of 100 to 500 acres; 36 per cent of these
small holdings are not connected with farms. Various studies show
rather clearly that most of the latter group of owners are not motivated
by comparative costs and returns from their forest land management;
they own the land for reasons other than financial returns. Moreover,
it is very difficult to establish an economic rationale for more intensive
forestry on their part; although returns can be comparatively much higher
than at present, in absolute terms the gains are often too small to
warrant the forest owner taking the time or trouble to achieve them.[6] On

[4]Harvey S. Perloff, Edgar S. Dunn, Jr., Eric E. Lampard, and Richard F. Muth, Regions,
Resources, and Economic Growth (Baltimore: Johns Hopkins Press, 1960). See especially
Chapter 33.

[5]U. S. Department of Agriculture, Forest Service, Timber Resources for America's Future,
Forest Resource Report No. 14 (Washington, 1958).

[6]Charles H. Stoddard, The Small Private Forest in the United States (Washington: Resources
for the Future, 1961).

the other hand, a substantial part of the larger private forest holdings
have already achieved a level of forestry comparable with that on most of
the publicly owned forests. Greatly more intensive operations are possible
on most private and public forests, and undoubtedly some shifts in this
direction will occur over the next few decades.

Large shifts of land into or out of forestry seem most unlikely. Most
of the lands physically capable for forestry but not so used at present are
now in crops; their shift from crops to forests will depend more upon the
impetus for agriculture adjustment, discussed above, than upon their
returns from forestry. Some encroachments upon forest land will be made
for urban, recreation, and transportation expansion. On balance, a
relatively small net shift out of forestry seems probable.

The situation for grazing lands is rather closely analogous to that
for forestry, at least in many respects. Major shifts of land into and out
of grazing seem unlikely. The only major additions can come from the
conversion of low-yielding wheat land and other croplands to grass, a
process that will be influenced much more by agricultural adjustment
programs than by the profitability of grazing as such. Some grazing lands
will also be taken for the same uses that will impinge upon forestry, and to
perhaps something like the same general extent. A small net shift out of
grazing is thus probable. Although there are many ranches too small to
constitute economic units under probable future conditions, grazing is not
plagued with the problem of small ownerships to the extent that forestry
is, nor does it have the great numbers of small absentee owners found in
forestry. The demand for the products of grazing lands will be moderately
up in the future, probably more so than the demand for all agricultural
commodities, thus providing some impetus for larger output. Comparatively
large increases in output are possible from present grazing lands; technology
has its effects upon grazing as upon cropland.

This section may be concluded by brief reference to several miscellaneous uses of land. Somewhat more land will be required for transportation purposes, especially for superhighways and airports. Railroads and
much of the highway system will show little change, and some local dirt
roads will revert to other uses. Additional areas are likely to be set aside
primarily for wildlife production; like recreation, this is more a political
than an economic decision. Additional areas will be required for water
management, particularly for reservoirs but also to some extent for
levees and flood control structures. Miscellaneous public uses, such as
for military defense, may also take additional areas. Rights-of-way for all
sorts of miscellaneous uses will either take land or at least impinge on
other uses of land. Individually these various changes will not be large,
but in total they will be sizable; and in some local situations they may be
dominant.

FUTURE LAND USE AND TENURE PROBLEMS[7]

No one man could list, let alone describe, all the probable land problems
of the next two decades in the United States; and if he could, there would be
no space within this chapter to do so. Moreover, for our present purpose it

---

[7]See Chapter 14, "A Program of Land Economics Research for the Next Decade", by Harry A.
Steele, for further discussion of this subject.

is unnecessary. Individual researchers and research teams over the next several years will isolate, describe, and analyze the problem situations most important to them. With the great geographical diversity which characterizes the United States, the importance of various problems will vary greatly from region to region and state to state. It is possible in this chapter, however, to give some examples of the kinds of land problems likely to be acute during the next few decades, and to suggest some of the more important lines of work.

Perhaps the most important land problems for the near future lie in the field of urban land use.[8] Most of our people now live in urban areas and essentially all our future net population growth will reside there; more than two-thirds of our physical property is now found in urban areas, and most of the net future investment will occur there. It is difficult to contrast present land use and land arrangements with any sort of ideal, yet the judgment may be offered that the present diverges more from the ideal in urban areas than in any other land use situation. For all these reasons -- personal welfare, capital efficiency, and opportunity for improvement -- it is hoped that a vastly larger share of all future land economics research will be directed toward the city. Land economics research is needed for each major land use; the need may be greatest for urban, suburban, and metropolitan areas. By and large, very little economic land research has been directed toward cities, especially in the macro as contrasted to the micro relationships. City planners, political scientists, sociologists, and others have each made valuable studies, although these have not been notable for their integrated and related character. There has been little or nothing for urban areas comparable to the many studies of rural land use -- and most students will agree that these fell short of our aspirations.

During the next several decades the older parts of virtually all cities will have to be rebuilt, other parts of the same cities must have their value and their productivity maintained by group action, and vast new additions will take place around the periphery. The objective of all this action is a pleasant city to live in, one whose costs are no higher than necessary to achieve the kind of living desired. The problems, by and large, cannot be met by individual action of land and property owners. The value of one's urban property, and the attractiveness of an area to live in, are due as much or more to the action of one's neighbors as to one's own actions. It is a peculiarly intensive form of external economy or dis-economy. However well one may maintain his own home, a deteriorating neighborhood robs his property of value and the home of attractiveness for living; and rundown houses in good neighborhoods still have considerable value.

These impending changes within and around cities will involve sub-stantial physical conversion of land. One major field of research will be directed toward the design of the most efficient and livable urban areas. Landscape architects, transportation and utility engineers, and other specialists may make the major contribution in this direction. Yet the land economist should have something to contribute, even on this matter of physical layout. He should be particularly concerned with avoidance of the massive waste of land which characterizes urban areas today. This will almost certainly lead him into measures to reduce speculation in land,

---

[8]For a most interesting and graphic semitechnical account of the land problems of the modern city, see House and Home, August, 1960.

methods of controlling and directing suburban expansion, and the difficult
problems of reconciling individual rights in property with society's rights
for sound resulting city form. Taxes on land will surely be one major
factor in the total situation, and probably in any control programs that may
be evolved.

The expanding city is particularly deficient in political and institutional structure to meet its difficult problems. During suburban expansion,
the form of residential, business, and public service areas is determined
for many decades ahead. The future residents of such areas, who presumably have the most at stake in the decisions reached, are not and cannot
well be involved in these decisions; they are, for the most part, not yet
in the area. The decisions are de facto mostly taken by individuals and
organizations with but a passing interest in the area. Our American political institutions largely evolved from a rural and small town background; we
have not yet adapted them to meet the problems of big cities and booming
suburbs, each with its racial, cultural, and economic minorities and
classes, and each with a rather rapidly revolving or transient population.

A mere recital of some of these broad problem situations in the urban
area of the future should surely suggest to the imaginative land economist
many fields of research and many specific research projects. Urban
problems seem particularly to call for a varied and flexible attack. Few of
the problems lie squarely and solely in economics. Urban planners, lawyers,
political scientists, and other specialists have not only an interest but a
major contribution to make. Group, team, or other co-ordinated approaches
to some of these problems would seem to be particularly promising.

Recreation use of land and water poses many problems requiring
economics research. The growing demand for such areas is evident to
anyone who has visited them or has looked at the available statistics; the
probable future trends in population, income, leisure, and travel all
support the idea of a greatly increased demand. But much of our knowledge is on a very superficial level, and we rely altogether too much on
inherited folklore. Just what place should leisure and recreation play in
the future society we want in this country? The amount and timing of
leisure is to a large extent socially rather than individually determined;
decisions have typically been made on an ad hoc or opportunistic basis. How
can a large and complex society such as ours ascertain its social alternatives, debate them with intelligence and knowledge, formulate group goals,
and implement them? Difficult as it may be to conduct research in such
fields, social scientists as a group have responsibilities here; and
economists must do their share. In some not-too-distant day, some major
labor union will press successfully for reduced working hours instead of
more pay per hour; and the form such reduction takes will do as much to
determine some kinds of land use as any direct land programs.

The whole problem of demand for outdoor recreation is a great un-
explored wilderness. How do we establish demand curves, in the economist's
sense, for recreation experience and for recreation resources? How can
we in practice obtain the needed data for any scheme of analysis? How can
we estimate future demand, and areas of land and water required to satisfy
such demand? These problems have a major economics content; they have
been almost wholly neglected to date.

Outdoor recreation is the business of many public agencies at federal,
state, and local levels, and also of many special interest private groups;
each has necessarily done piecemeal planning in the past. How can we

obtain a more co-ordinated approach, without unacceptable centralization in planning? Provision of adequate outdoor recreation facilities in the future will cost money, quite a lot of it; how can the necessary funds be raised? In particular, how can governments reserve land well ahead of need, so as to have it available when needed? How can the emotional and intellectual content of outdoor recreation experience be increased? Can we merely accept what people think they want -- which in turn is heavily influenced by what society has made available for them in the past -- or is there a public responsibility for the kinds of recreation available?

Although most attention focuses on public lands for recreation, private lands are used a great deal by people who do not own the land. This is especially true for hunting, but other forms of recreation are involved also. How can recreation as one use among several be encouraged on private land? Are new institutional arrangements between land owner and land user needed? What role, if any, should the state play in such arrangements?

Again, a mere listing of some of these present and future problems in outdoor recreation should be enough to suggest many specific research projects to the imaginative land economist. Also again, other specialists have large roles to play. Land economists will almost certainly have to sell their approach and results to park specialists, for instance; perhaps the most practical way to do so would be to involve such specialists in co-operative research projects.

In the case of agricultural land use, many of the problems of the past will continue to plague us in the future, but new and special problems seem imminent. The problems of the best major use of land, of land classification, landlord-tenant relationships, and many others which have had extensive study in the past will continue to merit attention. But American agriculture over the next several decades will face a different kind of problem, one with which we have had some limited experience since the war. One major problem, perhaps the most important one, lies in how best to withdraw from agriculture a substantial part of the labor force now found there, and how best to make the necessary farm reorganizations and consolidations? If total crop acreage is to remain constant or decline slightly, while labor force shrinks greatly and numbers of farms decline to a million or less by 2000, then American agriculture is faced with a series of problems it has not really had to cope with in the past. We have experienced land settlement, colonization, and subdivision; what we shall experience is largely the reverse, and on the whole it is much more difficult. New land tenure problems, as well as land use problems, will call for land economics research.

A host of problems as to best farm size, best farm shape and layout, necessary farm capitalization and how typical owners may achieve the needed capital, social services to rural areas, emigration from land -- all these, and others, will arise. Some will be primarily micro, or within the farm boundaries; but others will be macro, concerned with the total rural structure. Specialists in other fields will surely be concerned also. Research could well be directed toward a better understanding and evaluation of changes that have taken place in areas experiencing a substantial emigration; but it could also be inventive and look for new methods and new approaches.

The problems of commercial agriculture will be difficult also. An inflexible demand for farm commodities, probably growing more inflexible with the passage of time, and an inflexible supply curve, also apparently growing more inflexible with new technologies, combine to produce extreme price and income instability in the absence of governmental programs. But the latter have shown a serious tendency toward inflexibility also, with resulting mounting costs and economic wastage. Research on these problems will probably lie mostly outside land economics. But problems of incidence and capitalization of program benefits into land values, problems of land taxes and their effects, and problems of the effects of programs upon land use certainly are of direct concern to land economists.

Forestry in the United States has been but little exposed to economics, especially on a macro scale. Vast areas and volumes of timber are publicly owned, large programs of public aid for fire protection on public and private lands are undertaken, and much public effort is expended to try to induce private forest owners to practice "better" forestry, and all without any real economic analysis at any stage. Such programs have been advocated and approved by those with other objectives in mind; philosophical and ideological convictions, not economic analysis, have determined action. There has been no such rapport between foresters and economists as there has been between agricultural specialists and economists. Hopefully, forest economics in the United States is on the threshold of advance, roughly comparable to where agricultural economics stood in about 1920. But land economists have much to learn and much to do before they can fully sell themselves and their ideas to foresters, including forest owners.

The extensive margins, of forestry are fairly well known in the United States, but the intensive margins have been studied very little indeed. We know that some forest sites and some forest management methods produce very much larger output than others, but this has not had adequate comprehensive study. Moreover, because of the vastly longer growing and harvesting cycle, practical experience has not produced the kind of knowledge for forestry that it has for farming as to the relative capabilities of different soils, sites, and methods. Which forests in the United States can profitably absorb greater inputs of capital and management, and how much? We greatly need competent economic land classification of forests, tied into forestry practices and management.

For the vast number and large acreage of small forests, farm and nonfarm, how can we obtain management reasonably consonant with their physical production possibilities? Is there in fact any program that will succeed as long as these lands are in such small management units? Is there any way in which management could be extended for larger units, without necessarily changing the land ownership pattern? How can the objectives of small forest owners, for ends other than financial gain, be achieved and at the same time forest output stepped up? What new institutions, if any, might help solve these problems?

Co-operative fire control has reduced the fire hazard to the point where losses from fire are no longer the major hazard to successful forestry. Insects, disease, and even climatic hazards now loom larger, but fire control efforts cannot be relaxed. Can present institutional arrangements, with co-operative public and private efforts, be directed at these problems also? Or are substantial institutional changes need? Forests often have major recreational values; how can such values be realized, especially on privately owned forests, without undue interference with forest products output? What are the relative roles of the private landowner, government at any level, and organized groups representing the recreationist?

As with the other land uses, a mere listing of some of the major problems likely to arise in forestry over the next decades surely suggests many specific research projects to the land economist.[9] Also, as in the case of other land uses, the need to work with specialists from other fields should be obvious.

This section may well close by briefly considering a different class of probable future land problems. Over the past several decades, government, especially the federal government, has undertaken major investment in land and water resources. It seems highly probable the federal government will be called upon for major future investments in land and water resources, and possibly also for recreation programs. One cannot view the past record without many misgivings. Waste and pork-barrelling have been common, not to say dominant; results from investment have been less than readily attainable. The unnecessary costs have not been fatal to a rich country such as the United States, but they have been significant. Can we do better in the future? There are involved many problems of measurement of costs and benefits, analysis of alternatives, and decision-making. There is also a serious problem of securing greater repayment from beneficiaries. The latter is not unrelated to the problem of accurate estimation of benefits and costs. Research personnel cannot get into the operational aspects of such programs without losing their research role; but they can diagnose past errors and develop better ways of working.

---

[9]See also William A. Duerr and Henry J. Vaux, Research in the Economics of Forestry (Washington: Charles Lathrop Pack Forestry Foundation, 1953).

2.

Scope, Content, and Orientation of Rural Land Economics Research Today

by M. M. Kelso*

Land economics research has always had its urban, nonagricultural branch. In fact, the economics of resource use and property was central to the conceptual structure of aggregative economic analyses of the classical tradition and of many of its critics (Henry George, e.g.). Much of the economic research in forestry, urban planning, and mineral exploitation was--and is--"Land economics" research in the meaning given the term in this work. However, this chapter will center on <u>rural</u> land economics research and that in which agriculture is central because the volume of land economic research is far greater in this context than in all others combined and because the area of training and experience of the author is in this area and he is familiar only with the research output of this field. Nevertheless, the conceptual framework for land economics research developed in this chapter is equally applicable to all branches of the field; it is only in the illustrations used and appraisals made that its narrower focus on rural and agricultural land is apparent.

Land economics <u>research</u> implies something, often only vaguely felt, about science. In this frame of reference its goal is an elaboration of definitions and classes in their functional relations so structured as to be usable in realistic predictions of real world events. As such, its value goes beyond interest in itself for its own sake as a curiosity satisfying endeavor on the part of its practitioners (though this value is important, too.) It is also relevant to problem-defining and problem-solving in the world of man in society. Land economics research does not (and cannot)

---

*M. M. KELSO has been professor of agricultural economics at the University of Arizona since 1958. Born in South Dakota in 1905, he holds a B.S. from the University of Minnesota, an M.S. from Connecticut State College, and a Ph.D. from the University of Wisconsin. He served several years in the Bureau of Agricultural Economics, United States Department of Agriculture, part of the time as Head of the Division of Land Economics. He was professor and head of the Department of Agricultural Economics at Montana State College from 1946 to 1953, and Dean of Agriculture and Director of the Agricultural Experiment Station at the same institution from 1953 to 1958. He has also been a cattle rancher in eastern Montana. He has written extensively about various land economics matters.

stand by itself alone. As an exercise in science, it ramifies into and builds upon linkages with other scientific endeavors; as a problem-defining and problem-solving exercise, it is one tool in the kit of the social practitioner to be applied in the defining of problems, and in devising relevant solutions.

THE PAST IS PROLOGUE

To gain perspective on land economics research of today, it is well to begin with a look at that of yesterday. Just as the person is the image of his forebears and environment so is land economics research the image of transmitted and experienced influences.

It is a product of intellectual inheritance through the education its practitioners received from the land economics research workers under whom they studied, and it is influenced by the recorded experiences of the past in its recorded research literature.

But just as the child also differs from the parent, land economics research today differs from that of the past through influences brought to bear upon it from the contemporary environment--the problems peculiar to the times--and through learning from past mistakes.

Fortunately, an elaborate treatment of the history of land economics research is not required in this paper because of the definitive work by Dr. Leonard Salter written in May, 1946. (1)

Let us divide this brief review of the history of land economics research into two parts as does Dr. Salter in his work--research in land utilization and research in landed property.

Research in Land Utilization

Dr. Salter opens his discussion of land utilization research with the following definition:

> Land utilization research can be described as dealing with
> problem situations in which people in a given locality are in
> the process of transformation from activities with certain
> land requirements to activities with different land require-
> ments. (2)

Two things are significant in this definition--its reference to "locality", thus implying concern with an aggregate of people and firms, and its reference to "the process of transformation" from activities with "certain land requirements" to others, thus implying shifts in use between major uses such as normally require change in type and pattern of firms. Thus, land utilization research throughout this early period was concerned with shifts or the need for shifts in major uses of resources in the area and was centered on the problems of areas rather than of farms as individual firms.

Of major importance in land utilization research through this early period were two types of land utilization problems: the problems of development and settlement of new areas, primarily in the "cutovers", and the problems of abandonment from intensive agricultural use in old areas, primarily in the eastern highlands of the United States. Thus, the problems under investigation centered in uncertainties as to how to occupy lands agriculturally that had not previously been so occupied or how to disoccupy agricultural land that was changing use to something more extensive.

During the later years of this early period the focus shifted from study of land use problems in local areas, together with exploration of adjustments appropriate to that area, to study of the geographic delineation of all areas needing some kind of land use adjustment and, within many of these areas, studying the types of economic adjustments that might be appropriate.

Another popular area of land utilization research in this period was the development and application of "land classification" techniques. The intent was to map geographically the patterns of physical and biological characteristics of the environment. Often the problem-solving relevance of these classifications was vague, and in most cases their economic interpretation was more vague. Generally, they were descriptive inventories of resources described cartographically; to what purpose the inventory might be put--other than to satisfy a curiosity as to what there was--and how the inventories might be used in economic decision-making was quite unclear.

Characteristic of much of the land utilization research of this period was the "agriculture-forestry" dichotomy. In most early studies the two major uses between which shifts seemed to be important were agriculture on the one hand and forestry on the other. Rarely was attention given to other uses that might intrude. During later years of the period, with the more rapid development of suburban living, there appeared studies of rural residential use, urbanization, and recreational uses of land as uses that either were usurping or might be more appropriate than agricultural uses.

That the agriculture-forestry dichotomy was prevalent in early land economics research points up the peculiar absence of such research in the subhumid west where uses alternative to "agriculture" usually were not forestry but grazing, or where the alternatives were major shifts within agriculture, such as from grazing or desert to dryland farming or irrigation. To quote Dr. Salter: (3)

> In respect to the problems of land use adjustment in the subhumid areas of the West, the paucity of Land Economics research is noticeable. It is particularly so in view of the fact that the settlement of arid lands has always involved serious questions of public policy. . . . The relative inattention to land utilization problems of the subhumid regions is particularly noticeable in view of the fact that range management studies consistently stress the fact that the critical problems are those of general land use and tenure adjustment. Also, the large amount of range and irrigation investigational work done by physical scientists and engineers adds emphasis to the lack of work on these problems by social scientists.

Land utilization research of this period involved a merging of the traditional farm management (firm) approach with an "aggregative geographic" approach. The traditional farm management concern with the economics of decision-making in individual firms was merged in this aggregative process with concern for the patterning of uses in areas more broadly defined than that of the single firm. Thinking in "area" terms led promptly to concern in these "area" studies over the implicit and related problems of local government (local public finance), community organization and social patterning, and to concern over means for attaining land utilization change (zoning, tax reform, public service developments, etc.).

Research in Landed Property

Let us turn next in this brief history to a look at research in landed property. Probably most common was research in landlord-tenant relations concerned primarily with the efficiency and equity issues in leasing systems and rental rates and frequently concerned with the economic consequences of different systems and rates on landlords and on tenants.

The overwhelming importance in American land policy of ownership of farms by their operators dictated one of the important areas of interest in landed property research during this early period; viz., research into the progress and problems of attaining ownership of farms. A great deal of attention was spent on study of the "agricultural ladder"--whether or not such a ladder existed, the identity of the "rungs", the rate and pattern of progress made by persons attempting to climb it, etc. Interest in this problem led logically to consideration of other factors related to the attainment of ownership--the problems of credit and its adequacy, the processes of inheritance, etc.

In the 1920's, and more particularly in the 1930's, the property problems that moved into the forefront in research were those not of attaining but of maintaining farm ownership. The historical American ideal of farm operator-ownership was severely jolted during these decades by the difficulties farm people experienced in retaining ownership of the farms they already owned. Consequently, the problems for research shifted to those related to the processes of foreclosure and delinquency and to study of other devices including credit, particularly government credit, that might assist in forestalling the loss of ownership by those who already owned their farms.

An obvious corollary to this interest in attaining and maintaining ownership were studies of land values and the land market, for most farms moved into ownership through such a market. A good deal of such research was descriptive of the movements of land values although there were several studies that attempted to analyze the forces that might explain the level of values and of value changes. Research of this kind, of course, also stimulated interest in study of the structures and processes of the land market in order to cast some light on the trends in and levels of values.

Dr. Salter closes his discussion of research in landed property as follows: (4)

> The development of landed property research shows the close relation between investigational work and the pressure of existent social problems. Throughout the period there was some

continued attention to making available to owners and operators
of farms some information relative to their personal problems
of drawing leases. But in respect to social problems, interest
shifted from ownership and tenancy to land values and ownership transfers, to taxes and debts, to foreclosures and tax
delinquencies, again to ownership and tenancy, and back to
land values--as the country became successively aware of the
existence of tenancy, a land boom, falling prices, severe
agricultural distress, and signs of another wartime land boom.

The late 1920's and more particularly the 1930's saw the emergence of
studies of the actions of government that might direct use and tenure of
rural landed property. These devices, which came to be called "directional measures," included study of such devices as rural zoning, grazing
districts, etc.
Also during the 1930's, the emergence of research in water in the
West in the form of water utilization studies and of studies in water rights
were greatly stimulated by the emergence of flood control and water
facilities programs in the federal government. Prior to this period the
only substantial work by land economists relative to water was The
Economics of Reclamation, privately published by Ray P. Teele. (5)

Summing up the Prologue

We can sum up this résumé of the history of Land Economics research
in Dr. Salter's words: (6)

The history of rural land economics research shows a close
connection with current public issues. Before World War I
the existence of tenancy and the availability of land for
settlement took precedence in research interest. After the
land boom following the War, attention shifted from tenancy
to land evaluation and ownership and to the burden of land
debt and taxes that the boom had fostered. Also with the
decline in the demand for agricultural products, studies
of land abandonment and of agricultural decadence replaced
work on land settlement. Because of the overwhelming importance of these problems in certain localities, the idea
developed that land utilization research was a basis for
community organization and planning.

With the advent of the depression and the New Deal era of
public action, Land Economics research emphasized the
use of public land purchase, reforestation, rural zoning,
and subsidized relocation as a means for resolving local
difficulties associated with settlement on isolated or poor
quality land, tax delinquency, land abandonment, conflicting uses, and other phases of land utilization
adjustment. Such work came to be seen as a possible
basis for aligning various types of public activities into
an integrated attack on rural problems, and for a few years
prior to World War II, land use planning held a central
place of interest in Land Economics.

The depression also resulted in widespread foreclosures
of mortgages, and this phenomenon recreated an interest
in the problems of farm tenancy comparable to that which
existed before World War I. The parallel also extends
into the World War II period, when interest shifted from
farm tenancy to land values, and immediately following
World War II, to attention to land ownership changes.

It is evident that land economics research during its formative
period was concerned to a considerable extent with actual or "needed"
major use shifts in land utilization wherein such shifts centered around
an agricultural use as the major use or as one of the major uses. It
also is apparent that one of the centers of interest in early Land
Economics research was the question of who held what right in space
units, how those rights were distributed among individuals, and what
valuations were placed on them. Here again the focus was on agricultural
tenure.

Much of this early research was descriptive in character. It rarely
was explanatory in the sense that it uncovered functional relationships
making it possible to predict the course of change. It was frequently
concerned with recommendations as to "actions" to correct "problems"
but, characteristically, such recommendations usually were based on
ad hoc normative assumptions.

Recommendations for land use and tenure changes were arrived at by
comparing what the description showed to be the actual course of events
with what the normative assumption showed to be an ideal or appropriate
course; recommended actions were those that would (or might) bring the
actual more into keeping with the norms. Research into whether these
norms were those which the actors rather than the observers held were
noticeably absent.

It was during this period that land economics research became aware
that its concern centered in "space units"–the nature of their embraced
resource qualities, their locational attributes, and the nature and sharing
of rights in them. Its concern, clearly, was with space units larger than
those embraced by individual firms; it was with space defined as an
aggregate of firms in broader areas. Land economics research was
centered on the economic uses of the agricultural resource qualities and
the associated tenure structures and processes within such defined spatial
contexts. Its focus was on agricultural usage; other uses that were in or
might be made of these space units were considered as "alternatives"--
actually, frequently, as if they were "intruders" or as if they might "solve"
the agricultural problems of the area. Land economics research of this
early period looked at problems through the eyes of agriculture and considered other uses as alien in the environment. It thus had a strong
"agro-centrism."

Apparently during this early period, there were no research studies
centrally concerned with problems of the changing character of the
resource content of the space units except in those cases where major land
use or tenure adjustments are centrally involved. As Salter puts it: (7)

The lack of research of this type emphasizes the dominance in
Land Economics of those problems which do center in major
land use changes and in landed property relations. But it also

reflects the closeness of Land Economics to current public
issues, for during the larger part of the growth of Land Economics, public attention was not directed to soil erosion.
Furthermore, during the period since soil conservation has
come into public consciousness, action has been effected
through a specialized agency dominated by physical scientists
and engineers. And, as was earlier pointed out in respect to
irrigation and other western land problems, in all of these
instances little room has been left open for independent social
science research on the public aspects of these issues and
programs.

Also striking by their absence, at least as seen from this later vantage point, were studies of public in contrast to private evaluations of
resource use, adjustment, and investment, studies of interuse and inter-
area competition, and studies of "time" other than as it was involved in
studies of land values. Another strange absence was studies of the
public tenure of land, and of water as a land resource. Both of these
might have been studied in respect to their utilization and property
dimensions, but neither of them was.

THE PRESENT

A review of the present course of land economics research suffers as
do all studies of current processes because it lacks the perspective of
history. It is difficult for the analyst to see the forest for the trees. It is
time for another student of Dr. Salter's acumen to bring up to date the
critical appraisal of land economics research. It is impossible for me to
do so in this short paper; that is a problem for a major investigation like
Dr. Salter's work. Nevertheless, let us scan the land economics
research scene, note what we see, and make appraisals--objective we
hope, but inevitably somewhat subjective.

Conceptual Development

It is 40 years since land economics emerged as a sub-discipline of
economics under its own name. It is inevitable that the research activities
undertaken in its name are colored not only by the problems that attract
investigators but also by the conceptual framework within which these
problems are recognized and analyzed. It is appropriate after 40 years to
begin our discussion of today's land economics research with a review of
the conceptual framework for land economics research as it has evolved
in the course of 40 years of experience and evolution. So let us begin our
appraisal of land economics research by trying to answer the questions:
What is land economics research?" "Why is it pursued?"
   Land, as one factor in the production complex managed by man to
serve his ends, has come to mean the "natural environment" as it confronts him at each passing moment of his choosing. He is concerned with
whatever confronts him out of the natural environment including whatever
modifications may have been irretrievably incorporated into it by man
himself. Consequently, "land" is "space" with whatever resource content,

altered or unaltered, it contains. Modifications ex ante, insofar as they can be effected by incorporating inputs from outside the space unit, are capital until decision and subsequent action has effected the incorporation; then, they become "land" for purposes of land economics analysis.

This environment, which is synonymous with land, is three dimensional. Hence one of the basic postulates of the conceptual structure of land economies is the postulate of three-dimensional space and the problems of location and distance thus implicitly introduced.

It is this postulate probably more than any other that distinguishes land economics from other subcategories of economic theory--namely, its concern with the spatial attributes of decision-making and the spatial patterning of economic behavior. Much of economic theory has abstracted from space, assuming all economic activity collapsed to a point thus taking place in a time setting only.

However, it is evident that man's choosing can only be an act of the present and must have a past and a future, becoming past even as it is made. Hence, there must be a time dimension in all economic analyses of decision-making and land economics is no exception. The time dimension that appears in land economics is the same dimension treated explicitly in contemporary "dynamic" theory; in land economics, it has been teamed up with decision-making within and among space units.

Thus, the concept, "land," reduces to space and its content of natural forces which, in the real world of man's decision-making, always reduces to units of space together with the resources each contains. These space units are fixed in location though their resource content may be transient in nature or by virtue of man's actions. It is this conceptualization of land that leads some theorists to characterize land economics as the "economics of location," (8) which it is in the general sense that all resources, as well as the demanders whose wants they are sought after to satisfy, lie in space and that man's actions relative to them are for the purpose of bringing them together. The decision-making relative to the act of bringing them together is the economic problem of "location in space" that characterizes Land Economics.

In order, however, for any actor to bring resources and their demanders together within any space unit it is necessary that the resources be under his control. In a primitive society, this "control" could and might be enforced as a purely physical act on one man's part as against other men attempting to usurp the resources. In advanced societies, however, control over any space unit and the resources it contains is defined and realized through the institution of property. The characteristics of and the problems created by the institution of property in land consequently play a peculiarly important role in land economics research. Property in land, as is true of all property, establishes a degree of control over any one man's behavior vis-a-vis all other men and vice versa relative to their mutual interest in a property object. Property in land defines and regulates the relationships among men and their behavior relative to one another, to a specified space unit, and to the resources that it contains. The limits of the space unit and the resources within it to which any man's or group of men's control attaches is defined by the property institution; the requisite and permitted behavior of this man or group and of other related men or groups relative to one another and the land unit is spelled out by the property institution. Thus, the economic analysis of a land problem cannot be so much as begun unless the space unit, its resource content, and the behavior of men relative thereto are specified, and conversely the description of the space unit, its resource content, and the permitted behavior of men relative thereto will affect the character of economic decision-making relative to it.

In decades past, economic theory was bedeviled by a debate over the difference between "land" and "capital." One hears this debate less now, possibly because it has been largely accepted that capital is only that which, when brought under man's control, he can move about better to serve his ends and that capital once committed to a location by man's decision-making is, for purposes of economic decision-making, "land". This debate grew out of the historical definition of land as the "natural and indestructible powers of the soil." This unfortunate definition led to extensive pointless argument for the obvious reason that land once occupied and used by man is altered in character, thus raising questions as to the "natural and indestructible" properties, how to handle, in theory, those that are "destructible" by man's use, and how to distinguish between the removal of a "destructible" nutrient and the "depletion" of a sunk capital investment? Land economics research in these later days is concerned with economic decision-making relative to the "natural" attributes of space together with all immovable elements contained therein whether altered or unaltered, naturally or by man. This has led to the observation that land for purposes of modern land economics research includes "sunk capital ex post" whereas capital is liquid funds and movable instruments of production "ex ante" their irretrievable commitment to a location.

Another troublesome problem in the history of land economics in relation to other branches of economic theory has been its relation to farm management. If farm management is an application of the economics of the firm, it is the economics of managerial decision-making directed to the most efficient combination of land, labor, capital, and management within the firm. From this, it follows that farm management is concerned, as is land economics, with the use of resources within a unit of space. It is true that man's relations to land are, at their simplest level, "micro" relations of individual or small groups of men to small units of space to which their management is directed; but it is also true that these micro relations build up into "macro" patterns which reciprocally effect the micro-relations of man to space. Nevertheless, land economics research is peculiarly concerned with the macro aspect of this man-man-land relationship. Though land economics cannot cut loose from its micro base and hence is closely tied to firm analysis, its particular focus of interest is on the macro patterns and relations developed out of the micro decision-making and, in turn, on the impact that the macro patterns and relationships have upon the micro units. Hence, land economics is concerned with land in all its complex relations with men and with institutions in all their forms insofar as they are related to the complex land resource pattern. As a result of this concern, land economics has refused to confine itself even when agriculturally oriented, exclusively to "agricultural" or "rural" or any other single category of land problems. Because it is concerned with the macro pattern that emerges, it has been and will continue to be concerned particularly with the competitive relations among all classes of land uses as they operate in a spatial area larger than an individual firm and, hence, it will be concerned implicitly with all possible land uses and the property institutions related thereto including but not confined to agriculture.

Those problems that emerge from the aggregate of man-man-land relationships are grist for the mill of land economics research when they arise within space units larger than controlled by single firms wherein the central issues are functions of the "fixity" and "qualities" of the resource content and of the property relations relative thereto.

Current Emphases in Land Economics Research

We have defined land economics research as concerned with those aggregative problems of man-man-land relationships wherein "locational fixity" of space units, the nature of the resources therein contained, and/or the property controls relative thereto are the "limiting and strategic" factors in man's decision-making. Let us turn now to a brief résumé and characterization of current land economics research, noting as we proceed in what respect it differs from and is similar to the land economics research of the past so thoroughly described by Salter in his work. The "current period" is largely that of the decade of the 1950's although some landmark studies, advanced even in terms of 1961, were completed during the war decade of the 1940's.

Research into Land Resource Utilization

It is appropriate to divide the broad subject of land economics research into two major subclasses: land resource utilization, and property in land. We will begin by taking up the first of these subclasses. Utilization research usually abstracts from "property" or treats property as a given parameter.

Utilization in space with time implicit. It is not so simple to dispose of "time" as it is to dispose of "property" in utilization research. Utilization research is obviously concerned with questions related to the use of resources randomly disposed in space and sometimes it is possible to investigate such questions while abstracting from questions engendered by "time." In other words, one can concern oneself with problems related to instantaneous relations among resources, distance, and decision-making. But it is impossible for the investigator to go very far before running afoul of the problems of "time" inasmuch as resource utilization, both as regards distance elimination and manufacture, takes place in a time as well as a space dimension. But, nevertheless, let us concern ourselves first with research directed solely at the spatial configuration of resources abstracted from the problems of time except insofar as time may be implicit in the analysis through the imposition of assumed interest and depreciation charges. Here the focus of analysis is on utilization as it is affected by location and the patterning of uses that emerge in space.

The growth of a research discipline is partly a product of the development of its formal conceptual structure which is, in turn, partly a product of experience in empirical investigations into the problem. In part, the growth of a discipline can be measured by the development of the theory that underlies and guides the empirical investigations. Growth and development of the theory is characterized by refinements of concept and clarification of their interrelationships. This is progress in "conceptualization" of the discipline.

In land utilization research of the pure spatial variety great strides

have been made in the past decade or more in the conceptual framework of
understanding and analysis. Historically, the landmark figure in this connection and the only figure studied by most land economists has been von
Thuenen who wrote in Germany a century and a quarter ago. Following
von Thuenen, little or nothing was done in this area except by a scattering
of German economists of the German historical school, the outstanding
figure being Weber. But Weber's advanced work on location theory was
not written until 1909 and was not translated into English until 1929.
Following his work, several investigators in Germany undertook to extend
the conceptual framework for location analysis, but it was not until 1940
that the first edition of a reasonably complete theory of spatial location
appeared in Germany with the publication of the results of the analyses of
August Lösch; this was not translated into English until 1954 when it was
published under the title of The Economics of Location. Following on the
heels of Lösch's work, and largely since the war, have appeared several
landmark works by American analysts. Among them should be mentioned
particularly the works of E. M. Hoover, Walter Isard, and Edgar S. Dunn,
Jr. (8)

Why did neoclassical economic theory so long ignore the problems of
space? Why did concern for the spatial considerations of economic behavior develop slowly in a long line of German economic writers? Though
we can't answer the "why", a quotation from Dr. Isard casts some interesting side lights upon it. (9) He opens with a quotation from Marshall--

'The difficulties of the problem depend chiefly on variations in
the area of space, and the period of time over which the market
in question extends; the influence of time being more fundamental than that of space.

Isard continues--

Thus spoke Marshall, in line with Anglo-Saxon tradition, and
in the half century to follow, Anglo-Saxon economists were to
harken to his cry. Theoreticians of today are preoccupied
with introducing the time element in full into their analyses,
and the literature abounds with models of a dynamic nature.
Yet who can deny the spatial aspect of economic development;
that all economic processes exist in space as well as over
time?

Realistically, both time and space must be vital considerations
in any theory of economy. Unfortunately, however, aside from
those of the monopolistic competition school of thought, particularly Chamberlain, the architects of our finest theoretical
structures have intensified the prejudice exhibited by Marshall.
They continue to abstract from the element of space, and in so
doing they are approaching a position of great imbalance.
(Pp. 24 and 25.)

One might venture the hypothesis that historically had there
been a certain social class which owned all transport facilities and performed all transport services, the classicals
might well have thought of transport as a fourth factor of pro-

duction and have been more conscious of distance and the
spatial aspect of production. (P. 89).

In the last decade and a half, the conceptualization of the spatial element in our economic decision-making has been advanced immeasurably.
Though it has not yet advanced to a position of prominence equal to that
concerned with the problems of time and dynamics, it is on its way.

Conceptualizations, however, serve no useful purpose until they are
put to use to guide investigations into reality. Such investigations can take
place at one of two levels. The first is to take some beginning data specified by the theory and drawn from the real world and, by using the analytical framework specified by the theory, derive from these data the spatial
configurations that one "ought" to find. We can call this the "analytical"
stage.

The second level of investigation involves using the conceptual framework of the theory as a guide to what data to seek and what categories to
relate in order to explain the spatial configurations objectively observed.
This is the "explanatory" (positivistic) stage of investigation. Both levels
are empirical in the sense that they manipulate existent data derived from
reality. The analytical level concludes with the spatial configuration one
ought to find in the real world. The second level looks at the real world
to see if the explanation "works" in the sense that the spatial configuration
predicted to exist does actually exist within the limits of some acceptable
degree of probability. These levels usually differ in another respect in
that the analytical level is usually concerned with broad spatial configuration problems whereas the explanatory is confined usually to much more
narrowly defined spatial units.

There have been several analytical studies of note during the recent
period. Generally these have involved the analysis of spatial equilibrium
models of the locations, markets, and prices of agricultural industries.
Among these studies have been analyses of such spatial models for beef,
pork, eggs, and broilers. (10)

All of these studies are similar in that they conclude with a configuration of "point" locations of these industries that, the theory says, would
"maximize" satisfactions by "minimizing" the costs of overcoming distance in the assemblage of supplies and the distribution of products. That
these configurations do not conform with reality is readily admitted but the
next steps to explain why they don't conform with reality or what steps
would need to be taken to bring them into conformity with reality or to
bring reality into conformity with them are not undertaken.

In the more rigourously empirical and explanatory studies of space a
large number are purely descriptive in character. These are the land
utilization inventories. (11) They describe what is or what exists. As is
true of any inventory, it is necessary that classes be devised in which to
assemble the descriptive data. These classes will be those that the investigator feels to be important in relation to the problem that has insti-
gated his inventory. Consequently these inventories are of extreme diver- |
sity. Soils, natural vegetative cover, weather patterns, susceptibility to
erosion, use adaptability, adjustment problems,--any of these may be the
subject of a descriptive inventory of land utilization. In some restricted
areas, some addition to the inventories has been made as to why these
land use patterns or problems may have arisen or what might be a better
configuration of uses. In the latter category fall many of those "land

classifications" which attempt to portray a more suitable pattern of uses than that which currently exists in the area. In no case, however, [with the exception of the work in New York state described by Conklin and Nobe (11)] are the explanatory or normative classifications or inventories supported immediately and clearly by empirical economic analyses.

Another important class of land utilization research studies has been concerned with <u>interuse competitions within given space units.</u> (12) Here the focus has been on a defined unit of space and the problem has been to describe and explain the use of configuration of that space--why it is what it is with some attention given to what it ought to be. Studies of this kind, when concerned with "minor use" competitions within narrowly defined space units such as those typical of an individual firm, are "farm management" studies of intrafirm substitution choices--factor-factor, factor-product, and product-product substitutions, familiar in the economics of production. In land utilization research of this type, however, the concern centers on "major use" competitions within broadly described space units such that change in the nature and structure of firms normally is required. Examples of such "major use" shifts are the competition between game animals and livestock, suburban "sprawl" versus agriculture, idle land use versus some form of economic utilization, recreation uses versus other "wild land" uses such as forestry, grazing and water supply. Within the area of agriculture itself, some agricultural uses are so dissimilar as to constitute major use competitions even within the major field of agriculture--for example, irrigation versus dry-land farming, crop farming versus livestock grazing, "intensive" versus "extensive" systems. The same can be said for other broad major uses such as, for example, "urban use" where the difference between business district and residential use involves a similar major shift in firms.

Another form of utilization research is concerned with <u>interspace competitions of the same use.</u> Studies of this kind take some single major use like agriculture or, more specifically, dairying, and examine the competitive position of this use in various separate but related space units. Such studies, better known as studies of "interregional competition," were more prevalent a decade or two ago than they have been during the recent decade, although several pressing "interregional" competition problems deserving of research currently exist.

A striking current example of research of this kind into a vital problem is the study of regional adjustments in wheat and feed grain production in the United States. (13) Such "inter-spatial" competitions in meat animal production, in cotton, in recreation, in timber production are often referred to but so far not formally studied. The contemporary intellectual fashion in economic analyses is to center on problems of "development" both at home and abroad. Development is usually phrased solely as a problem in dynamics, meaning change (adjustment) over time. As development (growth, change, adjustment) progresses or as our intellectual grasp of the analytical framework pertinent to it matures, it is safe to predict that the next analytical fashion must shift its center of attention to the "inter-space" (inter-regional, international) parameters of the problems of development (growth, change, adjustment).

It is apparent from what has been said that most explanatory studies of land utilization have either taken space units as fixed and studied interuse competitions within them or have taken use as fixed and studied interspace competitions relative thereto. Studies that combine both variables, space and use simultaneously, are extremely rare. Some broad attempts in this direction have been undertaken by Leontieff, Hoover, and Isard. The most recent and most complete guide to such studies is Isard's Methods of Regional Analysis. (14)

Utilization in time -- space implicit. Let us turn now to the other extreme, namely, those studies of resource utilization in the time dimension that have been abstracted from space in the sense common to economic analyses that have been made in the neoclassical tradition. It is, of course, as impossible to eliminate space completely from the problem setting as it is to eliminate time. Just as time is implicit in purely spatial studies through the imposition of interest and depreciation charges, so is space implicit in purely time (dynamic) studies through the imposition of transportation charges as costs. But what we are concerned with here are studies in utilization of resources that focus on the time dimension, space being taken as given. As with the discussion of space above, we can start with consideration of the more purely conceptual developments in this area. One of the centers of conceptual development in the patterning of uses in time is the rotational uses of resources in the time dimension. This problem has often been studied from the intrafirm standpoint of product combination and substitutions. But it may be studied also in relation to the succession of major uses in areas more broadly defined than those pertinent to individual firms. In this connection, studies have been undertaken of the problem of transition from one crop to a succeeding crop such as the length of rotations in the growing of timber or orchards, or shifting from timber or orchard to nontimber or nonorchard agriculture, or the shifting from agriculture to various forms of nonagricultural uses, as well as the many types of shifts among nonagricultural uses. (15) In these problems the strategic question centers on waiting, ripening, and supersession costs which are, as a matter of fact, aspects of the general theory of the economics of investment.

Another center of conceptual development involving the time dimension is the economics of conservation. Here the central question has been the investigation of means by which returns from resource use within the space unit might be maximized over time whether with or without depletion and with or without investment. The problem investigated has been of this character--given a fund of resources within the space unit that might be depleted through use, what rate of depletion (a zero rate being one alternative) will maximize returns from the body of resources in that space unit over time, the problem implicitly encompassing the question of what kind and how much investment or disinvestment will be associated with this maximized return over time. The conceptual analyses of this problem have been the particular contributions of Bunce and Wantrup. (16)

Of recent major importance in this conceptual problem has been that of distinguishing between and characterizing public criteria of maximization in contrast to private criteria of such maximization. This problem centers in the different way economies and diseconomies impose directly on individual property managers in contrast to the way they impose indirectly on other individuals that compose the relevant political body. Also at the center of this problem is the differing impact of uncertainty and time preference on the indirectly affected "public" and on the directly affected private user. Bunce and, more fully, Wantrup have explored this problem but the issue is still far from clearly resolved.

Another area of conceptual development in this context has centered in

the economics of resource development. Attention has centered on investment in the space unit to enhance the "available" resource content of the
unit, or the efficiency of the economic use of that resource content, or to
reduce the transiency of the included resource. This problem obviously
overlaps on the problems of "conservation" and "depletion" in those instances when investment in the space unit is required to maximize returns
over time from the use of the included resource and simultaneously may
conserve or deplete these resources. There are many circumstances,
however, in which investments in the space unit will be divorced from
questions of a conservational character such as when they reduce the
waste of a flow resource. However, both the nonconservational and the
overlapped conservational issues in resource development are of concern
here.

The issue of outstanding importance in this connection over the past
decade or two has been that of the public and private criteria for decision-
making in the development of resources. The issue has turned largely on
the conflict that has emerged relative to public development of resources
particularly in relation to private development of the same resources.
There has been a large output of conceptual studies of this problem particularly in relation to the development of water resources. A long list of
books and articles dealing with this subject might be included here, but a
reasonably suggestive list of the more important contributions will be
found as a bibliography attached to the article by Kelso.[17]

Though the conceptual analysis of the public and private criteria for
decision-making in resource development has been worked out largely in
relation to water resources, there has been some, though a great deal
less, development of the conceptual framework relative to the development of grazing and forestry resources.

The more purely empirical studies of time in relation to land utilization can be considered under the same two categories used above to discuss the conceptual development of time in land utilization research,
namely conservation and resource development.

Empirical studies of the economics of conservation have been mostly
concerned with micro-firm analyses--that is, what constitutes conservation maxima within the decision-making limitations of the individual
firm? There is no good reason why such conservational analyses could
not be extended to consideration of the aggregative spatial patterning
generated by the application of conservational decision-making by managers of individual firms. Only a beginning has been made in study of this
type of problem in studies in Iowa and the Southern Piedmont.[18] These
studies have been tentative normative explorations of what a pattern of
uses ought to be assuming conservational decision-making optimum for the
entrepreneur. So far, no study has been made in which conservational
decision-making has been central to the explanation of the existing pattern
of uses in an area.

Empirical studies of the economics of resource development have been
of three general kinds: (1) Inventories of prospective development opportunities for additional agricultural land.[19] Most of these analyses have
been only incidentally economic in character or, more accurately, the
economic analyses that must underlie their classification as "development opportunities" have been implicit or submerged. (2) The problems of
financial progress among users of newly developed agricultural resources.
(20) In the early decades of Land Economics research this problem was

frequently explored but almost entirely within the setting of the "cutovers" and of areas that had experienced expensive drainage investment. Currently, the problem is centered largely in the areas of new irrigation development with little or nothing now being done on this problem in the "cutovers". (3) By far the most important, in terms of volume of studies undertaken in this connection, have been the extensive analyses of prospective water development projects. Over the past two decades, it has been required by the federal government that proposed water development projects be accompanied by investigations as to their "economic feasibility" to answer the question as to whether benefits "to whomsoever they may accrue" will exceed the cost of the projects (on whomsoever they may impinge). Consequently, numerous water development projects have been investigated and analyses to answer these questions have been made. Out of these investigations have been forged extensive empirical experience as to the economic evaluation of the feasibility of resource development over time. The literature of these investigations provides one of the best sources of empirical and conceptual developments in land economics research.(17) [For studies of the development of resources other than water, see (21).]

Research into Property in Land

The pattern and structure of property in land has an impact on the pattern of utilization of the same land and, conversely, the way in which land is used will influence the property structure that will evolve. However, in the research taken up first below, property has been abstracted from use and impact on use. Consequently, this "property" research takes some use pattern as given and studies the property institution in the setting of that parameter.

Research in property abstracted from use with which we are first concerned centers in the structure of the tenure institution in land, the relations among the participants in the structure, and the processes by which the structure evolves.

First is that research which describes the over-all tenure structure embracing all persons who are directly engaged in agriculture. This research describes the structure of property in land in agriculture and the property relationship held by the various participants from farm laborers to owners. It is largely descriptive of what exists in agricultural land tenure, but gives some empirical and analytical attention to the forces that explain the existing structure as well as some attention to the implications of the structure relative to accepted "norms" of agricultural tenure and to the policies required if these norms are to be realized in practice. (22)

Research into the processes by which a tenure pattern in agriculture evolves is best represented by two landmark Wisconsin studies that developed conceptual, analytical, and empirical explanation and description of the tenure processes in agriculture based on evidence from two localities in Wisconsin. These studies examined how and why the tenure patterns evolved in these agricultural areas in Wisconsin and the processes by which the patterns evolved or have been maintained over time.(23)

In the period since World War II when the problems associated with acquiring farms have become severe owing to large capital requirements, the disappearance of "free land," etc., considerable attention has been devoted to research into the problems of acquiring a tenure status in agriculture (often referred to as "getting started in farming"). In contrast to earlier land economics research called "acquiring farm ownership" these studies have been concerned not only with that problem, although it has played an important part, but also with the problems of "getting started" in farming at any reasonable and relevant tenure level. Empirical studies of the problems of farming, the problems they encounter in acquiring equitable and workable tenancy arrangements, and in acquiring ownership have been studied in many locations.(24)

A number of research projects in recent years have focused attention on the ownership-operatorship relation on agricultural land in circumstances where the owner and the operator have been different persons. Many projects have focused their attention particularly on the ownership side of this dual pattern. Most of these studies have been mainly descriptive of the classes that compose the ownership complex and of the changes that have occurred in them and in the complex over time. Most such studies have focused primarily on the private ownership of private land--the make-up of the ownership class, how the owners acquired their property, what they are doing with it, how they manage it, characterization of their tenants, etc.

A few projects have examined the public ownership side in the situations where the public is the owner and private persons are the operators. These studies have been entirely descriptive in character, portraying the volume of publicly owned land, what agencies of the government "own" it, and the character of the land "owned." Sometimes descriptive attention has been given to the nature of the arrangements under which private users make use of these public lands.(25)

Another class of research into the ownership side of the ownership-operatorship relation consists of studies concerned particularly with the processes of ownership acquisition and transfer. Some of these studies are concerned primarily with nonsale methods of acquisition and transfer such as inheritance; others have been concerned with purchase and sale methods by which ownership is acquired and transferred. Reference especially should be made to the many projects studying the land market and the forces and influences that determine land values. Such research has been largely descriptive and analytical, with occasional empirical studies centered in examination of what goes on in specific market situations.(26)

Another class of "market"studies centered on the purchase and sale of land use "privileges" has examined how privileges other than ownership of the full title have been acquired and transferred and how the values of such privileges were determined. Included among such "privileges" are the production of allotted crops, grazing on the public's range, etc.(27)

Concern over purchase and sale methods of acquiring and transferring ownership has also led to research centered in problems of land credit and land contracts. These have been studied from the point of view of the availability or lack thereof of credit, the suitability of various types of devices for acquiring credit or for acquiring title or contracts for title in land.

A principal class of research projects that fall under the general heading of the ownership-operatorship relation are those that focus not on either side of the relation but on the relationship itself. The relationship studied might be that on private land or on public land.

Extensive research has been carried out in the past decade or so on the ownership-operatorship relation and the problems pertinent thereto on private agricultural lands. These studies have centered largely on the terms of leases, the arrangements between landlords and tenants, the arrangements for guiding the behavior of the tenant on the land, the rental practices that the landlords follow, and the problems that these terms and arrangements and practices have created when measured against assumed norms of efficiency and equity.(28) One project, (29), devoted considerable attention to finding out what the commonly held norms of behavior by landlords and tenants might be, thus, giving a better empirical basis for discussing problems in relation to the actual norms of the persons involved.

Research on the ownership-operatorship relation on the public lands has dealt very little with the tenure-relation problem. It has been concerned largely with description of the relations that do exist with little or no attempt to interpret why they have occurred or what impact they have on the efficiency and equity of the relationship.

Research into the role of the public in private property and agricultural land tenure is another area that has attracted some attention in research since the war. Research undertakings in this field can be divided into three categories: (1) those concerned with the problems of assessment and taxation--the determination of values for taxation purposes, description of what these values are and sometimes of how they are arrived at, and studies of the taxation burden and its relation to problems of tenure and utilization; (2) the regulation of use by the public through use of the police power by such measures as zoning and various types of improvement districts; and (3) studies of eminent domain and the question of reasonable value thereunder especially when agricultural lands are taken for highway use.(30)

Although use by the public of private lands where title transfer is not involved (hunting, fishing, etc.) has long been a difficult problem and is growing more pressing as recreational pressures build up, I can find no examples of formal research attacks on the problem at descriptive, analytical, or empirical levels.

Most research on the structure, relations, and processes of tenure in land resources have been concerned with the land surface. Little attention has been given to that problem of growing importance--property in water. Such studies of this problem as have been made in recent years have been largely descriptive of the water rights that do exist frequently describing them largely from a legalistic viewpoint. Little or no empirical research has been undertaken in specific area contexts on who owns or uses what classes of water and how it has changed and is changing over time.

The classes of research described above have centered on the tenure structure abstracted from effects that the structure may have had on the use of the resource or the effect that the use may have had on the tenure structure. Some research has attempted to relax this abstraction and to examine the impact of the tenure structure on the use of the resource and vice versa.

For many years research has been undertaken in tenure in relation to efficiency wherein concern has centered on the leasing systems on privately owned land and the effect these systems have on the efficiency with which resources are combined within the firm. But no research has been undertaken to translate these micro-firm analyses into macro-aggregative patterns of land use that have been brought about by such tenure structures.

Strangely, although research in tenure in water has been much less extensive than has research in tenure in the land surface, the impact of water tenure on use has been studied a great deal more than has the impact on land use of tenure in the land surface. Considerable conceptual and analytical progress has been made in research into property in water, water administering organizations, and pricing practices relative thereto, centering on the impact the institution has on the allocation of the water among various uses and the uses to which the water actually is put. These studies have been largely undertaken in the Western United States where water is scarce and the question of its allocation to most efficient uses is of general concern.(31)

Summary of Current Emphases in Land Economics Research

In land utilization, research has been increasingly centered on the problems of urban and recreational competition for space units relative to agriculture, grazing, and timber uses; within the field of agriculture itself, the time factor in decision-making and the role of government decision-making in development have been of outstanding significance, especially in the field of water resources and land and water conservation. However, most of this research even when dealing with nonagricultural uses such as urban and recreational has viewed the problem from the standpoint of agriculture, these other uses being viewed as intruders into the rural scene.

Research in property in land has emphasized the problems encountered in obtaining an operating tenure in agriculture whether obtained from within family processes, by "equitable" leasing arrangements, or by "buying" ownership, the latter involving studies of the land market and of land values. Another interesting shift in current emphasis has been the shift of attention to problems of water, both surface and subsurface, both in respect to its utilization and its property. This has been a marked departure from the earlier period and has developed on a much broader base than simply concern with irrigation alone.

CRITIQUE OF LAND ECONOMICS RESEARCH TODAY

Upon looking over land economics research of today, one is struck by the surprising lack of research in the following areas: (a) Interspace competitions by the same use; the center of the problem here, is interregional competition and the resulting aggregative land use patterns but involving broad areas and several regions; (b) the aggregative spatial patterning of uses within single areas derived from time decision-making whether public or private and whether in the areas of conservation or development; (c) the aggregative patterning of the complex of uses within a given space unit, that is, interuse competition within a given space unit defined more broadly than a single firm wherein the question centers on how and why these space patternings have emerged from the decision-making by individual firms both public and private; (d) the lack of conceptual analyses of tenure in land, especially conceptual analyses of public

landlordism-private operator relationships and of private owner-public
user relationships; (e) studies of the tenure structure and processes in
property in water--who owns or uses what waters and how these structures
and patterns are evolving; (f) empirical analyses of the impact of tenure
structures on uses and vice versa studied from the micro-firm standpoint,
especially in the public ownership-private use and private owner-public
use situations, and from macro-aggregative points of view in private owner-
private user situations, especially where water is involved, where there is
changing competitive strength on the part of nonagricultural uses of land in
the area, etc.

Certain shortcomings of land economics research have existed for
many years and still persist. Current emphases in research still exhibit
these general deficiencies: (a) Most land economics research still views
the problem under study through the eyes of agriculture vis-a-vis "other"
uses, considering these other uses as intruders. Doing so leads to (or
derives from) implicit biases concerning agriculture as central in the
functioning development. In pursuing the conceptual and analytical problems relative to economic analysis of water and other resource developments by public agencies, agriculture cannot be central even though
irrigation may be one of the facets of the developmental activity suggested.
(b) Land economics research still relies too much on norms derived from
the traditional assumptions of economics (rather than derived empirically
from norms actually held by the actors) and has persisted too long in
measuring performance of the system against such posited rather than
positivistic norms. Proceeding as it does in this manner involves it in
setting up normative hypotheses as to the desirable ends of human action
in resource use or property and in defining the "problem" of the given
research activity in terms of performance "short" of these posited norms.

Little or no research has been done in the human process--what do
people do and why in relation to land use and property relations? Not what
they ought to do but what their norms are and why are they having difficulty in attaining them (if they are). What are the interpersonal institutionalized relations that curb individual human behavior in the realization
of their goals? Excellent examples of empirical analysis in this vein are
the Salter and Parsons investigations (23) and North Central Regional
Publication No. 50.(28)

Dr. Salter closed his 1946 study with the following charges to his
profession:

> In the future, the most important needed step is the adoption
> of a more comprehensive conception of social science inquiry.
> Research must be viewed in terms of its relevance to action.
> To do so means that the purposes and consequences of inquiry
> are given greater attention and that the mechanics of research
> are regarded not only as procedures for gathering data but as
> ways and means of observing processes of human experience as
> operating experiments.

> Secondly, it should be recognized that research has its roots
> in problematic situations; that is, it exists because of conditions
> under which there is doubt as to what people should do because
> there is conflict between the purposes they are striving to
> achieve and the consequences they are experiencing. There is

need for sharper attention to the preliminary exploration and clear definition of the problems--that is, to the statement of these doubts and conflicts. In rural land economics these problems will arise in connection with the establishment of new major forms of the utilization of space, with the development of landed property relations among men, or with the changing character of locational or resource qualities of the space which men control.

The next step is to encourage the functional use of hypotheses. Hypotheses are suggested alternative lines of action that will lead to the achievement of purposes. Their function is to direct the search for evidence as to what might be done. The aim of research is not just to affirm or deny a hypothesis, but to expand and modify it until it represents warranted assertions, grounded in experience, as to what actions will result in a satisfactory pattern of major land uses, will create desirable landed property relations, will overcome the problems engendered by changing attributes of space.

A fourth step in the improvement of research in rural land economics is recognition of the limitations and advantages of various forms of factual materials as evidence. Scientific investigators must stand ready to make use of all types of data and to judge their accuracy not merely in terms of metrical precision but on the basis of how well they reveal patterns of actual human experience. Secondary statistics, quantified data from interview schedules, qualitative information, newspaper files, public documents, participant observer reports, local histories, all kinds of maps--among these and other forms of data there should be no a priori choice, except that only information which is sequentially arranged can positively substantiate reported patterns of experience. The goal in respect to evidence is to examine the full range of experience in which alternative lines of action have been tried. In this view, exceptional cases become not merely extremes to be cancelled out, but potentially useful proving grounds and potential sources of new suggestions. The basic form for the presentation of research results will finally shift from successive discussions of various items, factors, or elements as they affect all the subjects of the study, to discussions of the various lines of actions and sequences of experience revealed in the evidence. (32)

These charges are as applicable today as when Dr. Salter penned them fifteen years ago. Were he alive today, he would join me in saying that progress has been made (thanks to the activities of the Farm Foundation) but that the mental blocks of custom and institutionalized conceptual structures have been battered but not breached.

CITATIONS

This selection of references is for illustrative purposes only. It is not implied to be either a complete bibliography or a carefully selected list of the "most representative" references.

(1) Salter, Leonard A. Jr., A Critical Review of Research and Land Economics. University of Minnesota Press, Minneapolis: 1948.

(2) Ibid., -.83.

(3) Ibid., p.173.

(4) Ibid., p.229.

(5) Teele, Ray P. The Economics of Land Reclamation. Chicago, 1927.

(6) Salter, op.cit., p.242-43.

(7) Ibid., p.241.

(8) Hoover, Edgar M. The Location of Economic Activity. New York: McGraw-Hill, 1948.

Isard, Walter. Location and Space-Economy; A General Theory Relating to Industrial Location, Market Areas, Land Use, Trade and Urban Structure. New York: John Wiley, 1956.

Dunn, Edgar F. Jr., The Location of Agricultural Production. Gainesville: University of Florida Press, 1954.

Weber, Alfred. Theory of the Location Industries. Carl J. Friedrich, Translator. Chicago: The University of Chicago Press, 1929.

Lösch, August. The Economics of Location. Wm. H. Woglom, Translator, New Haven: Yale University Press, 1954.

(9) Isard, Walter, op. cit., pp. 24-89.

(10) Judge, G. G., and T. D. Wallace. Spatial Price Equilibrium Analyses of the Livestock Economy. I. Methodological Development and Annual Spatial Analyses of the Beef Marketing Sector. Oklahoma State University. Tech. Bulletin TB-78. June 1959.

-. Spatial Price Equilibrium Analyses of the Livestock Economy. 2. Application of Spatial Analysis to Quarterly Models and Particular Problems Within the Beef Marketing System. Oklahoma State University, Tech. Bulletin TB-79. December 1959.

-. Spatial Price Equilibrium Analyses of the Livestock Economy. 3. Spatial Price Equilibrium Models of the Pork Marketing System. Oklahoma State University, Tech. Bul. T-81. January 1960.

Judge, G. G. A Spatial Equilibrium Model for Eggs, Storrs Conn. Agr. Exp. Station. Bulletin 318. 1956

Henry, W. R., and C. D. Bishop. North Carolina Broilers in Interregional Competition. Agr. Econ. Information Series No. 56, North Carolina State College, 1957.

(11) Reuss, L. A., et. al. Inventory of Major Land Uses in the United States. Bureau of Agr. Econ., U. S. Dept. of Agr., Misc. Pub. 663. 1948.

Wooten, H. H. Major Uses of Land in the United States. U. .S. Dept. Agr. Tech. Bul. 1082. October 1953.

-, and James R. Anderson, Major Uses of Land in the United States: Summary for 1954. Agr. Res. Service, U. S. Dept. of Agr., Agr. Info. Bul. 168. January 1957.

Marschner, F. J. Land Use and its Patterns in the United States. U. S. Dept. of Agr., Agr. Handbook 153. 1958.

Halcrow, Harold G., and H. R. Stucky. Procedure for Land Reclassification in Montana. Montana Agr. Exp. Station, Bozeman. Bul. 459. February 1949.

Ray Chaudhuri, S. P., and R. S. Murthy. "Land Classification for Agricultural Development: A Brief Review of the Work Done in Different Countries." Soils and Fertilizer. 23(4):235, August 1960.

Conklin, Howard E., and Kenneth C. Nobe. "Development of a Regional Concept for Farm Management Research in New York." Land Economics, 37(1):42, February 1961.

(12) Upchurch, M. L., and T. S. Brown. Land, Livestock, and Deer in the Milford-Doyle Area of Northeastern California. Office of the Farm Advisor, Agr. Ext. Service, Susanville, California. 1951.

Gertel, Karl, et. al. Use of Idle Land in Potter County Pennsylvania for Crops, Pasture and Forest. Pennsylvania Agr. Exp. Station, University Park. Bull. 642. February 1959.

Walrath, Arthur J. Impacts of Changes in Land Use: A Study of Urban-Rural Area of Southeastern Wisconsin. Agr. Res. Service, U. S. Dept. of Agr. ARS. 43-95. November, 1959.

Bolle, A. W. "The Cooperative Study of Multiple Use of Natural Resources in the North Fork of the Flathead Valley." Montana Business Review. 12(3), March 1960.

Price, P. H. and G. A. Hillery. The Rural-Urban Fringe and Louisiana's Agriculture, a Case Study of the Baton Rouge Area. Louisiana Agr. Exp. Station, Baton Rouge. Bul. 526. June 1959.

Kunkel, J. H. "The Role of Services in the Annexation of a Metropolitan Fringe Area." Land Economics. 36(2):208, May 1960.

Barlowe, R., and J. E. Hostetler. "Sub-division Trends in Southwestern Michigan, 1944-1958". Michigan Agr. Exp. Station Quarterly Bulletin 42(2):373, November, 1958.

Mason B. "An Example of Climatic Control of Land Utilization." U.N.E.S.C.O. Arid Zone Research 11:188, 1958.

Mavis, J. G. "Annexation: the Process of Reurbanization." Amer. Jour. Econ. and Sociol. 18(4):353, July 1959.

Frazer, W. J. "Changing Patterns of Land Utilization Within the Salt River Valley of Arizona." Diss. Abs. 20(5):1735, November 1959.

Doehne, H. A. "Relationships of Land Uses to Land Character of Lansing and environs." Diss. Abs. 20(8):2981, February 1960.

(13) Egbert, Alvin C., and Earl O. Heady. Regional Adjustments in Grain Production: A Linear Programing Analysis. Farm Economics Research Division, U. S. Dept. Agriculture, Technical Bulletin 1241. Washington. June 1961.

(14) Isard, Walter. Methods of Regional Analysis: An Introduction to Regional Science. The Technology Press of Mass Institute of Technology and John Wiley and Sons, New York. 1960.

Henderson, J. M. "The Utilization of Agricultural Land: A Theoretical and Empirical Inquiry." Rev. Econ. and Statis. 41(3):242, August 1959.

(15) Faris, J. Edwin. Economics of Replacing Cling Peach Trees. California Agr. Exp. Station, Giannini Mimeo. Report No. 232, Berkeley. June 1960.

—. "Analytical Techniques Used in Determining the Optimum Replacement Pattern." Journal of Farm Economics. 42(4), November 1960.

Gaffney, M. Mason. Concept of Financial Maturity of Timber and Other Assets. Dept. of Agricultural Economics, North Carolina State College. Agr. Eco. Info. Series No. 62. Raleigh. December 1960.

(16) Bunce, Arthur C. The Economics of Soil Conservation. Ames: Iowa State College Press, 1945.

Ciriacy-Wantrup, S. V. Resource Conservation: Economics and Policies. Berkeley: University of California Press, 1952.

(17) Kelso, M. M. "Economic Analysis in the Allocation of the Federal Budget." Water Resources and Economic Development of the West. Conference Proceedings, Committee on the Economics of Water Resources Development of the Western Agricultural Economics Research Council. San Francisco. Report #8, Jan. 28-29, 1960. p. 21.

42

(18) Coutu, Arthur J. , W. W. McPherson, and Lee R. Martin. Methods for an Economic Evaluation of Soil Conservation Practices. North Carolina Agricultural Experiment Station, Raleigh. Tech. Bulletin 137, January 1959.

Pavelis, George A. , and John F. Timmons. "Programming Small Watershed Development, " Journal of Farm Economics. 42(2):225, May 1960.

Haren, Claude C. Conservation Farming in Selected Areas of the Southern Piedmont. Agr. Research Service, United States Department of Agriculture, Washington. ARS 43-120. August 1960.

(19) Wootten, H. H. , and Margaret R. Purcell. Farm Land Development: Present and Future, by Clearing, Drainage, and Irrigation. United States Department of Agriculture, Washington. Circular No. 825. October 1949.

(20) Stewart, Clyde E. , and D. C. Myrick. Control and Use of Resources in the Development of Irrigated Farms. Montana Agricultural Experiment Station, Bozeman, Bul. 476. October, 1951.

Kristjanson, Kris. Development of Irrigated Farms on the Mirage Flat Project. South Dakota Agr. Exp. Station, Brookings. Bul. 410. June 1951.

Voelker, Stanley W. Settlers Progress on Two North Dakota Irrigation Projects. North Dakota Agricultural Experiment Station, Fargo. Bul. 369   June 1951.

Stewart, Clyde E. Recent Land and Ground Water Development in Utah Under the Desert Land Act. Utah Agricultural Experiment Station, Logan. Bul. 418. March 1960.

(21) Caton, D. D. , and Christoph Beringer. Costs and Benefits of Reseeding Range Lands in Southern Idaho. Idaho Agr. Exp. Station, Moscow. Bul. 326. May 1960.

Caton, D. D. , et. al. "Economics of Improvement of Western Grazing Lands. " Jour. Range Management. 13(3):143. May 1960.

(22) Maier, Frank H. , Sheridan T. Maitland, and Gladys K. Bowles. The Tenure Status of Farm Workers in the United States. Agricultural Research Service, United States Department of Agriculture, Washington. Tech. Bul. 1217. July 1960.

(23) Salter, Leonard, A. Jr. Land Tenure in Process. Wisconsin Agr. Exp. Sta , Madison. Research Bul. 146. 'February 1943.

Parsons, Kenneth H. , and Eliot O. Waples. Keeping the Farm in the Family. Wisconsin Agr. Exp. Sta. , Madison. Research Bul. 157. September 1945.

(24) Hill, Howard L. , and Sydney D. Staniforth. A Modification of Leasing Arrangements to Expand Farm Opportunities. Wisconsin Agr. Exp. Station, Madison. Research Bul. 213. August 1959.

Kanel, Don. Opportunities for Beginning Farmers, Why are They Limited? Nebraska Agr. Exp. Sta. , Lincoln. Bul. 452. Also North Central Regional Publication 102. May 1960.

Reiss, Franklin J. Getting Started and Established In Farming With and Without Family Help. Illinois Agr. Ext. Service, Urbana. Circular 822; Also North Central Regional Extension Publication 8. June 1960.

(25) Inman, Buis, and William H. Fippen. Farm Land Ownership in the United States. Bureau of Agricultural Economics, U. S. Department of Agriculture. Miscellaneous Publication 699. Washington. December 1949.

Timmons, John F. , and Raleigh Barlowe. Farm Ownership in the Midwest. Iowa Agr. Exp. Sta. , Ames. Research Bul. 361; North Central Regional Publication No. 13. June 1949.

Patteson, G. W. , and A. J Harris and Z. M. K. Fulton. Classification of Land Ownership in Rockbridge County. Virginia Agr. Exp. Sta. , Blacksburg. Bul. 510. December 1959.

Anonymous. Land Ownership in the Great Plains. Agricultural Research Service, U. S. Department of Agriculture. ARS 43-93. Washington. June 1959.

Strohbehn, Roger W., and Gene Wunderlich. Land Ownership in the Great Plains States, 1958. Agr. Research Service, U. S. Department of Agriculture. Statistical Bul. 261. Washington. April 1960.

Strohbehn, Roger W., and John F. Timmons, Ownership of Iowa's Farmland. Res. Bul. 489. Iowa Agric. Exp. Station, Ames. December 1960.

Federal and State Rural Lands, 1950. Bureau of Agricultural Economics, U. S. Department of Agriculture. Circular No. 909. Washington. May 1952.

(26) Ellis, Harold, Raleigh Barlowe, and E. B. Hill. Inheritance of Farm Property in Michigan. Michigan Agr. Exp. Sta., Lansing. Special Bul. 388. January 1955.

Pine, Wilford H., and James K. Logan. Acquiring and Transferring Farm Real Estate in Kansas. Kansas Agr. Exp. Station, Manhattan. Circular 367. November 1958.

Hill, Elton B., and John W. Fitzgerald. The Land Contract as a Farm Finance Plan. Michigan Agr. Exp. Station, East Lansing. Special Bul. 431. November 1960.

O'Byrne, J. C., and J. F. Timmons. Planning Farm Property Transfers Within Families in Iowa. Iowa Agr. Exp. Station, Ames. Bul. P-125. January 1959.

Krausz, N. G. P. Installment Land Contract for Illinois Farm Land; A Deal to Study. Department of Agricultural Economics, Illinois Agr. Exp. Station, Urbana. Research Report AERR-31. January 1960.

Southern, John H. Farm Land Market Situation in the Southwestern States, 1946-54. Texas Agr. Exp. Station, College Station. Bul. 797; Southwestern Regional Bul. No. 5, March 1955.

Sargent, Frederick O. The Demand for Land in Texas. Texas Agr. Exp. Station, College Station Miscellaneous Publication 235. October 1957.

-. The Land Market Process in Robertson County. Texas Agr. Exp. Station, College Station. Bul. MP-290. July 1958.

Lassiter, Roy L. Jr., and W. K. McPherson. Agricultural Land Prices in Palm Beach County, Florida, 1940-55. Florida Agr. Exp. Station, Gainesville. Bul. 608. February 1959.

Fischer, Lloyd K., Richard Burkholder, and John Muehlbeier. The Farm Real Estate Market in Nebraska. Nebraska Agr. Exp. Sta., Lincoln. Bul. SB-456. March 1960.

(27) Maier, Frank H., James L. Hedrick, and W. L. Gibson, Jr. The Sale Value of Flue-Cured Tobacco Allotments. Virginia Agr. Exp. Station, Blacksburg. Tech. Bul. 148. April 1960.

Gardner, B. D., "Price Policies and the Changing West," The West in a Growing Economy, Proceedings of the Western Farm Economics Association, Logan, Utah. July 14-17, 1959. 228.

(28) Klickenberger, R. S., and W. L. Gibson, Jr. Farming as a Part Owner. Virginia Agr. Exp. Station, Blacksburg. Bul. 504. April 1959.

Pine, Wilford H., and Warren L. Trock. Leasing Irrigated Lands. Kansas Agr. Exp. Station, Manhattan. Circular 370, June 1959.

McWhorter, Robert L., and Arthur G. Murphey, Jr. The Legal Nature of Farm Rental Contracts in Georgia. Georgia Agr. Exp. Station, Athens, Tech. Bul. NF-18. September 1959.

Berry, Russel L., and Vernon E. Bau. Tenant Interest in Long Term Cash and Flexible Cash Leases. South Dakota Agr. Exp. Station, Brookings. Bul. 480. June 1959.

(29) Hurlburt, Virgil L. Farm Rental Practices and Problems in the Midwest. Iowa Agr. Exp. Station, Ames, Research Bul. 416; North Central Regional Publication No. 50. October 1954.

(30) Jensen, M. C., et. al. The Equitable Obligation When Assessed Irrigation District Lands are Taken for Highway Use. Washington Agr. Exp. Station, Pullman, Circular No. 350. December 1958.

Leonard, Lawrence A. Assessment of Farm Real Estate in the United States. Agr. Research Service, U. S. Department of Agriculture, ARS. 43-117. Washington. February 1960.

44

Hill, E. B. Impact of Taxes and Legal Cost on Farm Transfers Under State Settlement. Michigan Agr. Exp. Station, East Lansing. Special Bul. 424. 1959.

Fischer, Lloyd K., and John F. Timmons, Progress and Problems in the Iowa Soil Conservation Districts Program. Res. Bul. 466. Iowa Agric. Exp. Station, Ames. April 1959.

(31) Kelsey, M. P. Economic Effects of Field Renting on Resource Use on Central Indiana Farms. Dissertation abstract 20(5):16-115. November 1959.

de Benedictus, Michele, and John F. Timmons, Identification and Measurement of Inefficiencies in Leasing Systems. Iowa Agric Exp. Station, Ames. Res. Bul. 490. April 1959.

Schickele, Rainer, "Effect of Tenure Systems on Agricultural Efficiency." Journal of Farm Economics. 23. February 1941.

Johnson, M. C. "Federal Land Ownership and Local Government in Montana." Montana Business Review. 12(2). February 1960.

Chastain, E. B. "Implications of Property Transferral Arrangements to Agricultural Efficiency in the Black Belt Region of Alabama." Alabama Academy of Science Journal. 31(2). October 1951.

Brewer, Michael F. Water Pricing and Allocation With Particular Reference to California Irrigation District. California Agr. Exp. Station, Berkeley. Giannini Foundation of Agricultural Economics, Mimeograph Report 235. October 1960.

Casamajor, Paul, and Dennis Teeguarden and John Ziznuska. Timber Marketing and Land Ownership in Mendicino County. California Agr. Exp. Station, Berkeley. Bulletin 772. June 1960.

(32) Salter, op. cit., pp. 252-53.

3

Objectives of
Land Economics Research

by John F. Timmons*

This is an inquiry into the objectives of land economics research. Adhering to the premise that research is purposeful, at least in a broad sense, this inquiry seeks to identify the objectives motivating research in land economics.

Throughout this inquiry land economics is viewed as an applied area of economics, the parent discipline. However, through land economics research, economics is extended in its application to existing problems by relaxing certain assumptions and by embracing relevant institutions in the analyses. Within this context, attention is focused on certain approaches to identifying objectives peculiar to land economics research. These approaches are (1) retrospective consideration of major and ancillary objectives, (2) reorientation possibilities of these objectives, and (3) prospective objectives of major and ancillary orders.

LAND ECONOMICS AS AN APPLIED AREA OF ECONOMICS

As an applied area of economics, land economics shares in the rich legacy of knowledge and methods developed over the years by the parent discipline. Land economics not only partakes of this legacy but helps extend the content of economics in its particular role of advancing knowledge and applying knowledge to affairs of man. [1]

---

[1] Knowledge is used in the philosophical context throughout this chapter, as meaning intellectual knowledge rather than sensoral knowledge. Used in this sense, sensoral knowledge gained from the five external and four internal senses provide raw materials used by the intellect in fashioning intellectual knowledge. Thus, intellectual knowledge becomes characterized by (1) abstract rather than concrete, (2) ideas and concepts other than things, (3) judgments wherein contents of concepts are joined or divided, and (4) reasoning wherein a new proposition is derived from two other propositions with a common term.

---

*JOHN F. TIMMONS has been professor of economics at Iowa State University since 1947. Born in Missouri in 1912, he obtained a B.S. and an M.A. at the University of Missouri, and a Ph.D. at the University of Wisconsin. He was also an instructor at the latter university. He served several years in the Bureau of Agricultural Economics, United States Department of Agriculture. He has written extensively in the field of land economics, and has served as consultant or on committees for a number of national and international organizations.

Two basic ideas of human behavior apply to land economics as a segment of economics.

First man prefers more to less of the goods and services which satisfy his wants. Or, stated another way, man prefers less to more of the things which dissatisfy him. This idea is the crux of the maximization principle which is the energizing core of economics. Actually, this principle is inherent in all disciplines through their indirect or direct and immediate or ultimate contributions to the satisfaction of human wants. This principle performs a unifying role for all knowledge in the Aristotelian sense of universality of knowledge. However, the principle reaches a primacy of relevancy to human welfare in the science of economics, which is concerned with the transformation of scarce resources (factors) into satisfaction of multiple and often competing human wants (products) and services.[2]

Ever since Adam Smith and the tenuous roots threading back to the Greeks, economics has been developing the logic and tools concerned with enlarging and distributing the wealth of nations and their citizens. In the process, many and elaborate systems of analysis have evolved including, for example, Hicksian equilibrium, Keynesian savings investment, Domar's growth model, and Reder's marginal conditions of maximum welfare. In the process, numerous and specialized tools have been borrowed or fashioned by economists, including, for example, marginal analysis and dynamic linear programing, in the interest of advancing knowledge and making knowledge serve man in his pursuit of maximizing his satisfaction.

Land economics as an applied area of economics is a legitimate heir of the entire reservior of knowledge, both methods and matter, developed in the parent discipline.

Second, man is rational[3] in the sense that he possesses an intellect (individual and collective) capable of appraising alternative courses of action which he (they) expects to satisfy him (them) most.[4] In other words, the science of economics identifies alternatives and provides probable consequences of each as an aid to the human intellect (individually and collectively) which analyzes alternatives prerequisite to using the will (individually or collectively) in making and implementing a choice between alternative

---

[2]The English term "science" is derived from the Latin "scientia" from the verb "scire" which means "to know." Since in English there is no etymological connection between the terms science and to know, not all forms of knowing are science but all science is knowing. Science, as the term is used in this chapter, imposes these requirements on knowledge: (1) must be intellectual, not merely sensoral, (2) must be certain if certainty is possible; if not possible, must be held in a provisional sense of certainty of probability, and (3) must provide insight into causation along lines of Aristotelian posterior analytics. Thus, science results from the thinking process of the intellect. However, it has meaning only insofar as it can be transferred to other beings through written or spoken language.

[3]Theories of why people behave as they do run through a wide continuum of rationality explanation. Economics attributes to man a high measure of rationality and stands at one end of the continuum. On the other end is psychology which offers emotions, motivations, and other causes of human behavior. In between, sociology and anthropology offer cultural and environmental factors as major determinants in explaining human behavior. See Herbert A. Simon, Models of Man (New York: John Wiley & Sons, Inc., 1955), particularly the "Introduction" and Part I, "Causation and Influence Relations."

[4]The use of the concepts individual and collective intellects and individual and collective wills warrants some explanation lest my ideas be misinterpreted. Obviously, the individual human being possesses an intellect and a will among the many faculties of his mind. These are the two important faculties underlying an understanding and application of economics. The collective intellect refers to the understanding and analysis by those people involved in and affected by appraising group courses of action. The collective will refers to group decision among alternatives of group action. Important elements of interaction, conflict, and compromise are involved in the appraisal and decision processes. The use of these terms does not imply that there exists a collective will or intellect apart from the individuals involved in the processes.

courses of action. Thus, land economics as a field of economics is a behavioral science concerned primarily with the intellect and will faculties of the human mind. As such, land economics is concerned with decision-making and particularly with providing the facts and ideas upon which decisions are premised.

Here again, land economics as an applied area of economics incurs the responsibility of contributing facts and ideas to the human intellect (individually and collectively) for use in making a choice between alternatives prerequisite to using the will (individually or collectively).

Land economics has been criticized (not without some justification) for not availing itself more fully of the legacy of content and methods from the parent discipline. More specifically, land economics has been overly involved with institutions and everyday problems and inadequately involved in making use of analysis proffered by the parent discipline. This may be due in part to the initial orientation of land economics around the property concept and pressing problems of land use and land tenure. This possibility is explored later in the chapter. Or, it may be due partly to recent trends in economics which have tended to veer away from institutions and political economy as legitimate areas of economic inquiry.

Regardless of the reasons for land economics not using modern developments in economic analysis more fully or for the parent discipline to veer away from institutions in recent years, I find no substance for any necessary conflict.[5] The logical analytical framework and tools provided by a Keynes or a Hicks are essential but not sufficient in providing man's intellect with the full basis for making decisions. Likewise, the consideration of institutions provided by a Wehrwein or a Commons are essential but not sufficient. Both are complementary within their total range of usefulness.

Professor J. R. Hicks has commented upon this matter by excluding institutions from his theoretical economic analyses. In the "Introduction" of his widely used book, Professor Hicks states:

> The programme before us is thus rather extensive, and we have, I think, a right to limit it in some direction . . .
>
> Another more important limitation is implicit in our sub-title. This is a work on Theoretical Economics, considered as the logical analysis of an economic system of private enterprise, without any inclusion of reference to institutional controls. I shall interpret this limitation pretty severely. For I consider the pure logical analysis of capitalism to be a task in itself, while the survey of economic institutions is best carried on by other methods, such as those of the economic historian (even when the institutions are contemporary institutions). It is only when both these tasks are accomplished that economics begins to near the end of its journey. But there is a good line of division of labour between them, and it is a line we do well to observe.
>
> It must be realized, indeed, that, as the price of this austerity, the purely theoretical economist becomes unable to say that any opportunities or dangers he diagnoses are or are not present in the

---

[5]This viewpoint has been developed more fully by this author in "Integrating Law and Economics in Analyzing Agricultural Land Use Problems," Journal of Farm Economics, Vol. XXXVII, No. 5, December 1955; and in Chapter 10, "Land Institutions Impeding and Facilitating Agricultural Adjustment," Problems and Policies of American Agriculture (Ames: Iowa State University Press, 1959).

actual world at any particular date. He is bound to leave that to a separate investigation. But he will at least have helped that other investigator in showing him some things to look out for (1, p. 7).

This means, as I interpret Professor Hicks, that economics science does not fulfill its responsibilities to human welfare unless and until institutions enter the analyses. Economic analysis achieves usefulness in its application to economic problems only as existing institutions are understood in terms of their economic consequences and only as alternative changes in institutions are evaluated. This idea permeates land economics research and remains a major characteristic of the field.

Professor Kenneth E. Boulding confesses that he has been ". . . gradually coming under the conviction, disturbing for the professional theorist, that there is no such thing as economics -- there is only social science applied to economic problems" (2, p. vii). Boulding attributes this conviction on his part to ". . . the failure of economics to integrate itself into the general body of social science" (2 p. vii).

Professor J. M. Clark views the field of economics in this manner. "The subject matter of technical economics consists of the operations of what we call, for short, the 'market.' But the market operates in a community setting . . ." (3, p. v). Clark finds the community setting made up of institutions, attitudes and mechanisms ". . . without which the things we call economic laws and principles would not work . . ." (3, p. v).

Thus, land economics helps carry economics toward the end of its Hicksian journey by making economic laws and principles work in the Clarksian sense through the means of institutions. More will be said on this point later as land economics takes a more limited role in discharging this type of responsibility.

NATURE AND OBJECTIVES OF SCIENTIFIC RESEARCH

Scientific research is interpreted as yielding knowledge using the terms as previously defined. This knowledge must add to the system of knowledge constituted as a coherent whole of interconnected parts appropriately ordered. [6] As knowledge expands, specialization in subfields necessarily develops because of the life (time) and capacity limitations on the individual mind. Land economics affords an application of this reasoning. According to Richard T. Ely, "Land economics, a new branch of economic science, is a product of the specialization which accompanies the development of all sciences" (4, p. 119). In earlier times, one mind, an Aristotle for example, could be complimented with "totum scibile scisti," "Thou knowest whatever can be known." However, today with the growth and specialization of knowledge, even an Aristotle could not become the universal doctor that he was in the pre-Christian Era.

Knowledge in the scientific sense is preferably expressed in universal statements. These statements must be true or probably true. Also, knowledge is concerned with causality. And the statements must be logically ordered. Finally, research must explain its investigations and findings in a communicable form.

---

[6] This reasoning follows that of Professor P. Henry Van Laer in The Philosophy of Science (New York: Ad Press, Ltd., 1956).

If this be the nature of scientific research, what then are its objectives?

Objectives of research have been treated profusely in the literature of the several disciplines as researchers are well aware. The labors of these discussions may be briefed into two general purposes. One is knowledge for its own sake. Two is knowledge for problem solving.

The former objective is justified by the fact that the human mind inherently is curious and seeks and finds satisfaction in merely knowing. This kind of research, sometimes known as basic research, is carried out without any test of utility in problem solving, albeit the results frequently generate the major breakthroughs providing necessary foundations for solving man's most difficult problems.

The second objective is justified by the fact that human beings encounter specific problems which are solvable, at least potentially. Through application of the existing reservoir of relevant knowledge to specific problems, solutions with probable consequences can be sought and ordered. But applied research infers that some elements of knowledge are available for application. This available knowledge may derive from basic research or from applied research.

The distinction we make between basic and applied research is one of intent, not methods and not subject matter. Both basic and applied research are necessary in all disciplines with which I am familiar and economics or its applications in land economics offers no exception.

The identification of objectives within a discipline whether they refer to basic or applied research is another matter. We now proceed into an examination of the means to identify and examine objectives with which land economics may be charged within the discipline of economics.

IDENTIFICATION OF RESEARCH OBJECTIVES

We consider three approaches (albeit there are others) which appear relevant to arriving at an identification of the objectives of land economics research.

The first approach derives the objectives of land economics research from the research completed and undertaken by land economists. This approach is in keeping with Professor Jacob Viner's observation that economics is what economists do.[7] Although land economics research studies completed or in progress provide material from which objectives may be imputed or generalized, this approach has one inherent weakness. It is this. What land economists do may carry them far afield from what could be considered land economics science because of their use of all kinds of personal skills on many types of personal interests. In other words, if there is a field of study in land economics, the field of study per se does not prevent the land economist, the practitioner, from venturing far afield in what he does. In identifying the objectives of land economics research, we must limit our search to land economics science and not wander afield with land economists who desire and proceed to follow their personal desires and

---

[7] See Jacob Viner, International Economics (Glencoe, Ill.: The Free Press, 1951). This approach is also in accord with Albert Einstein's views expressed in his The World As I See It, p. 30, in these words: "If you want to find out anything from theoretical physicists, about the methods they use, I advise you to stick closely to this principle: don't listen to these words, fix your attention on their deeds."

interests unless their particular skills developed as land economists guide them in their professional activities.

A second approach derives objectives of land economics research through examination of the skills of the land economist.[8] This approach has been suggested by Professor Kenneth Boulding in discussing the objectives of economics as follows:

> These skills may be employed in fields remote from the actual field of economics. This is one reason why I have chosen to emphasize the skill itself rather than the concrete subject matter from which the skill is derived. Skills developed in one area often carry over into other areas. A carpenter finds that some of his woodworking skills apply to metals; a pianist finds that some of his musical skill adapts itself to the violin. Similarly an economist may carry over part of his skill into other intellectual fields or even into the solution of practical problems of political or domestic life (5, p. 2).

Extending Boulding's reasoning, the contribution of the land economist to human welfare is gauged by his special skills developed through his study of land economics as a specialized application of economics. In line with this reasoning, land economics is that study which develops the skills of the land economist. This idea leads us to inquire into both what is a land economist and what is land economics. This we shall attempt to do presently.

The third approach was stated succinctly by Professor Salter as follows: "The content of a field of science consists of the problems to which the scienc turns its attention" (6, p. 227). Developing futher this idea, Salter reasoned that "Scientific inquiry must ultimately be related to the solution of experienced problems; its significance judged on the basis of its contributions to that solution; and its final test of validity set in the result obtained when the conclusions are put to test in purposive action" (6, p. 226).

These three ideas advanced by Viner, Boulding and Salter appear useful in our endeavors to articulate the objectives of land economics research. They involve inspecting (1) the work land economists have done, (2) the skills land economists have used and (3) the problems to which land economists have devoted their labors.

These three approaches become the complex, the modus operandi, and the major tool we use in identifying objectives of land economics research involving both the field and the practitioner in the field. We use this approach in both the retrospective and prospective parts of the examination although certain important modifications are made in the latter part.

MAJOR AND ANCILLARY OBJECTIVES: IN RETROSPECT

Pursuing the approaches suggested above that land economics is what land economists do (Viner), that land economics arises from the application of skills of land economists (Boulding), and that land economics consists of the problems to which it turns its attention (Salter), we shall

---

[8]See Kenneth E. Boulding, "Economics Is What Economists Do," The Skills of the Economist (Cleveland: Howard Allen, Inc., 1958), Chapter 1, pp. 1-31.

look briefly into what land economists have been doing, the problems absorbing their energies and how they have performed their work. From this retrospective excursion we expect to gain insight into what the objectives of land economics research have been.

Land economics as a field of study is relatively young even though its roots trace back to Ricardo, Malthus, J. S. Mill, Jones, Carey and other progenitors of the economics discipline. Beginning during the closing decade of the nineteenth century, land economics started to take form as a field of study within economics.

Three major developments during the closing quarter of the nineteenth century provided the mix from which land economics was fashioned.

First, certain land problems emerged on the national scene which attracted attention of legislators, scholars, and public minded citizens. The ideas deeply imbedded in economics of the later classical evolution of the science that private ownership and management of the nation's land resources without public interference would assure adequate development and use of these resources (a la Arthur Young) came under severe attack.[9] Likewise, the idea of universal family farm ownership (espoused by Thomas Jefferson and Thomas Hart Benton) became questioned particularly in light of the results of the first census of agriculture in 1880. The questioning of these two pillars of American land policy aggravated by the reasoning of Henry George and Karl Marx resulted in demands for public entrance into the management, control, and even ownership of land resources.

Second, trends in economics by English and Austrian scholars away from the political economy ideas of the earlier classical school and toward an orientation of laissez faire private ownership and management was not geared to the emerging land use and control problems demanding more rather than less action by government. Consequently, foresters, engineers, lawyers, and scholars in other disciplines were attracted to the vacuum created by the retreat of economists from consideration of public policy. For example, the Association for the Advacement of Science in 1890, petitioned Congress to effect substantial changes in the nation's land system, largely if not wholly through the action by physical scientists.

Third, certain American economists, notably Richard T. Ely, were not willing to define public policy issues outside the legitimate domain of economics. These insurgent economists had largely escaped the laissez faire reasoning of their colleagues in the private managerial approach to resource use following the English and Austrian influences. In contrast, they relied more heavily on the reasoning of the German historical school, particularly as influenced by Professor Karl Knies.[10] Ely and his colleagues engaged in analyses of the land policy issue of the times and, in the process, laid the groundwork for the development of land economics as a field within economics.

This reasoning, upon which land economics was founded, has been restated more recently by Professor J. M. Clark as follows:

The traditional "economics" laws are not wholly obsolete, but they

---

[9]These classical ideas still linger in our society as illustrated by Mr. Wilson's widely quoted remark to the effect that what is good for General Motors is also good for the nation.

[10]It is interesting to note that Ely and his public-policy-minded colleagues founded the American Economic Association in 1885, largely in protest of prevailing trends in nonclassical economics.

can no longer be presented as representing the dominant tendencies of the actual economic system now existing . . . . Very broadly speaking, the economic system used to be presented as a scheme of unplanned cooperation in which "economic laws" automatically convert the self-seeking efforts of individuals into an efficient organization and distribution of the resources of the community. Growing recognition of the shortcomings of the system and of the need for growing measures of public intervention have for some time changed the character of this picture . . . . (3, pp. 3-4).

Ely identified land economics as emerging during the concluding decade(s) of the nineteenth century in these words. "I am confident that very soon after I came to Wisconsin in 1892 we began a systematic treatment of what is now called land economics. I treated the whole subject under the awkward title, 'Landed Property and the Rent of Land'" (7, p. 191).

In 1916, Ely presented a paper to the American Economic Association (the association which he earlier helped found) entitled, "Landed Property as an Economic Concept and as a Field of Research" (8). In this paper Ely stressed his reasoning that economics had offered little help in dealing with the economic problems arising from property and land resource use. This paper stressed resource conservation, land taxation and income, ownership interests in land, and public controls over private land.

During the same period, Lewis C. Gray who was associated with Ely, published two important papers, "Economic Possibilities of Conservation" and "Rent Under the Assumption of Exhaustibility" (9, 10). These papers which have become major reference points in land economics research dealt with resource use. Thus, the Gray papers complemented the work of Ely which dealt more with land as property.

In its initial development, land economics thus became concerned primarily with land resource use and with property in land and with the interrelationships between the two.

It was perhaps not unexpected to find land economics recognized administratively as a field of study in the U. S. Department of Agriculture in 1919 (11). The Division of Land Economics, as the field of study was known administratively, was headed by L. C. Gray who remained in charge for two decades. During the same year, 1919, land economics first became a major course offering at a university (Wisconsin) (4, p. 119). Thus, after nearly three decades of evolutionary development, land economics became christened in 1919 both as a field of research and as a course of study within the economics discipline.

During the period, Ely defined land economics as ". . . that division of economics, theoretical and applied, which is concerned with the land as an economic concept and with the economic relations which grow out of land as property" (12, p. 4). Another development was taking place during the third decade of this century which extended land economics in a specialized manner into the urban field. Following closely the Ely definition of land economics, Dorau and Hinman defined urban land economics as ". . . that division of land economics which embraces that class of land defined and described as urban land" (13, p. 31). Later on, Ratcliff reinterpreted urban land economics as follows: "Urban land economics deals with the processes and patterns of land utilization where man and his artifacts are assembled in communities" (14, p. i).

During the two decades between World War I and World War II, land economics became entrenched in the USDA and the university research programs. During this period land economics became highly oriented to problems of land use and land tenure in both urban and rural context. Salter's excellent review of the content of land economics research during this period and the methods used by land economists provides insight into the objectives characterizing the work (15).

Salter characterizes land economics research during the period as research in land utilization and research in land property. Thus, land economics research developed close to the format provided earlier by Ely and Gray.

More recently Professor Schultz has emphasized the major contributions and concerns of land economists in terms of land tenure, soil conservation, land use, the nature of land inputs and outputs, and the problems of measurability of land inputs and outputs (16) (17).

In reviewing the work of land economists, the skills they have used, and the problems which they have attacked, a pattern of objectives begins to emerge. The land economist has started from two important philosophical points of reference which may not always have been obvious to him as he went about his work. These references consisted of (1) the property concept involving the exclusive use of an economic good and (2) the spatial concept involving all land resources arising within the three dimensions of space.

In pursuit of knowledge guided by these two referential concepts, land economists have followed two major objectives. First, they have been deeply involved in the classification of land resources and the uses of land resources and the classification of property in land in terms of institutions and the controls exerted by them. Second, they have been equally deeply involved in alleviating problems arising from land resource use and existing property institutions in land. Within this latter objective, numerous ancillary objectives have evolved. Land economists have emphasized in their studies the differences between existing land uses and the desired land uses, between the existing tenure arrangements and desired tenure arrangements. In this process of study, conflicts of interest among individuals and between groups and among individuals and groups become obvious. Equally obvious became the use of public interventions generated from the nature of the property concept of exclusive but not absolute control by individuals, to resolve conflicts of interest.

REORIENTATION OF OBJECTIVES

Self-examination is an important aspect of the development of any field of knowledge. This task involves initially the consideration of the objectives of a field and, particularly, possible reorientation of these objectives. Self-examination of the field of land economics appears particularly apropos. This field has grown very rapidly and developed frequently under considerable pressure for answers to pressing problems.

Referring to this need for examining the content and objectives of land economics research, Professor Salter reasoned thusly:

The development of land economics in the United States has been
such as to accentuate the need for a review of the research that
has been done. Land economics is not only relatively new but
has experienced a phenomenal expansion during its brief course.
The tempo of this growth has been set by rapid and sharp social
changes during the past few decades. Far from having a slow
and gradual maturation period, land economics research has
mushroomed under a demand for results which has been so
pressing that only inadequate attention has been given to the
re-examination of scientific requirements, to the ordering of
knowledge gained, and to the training of scientists (15, p.1).

Professor Wehrwein came to a similar conclusion regarding the
need for appraising land economics research in these words: "In conclusion, it must be said that there is as yet no complete body of theory
setting forth in a systematic fashion the principles of land economics,
partly because land economists have been so busy with direct attacks on
land problems that they have not had much opportunity to convert experience into theory" (18, p.169).

In keeping with the reasoning of Salter and Wehrwein, our retrospective excursion into the development of land economics research
strengthens the need for examining the objectives of land economics
research in terms of possible reorientations. In pursuing this examination, certain reorientations of objectives become apparent. The
general nature of these changes involves important shifts in emphasis
and in content. These shifts are as follows: from description to
analysis, from ordinal to cardinal measurement and identification, from
normative to positive characterization of data, and from applied to basic
studies including the development of analytical tools and concepts.

These suggested shifts in emphasis and content are not intended to be
in any sense complete shifts but are intended to suggest a degree of redirection of land economics in the years ahead. This redirection is the
concern of the remainder of this and the following sections.

Initial stages in the development of a field of knowledge frequently
rely heavily on the nature, description, and classification of data within
the field. This is a logical orientation phase. Land economics has
experienced description and classification in abundance. It appears that
this science has reached the stage of development, however, whereby its
research can move more aggressively into the analysis of structural
relationships, into the precision of identification and quantification, into
the development of methods and into basic research in quest of knowledge
for its own sake rather than research under duress and pressure of
current problems to be solved even though problem-solving remains one
of the important aspects of the work.

One of the suggested reorientations is a shift somewhat from normative to positive considerations in land economics. I use these terms in
the context developed by J. M. Keynes and Milton Friedman. That is,
positive economics ". . . deals with 'what is' not with 'what ought to be.'
Its task is to provide a system of generalizations that can be used to make
correct predictions about the consequences of any change in circumstances. Its performance is to be judged by the precision, scope, and
conformity with experience of the predictions it yields" (19, p. 4).

Following further the reasoning of J. M. Keynes and Friedman, normative economics deals with what "ought" to be.

Interrelationships between normative and positive economics are necessary and complementary. As Friedman points out,

> The conclusions of positive economics seem to be, and are, immediately relevant to important normative problems, to questions of what ought to be done and how any given goal can be attained . . . any policy conclusion necessarily rests on a prediction about the consequences of doing one thing rather than another, a prediction that must be based -- implicitly or explicitly -- on positive economics. There is not, of course, a one-to-one relation between policy conclusions and the conclusions of positive economics; if there were, there would be no normative science. Two individuals may agree on the consequences of a particular piece of legislation. One may regard them as desirable on balance and so for the legislation; the other, as undesirable and so oppose the legislation (19, pp. 4-5).

This is the type of shift of emphasis to which we refer in providing land economics an improved scientific balance between normative and positive considerations.

The shift from applied to basic research objectives (as defined earlier) is in keeping with the earlier reasoning of Ely as follows: "As science, land economics seeks the truth for its own sake. It aims to understand present facts in regard to land ownership in all their human relationships, to explain their development in the past, and to discuss present tendencies of growth" (4, p.122). This is the type of shift in objectives that Wehrwein was suggesting when he lamented the fact that land economists had not experienced the opportunity "to convert experience into theory." Salter likewise recognized the need for this type of shift in land economics research objectives where he concluded that land economics had given only inadequate attention to the "re-examination of scientific requirements to the training of scientists." Both Wehrwein and Salter attributed the incompleteness of theoretical developments in land economics, partly at least, to the pressure of problems to solve and programs to administer.

Science as defined earlier is communicated to other beings. In the process, other beings assimilate, modify and develop results received. Thus, any field of science is a changing system of knowledge in terms of what is known and how it is known. Professor Henry Van Laer describes science thusly,

> This science as a system is not at all something rigid or static, but on the contrary it is a dynamic whole which is born and grows, is subject to all kinds of changes and is developed in scope and depth in and through the intellectual activity of human beings. Taken in this sense, therefore, science is never something purely objective, but, as it exists in reality, i.e., as it is possessed by man, it is always a web of subjectivity and objectivity (20, p. 6).

The shift from ordinal to cardinal measurement and identification of factors, functions and other aspects of the system of knowledge involves shifts in methods.[11]   The shift in methods draws upon mathematics in both processes of analysis and of communication.

In the process of making this shift, we must be cognizant of the limitations as well as the contributions to be realized from methods borrowed from mathematics. Mathematics as a system of logical knowledge is ordained by arbitrarily chosen postulates and conventions. For example, only in Euclidean geometry is the sum of the angles of a triangle equal to two right angles and this because of the postulate of parallel lines. In the case of numbers, the sum of 3 and 4 is 7 only in terms of natural numbers. In case of vectors of the magnitudes of 3 and 4, the sum depends upon their direction. Thus, the sum is 7 only if the vectors run in the same direction. Thus, the use of quantification analyses involves the appreciation of limits as well as the contributions of the analytical models and procedures. As John Dewey once observed:

> . . . an adequate set of symbols depends upon prior institution of valid ideas of the conceptions and relations that are symbolized. Without fulfillment of this condition, formal symbolization will (as so often happens at present) merely perpetuate existing mistakes while strengthening them by seeming to give them scientific standing (21, p. iv).

We now proceed to try and visualize how these kinds of shifts in objectives of land economic research may be articulated in terms of major and ancillary objectives for the future.

MAJOR AND ANCILLARY OBJECTIVES: IN PROSPECT

There are several ways in which we could go about suggesting objectives for future land economics research. We could suggest basic and applied objectives as defined earlier. However, this kind of characterization of objectives could be applicable to any research field, hence, we should endeavor to find and use a means which would be more indigenous to land economics.

We return to the approaches used earlier to examine land economics research from the retrospective point of view. Thus, we consider further the Viner, Boulding, and Salter complex. Here we encounter some difficulties. The Viner approach becomes largely ineligible since it is limited to a retrospective orientation in terms of what land economists do and have done as evidenced by research undertakings. Thus, we have remaining the Boulding and Salter approaches.

Since the Boulding approach leads us to deal with the skills of the land economist and since the land economist is first an economist, we identify the skills of the land economist with the skills of an economist. Thus, the land economist may draw and develop his skills from the total methods, techniques, and procedures found in the parent discipline of economics with two special extensions into institutions and natural resources.

---

[11] The word "method" is derived from the Greek "methodos" which means "road to." Method in the research context means the procedures used to reach the intended end.

We have extended the Salter approach into the Ely philosophy to include land economics research for the sake of knowledge as well as for the solution of problems. Hence, we need not be overly anxious about the application of knowledge to concrete problems; our major concern is to identify the elements of problems with which land economists are concerned and then proceed to develop both basic and applied considerations relevant to these elements.

THE CORE ELEMENTS

The major ingredients of the mix from which land economics is fashioned involve: (1) maximization of human satisfactions from (2) products and services arising from land resources in light of (3) conflicts of uses and interests between individuals and groups which are (4) resolved by collective action.

Oriented in the maximization core of economics, land economics seeks an improved understanding of the resources of land and how these resources may be transformed into human want satisfactions. Even though the processes of use including factor control and product distribution have been regularized to a degree by "working rules" embedded in land institutions, many conflicts develop between uses and between users. These conflicts arise between individuals, between groups, and between individuals and groups. Presumably, land institutions have developed for the purpose of aiding man to maximize his want satisfactions in the use of land resources. However, these institutions frequently lag behind technological and economic change and thereby become impediments rather than facilitators to man's want satisfactions. Since land institutions were made by man, they may be changed by man to administer to his needs more adequately. Thus, through collective action man may bring about changes in land institutions more in keeping with his needs.

If these be the core elements of land economics, then what are the implied objectives?

THE IMPLIED OBJECTIVES

The major objectives in prospect suggested by this analysis are fourfold.

The first objective concerns land resources, their nature, their response to stimuli of technology and innovations, their elasticity, their substitutions and their transformations all viewed in light of human wants. Pursuit of this objective relies upon positive economics, cardinal measurement, and basic research as these concepts have been defined earlier.

The second objective concerns alternative courses of progress in allocating and organizing land resources. This objective appraises alternatives in terms of their probable consequences. Pursuit of this objective uses the results of the first objective and proceeds with a normative approach.

The third objective concerns institutional means for attaining alternative courses of progress. This objective embraces the identification and nature of present institutions in terms of their functioning as means which inhibit or facilitate the achievement of economic objectives. This objective also includes the development, discovery, and invention of additional institutions which will inhibit less and facilitate more the achievement of economic objectives.

The fourth objective concerns the development of models and analytical procedures which will accommodate the kinds of analyses implicit in the three preceding objectives.

The nature of these four major objectives and their ancillary objectives is developed further below. The development of ideas under the major objectives frequently overlaps. However, an attempt is made to provide an initial home for each ancillary within the objective in which it is placed initially.

What Are Land Resources?

This objective seeks to identify the kinds and characteristics of land resources. These include surface, subsurface, and suprasurface resources. The characteristics sought embrace all kinds of present and potential uses of these resources. Land resources might be regarded as knowledge that gives man some measure of control over his natural environment. Thus, resources become as unlimited as man's capacity to extend his knowledge. This concept brings technology and innovation directly into the analysis. Productivity coefficients of land in alternative uses are required. Supply elasticities of land in various uses are needed. Also, the land input requires definition and measurement. What is the range of and what are the substitution ratios between various kinds of land resources?

Professor Schultz asked a relevant question as follows: " Are the natural and original differences in the physical properties of particular parcels of land employed for farming related in some consistent and necessary way to the differences in the value productivity of human agents in agriculture" (17, p. 207)? Answers to this type of question help satisfy the objectives of land economics research.

What Courses of Change?

In terms of possibilities procured from objective 1, this second objective considers and converts possibilities into alternatives with probable consequences linked to each. This objective embraces the matters of economic growth insofar as land resources and land institutions are concerned. The organization and allocation of resources are considered at the multiple firm and regional as well as national levels for this and other countries.

This objective embraces the questions raised by Schultz in his retardation hypothesis (17, p. 207). Does development occur in a specific locational matrix? Are these matrices primarily industrial-urban in composition? Does existing economic organization function best at or near the center of a particular matrix of economic development?

As stated by Professor Loomer,

The "retardation hypothesis" will, of course, be welcomed by the land economists who, among others, have given their atten-

tion to economic locations, site and transportation as factors
related to economic welfare. Professor Schultz, however, has
given the old idea a new twist. He is not so much interested in
the relation of location to cost and price differentials -- the
conventional approach -- but in the relation between location
and "imperfections" in the capital market. When an investigator sets himself to look into "imperfections," he has apparently
begun to question the traditional assumptions of perfect competition, perfect mobility of the factors, and perfect economic
rationality in the part of decision makers. Furthermore, the
"retardation hypothesis" implies some kind of regional approach
to economic analysis. The proposition rests on the assumption
that one area is not like another, and that insight into economic
affairs demands a willingness to inquire into the specific circumstances of a given situation (22, p. 396).

Under this objective, we consider land resources in multiple as well
as in alternative uses. Can land in one use, i.e., farming, be assigned
a negative value product through land retirement as long as positive value
products exist, albeit low, in other uses? What are the possibilities of
substituting land for capital on extensive margins of use if land develops
negative returns through the substitution of capital for land on the
intensive margins?

To what extent and in what manner is technological progress as well
as program benefits capitalized into land values? In this respect, the
study recently completed by the Southeast Land Tenure Research Committee is a pioneering example fulfilling this objective (23).

Identification and appraisal of the courses of progress in the use of
land resources necessarily involve consideration of demands for the
products and services contributed by land resources. These demands in
terms of alternate estimates under differing assumptions including
contingency reserves must be translated into land resource needs in
meeting these demands. In the process, joint, multiple, and single purposes require consideration.

What Are Land Institutions?

In this objective, we proceed to identify and characterize the many
land institutions. We identify and appraise them as means in the process
of maximizing human satisfactions. We fashion new institutions through
sheer speculation and through purposeful invention to remove present
defects.

Here we consider the defects in agrarian structures throughout the
world as impediments to progress. These are the defects suggested by
the United Nations and may be identified in a general sense as uncertainties of tenure, high fixed costs of operating noncontiguous holdings,
undersized holdings, underutilized reserves, insecure land titles, high
fixed costs of ownership, inadequate legal protection for guaranteeing
rights, occupational immobilities and inadequate knowledge of existing
improvements in agrarian structures.

Specific identification of these defects throughout this and other
countries and the nature of the institutions engendering these defects

suggest important objectives for future land economics research.
Possible means for overcoming these defects constitute additional
objectives.

When technological improvements flow through land as property,
how may these benefits be released and sprayed among resource contributors in relation to their contributed productivity? How may social
benefits be distributed?

Do land institutions induce dissociations of inputs and outputs in the
intellect(s) of the planning agent(s) and thus produce a motivation to stop
short of or go beyond the optimum allocation from the best interests of
the firm? From society? Examples of studies which move in the
direction of this objective include recent North Central Land Tenure
Research Committee publications (24) (25). These studies endeavor to
measure as well as identify tenure-engendered inefficiencies in resource
use.

To remove these dissociations, what may be done with the multiple
firm planning unit such as a watershed firm? Recent studies of regional
resource analysis applied particularly to waterhsheds are suggestive of
the kinds of objectives which challenge land economists in the years
ahead (26). These objectives include the formulation of optimal development programs which maximize discounted net returns from resources
considered, which allocate development costs among various public and
private participants, and which provide for the management of the
multiple firm including financing, installation, and maintenance.

Does the inheritance system tend to make the home farm a refuge for
the less competent farm youth, thus inducing inferior managerial capacity
into the farming industry?

What are the relative advantages and disadvantages of alternative
forms of business organization in farming and other resource organizational units? Consider the corporate, sole proprietor, partnership,
co-operative and other forms.

What are the public controls applicable to private land resource use?
What are the varied applications of these controls and the consequences?
Consider public versus private ownership of land resources and of
productive rights in these resources. These are suggestive of the many
ancillary objectives encompassed under the major objective concerned
with land institutions.

What Models and Procedures?

Even though the economics discipline contains a wealthy reservior
of methods available to the land economists, application of these methods·
to land economics problems may require considerable modification,
adaptation, and invention to derive the tools necessary for the tasks at
hand.

One type of method which upon initial application promises to be of
valuable aid in land economics analysis is dynamic programing wherein
institutions are carried as restriction in the analysis. However,
several problems in wider application of the method demand attention.
One problem involves the discreet continuous additions of land. For
example, the addition of 21. 3 acres of land in the maximizing process
may be as unrealistic as the addition of 0. 4 of a litter of pigs or 0. 34 of
a dairy cow.

In the area of regional and aggregative resource development, several promising methods are suggested including Leontief's input-output model extended by Isard's regional data and Losch's location factor (27) (28). In resolving the partial equilibrium difficulties which Alfred Weber faced, Losch has suggested the theory of economic regions, which offers opportunities for further work. The Leontief approach is largely static and positive despite certain normative assumptions like constant costs of production. Proceeding into nonstochastic programing, optimization of certain objectives subject to certain restraints becomes a guiding objective. Here, institutional restraints may be utilized at the regional level just as institutional restraints were utilized at the intrafirm level in the de Benedictis-Timmins study (25).

Although programing, particularly dynamic programing, and input-output models provide initial foundations for accomplishing major objectives 2 and 3, much work remains in developing an integrated model which makes use of normative as well as positive approaches and data.

In the area of public and private and intraprivate conflicts in resource allocation and income distribution, welfare economics offers useful starting points. The problem of interpersonal utilities and measurement remain to be solved, but they provide the challenge as well as the direction for methodological developments.

CITATIONS

(1) J. R. Hicks, Value and Capital (Second Edition - London: Oxford University Press, 1946).

(2) Kenneth E. Boulding, A Reconstruction of Economics (New York: John Wiley and Sons, 1950).

(3) J. M. Clark, Economic Institutions and Human Welfare (New York: Knopf, 1957).

(4) R. T. Ely, "Land Economics," Economic Essays Contributed in Honor of John Bates Clark (New York: The Macmillan Co., 1927).

(5) Kenneth E. Boulding, The Skills of the Economist (Cleveland: Howard Allen, Inc., 1958).

(6) Leonard A. Salter, Jr., "The Content of Land Economics and Research Methods Adapted to Its Needs," Journal of Farm Economics, Vol. XXIV, No. 1 (February 1942), pp. 226-47.

(7) Richard T. Ely, Ground Under Our Feet (New York: MacMillan Co., 1938).

(8) Richard T. Ely, "Landed Property as an Economic Concept and as a Field of Research," American Economic Review, Vol. VII, No. 1 (March 1917), pp. 18-33.

(9) Lewis C. Gray, "Economic Possibilities of Conservation," Quarterly Journal of Economics, Vol. XXVII, No. 2, (May 1913), pp. 497-519.

(10) Lewis C. Gray, "Rent Under the Assumption of Exhaustibility," Quarterly Journal of Economics, Vol. XXVIII, No. 2 (May 1914), pp. 466-89.

(11) U. S. Department of Agriculture, Report of the Committee Appointed by the Secretary of Agriculture, USDA Circular No. 138 (Washington, June 1919).

(12) R. T. Ely, et. al., Outlines of Land Economics, Vol. 1 (Ann Arbor, Michigan: Edwards Bros., 1922).

(13) H. B. Dorau and A. G. Hinman, Urban Land Economics (New York: The Macmillan Co., 1928).

(14) Richard V. Ratcliff, Urban Land Economics (New York: McGraw-Hill Co., 1949).

(15) Leonard A. Salter, Jr., A Critical Review of Research in Land Economics (Minneapolis: The University of Minnesota Press, 1948).

62

(16) Theodore W. Schultz, "Scope and Method in Agricultural Economics Research," Journal of Political Economy, Vol. 47, (October 1939), pp. 705-21.

(17) Theodore W. Schultz, "A Framework for Land Economics -- the Long View," Journal of Farm Economics, Vol. XXXIII, No. 2 (May 1951), pp. 204-15.

(18) George S. Wehrwein, "Institutional Economics in Land Economic Theory," Journal of Farm Economics, Vol. XXIII, No. 1 (February 1941), pp. 161-70.

(19) Milton Friedman, Essays In Positive Economics (Chicago: The University of Chicago Press, 1953).

(20) P. Henry Van Laer, The Philosophy of Science (New York: The Ad Press Ltd., 1956).

(21) John Dewey, Logic, the Theory of Inquiry (New York: Henry Holt, 1938).

(22) C. W. Loomer, "A Comment on Professor Schultz -- Framework for Land Economics," Journal of Farm Economics, Vol. XXXIII, No. 3 (August 1951).

(23) Frank H. Maier, James L. Hedrick, and W. L. Gibson, Jr., The Sale Value of Flue-Cured Tobacco Allotments, Technical Bulletin No. 148, Virginia Experiment Station, V.P.I., April 1960.

(24) Walter G. Miller, Walter E. Chryst, and Howard W. Ottoson, Relative Efficiencies of Farm Tenure Classes in Intrafirm Resource Allocation, North Central Regional Publication No. 84, November 1958.

(25) Michele de Benedictis and John F. Timmons, Identification and Measurement of Inefficiencies in Leasing Systems -- An Application of Linear Programming. Iowa Agricultural and Home Economics Experiment Station Research Bulletin No. 490, January 1961.

(26) George A. Pavelis and John F. Timmons, "Programming Small Watershed Development," Journal of Farm Economics, Vol. XLII, No. 2, (May 1960), pp. 225-40.

(27) Walter Isard, Methods of Regional Analysis: An Introduction to Regional Science (New York: Technology Press and John Wiley, 1960).

(28) August Losch, The Economics of Location, translated from the second revised edition by W.H. Woglom (New Haven, Connecticut: The Yale University Press, 1954).

4

Land Economics Research
for Urban and Regional Planning

by Coleman Woodbury*

Because in recent years planning for urban and other regional areas
has been changing markedly in scope, character, and method, many
persons, even knowledgeable and thoughtful citizens of these areas and
students of the urban and regional scenes, find difficulty in keeping it in
focus. This difficulty is shared by some practicing members of the
planning profession as well. The writers of several recent articles and
books say many acute, wise, and provocative things about planning problems and possibilities without ever quite coming to grips with the essential nature of planning--what it basically is, what its principal relations
with other institutionalized activities are or might become, what its
limits are in our society. Certainly, however, these are precisely the
questions with which any serious consideration of the relations between
land economics research and urban and regional planning should start.

Although relatively rapid change in planning probably is the principal
factor in this confusion, it is not the only one. At least four others should
be noted:

(1) Planning as a professional activity grew out of or evolved from
older professions--notably civil engineering, landscape architecture, and
architecture. In this country this evolution went on over some four or five
decades or more. Only quite recently have the leading strings been cut.
Even today many able and productive practitioners and teachers of planning were educated for one of the older professions and practiced it before
turning to planning. Naturally their view of many of the diverse needs and
problems of planning is colored by their earlier training and background.

(2) While this process of evolution to recognized professional status
was going on, planning was influenced strongly by still other professions

---

*COLEMAN WOODBURY is a professor of political science at the University of Wiscon-
sin. Born in Illinois in 1903, he obtained his B.S., M.A., and Ph.D. from Northwestern
University; he was also a Rhodes Scholar at Oxford for one year. He has long been concerned with urban planning and housing, at various universities, federal agencies, and
planning agencies. Author or editor of several books, he is also well known abroad for his
work in this general field.

and activities. A clear example was the development by lawyers and others of land-use controls--zoning, height limitation, building and housing codes, and other police power measures--many of which are now among the chief implementing measures or devices of planning. To be sure, some of the leading planners and students of planning have had a strong hand in shaping these tools, but the fact remains that many of them were started outside planning circles, and their consolidation with other lines of planning thought and practice was slow and is still incomplete. Evidence of this is the substantial number of zoned localities that have only the most rudimentary, if any, formal planning. Similarly, housing reformers of various stripes, from the public housers to the formulators of the risk-rating system of FHA, have had substantial effects on planning. Again, however, although their earlier efforts were aided by a few leaders in planning, up until at least World War II many planners looked upon such developments with indifference or skepticism, and the task of fitting housing programs into urban planning went slowly and still presents problems in many areas.

(3) While planning thought and practice were being shaped, primarily not in universities but by the hard, pragmatic, cut-and-fit experience of planning officials and consultants, university scholars and researchers in the social sciences have been producing studies of various kinds and of varying degrees of usefulness to planners. These studies go back many decades, but became notable in number during the 1920's, continued through the 1930's with marked changes in orientation and content, and since World War II have increased to several times their earlier volume.

Rather curiously, scholars have paid relatively little serious attention to the planning process per se, but have inquired into many aspects of the kinds of communities and localities for which planning is now being done. Urban sociology seems to be having a renaissance. Working the rich vein usually labelled political behavior, political scientists and political sociologists have concerned themselves with studies of local community leadership, pressure group activities, various kinds of elites, the complex processes of policy formulation or decision-making, community power structures, etc. Local government structure and functioning are receiving more probing attention than they have for many years. Intergovernmental relations, fiscal and other, also are being inquired into. Demographers and urban geographers are keenly interested in urban in-migration, suburbanization, and the even more remarkable growth of the rural-urban fringe. A relatively small but able band of urban land economists have addressed themselves to questions of housing policy, urban decentralization, and the economic base of urban and regional areas.[1]

Incidentally, one of the indications of the relevance of much of this

---

[1]For an introduction to the more recent literature see Government Affairs Foundation, Inc., Metropolitan Communities: A Bibliography (Chicago: Public Administration Service, 1956) particularly Part Two, and its Supplement: 1955-1957 (Chicago, 1960); Paul K. Hatt and Albert J. Reiss, Jr., Cities and Society (Glencoe, Ill.: The Free Press, 1957); Ralph W. Pfouts, The Techniques of Urban Economic Analysis (West Trenton, N. J.: Chandler-Davis Publishing Co., 1960); U. S. Department of Agriculture, Land: The Yearbook of Agriculture, 1958 (Washington: U. S. Government Printing Office, 1958); Morris Janowitz (ed.), Community Political Systems (New York: The Free Press of Glencoe, 1961); Harold M. Mayer and Clyde F. Kohn, Readings in Urban Geography (Chicago: The University of Chicago Press, 1959); William Dobriner, The Suburban Community (New York: G. P. Putnam's Sons, 1958); J. H. Beuscher, Land Use Controls--Cases and Materials (Madison, Wis.: The College Typing Co., n.d.); Charles M. Haar, Land-Use Planning: A Casebook on the Use, Misuse, and Re-Use of Urban Land (Boston: Little, Brown and Co., 1959).

scholarly output to planning is the increasing frequency with which articles of these kinds now appear in The Journal of the American Institute of Planners, as well as its coverage of the larger works in its book review columns. Notable, too, is the fact that in the Journal and elsewhere substantial articles by members of university departments of city and regional planning as well as by practicing planners are now quite common.

Undoubtedly many of these studies have added materially both to the equipment of planners and to the range of their responsibilities. Almost as surely, however, they also have opened new areas of knowledge without going into them far enough to establish firm guides for the practicing planner, and have added to the profusion (or confusion) of tongues already a difficulty in planning and other local public affairs. Thus, although on the whole they have enriched planning, they, too, have pointed to the need for analysis and restatement of its nature and essentials.

(4) Finally, and fortunately of declining significance, is the influence of those who have tried to make of all or nearly all forms of public planning an ism--to equate it with certain doctrines or dogmas as to the scope and nature of government concern and activity in economic and social affairs. Although the proponents of this view have been more numerous outside than within scholarly circles, not many years ago they were quite vociferous in both locales and had succeeded in putting on the defensive many advocates of even very limited kinds of planning. Now their influence seems to be waning, but its after-effects still blur many persons' conceptions of the nature of planning.

Without going further into the history of urban and regional planning, its recent changes, or the factors contributing to them, let me now propose and explain briefly a definition of urban or regional planning. Except as noted, I have in mind primarily public planning--i.e., planning by governmental bodies or entities. My emphasis is on general or, as it is usually called, comprehensive planning for the development and welfare of these areas as distinguished from planning for one or a few of their functions or sections--e.g., for highways or transport, recreation, or water supply.

Urban, as here used, refers to more than municipalities. It includes cities and all adjacent, continuous area that is urban in character, undergoing urbanization, or under strong and direct urban influence or "dominance" economically and socially. Urban planning, then, is planning for urban regions--for areas or communities that include what the Bureau of the Census defines as standard metropolitan statistical areas plus similar areas the central cities of which have populations less than 50,000. Regional refers to larger geographic areas that usually are more heterogeneous in character--river basins, states, sections (of one or more contiguous states) that have identifiable economies, social characteristics, and problems. They ordinarily contain cities and relatively more nonurban territory than do urban or metropolitan areas. Admittedly the line between urban and regional is sometimes hard to draw and is becoming more so as urban development disperses over larger and larger areas. Nevertheless, the distinction is usually clear enough--at least for the purposes of this paper.

Probably I should point out here that in the discussion that follows rather more attention is given to urban than to regional planning. Two reasons account for this. Now and for a decade and more past, urban planning has been much the more active field. Also, it is the field in which I have had more experience and have given more study. In many important respects, however, urban and regional planning share the same or very similar characteristics, potentialities and problems. They can usefully be considered together, even by those whose interests lie more in one than in the other.

PLANNING--A DEFINITION

Although formal definitions have their limitations as well as their uses, one is necessary for the purposes of this paper.[2] Of course my definition covers much ground that is well known to most of its readers. Perhaps, however, it will suggest to some others one or two aspects of the subject that they have not fully explored. At least, it will give my conception of planning, which underlies the later proposals for needed research by land economists and allied scholars. It is closely limited to what seem to be the essentials. Only incidentally does it touch on procedures, methods, or techniques.

Reduced to its essentials, urban or regional planning is the process of preparing, in advance and in a reasonably systematic fashion, recommendations as to policies and courses of action to achieve accepted objectives in the common life of urban or regional communities. A few comments on key words and phrases in this definition may give it more substance and meaning.

Process certainly implies a continuing activity, not the ad hoc drawing of a master blueprint or other document, which then only needs to be carried out or "implemented." It means continuous study of the urban or regional scene as it is affected by population growth and migrations, scientific and technical developments, by changes in national income and in its distribution, by changes in the preferences and value systems of various classes of urban or regional residents, by shifts in industrial and commercial location, etc. Making the necessary adjustments and revisions in plans, however, requires rather more than further study, essential as that is. It calls for rare qualities of judgment. In respect to revisions as in the preparation of the initial plans, every effort must be made to look ahead, to try to foresee how the community will develop under existing trends, and then what influences can be brought to bear that seem likely to guide that development closer to the desired objectives.

Much has been said, possibly too much and too glibly, about the ability of planners to look ahead, to plan in advance of coming events. Without belittling this responsibility of urban and regional planners, two observations seem in order.

1. In very few localities can planning start with a fairly clean slate. Nearly always planners are, in fact, pushed into devising corrective measures to deal with the mistakes of the past--e.g., to clean up areas

---

[2]This section follows quite closely a paper (The Fundamentals of Healthful Residential Development: Town Planning) prepared for a meeting of the Expert Committee on the Public Health Aspects of Housing, World Health Organization, held in Geneva, June 19-26, 1961.

of residential blight and slums, to relieve traffic congestion; to reduce
shortages of public recreational and open space.

2. Foresight in respect to trends and needs of an entity or organism
as complex as a sizable urban or regional community is not only dependent on hard work, experienced judgment and what might be called educated intuition, it also is a function of the depth and breadth of one's
knowledge and understanding of local community life. Perhaps here is the
Achilles' heel of most, if not all, urban and regional planning. Not long
ago, one of the most perceptive critics of planning said, in effect, that
earlier in this century various individuals and agencies were operating
on the urban body social and corporate in light of a knowledge about its
anatomy and physiology roughly comparable to the notions about the
human body held by an old-time medicine man at a country fair.[3] This
may be an exaggeration, but not a gross one. Altogether too much of
what passes for knowledge of urban communities even today is superficial, spotty, and unreliable.

An urban or regional planner, however, is more than a part-time
student of local community life and affairs. Our definition indicates that
he makes recommendations as to policies and courses of action and,
further, that he prepares these recommendations in a reasonably
systematic fashion.

"Recommendations, " however, raises a substantial question that has
been debated for years in planning circles--and the end is not yet. The
word clearly implies that planning is advisory, that the final determination of policies and courses of action lies with others. The others, the
nonplanners who make the final decisions in all major planning matters,
are those legislative and administrative officials responsible to the citizens of a locality or community.[4] On some points, to be sure, they may
share some of this responsibility with judges as well as with representatives of elected officials of a larger political unit of which the local or
regional community is a part. The principle, however, is clear.
Planners as an identifiable professional group are advisers, and by no
means the only advisers, of politically responsible officials.

In this context, therefore, planning is one component or factor in the
complex and evolving processes of policy formulation. Other influences
can readily be identified. They include the opinions, preferences, and
ideas of the elected officials themselves, the positions taken on major
issues by political parties, the less clearly articulated notions of political
leaders, the recommendations of administrative heads of operating agencies of local government, the pressures of organizations of business, labor,
and professional groups as well as those of civic, neighborhood, and district associations. In the most general terms, this is the political or
social environment in which urban planning plays its part.

The phrase "in a reasonably systematic fashion" suggests (possibly
rather indirectly and clumsily) that the role of planning agencies differs,
in some respects, from those of other groups in this process. In my

---

[3]Lewis Mumford in The New Yorker, May 5, 1951, p. 80.

[4]The degree or directness of the lines of responsibility of these other officials obviously varies
considerably. For members of city councils and mayors the line is short and direct; for appointed
heads of departments or members of boards and commissions it clearly is less direct and sometimes, for example, for members of boards of ad hoc agencies appointed by more than one official,
it may be tenuous; for officials of agencies charged with administering programs, often with a
substantial degree of discretion, and for appellate court judges the lines of responsibility may be
quite indirect and even circuitous.

opinion, there is a difference, but the line cannot be drawn too sharply and the contrast is not that of black and white.

In general, however, the proposals put forward by most of the other groups and organizations tend, naturally, to be colored by a strong concern for their own welfare and, sometimes, for their advantage vis-a-vis other elements in the community. Also, they often are argued for in short-run terms. Finally, they seldom reflect much care in identifying the ends sought--these are more or less taken for granted--let alone much consideration of other possible ways of reaching them.

Planning, on the other hand, is first of all rational in the sense that the planners identify certain objectives or ends to be sought, consider various possible ways and means of reaching them, as well as the costs and benefits of each, and recommend the one that, on balance, seems best.[5] Furthermore, a planner pays careful attention not only to the measures and courses of action at hand but also to the interrelations of any one proposal with others. For example, what will a major public investment in additional traffic and transport facilities do besides facilitate the movement of more goods and people into, out of, and within the area? Will it lead to traffic congestion in other districts not now so afflicted? Will it eliminate some slums, and, possibly, accelerate the blighting of other property adjacent to rights of way? Will it strengthen the tax base in the central business district? Will it encourage further urban sprawl? These questions only indicate some of the complexities that have to be considered--not in general terms but specifically. Concern with interrelationships among programs and projects and with the by-products of courses of action are among the hallmarks of good planning.

Objectives in the planning process have been mentioned several times above. It seems to some students of urban and regional planning that one of the more notable advances in thought and practice during recent years has been in more explicit and sophisticated recognition of the central place of goals or objectives in the whole process. After all, when an individual or group or public agency or government plans, it plans for something. Certainly the range of objectives of public planning is wide. What are the more common kinds or classes of objectives for urban planning today? What is the proper part played by planning agencies in the setting of goals or objectives?

One classification of urban and regional planning objectives, with some illustrative but by no means complete detail, follows:

1. Livability - reasonable convenience for all persons in their normal activities, including recreation and the journeys to work of those gainfully employed; sufficient space, particularly in and around dwellings, to give some sense of relaxation from the routines of work and from the constant stimulation of interpersonal contacts; the separation of incompatible land uses; safety and pleasant facilities for all children's activities--at home, in the neighborhood, at school, and going to and coming from it;

---

[5] I hope no reader of these paragraphs is so naive as to imagine that they imply that planners are simply two-legged calculating machines without preferences, opinions, and value systems of their own. Of course they have them--almost as many combinations of them as there are practicing planners. Quite as clearly, however, a large majority of planners do accept the role outlined here and do their work in conformity with it. The view that because everyone has preferences and values as to urban or regional affairs, everyone tries, in the same ways and by the same means, to further his own ends is both a logical fallacy and contrary to easily ascertainable facts. For a brief consideration of the planners' part in the determination of goals or objectives, see below.

opportunities for, but no compulsion to, neighborliness; the removal and
prevention of slums and blight.

 2. Efficiency - a physical structure of such densities of population and
of land uses in its component districts that it makes for reasonable efficiency in the provision of public services and in the activities of business
and industry.

 3. Amenity - a setting for all land-use districts that encourages
development marked by a degree of both variety and unity as well as by
"character," beauty, and a sensitive and imaginative treatment of the
natural site.

 4. Flexibility - again, a structure and density pattern that allows
many use districts to grow or change at least moderately without drastic
disruption of adjacent areas; at least some range of choice open to families and unattached individuals in all income groups as to where, in what
kind of housing , and under what kind of tenure they wish to live.

 5. Optimum Use of Resources - a distribution of capital and human
resources among the various types of public and private investment and
between new development and redevelopment that represents some
approximation to their optimum use; priorities among the needs for public
investment at any one time that will both meet the most urgent needs first
and minimize future shortages; a system of local public revenues that
will both distribute the costs of local government in some fair relation
to ability to pay and encourage private development to accord with other
planning objectives.

 6. Public Participation - Public here refers to non-officials, non-
professionals in planning; participation refers to some meaningful part in
the planning process itself through regular rather than occasional or chance
opportunities for criticism and voicing of preferences, either directly
(whenever possible) or through acceptable representatives; implies nearly
everywhere the need for inventiveness and experimentation with political
devices--new or revised--for this purpose; both an objective of urban or
regional planning and a means of setting and achieving its other goals.

 This or any other classification of planning objectives touches upon
many sectors of urban and regional life in which at present we have no
satisfactory units of measurement or comparison. Nevertheless, it is
apparent that pressing too hard for any one group of goals often would
endanger some or all of the others. For example, the highest degree of
efficiency in an urban structure quite surely would not be compatible with
a corresponding degree of livability or amenity. On these, as on other
parts of the planning process, our reliance must be on the planning
officials' judgment and devotion to the general welfare, plus, of course,
on the controlling institutions of public discussion, debate, and decision.

 If this listing or something like it indicates roughly the range and
character of objectives for urban planning, what is the responsibility of
planning officials in determining specific goals for any local community?
The whole thrust of the argument here rules out the planner as the deter-
miner and imposer of major objectives. But what should he do on this
vital front? Should he make up his own mind as to objectives and then
try his best to persuade others, including legislators and community leaders, to his opinion? Should he stand aside from the whole matter, saying
in effect: "When you responsible officials decide what should be the objectives of development in this locality, I will be at your service to advise
you how you may attain them most rapidly and effectively. " Should he pre-

pare several sets of possible objectives, with the priorities within each
set clearly indicated and with a judicious analysis of the pros and cons for
each set, and then present this statement to the decision-making officials
and possibly to others as well? Should he prepare such a document and
then add to it his judgment as to which set seems to him, on balance, the
best for that community at that time? This last possibility seems usually
preferable to any of the others. But it does not exhaust the potential usefulness of planning in goal determination.

The objectives set forth by legislative bodies and top administrative
officials are often broad and general. Even more so are those assumed
to exist in some general community consensus. It is a proper and necessary function of planning to make them more precise and often, in so doing,
to set intermediate, middle-range goals consonant with the more general
objectives in time and inclusiveness. For example, in a comprehensive
housing law passed in 1949, the Congress declared the broad objective of
"...a decent home and a suitable living environment for every American
family..."[6] Similar language can be found in many supplementary state
laws and in resolutions adopted by local governing bodies requesting aid
under the federal statute. Well and good, but what is a decent home or a
suitable living environment? What are reasonable standards for judging
housing and neighborhood quality? Further, once the areas of substandard
housing are clearly marked out in a locality, what should be the strategy
of attack on them? Should the worst slum areas be cleared first and
rebuilt? If so, should they be rebuilt with housing or for other purposes?
Should the occupancy in these areas be reduced before acquisition for
clearance starts in order to ease the problems of relocation and of high
asking prices? At any one time, how much public outlay is justified for
clearance and rebuilding operations in proportion to that used for opening
up areas for new development? Should the initial program--say, for the
first three years or so--emphasize rehabilitation of badly but not hope-
lessly blighted areas? What should be the quantitative objectives of the
first five, seven, or ten years? In other words, how fast should the
program go?

It would be easy to list literally pages of questions of this order. In
the context of this paper, they clearly are planning questions. Unless they
are asked and intelligently answered, any program to realize the fine-
sounding general goal could easily fail, or even make matters worse.

Over a period of years, planning can and should influence the selection
of goals in still other ways. Planners can propose working programs that
would keep the activities in behalf of all the objectives in some kind of
balance. They can warn against the easy optimism that occasionally
seizes well-intentioned officials and citizens when a long-debated program
finally is approved and started. From time to time they can suggest new
objectives or modifications of those already established. By no means
least important, they can educate other officials, leaders, and groups in
the possibilities of urban and regional development. Many persons, even
intelligent and sensitive persons, find it difficult to appreciate the range
of urban and regional goals that are now quite attainable. Not being very
knowledgeable in such matters, their imaginations are often limited by the
conventional, by what they have known and seen around them. They readily see only the possibilities of relatively minor or more or less tradition-

---

[6] Housing Act of 1949 (Public Law 171, 81st Congress) Sec. 2.

al changes or improvements. In addition to his primary responsibility for program and policy recommendations, the professional planner is now taking seriously his opportunities to be an educator, helping to shake off these blinders, making real and vivid the possibilities of urban and regional forms of development, including some of those now in the stage of experimentation, invention, or intellectual exploration. [7]

In the common life of urban or regional communities, raises the question: What things on the urban and regional scenes are being planned by local public agencies? Questions of process and objective aside for the moment, in what substantive areas of urban and regional life is planning by governmental bodies necessary or desirable?

The conception of urban and regional planning put forward in this paper recognizes at least seven areas in which planning agencies have definite responsibilities. They are parts of the common life because whatever is done within or to them affects, more or less directly, the welfare and ways of life of most people in the locality or community. They are:

1. Land Use - the allocation of land to fairly broad categories of uses --e.g., residential, industrial, commercial--within which the market mechanisms can continue the process; the sizes of such use districts and the linkages among them; selection of sites for public uses and facilities-- e.g., schools, hospitals, public parks, parkways, playgrounds, water supply and sewage disposal facilities, etc; less well developed but receiving increasing attention is what Professor J. H. Beuscher, my colleague at the University of Wisconsin, calls "the pacing of urban development"--i.e., regulation and guidance of the rate of urban expansion or development (changes in land use) in and around urban centers.

2. Standards for Development - closely related to area (1); minimum and desirable standards as to land uses both public and private - density of development, setbacks, floor-area ratios, minimum lot sizes, off-street parking of motor vehicles, etc; made effective by means of such police power measures as zoning and housing ordinances and subdivision regulations as well as by inducements such as the acquisition of sites and "write down" of land prices (as in urban redevelopment or renewal programs) and the preparation of sites for new towns; in many parts of this work, notably in the provisions of police power ordinances, planning officials must collaborate closely with others who have more expertise in such fields as public health, public recreation and schools; poses questions of how best to protect the public health or welfare without unduly limiting imaginative design and innovation in building and other kinds of development; the protection of sites and buildings of special historical or architectural interest or value.

3. Circulation - i.e., space and facilities for traffic, transit, and transport--the moving of people and goods into, out of, and within urban and regional localities; might be considered a subtopic of land use but seems to deserve separate listing; closely related, nevertheless, to both (1) and (2).

---

[7] Again, I hope no reader of this essay will take these comments on goal-setting to imply some mechanical process in which all objectives are first established, once and for all, and then are followed by other steps in the process--all proceeding in some sort of lock-step. A reasonably careful reading of the essay up to this point will make clear, I think, that this is not what is said or implied. Of course many community or locality goals will change over time, in varying degrees, and in response to many forces and influences, including those in the planning process. Social scientists, who after all will make up most of the readers of this volume, will not need this warning; others are hereby warned.

4. The Economic Base of Communities - useful and often essential to population forecasts both of numbers and of probable family and income status; means of strengthening and diversifying major sources of employment; obvious implications for over-all tax-paying ability of the community, which, in turn, conditions many other possible policies and programs.

5. Capital Programing - sometimes called capital budgeting; establishing time priorities for major public investments or capital outlays; recommending ways and means of financing, including utilizing grants-in-aid from federal or state governments; one experienced planner has remarked that any urban planning that neglects or omits capital programing is simply the adult equivalent of writing letters to Santa Claus.

6. Special Problems or Urban Redevelopment - determining in some detail the extent and character of blight as a step in deciding on the appropriate method of treatment in specific areas--e. g., clearance and re-building, clearance alone, rehabilitation, combinations of clearance and rehabilitation; the terms and conditions, including land prices of sites, for rebuilding; relocation policies and practices; measures for prevention of deterioration in rebuilt districts.

7. Site Planning - in some respects on the borderline between urban planning and the functions of architects, landscape architects, and engineers in designing large-scale projects for residential, and other purposes; important, however, in assuring economy, variety, and amenity in residential neighborhoods and other forms of development.

Urban or regional communities indicates very roughly the areas for which this kind of planning is done. Unfortunately the word community has more than one meaning in common and scientific usage. Here, of course, it means a local community--i. e., one that has a geographic or areal base--rather than a professional or functional community--as one might speak of the scholarly community or the scientific community. Even when the word is limited to local community, however, it is not unambiguous. At least two broad, related, but distinguishable meanings are common.

In one, community is used in the sense of place--a locality. MacIver's well-known definition indicates the second: "Any circle of people who live together, who belong together, so that they share not this or that particular interest, but a whole set of interests wide enough and complete enough to include their lives, is a community. Thus we may designate as a community a tribe, a village, a pioneer settlement, a city or a nation. The mark of a community is that one's life may be lived wholly within it."[8] Here the emphasis clearly is on people and their shared interests, sense of identification, and recognized responsibilities.

In this paper the phrases urban communities or regional communities are used in both of these senses. The context should indicate which meaning is intended. It should be clear, however, that planning of the kind outlined here will reach its full effectiveness only in a local community like or approaching MacIver's conception.

---

[8] Robert M. MacIver, Society: Its Structure and Changes (New York: Richard R. Smith, 1932) pp. 9-10.

COMMENTS ON THE DEFINITION

Without extending the length of this essay unduly, possibly four comments on this definition may be in order.

1. It outlines a conception of the nature of urban planning, not a description of any one or any group of planning agencies or of their practices. To be sure some planning agencies exemplify better than others the kind of planning indicated--in fact some illustrate it very well--but the conception is, nevertheless, a construct or, if you will, an ideal-type that reflects trends and needs in the field as well as current activity. In this paper, as has been pointed out above, very little can be said about techniques, methods, or procedures.

2. The paragraphs above have emphasized the over-all, comprehensive or general planning for urban and regional communities. It is carried on usually for urban areas by officials of general purpose local governments and for regions by various kinds of commissions and authorities. No reader should infer, however, that this is all the planning or all the significant planning for the development and improvement of urban and regional communities that is being done or should be done. Functional or operating departments of local governments--e.g., departments of water supply and waste disposal or of streets and highways--plan for their objectives; so do semi-independent, ad hoc or special purpose authorities; so do civic and semipublic organizations concerned with local affairs; so do many private enterprises having to do with urban growth and development.

Urban or regional planning, as set forth here, can provide important aids to these other kinds of planning: clearly defined programs and policies--a framework, if you wish--within which they can go ahead with some confidence, reliable information, analyses and estimates of the future of the community and its economy; co-ordination; professional collaboration and encouragement. Conversely, these other agencies can help the general planning office materially. Many of them have valuable, specialized knowledge on which the general planning should draw. Continuing informal discussion and interchange of information, ideas, and proposals can strengthen the entire fabric of the planning process.

3. Sometimes it is objected that planning of the kind considered here is beyond the capabilities of men. The variables to be dealt with are too many and varied; the systems of relationships in sizable communities are too complex; the questions of values are too puzzling for human judgment overall. According to this view, planning, in the larger urban and regional localities at least, should only be expected to accompany, so to speak, the great, uncontrollable forces of growth and change and to content itself with making them a little more orderly and correcting some of their most obvious crudities. Someone has called this role "collaboration with the inevitable."

This question is often posed in terms of the qualifications and responsibilities of "the planner." Is there or can there be any such animal as "the planner", who can, in fact, make the conception of planning outlined above a reality--not on paper but in the rush, bustle, and pressures of a changing world? A large part of the answer is that planning is not a one-man job; it is a team task. (Where the word, planner, appears above, it should be read as the planning team, the planning office, or the planning department.)

To be sure, a team must be led, and the leader, although not a master of all the tasks and techniques, must know quite a bit about them, including how to combine their results into a balanced and consistent whole. This, admittedly, calls for men of extraordinary abilities, but the planning profession has some of them, and could use more. A corollary of this view is that not enough time, effort, money, and attention have been given so far to recruiting and educating men of the caliber needed for planning in the near and middle-range future.

4. Another criticism of this paper's conception of urban and regional planning is somewhat similar to the one just noted but quite distinguishable from it. Often it is said that urban planning (less frequently, regional planning) really is "physical planning" and that the urban planner is or should be a "physical planner." In other words, the end result or true goal of urban planning, the urban environment, is physical--houses, streets, schools, water mains, parks, business and industrial districts, and other buildings and facilities as well as the spaces around and among them. The purpose of planning is to assure that they will be so designed, built, and arranged on the land that the final composite will be useful, convenient, and beautiful. Of course urban planning has to pay some attention to such matters as population forecasting, the analysis of slums and residential blight, legal controls of land use, public participation, and many related policies and programs, but only as they may aid or facilitate the physical result and only to the degree necessary to enable planners to achieve their conceptions (in arriving at which, they will take into account the views of others) of the good, the beautiful, the appropriate physical setting for urban or regional life. Thus planning is design, and the true planner is a designer in the grand manner. Although this view is no longer the dominant one, it still does have able and influential proponents.

My counter-argument does not deny the high importance of the well-designed physical city or locality. Neither does it deny the physical designer an important role as a member of the urban or regional planning team. Quite the opposite. It does dispute, however, the assumption that the only dimension of environment is physical. Urban and regional man does live and work and play in houses, neighborhoods, shops, factories, parks and playgrounds; it is highly desirable that they and the localities of which they are component parts be well and beautifully designed. But quite as truly urban man lives also in an economic environment, a social environment, and a political environment. To the quality of these too, planning can make contributions. It cannot, of course, determine or even directly affect all of their nature and characteristics; neither can it determine all aspects of the physical environment. But to all these environments or, more accurately to urban or regional environment seen in these several dimensions, planning, as defined in this paper, can contribute much today, and, quite surely, more tomorrow.

Although what can be properly and effectively planned by public agencies varies from one of these environments to another, it seems just as much a mistake for planning agencies to concentrate on one and neglect the others as it would be, within the physical environment, to plan only for traffic and transport and to ignore housing development and recreational facilities and open space.

If, as seems unlikely, urban and regional planners should adopt the narrower conception of their role, one of two results probably would follow. Either their efforts as physical planners would be largely frustrated or defeated by economic, political, and social forces or, more probably, other agencies and officials would come forward, under other banners than planning, to undertake the larger job.

RESEARCH AREAS

If one takes something of this order to be the scope and character of urban and regional planning, little reflection is needed to outline a formidable range of research needs. To decide which items of this range could most properly be called land economics research would be a more exacting and troublesome task--and one that would seem likely to produce more controversy than it would be worth at this stage in the development of the discipline. Instead of trying this, I propose to list several major research areas in which competent work would be very useful to urban and regional planning and in all of which land economists could make substantial contributions. To be sure, scholars in many other social sciences as well as those in such "technical" fields as architecture, engineering, landscape architecture, and planning itself, could also play major parts. The most productive combinations of talents would depend on many considerations, including the exact nature of specific research projects or programs--subjects well beyond the scope of this paper. It should be clear, however that genuine collaboration is not only desirable but essential if the research is to lead to true knowledge and understanding of phenomena as complex as current urbanization, the development of regions in our times, and the attempts of man to guide the powerful forces of these movements in ways that will further his welfare.

Before turning to the research needs may I suggest one way of looking at urban areas that has been a partial antidote to narrow vision and myopia on the urban scene. It is usually the four cities. In other words, a city or an urban or metropolitan area may be looked at in at least four ways: (a) as an economic unit or entity producing goods and services and exchanging them within its own boundaries and outside of them; (b) as a congeries of local governments and of public and quasi-public agencies - most of them corporate, legal entities with various powers, functions and responsibilities; (c) as a gigantic physical plant - the land, buildings, streets, transit and transport lines, parks, public buildings, utilities, and other artifacts within and through which the economic, governmental, and other social activities are carried on; (d) as a social structure or, if the term be properly qualified, a social organism made up of various groups and institutions in various stages of growth, equilibrium and decay and with almost numberless ties and relationships among themselves and with communities outside.

These four cities, of course, are not separate, discrete entities; they are simply different aspects of the complex reality. They are tied together and influence each other in numberless ways. No research in urban affairs will be very useful if it fails to recognize all four cities and at least the principal ties and influences among them. Furthermore, nonurban regions may be usefully considered in the same dimensions or aspects.

Without any claim of definitiveness in either content or classification,

research for this field might be grouped under four headings:[9] (1) patterns
of land use and population distribution, including the processes of land use
change, in-migration and the assimilation of migrants; (2) local public
finance; (3) the urban and regional planning process, including standards
and implementing measures; and (4) public policy formulation affecting
the scope, objectives, methods and results of planning. A brief sketch of
each of these groupings may indicate their potentialities. Each could be
the subject of an essay at least as long as this paper without exhausting its
possibilities.

Patterns of Land Use and Population Distribution

Although marked change in these patterns in and around urban centers
have been underway for about two decades, only quite recently have they
begin to attract any considerable attention. Quite possibly this is because
the fact of urban dispersal is now apparent to any reasonably observant
person who rides about or flies over even a few urban or metropolitan
areas. He sees a great, largely formless, and markedly uneven
spreading out of residential development punctuated, here and there, by
large new manufacturing and wholesale establishments and shopping
centers, interlaced with major highways, and, usually, with all too few
schools, hospitals, parks, and other recreational facilities. Many persons for whom this is an unpleasant if not appalling sight commonly call it
urban sprawl; some Britishers seem to prefer subtopia. Others who rather
welcome the general trend if not all of its manifestations speak of decon-
centration or, maybe, decentralization. Maybe urban dispersal is a reasonably accurate and dispassionate label. It should be clear, however,
that this movement is not limited, by any means, to the environs of very
large cities. In many respects it is a regional development, in scope and
implications.

Possibly the most telling single index of this phenomenon comes from
comparing an estimate made by the Bureau of the Census of the population
of this country by place of residence in April 1959 with data from the 1950
decennial census.[10] During these nine years, the population increase of
the 168 metropolitan areas recognized by the Census in 1950 was
16,124,000 -- quite probably, in light of 1960 data, an underestimate. Of
this substantial total, only 4.7 per cent was accounted for by the central
cities of these areas, which, incidentally, in 1950 had 56 per cent of the
aggregate metropolitan population. The remainder of the increase - 95.3
per cent - went into parts of the metropolitan areas outside the central
cities. If we break down that noncentral city area into the suburbs (the
1950 urbanized area outside the central cities) and the rural-urban
fringes (the remainder of the metropolitan areas, outside both central
cities and suburbs in 1950), we find that the suburbs accounted for 37.3
per cent of the nine-year increase and the rural-urban fringes for 58 per
cent.

---

[9] A somewhat similar outline of research needs, limited to urban areas and not focussed on
planning, is in my Wherrett Lecture on Local Government, the sixth in this series, entitled
Urban Studies: Some Questions of Outlook and Selection (Pittsburgh: Institute of Local Government, University of Pittsburgh, 1960).

[10] U. S. Bureau of the Census, Civilian Population of the United States by Type of Residence,
April 1959 and 1950 Series p. 20, No. 98 Rev., February 25, 1960. Data published so far from
the 1960 census of population do not make possible a similar breakdown for the entire decade of
the 1950's, but do indicate that the estimates for 1959 were not far off.

It is this rapid growth and massive redistribution of population plus
its attendant changes and problems in the economic, political, and other
social life of urban centers that led Harrison E. Salisbury, the well-known
correspondent of the New York Times, to write not long after he returned
from an assignment in Russia: "It could be argued that the greatest
revolution in progress today is not in Soviet Russia, Red China, or the
emerging national states of Asia and Africa, but right here at home in
your city and mine, in your suburb and the one next door . . . ."[11]

Another significant fact is that, unlike the more sedate suburban
movement of earlier decades, this spreading out of population is accompanied by a major dispersal of many commercial and service activities,
particularly retailing, and by a less marked but substantial diffusion of
industrial employment. Just one bit of evidence here: Murray D. Dessel
in the Office of Area Development of the Department of Commerce compared retail store sales in 45 metropolitan areas for 1948 and 1954.[12]
Over this six-year period the dollar volume of retail sales for the United
States increased by 30.8 per cent. For the 45 metropolitan areas the
corresponding figure was 32.3 per cent - not far from the national
increase. For the central business districts in the central cities of these
same metropolitan areas, however, the increase was only 1.6 per cent,
which, taking account of the rise in price levels during this period, indicates a decline in the volume of goods sold in the "downtowns" of these
areas. The burgeoning, outlying shopping centers plus most of the
established, suburban retail areas are increasing their proportion of total
sales. Quite surely this trend has continued and, probably, accelerated
since 1954.

This dispersal or diffusion of residential and other urban land uses is
no simple phenomenon. The trends just mentioned are the net consequences of many shifts or movements of population into, out of, and within
metropolitan areas and regions. We do not know much about some of
these shifts, and undoubtedly they vary considerably among localities.

In broad perspective, however, one other characteristic of metropolitan and regional growth is highly significant for our purposes: among
the three major subareas current growth is selective. It is concentrating
a large proportion of the recent migrants to metropolitan areas in the
central cities. Most of these newcomers are poor, unskilled in urban
vocations and in the ways and manners of urban living. Many of them,
but by no means all, are Negroes and Puerto Ricans. The central cities
are coming more and more to fit the phrase first applied, I believe, to
New York City: the home of the rich, the poor, and the childless. The
old image of the suburbs as predominantly bedroom towns of the wealthy
and well-to-do is no longer valid. More and more suburbanites are now
in the middle and lower-middle income ranges. Some students of the
metropolitan scene predict that before long many suburbs will be receiving an increasing proportion of low income in-migrants. Today's suburban populations have a disproportionate share of young families with
children. One study of nearly 400 suburban communities of 10,000 and
more showed that only 46 per cent of them were, by one method of meas-

---

[11] New York Times Book Review, October 5, 1958.

[12] Murray D. Dessel, Central Business Districts and Their Metropolitan Areas: A Summary of
Geographic Shifts in Retail Sales Growth, 1948-54 (Washington: Office of Area Development, U. S.
Department of Commerce, 1957.)

urement, essentially dormitory towns.[13] Heterogeneity seems to be the chief characteristic of the rural-urban fringes. Their populations range from the very wealthy to the very poor. They include refugees from central cities and older suburbs, often a sizable indigenous population, and, in at least some fringes, a substantial number of recent migrants from rural and small town localities.

Maybe because some of the recent semipopular writing on this subject tends to be alarmist, some scholars have reacted by pointing out that urban areas have always grown at their peripheries and are still doing so. In my opinion, however, it is a mistake to write off all current changes in suburban and fringe populations as "just more of the same." This warning may be emphasized by a short quotation from Dr. Thomas H. Reed's article on "Metropolitan Areas" in the Encyclopaedia of the Social Sciences. In a volume dated 1933, his article dealt chiefly with the conditions that had developed in the 1920's and before. He wrote:

> . . .At the same time the old city i.e., the central city has not only maintained but actually increased its dominance as a center of trade, banking, amusement and culture. The whole increasing population - the overtaken farmer as well as the invading suburbanite - more and more seek the stores, theatres, churches and professional services of the center to the detriment of the crossroads store, the wayside church and the country doctor. . . .[14]

This, indeed, must have a comical or even a bitter ring today to many central city merchants suffering from the competition of new outlying shopping centers and suburban retail areas, to redevelopment and other city officials in the older centers trying to combat serious and spreading blight, to church leaders in many central city congregations and parishes, and to many others. Yet undoubtedly it was a true statement at the time it was written. The change to the situation today admits of no simple explanation, but clearly a major factor is simply the difference in the relative size of central city populations, on one hand, and those of suburban and fringe areas, on the other. In many of the latter, something analogous to a "critical mass" has been reached. Some of its effects are now unmistakable. There is no reason to believe we have seen all of them yet.

These, then, in broadest outline, are some of the principal characteristics of current metropolitan and urban regional growth. It is a rapid, almost headlong growth heavily concentrated in the fringe and suburban sub-areas. It is producing a dispersed, land-devouring pattern of settlement, which in many respects deserves that derogatory label - urban sprawl. Although many of the most dramatic forms of this development are residential, it is not limited to this kind of land use. From the point of view of public policy, the dispersal, itself, is not more significant than the selective or sorting out process that is changing markedly the population, economic, and social characteristics of central cities, suburbs, and fringes, alike.

Nearly all of this section on Land Use and Population Distribution has

---

[13] Victor Jones, "Economic Classification of Cities and Metropolitan Areas," The Municipal Year Book (1953), pp. 49-57.

[14] Encyclopaedia of the Social Sciences (1933), Vol. 10, p. 396.

dealt so far with happenings and trends in the standard metropolitan (statistical) areas as generously defined by the Bureau of the Census. This heavy emphasis stems primarily from the fact that for these areas we have the most easily available data--both from the Census and from special studies. May I stress that this emphasis does not mean or imply that significant changes in land use and population are taking place only in these areas. Neither does it mean that, in my opinion, nearly all research useful to urban and regional planners should be focused on the metropolitan areas. Not at all: although our knowledge of these phenomena in smaller (i.e., less populous) urban-centered areas and in larger geographic areas or regions is painfully inadequate, there are grounds for believing that they, too, are undergoing notable changes in these respects. Also, a few scholars are pointing out that in several parts of this country--most obviously along the northern Atlantic seaboard--metropolitan growth and dispersal are producing great strips of urban and urbanizing areas that are sometimes called regional cities. Their scale and emerging character-istics seem likely to make them clearly distinguishable from metropolitan areas as we have known them to date.

It may well be that some of the richest veins for research by land economists lie in the phenomena of land use and population distribution in these three kinds of areas (the smaller urban centers, the larger geo-graphic regions, and the regional cities), as well as in the rural-urban fringes of metropolitan areas. By their very nature, it seems to me, they may be especially well adapted to collaborative work between the many land economists strongly oriented toward agricultural land, on the one hand, and urban land economists, demographers, urban sociologists, urban geographers and local government specialists, on the other.

Even a rapid sketch like the one in the preceding paragraphs, done in the very broad brush strokes of census figures and a few, rather general studies, shows a scene of rich research possibilities for scholars in the social sciences. Even those not attracted personally may agree on two statements: (a) If urban and regional planners are to work effectively in and on a social, economic, demographic, and physical terrain of this complexity and fluidity, they must have a wide and deep knowledge of its character and changes; (b) today neither planners nor others have the required knowledge, except in relatively small sub-areas of the whole. In general terms, what kinds of research are called for?

First, it seems to me, we need much more detailed, accurate, and sensitive descriptions of what is going on in land use changes and popula-tion redistribution in urban and regional areas. Some researchers, to be sure, use descriptive as a term of derogation and reproach, and in some circumstances not without some justification. Here, however, the situa-tion is different. It seems clear that knowledge, understanding and explanation of these phenomena are most likely to come only after the broad patterns of dispersal are analyzed and broken down into their com-ponent parts. Not only will this more detailed information aid planners directly, but it may also give imaginative researchers the leads to hypotheses and further methods of inquiry, some of which may produce significant knowledge.

Beyond description, of course, we need explanation, theorems, and eventually a theory of growth and change in these vital areas of our economy and society. Then, and only then, will planners be able to make their recommendations and local and state governments and private agen-

cies their investments with the highest chances of optimum benefit.
Several avenues or approaches that may lead to explanation and theory
are easily identified. How far they may lead can be told only after further
exploration along them.

Land economists naturally will turn to several aspects of the current
scene as more or less promising take-off points: the institution of home
ownership, particularly as it has been fostered and promoted in recent
years by FHA and others via the small down payment, long-term,
amortized mortgage; industrial location theory; the motivations and behavior of real estate investors - both with regard to equity and mortgage;
obsolescence and blight in older urban districts and their relations, if
any, to dispersal; highways and other facilities and means of circulation
as factors in land use--avoiding, of course, the simplistic view that the
motor car is "the cause" of population dispersal;[15] the Murray Haig
hypothesis of real estate market competition among users in a hierarchy
of rent paying ability; the implications of do-it-yourself housing, which in
the immediate post-World War II years apparently was accounting for
more than one-quarter of the nonfarm housing production of this country;[16] the organization, personnel, finance, and production methods of
the house-building industry, so-called, which despite its crucial importance, enormous growth, and substantial changes since World War II has
received little attention except in two or three Fortune articles.

Other social scientists may start from other angles and with emphasis on other possible factors: the sharp increase and wider distribution of
leisure time; state and federal grants-in-aid to local governments for
schools and other purposes; other technical influences on fringe-area
living than the automobile--e. g., widespread availability of electric
power, the lowly septic tank, the telephone, radio and television, and
what a perceptive Britisher calls the "passion for space;"[17] the alleged
need for "human scale" in one's physical, governmental and other
institutional environment; "exclusionism"--the suspicions, prejudices,
dislikes, and antipathies among various racial, ethnic, and economic
groups; the relations, if any, between the rate of assimilation of in-
migrants and the dispersal rates of older residents and of the in-migrants
themselves; the hypothesis that the mechanization of living has two related
effects on many people: some forms--e. g., the assembly line and the
time clock--control and regiment people's lives, while other forms--e. g.,
the automobile, motor car, and wood-working machinery--give people the
satisfactions of controlling and directing sources of power; as the first
form increases, many persons may turn to the other as a compensation
and, therefore, seek residential areas that either call for or facilitate
such activities.

Another aspect of current urban and regional development deserves

---

[15] Some recent work in this sector represents, in my opinion, remarkable advance in conception, rationale, and method. For a general introduction to it see Melvin M. Webber, "Transportation Planning Models," Traffic Quarterly (July 1961), pp. 373-90; Hans Blumenfeld,
"Transportation in the Modern Metropolis," Queen's Quarterly, Vol. 57 (Winter, 1961), pp. 640-53;
and Journal of the American Institute of Planners, Vol. 25 (May 1959), a special issue on Land Use
and Traffic Models: A Progress Report, Alan M. Voorhees, ed.

[16] Housing in the United States (Washington: Housing and Home Finance Agency, 1956), pp. 54,
75. The study summarized here was made by the Bureau of Labor Statistics.

[17] Peter Self, Cities in Flood: The Problems of Urban Growth (London: Faber and Faber, Ltd.,
1957). See also Amos Hawley and Basil Zimmer in Land Economics, February 1961, and in other
articles.

mention: To a much greater degree than is often recognized, various standards set by public and private agencies influence markedly the character of urban and regional growth--particularly physical growth. Zoning and subdivision control ordinances are the chief but not by any means the only devices for such standards. Mortgage lenders, insurance underwriters, local and state departments and agencies for education, recreation, conservation, redevelopment, public health, fire protection, and highways all have a hand in this process. Some of these standards are quite effectively enforced; some are often evaded or watered down; some are little more than distant ideals recognized more in the breach than in the observance. Some are controls on or requirements for private developers; some are self-imposed conceptions of good practice for public or private agencies.

Most of these standards have accumulated over the years. Often some of those in one locality are copied in another and so on almost ad infinitum. Some are clearly and directly grounded in careful studies; the rationale of others seems uncertain or has been lost over the years.

The studies needed would deal with the substance of the standards, how they are determined, and with their administration. Some studies would try to assess the results, direct and by-product, of particular standards; others might review their bases and rationale in light of present-day knowledge from the natural and social sciences. Some might point to simplification or cutting out of deadwood; others might indicate holes to be filled or neglected areas to be dealt with--some of them probably the consequences of recent changes in the character of urban and regional development. Others might try to devise and estimate the consequences of radically new formulations aimed at the same objectives as some orthodox standards. Certainly some should be concerned with the newer forms of regulatory standards--e. g., performance and "progressive" zoning. Others would look into the misunderstandings of prescribed standards of various kinds and the resistances and opposition to them.

Unfortunately, this area of study has been relatively neglected in recent years. Possibly this has been due to a feeling by professional scholars that it involved "value judgments" and, therefore, was not sufficiently "scientific." Whatever the causes, it is time that neglect be replaced by concern and activity. The present formulations of too many standards are poor and obsolete. In the absence of straightforward study and discussion based on it, the formulations remain relatively rigid and revisions are made, in practice, by various forms of evasion and pressured interpretations.

A prima facie case can be made for nearly all of these and other influences or forces as factors in dispersal and in the new and emerging patterns of land use. For some, more positive relationships already have been demonstrated; for others, this seems quite possible in the near future. Simply identifying contributing factors, of course, is only a first step. We also need comparative studies and other means of assessing their relative effectiveness in various contexts and of searching for combinations or systems of them as well as for underlying forces that might open the way to a more satisfactory explanation or theory.

Local Public Finance

As suggested above, local systems of public finance directly and indirectly affect urban and regional planning. When planning was looked upon as a province or offshoot of architecture or civil engineering, this relationship often was ignored--at least by many planners. Now it is only too evident, and is admitted by all persons concerned. Unfortunately for years most students of public finance have been so engrossed with national policy that local government and even state public finance has been relatively neglected. Fortunately this situation is now being corrected, but much remains to be done.

Looked at in broad perspective, the present situation in urban government finance appears as a paradox. Although our urban localities today are the greatest aggregations of income-producing power the world has ever seen, the overwhelming majority of urban governments, from those of new, lower and middle income suburbs and fringe areas to the mightiest central cities of metropolitan areas, are in financial stringencies that apparently are becoming more and more severe. Almost the only exceptions are traceable to the Balkanization of local government structures in most urban regions. This results in an occasional small suburban or fringe area municipality that is fortunate enough to have a major shopping center or industrial plant within its jurisdiction. Its property taxes are sufficient, when paid to a relatively small governmental unit, to ease its financial position materially. This condition of affairs, however, often only accentuates the plight of adjacent or near-by municipalities. Their residents contribute to the property value and tax-paying ability of the shopping center or factory by making purchases or working in it, but they receive no tax revenue from it. The exceptions aside, what accounts for the basic paradox? What can be done to remove the injustice of the exceptions? Various proposals for changes in local taxes and fiscal policy are being made quite frequently. Quite surely, many more will be put forward in the future. One does not have to subscribe to a strict economic interpretation of urban affairs to believe that the response to some of these proposals by different groups of urban populations, if intelligently studied, might add measurably to our understanding of urban society, quite aside from the practical usefulness of such research to planning officials and agencies.

Likely sub-areas of research in urban public finance include:

(a) comparative studies of the newer forms of local revenue measures: their impact and incidence, administrative expenses, methods of evasion, and their influence, if any, on various forms of land use and development;

(b) various forms of grants-in-aid and shared taxes now in operation in this country, Canada, and Great Britain: their impact and incidence; their effects, if any, on local budget practice, on standards of administration, and on local legislative and administrative discretion and responsibility;

(c) city size and density of development as factors in the expenses and efficiency of public services;

(d) local public debt policy and management, including the evolving practices and problems of capital budgeting and programing, the uses and limitations of revenue bonds, various forms of debt limitation and their effects, if any, on other parts of the local finance system and on local government structures in urban areas.

For some regional planning areas that are not predominantly urban (as well as for a few that are) the paradox does not appear. They are not

strong economically, and may have little chance of becoming so in the
near future. These facts, however, emphasize rather than reduce the
need for thorough and competent study of local finance, with particular
attention to (b) above.

The Urban and Regional Planning Process

The discussion above of the nature of planning certainly suggests
many subjects for research. On practically all of them a scholar wishing
to undertake a reasonably thorough comparative study could proceed with
the assurance that he would not be in danger of unnecessary duplication.
In recent years systematic inquiry into the urban and regional planning
process in action has been almost nonexistent. Planning literature does
include, of course, useful articles by practicing planners and others on
various techniques, methods, and problems, but nearly all of them draw
largely on personal experience plus limited comparisons with a few other
usually similar agencies. A few exceptions are to be found, notably in
economic base studies and zoning, but the generalization, in my opinion,
is valid. Here is a wide-open field for promising work by land economists,
political scientists, sociologists and others.

As suggested above, the so-called implementing measures affecting
private land utilization, traditionally zoning and subdivision control,
should not be overlooked. In recent years zoning practice, especially,
has been undergoing considerable change. Performance zoning, the elimination of nonconforming uses, methods of controlling the direction and
rate of urban development--"progressive zoning," exclusive agricultural,
industrial, and commercial zones, the protection of areas of historical
and architectural importance--these and other devices are now being
developed and tried out. So are various kinds of "snob-zoning," attempts
to keep out modest housing by setting large minimum lot sizes and other
provisions. Zoning administration, particularly the operations of boards
of appeal, and the so-called veto powers of some planning agencies on
variations, exceptions, and revisions, also should be looked into.

Equally deserving attention as implementing measures, in the forms
both of regulation and inducement, are the various urban renewal powers
now being tried out, often rather gingerly, in literally hundreds of urban
localities throughout the country. So much attention has been given to the
"write-down" of land acquisition prices as an aid in clearance and rebuilding projects that the other inducements and controls for assuring the
needed types of rebuilding, have been largely neglected by serious students
of urban affairs. Recent practice in housing codes and their enforcement
in (urban) conservation and rehabilitation programs, tax and other aids
for housing co-operatives, middle-income housing, and public housing,
as well as the vital questions in determining re-use patterns, also offer
opportunities for significant work. Furthermore, literally scores of
thoughtful officials in renewal agencies would welcome competent studies
on these matters and would be able to help materially in formulating them.

Although capital programing was mentioned under Local Public
Finance, it is potentially so important and now, in many localities, is in
so embryonic a stage of development that it may be emphasized here. In
the first few postwar years, most of the heavy volume of nonfarm housing construction and, to a lesser degree, the new retail and industrial
development were served by excess capacity in existing public facilities.

Now, in most localities that excess capacity has been used up. New
expansion, therefore, requires additional public investment more or less
across the board. To aggravate the difficulties, construction costs are
now at or near all-time highs and yields on good municipal bonds are nearly double those of 1950. In these circumstances, establishing priorities
among various kinds of public outlay and determining the most economical
means of making any volume of public investment are tasks of great importance and difficulty.

Public Policy Formulation

If planning is "one component or factor in the complex and fascinating
process of policy formulation," it seems axiomatic that planning officials
and students of planning ought to know as much as possible about the other,
related parts of the process, particularly about those that bear most
directly on the scope, objectives, methods, and results of planning.
Although this is now a field of lively interest and some excellent research,
it has only been well opened up. Of course some planners, like some
other public officials, believe that their practical experience has taught
them quite a bit on this front. Often it has, but many of the more thoughtful and experienced planning officials readily admit that their knowledge
is relatively superficial and not too reliable. They would welcome more
searching inquiries into many phases of the process, including their
relations with other actors on the scene.

These relationships, of course, reflect not only the planners' attitudes and actions but also those of the nonplanners--elected officials,
heads of operating departments, influential nonofficial citizens, representatives of organized groups and associations. How do they perceive the
planner and his works? How and where were their ideas of and attitudes
toward planning formed? How much effect do and can the planners actually have on most of these attitudes and notions? Equally pertinent are
these questions in reverse--i.e., directed toward the planners' attitudes
and views of elected officials, citizen leaders, lobbyists, etc.

These questions, it seems to me, are considerably more than reflections of the curiosity of some social scientists. On the cogency of the
answers made to them may depend, in part, our position on a centuries
old problem of man in a highly organized society: how to combine most
effectively into wise and just policies the special knowledge and competence of the few with the conflicting values and aspirations of the many.
Seen in this light, the urban and regional planner has a dual, maybe an
anomalous, role. Vis-à-vis the elected official or influential citizen he
is one of the experts; vis-à-vis the staffs of many departments and ad hoc
authorities he is one of the nonexpert combiners or co-ordinators. Is this
a viable position? From it can able men do more than "collaborate with
the inevitable?"

These, I would suggest, are more than rhetorical questions. Some
persons, planners and others, have assumed answers. Defensible
answers may well depend on more research and its resultant knowledge
about the processes of public policy formulation for urban and regional
communities.

In the earlier parts of this section I have sketched some of what seem to me to be major research needs and opportunities today in the affairs of urban and regional communities. With only a few exceptions they have not been stated in the technical language of land economics or of any other scholarly discipline. This was done deliberately--and for two reasons.

The first was implied above: I believe firmly that much (not all) of the most needed research in these fields should be collaborative or team research utilizing talents, concepts and methods of more than one academic discipline. To outline such research in the language of only one discipline might well obscure this point and even discourage interested researchers in other disciplines.

Also, it seems to me likely that prospective researchers in these areas and urban and regional planners will make more headway toward formulating significant and useful studies if both researchers and planners avoid their technical jargons as much as possible in the early stages of exploration.

This symposium, however, deals primarily with land economics. It does seem appropriate, therefore, to point out that a very large part of the research that I have very roughly outlined falls readily into the categories put forward by the writers of other essays in this series--notably Messrs. Clawson, Kelso, Timmons, Huffman, and Steele. Without rewriting this section of my essay, let me illustrate this.

Quite clearly the principal foci of land economics from its earliest days on have been: (a) land utilization--including classification, patterns of use, what Kelso calls "interuse competitions within given space units" and "interspace competitions of the same use," as well as the processes, motivations, and interests of actual and prospective land users; (b) landed property or rights in land--including conflicts of interests, legal and other means of defining and redefining the rights of individuals and public agencies in land, changing conceptions of the proper exercise of the police power on real estate, and the relations of these changes to the evolution of an economy or a society. Of course these concepts have changed in content, scope, and sophistication over time and in the light of research and study, but no one, it seems to me, could deny their central position in the field and in the discipline of land economics.

I would suggest that much of the land economist's part in the studies suggested and implied in this essay could be subsumed under one or the other of these basic ideas or categories. Where, for example, is there more active and vigorous competition among land uses than in the rural-urban fringes of rapidly growing metropolitan areas? What more drastic and imaginative redefinitions of property rights in land have been taking place than in urban redevelopment or renewal programs or in the British attempt at nationalizing development rights in and around urban centers or in current proposals to assure open space in urban and regional areas by ad hoc purchase of development rights or by various kinds of "conservation easements?" In recent years what attempts to provide a "ladder" for persons of moderate income toward fee-simple ownership have been more effective or have had more significant by-products than FHA, the Home Loan Bank System, or various state and local aids to co-operative housing? Where have public measures and programs affecting land use combined in a more complex fashion with the operations of the market than in urban and urbanizing areas?

LOOKING AHEAD

In closing this paper, let me suggest two more considerations that seem to me to deserve the attention of all scholars and others interested in the field.

The first has to do with scale of the phenomenon we are dealing with. It can, of course, be measured in several differing dimensions. If we take a relatively simple and obvious one--population size--the results are approximately these.

According to the latest projections of the Bureau of the Census, the population of the United States in 1975 may be between 215.8 million and 243.9 million people.[18] For our purposes we may take 220 million as a round and conservative figure. This would mean an increase of roughly 70 million over 1950. If the Census' metropolitan areas alone should continue to get 85 per cent of the national population growth (the proportion they are thought to have received over roughly the first third or more of this 25-year period), their increase would be about 59.5 million.

An increase of 59.5 million in metropolitan populations in a short generation may seem offhand a substantial volume of growth. Two comparisons may give it more meaning.

(a) In 1950 the officially designated metropolitan areas had an aggregate population of 83.8 million. Thus the increase projected for 25 years is approximately 71 per cent of the total metropolitan population at the beginning of the period.

(b) If we array the standard metropolitan areas by size of their populations in 1950 and then start at the top and add these population figures, we would include in our addition 38 areas before we reach a total of 59.5 million persons. In other words, the projected metropolitan population growth from 1950 to 1975 is slightly more than the 1950 populations of the metropolitan areas (not of their central cities alone, but of the entire areas) of New York-Northeastern New Jersey, Chicago, Los Angeles, Philadelphia, Detroit, Boston, San Francisco-Oakland, Pittsburgh, St. Louis, Cleveland, Washington, Baltimore, Minneapolis-St. Paul, Buffalo, Cincinnati, Milwaukee, Kansas City, Houston, Providence, Seattle, Portland (Oregon), New Orleans, Atlanta, Dallas, Louisville, Denver, Birmingham, San Diego, Indianapolis Youngstown, Albany-Schenectady-Troy, Columbus, San Antonio, Miami, Rochester, Memphis, Dayton, and Norfolk-Portsmouth.

When one tries to visualize the aggregate of the residential development of all these great centers plus a substantial proportion of their public and private facilities for nonresidential purposes, and realizes that it is approximately equal to the physical metropolitan growth needed in this country over a short generation that we are now rather more than one-third of the way through, he may grasp something of the truly enormous pressures that soon will be thrown on the local governmental structures, including planning offices and departments, and on much of the private institutional and other social fabric of our major population centers. When he also tries to see in his mind's eye this vast army of

---

[18]U. S. Bureau of the Census, Illustrative Projections of the Population of the United States, by Age and Sex, 1960 to 1980. Series P-25, No. 187,(1958).

nearly 60 million human beings and to imagine something of their individual family, and group activities, needs, aspirations, ambitions, and
conflicts, he may sense how important it is, in terms of human welfare,
that the problems of urban growth in this country be dealt with intelligently, humanely, and in time.

With growth of this magnitude and the current and prospective changes
in urban and regional patterns, it does not seem to me an exaggeration to
say that by 1985 or so most of the sizable urban areas of this country may
be as unlike the cities of the last quarter of the nineteenth century as they,
in turn, were unlike those at the end of the eighteenth century. Will the
changes on the whole make for cities more favorable to the multifarious
activities carried on within them and more kindly in the lives of their
citizens? Nobody, I believe, can answer that question authoritatively
today, but the answer is being pieced together now and the verdict for
many years, maybe for decades to come, will be largely determined
before many more years are past.

These figures for metropolitan areas, of course, are only a part,
though a large part, of our grand total of populations that need urban and
regional planning for many sectors of their common life. Smaller urban
areas and nonurban populations in regional areas would increase the total
considerably. There is no quick and reasonably reliable way to estimate
that increase, but surely the figures are impressive enough even without
it. Some persons, of course, would argue that all of the population of
the country might well be under some form of urban or regional, including
state, planning. If so, the Census figures we started with provide the
over-all dimensions.

It is a measure of the relative neglect of planning in scholarly or
scientific circles that no one knows what proportion of any of these totals
is, in fact, under local, public planning. Certainly the proportion is
large if we equate "under local, public planning" with living within jurisdictions and areas that have some kind of more or less formal planning
agency. If, however, we should try to go beyond the mere existence of
planning agencies, and to classify by even the most crude criteria, the
planning actually being done, we would be simply guessing.

Certainly, however, except in a relatively few areas the quality and
the quantity of local planning are not commensurate with the need for it.
From almost any point of view that need is gigantic, and the giant is still
growing.

This brings us to the second consideration: how can land economic
and related research be made to contribute more, and more effectively,
to urban and regional planning? Of course such research needs more
money and other resources, but if my evaluation of the research output
in this field in recent years is at all defensible, simply more of the same
will not be enough. In my opinion, we should consider at least two other
changes.

Scholars in the social sciences would be well advised to pay more
attention than many of them have to planning and its place in urban and
regional communities. This would enable them to orient and organize
some of their individual research in ways that would make it more useful
to planning--without in any way reducing its scientific quality. Also,
more knowledge about and contact with planning almost surely would rub
off on some of their more able students. Today, in my opinion, man-

power shortages, both in the practice of planning and in research related
to it, are more crippling than shortages of money.

Finally, it seems clear to me that some ways and means must be
found or invented for focusing a larger proportion, but by no means all or
nearly all, of the available and interested research talent on relatively
large-scale, multi-disciplinary projects in at least all of the four research areas outlined above--and probably in others as well. Size, in
and of itself, is no merit, but we are now scattering our not too abundant
resources of research skill and interest far too widely. As a result,
both our understanding of urban and regional life and the usefulness of our
product in planning are materially less than they might be and less than
many informed persons think they should be. This unfortunate state of
affairs, I am sure, could be corrected without jeopardizing the freedom,
initiative, or responsibility of the individual researcher. What is called
for is a little planning within the scholarly community.

5

Better Utilization of Results
of Land Economics Research

by Roy E. Huffman*

Land economics research is usually problem-oriented, as other essays have pointed out.[1] Since the purpose of such research is to assist in solving problems, the mechanism whereby research results are carried into action deserves the careful consideration of both the researcher and the administrator. Failure to bring such research results into the decision-making and action processes means that society does not get full value for the funds it has invested in research, and that the research worker fails to get full public recognition for his work.

The procedures whereby research results can most effectively enter decision-making and action processes are not well developed. Part of the responsibility - but only part - rests with the research worker himself, as we shall try to show; but the form and functioning of the organization by which he is employed is highly important also. In the specialized world in which we live, it may be the responsibility of the Agricultural Extension Service to carry the results of Experiment Station research to farmers, or of the State Recreation Service to carry them to citizens interested in parks, for instance. Yet the creation and operation of efficient bridges to other groups should be the concern of the research man also.

Unfortunately, much land economics research has not been used as fully as it might have been. In general, suitable mechanisms for piping

[1]See particularly "Scope, Content, and Orientation of Rural Land Economics," by M. M. Kelso; "Objectives of Land Economics Research," by John F. Timmons, and "Interdisciplinary Approaches to Land Economics Research," by Glenn L. Johnson.

*ROY E. HUFFMAN has been Dean of Agriculture at Montana State College since 1958 where he has administrative responsibility for resident instruction in agriculture, The Agricultural Experiment Station System, and the Agricultural Extension Service. Born in Montana in 1916, he has been a Montanan nearly all his life. He graduated at Montana State College in 1938, received an M.S. at the University of Maryland, and a Ph.D. at the University of Wisconsin. He has had a unique experience in his combination of research, teaching, extension, and administration. He has been particularly concerned with western irrigated land problems, having written one book on the subject.

research results into decision-making processes have all too often been inadequate. In agriculture, the traditional, developed Agricultural Extension methods have mostly involved work with farmers on their individual problems - agronomic, animal husbandry, plant disease, insect pest, and even farm management. Procedures for working on group problems are less well established; yet much land economics research deals with group problems and group-action solutions. Moreover, much land economics research gets into governmental action of one kind or another; "politics" enters, and many research and extension organizations immediately grow hyper-cautious. In fields other than production agriculture, organizations comparable to extension are less fully developed and the problems of transferring research into action are accordingly more difficult.

The problems of concern to research workers in land economics are generally those of rather immediate impact and broad public interest. They are closely related to public policies and programs and to the political process itself. It is doubtful that this is true to an equal extent in any other specialized field of economics. Land economics is alive and vibrant and a poor example of economics as a dead, dull, and dismal science. Problems in land economics research are of broad interest because they involve the development, management, and use of natural resources. They are controversial problems because a whole complex of institutional arrangements is oftentimes as important as the resources themselves.

These points would suggest that the results of land economics research would be eagerly and widely sought after by our public officials and elected representatives. As noted previously, this is not the case. The findings of research workers frequently show the need for changes in cherished institutional patterns and in resource use with major implications regarding ownership and investment. Thus, the central focus of applying the results of land economics research is most frequently related to those matters which are of emotional and financial concern to people. This tells us a great deal about the difficulties of securing better utilization of the results of land economics research. There are many instances, of course, where results from land economics research have been utilized effectively. There are also other instances where land economics research has been ignored to the detriment of the long-run public interest.

Major problems of the present day and the immediate future can be solved more quickly and more equitably if there is greater use of the results of land economics research. These problems are related to agricultural adjustments in a technological age, to the expanding and changing use of the land resource base in relation to a growing population, and to the task of keeping institutional arrangements adequate to serve the needs of an increasingly complex economy and society.

Land economics as a specialized field in economics received its greatest impetus from the twin dislocations of a nationwide depression and a regional drought in the Great Plains during the 1930's. The emergency character of the resulting problems caused an expansion of land economics research. The pressure for answers to the many and difficult problems brought rapid use of the results of research. In many cases, research and application were an almost simultaneous process.

The period since 1945 has brought another set of twins which have created many problems of concern to research workers in land economics.

They are the technological revolution in agriculture and the nationwide
population explosion. But the problems of the past fifteen years have not
seen the ready acceptance of the results of land economics research which
characterized the preceding period. This is true because there is not an
emergency of tremendous impact and because the public interest and
public action have not been dominant.

ANALYTICAL FRAMEWORK FOR LAND ECONOMICS RESEARCH

Much of what has come to be called institutional economics has application to land economics. The basis for institutional economics is found
in the work of John R. Commons. Selig Perlman has observed that
"Perhaps Commons' greatest contribution as a scholar dealt with the life
cycle of economic institutions. He defined an economic institution as
'collective action in control of individual action'."[2] Commons was concerned first with labor institutions but he also delved deeply into the fields
of public utility regulation and social security. Commons did not concern
himself directly with the institutional aspects of land but his colleagues,
students, and readers found much that was applicable to land economics in
the ideas and concepts he presented and the analytical procedure he used.
For example, his writings on value and valuation are significant in working with today's problems of recreational use of land and water resources.
His studies of co-operation in public and private administration of labor
activities have application to land and water problems.

The role of institutional economics in an analytical framework for
land economics research involves two important relationships; (1) the
fitting of the results of economic analysis into the existing institutional
situation and (2) the problems of institutional adjustment to meet changing
economic and social needs.

Economists have moved steadily in the direction of achieving greater
exactness in research results and their application through emphasis on a
mathematical approach. Involved in this development has been the use of
mechanical analogies which may give a false sense of exactness in the case
of many economic and social problems. To a considerable extent, the
mathematical approach has been forced by the emphasis on dollar values
in our public decision-making process. The Federal Congress and state
legislatures depend on statistical measures as the basis for choosing
among alternatives. The benefit-cost ratio for resource development
projects is a case in point. Once a benefit-cost ratio has been computed,
there is no indication of the relative importance in it of values which are
derived in the market place and the nonmonetary values which must be
determined in some other way. Likewise, there is no way of knowing what
consideration may have been given to a variety of institutional factors.
The same question can be raised with regard to the building of regional
and national economic models such as those based on the analytical procedures developed by Professor Leontief. It is not the purpose of these
comments to discount the value and importance of mathematical economics.
It does seem necessary, however, to emphasize the crucial position of
institutional relationships in land economics research and the limitations

---

[2]Selig Perlman, from the Foreword to John R. Commons, The Economics of Collective Action
(New York: The MacMillan Company, 1950), p. 2.

they impose. Research on problems of land tenure, agricultural credit, land values, and resource development and use will produce more usable results if the approach is designed to give due consideration to the predominance of institutional factors.

Land economics research has been concerned with numerous problems of institutional adjustment as they relate to land and water resources. Problems of zoning, governmental reorganization and control of water are involved in the widespread institutional adjustments necessary in a changing society. These problems were emphasized by the depression and drought conditions of the 1930's and have continued as matters of major concern. These are the sort of problems closely related to emotional and financial concerns of people.

Specific examples of research in the area of institutional adjustment are numerous. Studies of rural zoning in the cutover areas of the Lakes States are well known. A rapidly growing interest in rural zoning in the Great Plains waned with the end of the drought conditions of the 1930's and the return of more prosperous times. Such problem areas as the Lakes States and the Great Plains also generated interest in governmental reorganization, particularly as related to counties. There are a few cases where counties were combined, or changed to a new governmental organization such as the county manager. Growing demand for water everywhere brought studies of ways to make the institution of water rights more responsive to the needs of the day. In the western states, the need was for greater flexibility than is permitted by the doctrine of priority. One development was the use of water sales contracts as set forth in Section 9(e) of the Reclamation Act of 1939. In the eastern states, the need was for modification of the riparian doctrine of water rights to permit use for such purposes as humid area irrigation. As a result, state laws relating to water rights have been changed in a number of states.

All of these institutional factors, and more too, are involved in the broad problem of resource planning. The exploitation of resources at the turn of the century brought a recognition of the need for orderly planning in the use of resources. The drought and depression of the 1930's served to re-emphasize this need. The current population growth and pressure on resources has added new urgency to the need for comprehensive planning of resource development and use.

Resource planning in the broadest context involves a great many disciplines. The co-ordinating or integrating features, however, are more closely related to land economics than to any other area of the social sciences. Many of the problem situations require an analytical framework ranging from physical and biological data on the one hand to sociology, political science, and law on the other.

For the future, the major research problems in land economics will be concerned in one way or another with resource planning and development. Many of these problems will grow out of public policies and programs. Others will be related to privately held resources as they are affected by public pressures and private conflicts. Comparatively recent additions to the institutional complex affecting private use of land are to be found among the national agricultural programs (i. e., soil and water conservation, production controls, marketing orders, etc.). There seems little doubt that public values and interests will have a growing impact on private economic activity.

The role of the public in land and water development, control and use is a nebulous matter. The "public" is a difficult concept to identify in actuality. The problem of distinguishing between public and private interests and between various publics will complicate the approach to any research undertaking. This writer attempted to delve more deeply into this area by considering the four concepts of the public vs. the private, the public vs. the state, the public vs. the public, and the long-run vs. the short-run public interest to illustrate the difficulty of determining just what the public interest is in a given resource situation.[3]

The importance of relating land economics research to public and private aspects of economic activity and social organization comes further into focus when the informational needs to achieve understanding and provide the basis for planning are considered. This problem will be given further consideration later in this paper.

EXAMPLES OF LAND ECONOMICS RESEARCH

It is not easy to tie specific examples of land economics research to specific examples of application. Most often, the impact of research in land economics can be traced to many studies in many places which flowed together into a body of information that could not be ignored. Leonard A. Salter wrote that "The research work done on land tenure problems represents the first real substance, in research, of what later came to be rural land economics".[4] The widespread interest in tenure problems among research workers in almost every state grew out of the longstanding national goal of private land ownership and concern about the steady growth in tenancy. By the time the "golden era" of land economics arrived (the 1930's), there was a considerable volume of research reports available on the subject of land tenure and tenancy.[5]

The 1930's saw application of the new knowledge concerned with land tenure and tenancy and continuation of the research in this area. As a matter of national policy, the tenure and tenancy problem was brought into focus by the Report of the President's Committee on Farm Tenancy.[6] Research was widespread on landlord-tenant relations, length of leases, forms of rent payment and the broad problems of land tenure. Public programs were instituted to aid farm operators in gaining ownership of their units and to reverse the trend toward a higher percentage of tenant operations. Included was the Tenant Purchase Program which provided financing for the purchase of farms.

Greater benefits in total were achieved through educational efforts designed to improve the whole spectrum of landlord-tenant relations. Written leases, longer leases, more frequent use of crop-share rentals and reimbursement for unexhausted improvements were emphasized and encouraged. Stability of agricultural operations was increased substantially in many situations. This increased stability was reflected in greater

[3]Roy E. Huffman, Irrigation Development and Public Water Policy (New York: The Ronald Press Company, 1953). See Chapter 11.

[4]Leonard A. Salter, Jr., A Critical Review of Research In Land Economics, (Minneapolis: The University of Minnesota Press, 1948), p. 175.

[5]Ibid. See pages 175-210 for a review of research beginning in 1910.

[6]Report of the President's Committee, Farm Tenancy, (Washington: National Resources Committee, 1937).

production, better living conditions, conservation of soil and water resources, and increased equity in the distribution of farm income between
landlord and tenant.

As a second major category, land economics research has been concerned over the years with problems related to land values and appraisal.
Research has emphasized methods of determining land values and the
factors influencing land values. Results of such research have been important in the development of land appraisal methods to determine values
for purchase and sales, for tax assessments, and for real estate loans.
An example of classification and valuation of land for tax purposes is to be
found in research by the Montana Agricultural Experiment Station. The
existence of several state-wide levies on property made evident the need
for uniform classification and valuation procedures among counties.
Research workers developed a classification system based on productivity for each of five kinds of land. Dry cropland was classified on the
basis of wheat yields, irrigated land on the basis of alfalfa yields and
grazing land on the basis of animal unit carrying capacity. There are
also classifications for meadow and forest lands. Informational and
educational assistance was provided through the Extension Service.
Several counties entered into a reclassification program on a voluntary
basis. Later, an act of the Montana Legislature required that all counties
reclassify land for tax purposes by a specified date. The evolution of the
reclassification and valuation programs for tax purposes has been an
excellent example of the merging of research and education with the
political process. At times, research and extension workers found
difficulty in maintaining their role apart from public action because of the
controversies involved.[7]

Land values in a growing and changing economy present a complex
problem for the researcher. The strictly economic factor of ability to
produce income is complicated by social pressures and psychological
factors which are difficult if not impossible to value in monetary terms.
The growing demand for land to be used for other purposes than agricultural production is placing increasing emphasis on nonmonetary
values. Site values, recreational uses and community needs are of
increasing importance. They are a continuing basis for uncertainty and
conflict in relation to many public issues and many public-private relationships as in the case of taxation. Land economics research has a big
task ahead to provide adequate information in the area of land values and
appraisal as the nation faces the growth pressures forcing widespread
shifts in the use of land.

Farm credit is another important problem area where the ideas and

---

[7]The following publications indicate the history of this research effort: R. R. Renne and Bushrod
Allin, Montana Farm Taxes, Montana Agricultural Experiment Station Bulletin 286, March 1934;
R. R. Renne, Readjusting Montana's Agriculture - Tax Delinquency and Mortgage Foreclosures,
Montana Agricultural Experiment Station Bulletin 319, May 1936; R. R. Renne and H. H. Lord,
Assessment of Montana Farm Lands, Montana Agricultural Experiment Station Bulletin 348, October
1937; R. R. Renne and O. H. Brownlee, Uncollected Property Taxes in Montana, Montana
Agricultural Experiment Station Bulletin 382, August 1940; H. H. Lord, S. W. Voelker, and L. F.
Geiseker, Standards and Procedures For Classification and Valuation of Land For Assessment
Purposes, Montana Agricultural Experiment Station Bulletin 404, June 1942; Layton S. Thompson,
Changing Aspects of the Farm Real Estate Situation in Montana, Montana Agricultural Experiment
Station Bulletin 440, January 1947; H. G. Halcrow and H. R. Stucky, Procedures For Land
Classification in Montana, Montana Agricultural Experiment Station Bulletin 459, February 1949;
Proceedings Land Classification Conference, Great Plains Council Publication No. 3, June 21-24,
1950; Proceedings Land Valuation Conference, Great Plains Council Publication No. 7, June 17-19,
1952.

findings of research workers have found application. The decade of the 1930's brought final recognition of the fact that credit for agriculture must be tailored to fit a number of different situations. For the first time, such features as long-term loans, variable repayment, amortization, and management supervision became accepted features of various kinds of loans. They were incorporated, first, into public action programs including the Farm Security Administration and Farm Credit Administration lending programs, and the development programs of the Bureau of Reclamation and other agencies. Gradually, most of the features mentioned above have been accepted and used by private lending institutions. In recent years, this has included some aspects of management supervision through the agricultural representatives of commercial banks. The result has been an increase in the likelihood of success on the part of many borrowers.

Perhaps the most comprehensive use of research results available regarding land tenure, classification, valuation and farm credit occurred in the development of the Columbia Basin Irrigation Project. The history of irrigation development in the West had shown that unguided, unrestricted and unaided development and settlement of irrigated lands was often a costly matter for both the settlers and the public. In many cases, the third settler was able to "make a go of it" because he would build on the investment in labor and money expended by two predecessors on the land. An intensive series of studies of the Columbia Basin Irrigation Project provided for land classification as the basis of repayment schedules, for a carefully designed plan of farm units and tenure, for valuation of lands to prevent speculation at the expense of the settlers, and for a program of adapted credit.[8] Experience has demonstrated that some of the programs initiated are too restrictive as a result of the continuing technological revolution in agriculture. Certain social goals, including settling the maximum number of people on the land, have resulted in units which are too small and have several barriers to the land transfers necessary to enlarge them. This situation does not mean that effective research and application are impossible but it does emphasize some of the difficulties of doing research in a world of change.[9]

IMPROVING THE USEFULNESS OF LAND ECONOMICS RESEARCH

The land problems of the nation today are only partially agricultural and, in many cases, not agricultural at all. Land adjustment problems are, more and more, a part of the broad complex of public affairs and public policy. The impacts of adjustment on individual landowners are being outweighed by the problems created for the group and the need for public action. If the utilization of the results of land economics research is to be improved, large numbers of individuals must be cognizant of the facts. This suggests an educational effort tailored differently from the traditional agricultural extension programs. In many cases, the necessary

---

[8] Bureau of Reclamation, United States Department of the Interior, Columbia Basin Joint Investigations. This series of studies on the development and settlement problems of the Columbia Basin Irrigation Project involved research workers from the Department of Agriculture, Department of the Interior, and Washington State University and Agricultural Experiment Station.

[9] Report to the Secretary of the Interior, Repayment Problems - Columbia Basin Project (The Columbia Basin Board of Consultants, August 1, 1961).

involvement of people may be secured through the technique of self-administered discussion groups such as several states have used on an experimental basis in the public affairs area.[10]   This kind of an educational process requires specially prepared materials which can provide the basis for study and discussion without interpretation and explanation from a professional person.   There is a challenge here for both research and extension workers to present the results of land economics research in such a form.

The first and critical step to greater usefulness of land economics research is to carry out research of real significance for the problems of today and tomorrow.   All too often, land economics research seems designed to meet the researcher's personal interest, or deals with problems once important.   In an avowedly problem-solving field, this dooms the results to near impotence.   Three conditions seem necessary, if land economics research is to be useful: (1) it must be, as we have said, directed to important problems; (2) it must be competent, in a strictly professional sense; and (3) it must be available to its potential users in form that can be used.   Absence of any one of these attributes is likely to be fatal; their presence may not be sufficient.

There are two extreme approaches to land economics research which would seem to limit its effectiveness.   On the one extreme, there is highly descriptive research which presents an excellent picture of a problem situation but provides little basis for decision making.   On the other extreme, there is the highly statistical presentation of facts which provide all of the available data but give little basis for putting the data in perspective.   To this writer, the secret to improving the usefulness of land economic research lies in achieving a proper balance between the quantitative and the qualitative, between the statistical and the descriptive.   The necessary balance will vary with the problem being considered.

Obviously, the usefulness of land economics research will be enhanced greatly if the emphasis is on problems related to the rapidly changing economy and society.   Problems of development, management, and use of land and water resources for agricultural production will always require considerable attention.   But increasingly, the difficult land economics problems are concerned with the nonagricultural pressures on resources. This is reflected in the increasing attention given by researchers to problems of urban development, industrial needs, recreational values and national goals in the resources field.   Much of the research emphasis, however, is on the broad national and regional implications of these problems.   These research projects are important to the framing of public policy and in providing a basis for program development.   As yet, there is inadequate research available to cities, communities and other local areas in their consideration of necessary adjustments.

Specifically, more research is needed on the problems related to the expansion of nonagricultural land uses onto agricultural lands.   Suburban development, industrial growth, and highway construction are changing the face of rural America.   The effects on individual farm units are obvious and usually drastic.   Some people are concerned that the lands going out of agriculture may be needed for food and fiber production in the

---

[10]Among recent self-administered discussion programs carried on by agricultural extension services have been (1) "Vital Issues" in Montana, (2) "Operations Advance" in New York, and (3) "Pennsylvania Growth is Up To You" in Pennsylvania.

future. Others find it difficult to imagine such a need in view of the current surpluses in agricultural production. Little attention has been given, however, to what this upheaval in land use patterns means to local units of government, to public services and to the goals and values of people. Here is a whole new array of problems requiring study in such traditional areas of land economics research as taxation, tenure, credit, land values, and zoning. The problems are acute enough that the results of land economics research should find ready use. Without adequate information, individual and group action may well be creating problems which will be with us for a long time.

Another problem area requiring additional research is concerned with institutional adjustments needed to cope with the technological revolution and changing social goals. Walter W. Wilcox has asked these questions:

"Why do we embrace new production and distribution technology with outstretched arms, yet usually face the economic situation it creates with closed minds? Isn't it true that we want more effective bug killers, more potent fertilizers, and more powerful farm machinery but resist mightily proposed changes in economic, political, and other arrangements needed as a result of new technology?"

"Isn't one of the great challenges facing Land-Grant institutions that of getting farmers and the public generally to understand that if they embrace new technology, they should also embrace new governmental arrangements, new rules of the game, so to speak?"[11]

Assuming that the land economics researcher chooses a significant topic and that he does work which commands the respect of his professional colleagues, and assuming further that his organization is geared to help transmit his research results to decision-makers, what specific steps may improve the effectiveness of his research? Let us say at once, there is no simple, magical formula guaranteed to produce results in every situation. Some procedures seem to work better than others but one may prefer one approach and another man a different one. What works well one place may not be effective elsewhere. But I suggest the following steps - all of them, preferably, or as many as the situation permits - as generally helpful:

1. Wherever possible, the research project itself should be planned with the potential users of the research results. If the research project deals with farm leases, then consultation with country lawyers, landlords, tenants, farm organizations, agricultural extension workers, and others may be desirable. If the study aims at improved land use in a suburban zone, then city and county planning officials may be consulted. These potential users of research results cannot tell a trained researcher how to conduct a research project. But they can tell him what parts of the general problem are of most concern to them, they can sometimes give him leads to valuable information, and he should be able to find out what kind of information and style of presentation will get across to them. Moreover, personal contacts established at this stage may go far toward later acceptance of research results or avoidance of criticism and controversy.

2. These same potential users of research results should be kept informed of progress on the research project, at suitable intervals and

---

[11]Walter W. Wilcox, "Opening New Doors To Farm Know-How", Coop Grain Quarterly, Summer 1961, p. 21.

occasions. A single contact, with a long interval until the research report is published, is not enough. The reporting can perhaps best be informal, when the persons involved meet at other occasions. In many instances, a full-time professionally-trained research worker spends many months carrying out a project and writing a report. He presents it to potential users and is shocked and disappointed that they do not quickly understand it and grasp its meaning. The research man is understandably hesitant about revealing partial results before the study is finished. Yet he could often discuss his work, while in progress, with the same people he consulted before he began.

3.   The basic research report should be as readable, for the audience to which it is addressed, as possible. This is a large subject in itself, as other essays in this book point out.[12]   If the report is a technical one, addressed to professional colleagues, then the language, statistical materials, graphic materials, and other aspects of the report should be aimed at such an audience. Similarly, if it is addressed to farmers, the materials and the style of presentation should be governed accordingly. I assume that each research project results in one report that may be considered basic or prime; other uses of the same materials are considered below. More attention should be given to the "launching" of a research report than is customarily the case. Researchers and administrators are each interested in prompt release of reports; yet sometimes modest delays, or even modest accelerations, of release dates will permit using the report with a group or in a way that will bring it more directly and forcibly to the attention of the group to which it is aimed. A farmer's bulletin might be released for the annual meeting of a major farm group, for instance.

4.   The research results presented in the basic report may often be used in other media. If the basic report is a technical one, one or more popular reports can sometimes be prepared. If the basic report is a more popular one, perhaps journal articles or other means can be used to reach the more specialized professional audiences. Research workers are often unfamiliar with the possibilities of leaflets, newspaper articles, radio, and television, for reaching wider audiences. Many research workers lack the skills for use of such media, and some lack interest in using them. In many instances, specialized information workers can best prepare materials for such media, but they will require help from the research worker. It may sometimes be difficult to draw a line between research work and extension or information work. But the research worker cannot fairly refuse to work with information specialists and at the same time complain that his work seems not to reach the people for whom it is intended.

5.   The research worker should be prepared, within some limits, to discuss the results of his research work personally with interested groups and with public officials.   There is no substitute for personal contact. The chance to hear, as well as to read, and above all the chance to ask questions - questions which sometimes seem unnecessary to the researcher but which are quite important to the person who asked them - may make the difference between major use of research results and no use of them at all. Obviously, there is some limit to the amount of such work a researcher can do, and still have time for new research; yet in many

---

[12]See particularly Chapter 13 by Marshall Harris.

instances time spent in this way may be the most productive use of his time. Care may be required in choosing among potential audiences, to reach serious ones and for efficiency in use of the researcher's time. The action-oriented nature of research in land economics must constantly be borne in mind. If the researcher has proposed a better method of land assessment for tax purposes, for instance, then he must get his message across to tax assessment officials if his research is to bear fruit.

6. Finally, the research man in land economics can often profitably cultivate the acquaintanceship of leaders in all groups concerned with his work, so as to discuss with them, whenever opportunity presents itself, the results of his research and the problems which they face. This is both the last step in better use of results from completed research and the first step toward new research. Although most research moves forward on a project basis, each project is not a final goal, but rather a stage in progress. Consultations and discussion can be a continuing part of this process. The research man need not, perhaps should not, live in relative isolation from his clientele.

This discussion may well end by pointing out again that there is no royal road to effective use of research results, any more than there is a royal road to significant research itself; but research workers generally might well give more thought and imagination to better use of their results than they have customarily done in the past.

6

Land Economics Research for World Agricultural Development

by Rainer Schickele*

DELIMITING THE MAJOR ISSUES

What can research in land economics contribute to the acceleration of economic progress in the underdeveloped agrarian regions of the world? What types of land economics research can meet the pressing needs for solving strategic land policy issues? What kind of questions must be asked, and what methods used to answer them?

Land policy problems in the underdeveloped world center around two major and very complex issues: (1) the adaptation of tenure and settlement patterns to the requirements of modern agriculture; and (2) the economic and institutional arrangements needed to bring about changes in land use and development of land and water resources. These two broad issues dominate the planning discussions on land policy matters to such an extent that other issues become subordinated to them. This is the way it should be. These emerging countries are so pressed for time and human talent that they cannot afford to be sidetracked to matters of minor urgency.

This means cutting corners. There is not a fraternity of professional land economists who can set out a long-time research program for a detailed description and analysis of past and present land tenure systems, land use patterns, property rights in all their private and public aspects, land value trends, land taxation, and many other land economics data which have been so diligently assembled in the United States over the last

*RAINER SCHICKELE has been Director of Land and Water Development Division, Food and Agriculture Organization of the United Nations, Rome, since 1954. Born in Germany in 1905, he received much of his formal education there, culminating in a Ph.D. from the University of Berlin. He has been a research fellow at Brookings Institution and a post-doctoral fellow at Harvard. He has done research and teaching at Iowa State College; research in the Bureau of Agricultural Economics, USDA; and was Head, Department of Agricultural Economics, North Dakota College of Agriculture, for several years. World-travelled, he is world-known as a scholar concerned with land economics matters.

forty years. The few research workers they have, and the few whom the
Western countries might make available to them, must concentrate on
applied research specifically designed to help solve urgent land policy
problems, for the purpose of accelerating agricultural progress and lifting farmers out of the human and social degradation in which hunger,
poverty and outworn tenure systems have kept them for so long.

The challenge to research workers in the newly developing countries
is exciting and taxing their intuitive faculties and scientific imagination.
Western researchers will have to free themselves of their ethnocentricity
and must delve into the nature and the spirit of problems to be solved in
the countries they deal with. They will have only scant data on which to
build, and will have to develop new fact-gathering and analytical methods
adapted to local conditions. There is practically no research work done
in most of these countries which could be of real help in tackling the important issues facing them. And the conclusions they can draw from
relevant research in the Western world are tenuous at best, and may often
be dangerously misleading, in their application to the socio-economic conditions of the respective countries.

I shall sketch the nature of the main issues of land tenure and land
resources development and suggest some types and methods of research
which promise to be of direct usefulness in the shaping of land policies
and programs.

TENURE AND SETTLEMENT PROBLEMS

Land tenure, in the broad sense, comprises the dominant aspects of
the economic and institutional framework within which farmers work and
live on the land, and largely determines their motivations and incentives,
their opportunities for developing and exercising entrepreneurship and for
initiating and participating in group action. Land tenure conditions also
affect the bargaining position of farmers vis-à-vis landlords, merchants,
creditors, and the State, and the volume and kind of government services
and infrastructural facilities available to them. This is a reason why in
countries where political developments led to a dramatic attempt at pro-
pelling agricultural progress and economic development, major land
reform programs were usually among the first measures taken by the new
regimes. This applies to Russia, Mexico, India, Japan, Egypt, Bolivia,
China, Iraq, Cuba, and several other countries. The puzzling thing is
that although these countries all enacted rather sweeping land reform programs, their success in raising agricultural production and the well-
being of farmers has shown wide variations. It suggests that the legal
transfer of land ownership to tenants or the State, or the establishment
of collective farms in itself, is often not enough, and in some cases may
actually be harmful. Still, we know very little about why certain land
reforms succeeded fairly well and others failed to accomplish the goals
they were expected to serve.

A systematic comparative research project on the nature, scope,
means and degrees of accomplishment of major land reform programs,
especially of those in newly developing countries since the war, would be
extremely revealing and useful. Whatever research has been done is
rather sporadic, incomplete, at times unreliable. What is really needed

is a centrally planned, but locally executed international project for comparative research in this field - a challenge to one of the large foundations
and to the Food and Agriculture Organization of the United Nations. We
shall return to this problem again later.

The need for various types of agrarian reforms as a prerequisite, or
at least a necessary corollary, for general economic development is becoming widely recognized. A dramatic evidence of this growing recognition
emerged in the August 1961 conference of Latin-American States at Punta
del Este in Uruguay. [1]

For the sake of brevity and simplicity of exposition, let us concentrate
on a few agrarian reform problems of crucial importance in many countries today.

Large-Scale Versus Family-Type Farming

This is a dominant issue today throughout the underdeveloped world.
By "large-scale farming" I mean a centrally-operated estate in which the
farm worker is de facto a wageearner and has an employee relationship to
management. Private plantations and collective and co-operative farms
are subsumed under this term. "Family-type farming" means a farm unit
where the bulk of labor is provided by the members of the farm family,
where little wage labor is employed, where the family head is an entrepreneur and at the same time a farm operator and worker. Owner-
operators as well as tenants of various kinds are included in this term.
The tenure implications of these two classes of farms are sharply different, especially with respect to the individual's managerial functions, his
attitude toward the land, his motivations and incentives to produce.

The argument for large-scale farming runs as follows:

(1) Modern production techniques can be introduced much faster
    than in family-farms because of centralized management.
    Instead of training millions of individual farmers in scientific
    farming, only some thousand managers have to be trained;
(2) Large-scale farming is more efficient because full advantage
    can be taken of mechanization;
(3) Capital and credit are more accessible at more favorable
    terms because of the larger size of the farm unit;
(4) Marketing and quality control of farm products can be
    achieved more efficiently;
(5) Planning of agricultural production in line with national re-
    quirements can be more effectively implemented through the
    control over relatively few large farming units.

These aspects have a strong appeal to governments bent upon accelerating agricultural progress and increasing food production rapidly.
Stories of phenomenal production increases in Mainland China following the
collectivization of farming into "communes" in 1958 were widely publicized

---

[1] A good exposition of relationships between agrarian reforms and economic development is
found in United Nations, Department of Economic Affairs, Land Reform - Defects in Agrarian
Structure as Obstacles to Economic Development (New York, 1951), and in E. H. Jacoby, Inter-
Relationship between Agrarian Reform and Agricultural Development, FAO Agricultural Studies
No. 26 (Rome: Food and Agriculture Organization of the United Nations, 1953).

throughout India and other agrarian countries in Asia and Africa. After
the world had become a bit skeptical of the performance of collective farming in Russia, the Chinese experience seemed to rekindle the confidence in
collective farming. The recent reports of poor crops in China may dampen
the enthusiasm of some collective farming proponents somewhat, but the
Chinese authorities blame the setbacks on floods in some regions and
droughts in others.

The Indian Government policy promotes "co-operative farming"
through voluntary action and through the use of land reverting to the
villages as a result of applying ceilings to individual holdings, with but
little demonstrable success. Neither in India nor elsewhere does there
seem to be any genuine interest of farmers to band together voluntarily
into co-operative or collective farming units.[2] On the contrary, wherever
the political events permitted it, de-collectivization has occurred as in
Yugoslavia and Poland, as a result of farmers' deep-seated preference for
family-type farming. Nevertheless, where governments have land available for establishing new settlements, they often lean toward large-scale
mechanized farming, as in Indonesia and some other countries in Asia,
Africa, and Latin America.

The argument for family-type farming runs as follows:

(1) Family-type farming can become highly efficient if farmers
    are educated and trained in modern production techniques,
    because internal economies of scale in the production proc-
    ess are very limited in agriculture, and individual incen-
    tives to produce can be more effectively mobilized;

(2) Adoption of modern production techniques can be acceler-
    ated by training farm advisors and organizing an efficient
    extension service;

(3) In most farming regions in the underdeveloped world,
    there is a large underemployed farm labor force which
    for many years to come will make the use of large farm
    machinery and general farm mechanization unnecessary
    or even economically wasteful;

(4) Capital and credit needed for scientific farming can be
    made available through government farm credit programs
    and co-operative credit. Also, the use of tractors and
    specialized machinery on family-type farms can be organ-
    ized by hire-service through government, co-operative
    or private agencies;

(5) Marketing and quality control of farm products and other
    external economies of scale can be achieved for family-
    farms under co-operative or government organization.

These aspects have a strong appeal to farmers and to civic leaders
placing a high value on the human and social role of the individual in community life. Japan is an outstanding example of agricultural achievement
of family-type farming, as are Taiwan and many of the Western countries.
A comparison of the performance of Western family-type farming with that
of Russian collective large-scale farming since 1920 would probably turn

---

[2]H. S. Mann, "From Service Cooperatives to Cooperative Village Management," All India
Congress Committee Economic Review, March 1, 1959.

out in favor of the former. At any rate, output per man on adequate-size family farms in the U.S.A., Canada, and Western Europe is likely to be higher than on Russian collective farms. Within the national context of the United States the average rate of increase in per capita productivity has actually been somewhat higher in agriculture than in industry in recent years.[3] India is embarking upon a most promising venture to raise production on millions of small family-type farms through its "package program".[4] Seven districts in as many states have been selected where village-level workers and extension agents are concentrating to mass-introduce a selected number of farm practices, along with farm planning and budgeting. This program is supported by supervised credit, multi-purpose service co-operatives, minimum price guaranties and the general community development program.

Let us look a bit closer at the tenure and motivation aspects of these two types of farming structure.

Issues Surrounding Large-Scale Farming

The expansion of large-scale farming in the Far and Near East and Africa is usually not visualized in the form of private plantations, but of collective or co-operative ownership and management.[5] The legal seat of ownership appears to be of little concern. In most cases, government is thought of as retaining some measure of control over general standards of husbandry and land use, of tenure and employment terms and wage and other incomes of the members of the collective, of allocation of individual usufructuary rights of part of the land, etc., whether land ownership rests directly with the State, or with a public corporation, or with a co-operative. The major points at issue are membership eligibility, security of occupancy and employment, wage scales classified by skills and supervisory responsibility, partly in money and partly in kind and in amenities (housing, garden plots, etc.), bonuses and penalties for individual or crew performance, distribution of net income to members, and the whole complex of questions surrounding the function and organization of management.

Past experience in large-scale farming in Southeast Asia and Africa has been limited mainly to more or less monocultural plantations originally established by Europeans under colonial regimes. The large holdings of indigenous landlords were usually not centrally operated estates, but divided into family-type tenant farms. The tenure aspects and economic and social conditions of the farm worker on private plantations were not such as to solicit emulation from the newly independent regimes. Hence, many planners turn to what they have heard or read or seen during short

[3]Mordecai Ezekiel, "Distribution of Gains from Rising Technical Efficiency in Progressing Economics," American Economic Review, Vol. 47, No. 2, May 1957, p. 361. Ezekiel found that from 1935 to 1955 output per man-hour in agriculture increased at a rate of about 4.5 per cent, as compared with about 2 per cent in manufacturing.

[4]The Government of India, Report on India's Food Crisis and Steps to Meet It, by the Agricultural Production Team sponsored by the Ford Foundation (New Delhi, April 1959).

[5]There is considerable ambiguity in the meaning of these terms in the literature. A good working definition of "co-operative farming" can be found in H.S. Mann, op.cit. p.1. where he quotes the definition that emerged from a research seminar of the Indian Society of Agricultural Economics at Poona in May 1958: "It is an essential element of cooperative farming that its constituent members agree to surrender their individual rights and capacity to make major decisions in respect of farming enterprise to a common body constituted by them and accepts its decision instead." The term "collective farming" usually connotes a fairly direct government control over the management of large-scale farming units.

well-conducted tours in Russia and continental China. There is very little
systematic research available on the relevant aspects of collective farming
in Russia and Mainland China which would be of constructive use to Asian
and African countries in formulating policies concerning the role and scope
and type of large-scale farming suitable for enhancing economic and social
progress in agriculture.

What we observe today is that as governments embark upon settlement
schemes, they tend to favor large-scale farming for the reasons outlined
above, but they also find themselves under pressure from farmers to establish family-type farms.[6] The result is the groping for a compromise
which may lead to new types of tenure arrangements and production
organizations combining various elements of both systems. Land economists could be helpful in devising such new tenure systems adapted to
specific local conditions.

In Latin America, the issue has a somewhat different complexion from
that in Asia and Africa. Large-scale farming under private ownership of
nationals is much more prevalent. Current government policies in the
majority of countries still retain some hope that agricultural, and perhaps
even social, progress can be achieved by gradual internal reforms of this
tenure type, through such inducements as education of the hacienda owner
and his major domus, minimum wage and housing laws for farm workers,
taxation according to land use capabilities and other measures. It is hard
to judge how realistic such an approach might be. The rate of progress
along these lines may well have to be speeded up considerably, if the
external impact of the Cuban events and the rumblings in several other
Latin-American countries are to be met by effective though milder reforms which serve both the legitimate aspirations of farm families and
production needs of the nation.

The proponents of large-scale farming in underdeveloped countries
are prone to underestimate the demands on education, technical knowledge,
organizational and administrative skill, and leadership qualities of the
management and technical officers on the one hand, and the difficulties in
obtaining from the workers the necessary quality of performance, attitude
of personal care for plants and animals, and incentives to work, on the
other. There is ample evidence that these are the weak points of large-
scale farming, as compared to family-type farming.

Still, there is no question that, starting from a very low level of
agricultural technology, production efficiency can be increased substantially through large-scale farming, if tenure and incentive conditions are
worked out that will solicit genuine support of the farm family. The
question is, however, whether there are not alternative ways to accomplish a rise in efficiency and income of farmers which are more effective
and more desirable from the viewpoint of the aspirations of farm people.

To put the issue in a nutshell, agricultural progress in any case needs
more trained people. The question is: Can agricultural officers be used
more effectively by running large-scale farms as managers with farm
workers as employees, or by giving technical assistance to family farmers
through extension service and vocational training? To make such a com-

---

[6]In the initial stages of collectivization in China, farmers were given dividend-bearing ownership
certificates for the land they were called upon to contribute to the farm co-operative, obviously as a
means to overcome, in part, the deep-seated ownership preference of farmers and to offer some
compensation for the land previously owned by the individual peasants.

parison meaningful, other relevant conditions must be kept comparable, such as availability of capital, common use of machinery, marketing services, and number of farm workers per technical officer.

We lack systematic research findings to answer this question. I am confident, however, that such research could be undertaken, with very useful results.

So far, we can only speculate about an answer. Perhaps in the short run of 3-5 years, the large-scale farming approach, if applied in relatively few cases and under the control of highly qualified managers and technicians, could show faster adoption of modern practices. But in the longer run of 5-10 years, and covering larger regions as a predominant tenure system, the family-farming approach with effective extension service, supervised credit, and co-operatives might show a better performance in over-all productivity. The advantage of large-scale farming - where use of fertilizers and better seeds and machinery can be ordered - may often be offset by the workers' lack of incentives to carry through all the various improved practices so as to get maximum results. Under family-type farming, the incentives to farmers are much stronger, and they develop managerial skills and responsibilities of their own which enable them to control all the production processes of the farm as an organic whole in their own interest.

For instance, it is not likely that over-all production efficiency in Japanese agriculture would be higher today if agriculture had collectivized into large-scale farming after the war. It might, indeed, have been lower. The striking progress of Japanese family-type agriculture invites systematic study with a focus on those institutional arrangements which brought forth the production incentives and enabled farmers to adopt modern farming methods. Among these, extension services, co-operative services, land reforms, and supervised credit would be found to play decisive roles, aided by some strategic price supports and cost subsidies.

A general transformation of family-type farms into large-scale farming, whether of the collective or co-operative type, will rarely be possible through voluntary means, but requires coercive measures of one form or another. Since the newly developing countries are typically agrarian, and their governments must rely more and more upon majority support of the people at large, including those in the countryside, the search for tenure arrangements and incentives which will accelerate progress without eliminating the basic nature of family-type farming becomes a key issue in land policy.

This is an interpretation of factual evidence not based upon any biased notion I may have of the value of family-type farms, but upon direct observations and many discussions with government officials, peasants, and large and small landowners throughout the underdeveloped world. It is evident that the decisions between collective and family-type farming in every case will be made on political rather than economic grounds, that the difference in the potential production efficiency between the two systems is not sufficiently great to dictate the choice, and that the overwhelming majority of peasants have a strong preference for family-type farming.

The Large-Scale Family-Type Farming Combination

The wondrous ways of life are such that where the theorist constructs dichotomies of mutually exclusive types, people often find ways to synthesize elements of the one and the other into a new type that combines good features of both. A very promising prototype of such a synthesis is the Gezira Scheme in the Sudan. Although it is unique in several aspects, and has, after 35 years, not yet found its final shape nor reached its full potential performance, it is a grand experiment with far-reaching significance throughout the underdeveloped world.

Farm families in the Gezira produce cotton under large-scale farming conditions, under central management and supervision, but produce forage crops, maize, vegetables, and animal products under family-type farming conditions.

The land and irrigation water are owned by the state, and the management of the Scheme rests with the Sudan Gezira Board of seven members, including a Managing Director and four other persons appointed by the Governor-General, a representative of the Financial Secretary (Ministry of Finance), and the Governor of the Blue Nile Province. This nonpolitical Board has three functions: management, promotion of social development of the tenants, and promotion of research. The second function is placed into the hands of a Social Development Committee composed of selected Board members, and is advised by the Gezira Local Committee composed of representatives of tenants, local government, and the Provincial Governor as Chairman. Since 1952, a Tenants Union is the recognized negotiating body, with voluntary membership and elected president and other officers.

The profits of the Scheme derived from cotton, are divided: 40 per cent to the tenants, 40 per cent to the state, and 20 per cent to the Board. The Board's share is earmarked for research, social development of Gezira families, and interest and tax payments. There are no wage payments to the tenants, only loans to be repaid out of their profit share. Tenants are assigned their individual holdings, but all work on the cotton crop they do under close supervision of the Managing Director and his "block officers." Rotations are standardized and arranged to suit the irrigation water distribution system and to maximise cotton production.

But within these land use restrictions, the individual tenant can use the land and produce animal products as he wants, and the returns from such non-cotton enterprises are entirely his and at his disposal. This is the family-type farm aspect of the scheme.

The individual holdings fall mostly between 30 and 40 acres, of which rarely more than one-third are in cotton. Another one-quarter or one-third are in fallow, but can produce some pasture for livestock. This leaves 10-15 acres for sorghum (dura), leguminous grain or fodder crops (e.g., lubia), various vegetables or other crops which can be accommodated in the rotation without interfering with cotton production, and which belong to the tenant.

The history of this Scheme is peculiarly relevant to tenure and land economics problems, and many of its lessons apply, in principle, to a wide variety of conditions elsewhere. Arthur Gaitskell, one of the founders and leading spirits of the Scheme, has published recently an excellent evaluation of this pioneering tenure and settlement venture, which still today, with its over one million acres of rich irrigated land and over 25,000 tenant families, represents by far the most progressive farming system in the Sudan and the main source of the country's export earnings and government revenue.[7]

What gives the Gezira Scheme its world-wide importance is the experimental approach of settling peasants in a large-scale modern farming enterprise as family-type farmers instead of hired workers. The centralized management of the production of one basic cash crop through well-trained technicians and administrators introduces a modicum of economic and technical efficiency, produces a dependable core of income to tenants and the government, and provides a practical means for educating the peasants in the ways of scientific farming and commercial market transactions. The family-type tenancy status offers the individual tenant wide areas of opportunities for developing managerial skills, initiative and responsibility, and a number of supplemental sources of income from farming on his holding.

This is the general idea, the basic conception of the Scheme. But life is never perfect. King Cotton rules so sternly in the Gezira that neither management nor the government has really emphasized the development of the family farming part of the Scheme. The Board may feel that such a development would divert too much of the tenant's labor, perhaps also make him too independent, so that cotton production might suffer. This is the same argument that Kolkhozes in Russia make against larger garden plots and unrestricted livestock for the farm workers' families. I do not believe it is a good argument in either case. There is no better way of keeping the management of the collective part of the Scheme sensitive to the interests and needs of the farmers than providing supplementary work and income opportunities under their individual control. This also produces incentives to the central management for improving the efficiency of labor use and the terms of employment on the collective part of the Scheme.

All these are basic issues which apply in many other regions of the underdeveloped rural world. The Gezira experiment has a great deal to contribute to the finding of fruitful solutions elsewhere, and to developing experimental and democratically inspired approaches.

A comprehensive research project under independent auspices and concentrating on the present status of economic and social conditions of Gezira families and possibilities for their improvement would be extremely valuable, for the Sudan as well as for many other countries.

There have been other attempts of combining some of the advantages of large-scale farming with those of family-type farms. For instance, under the Egyptian Land Reform, the new cultivator-owners to whom the expropriated lands were assigned, had to agree to follow prescribed standard rotations in line with the requirements of efficient irrigation water distribution, to use approved seeds and minimum amounts of fertilizer for certain crops, to become members of co-operatives through which they had to sell certain key cash crops (especially cotton), and to do various other things considered necessary for maintaining adequate

---

[7]Arthur Gaitskell, Gezira, A Story of Development in the Sudan (London: Faber and Faber, 1959). The practical effectiveness of the Gezira Tenants' Union in its participation in the affairs of the Scheme is not easy to assess. Gaitskell refers to a study by G.H. Van Der Kolff, The Social Aspects of the Gezira Scheme in the Sudan (Amsterdam: Royal Tropical Institute, 1957), No. CXXIV, who "found the village councils flourishing in some respects," but Gaitskell reports that these councils "developed more as a convenient medium for consultation and for circulation of official viewpoints than as a spearhead of self-management" (p. 310). My own impression during an intensive two days visit in 1959 was that the social aspects, the drawing of the families into active participation in all kinds of community affairs, and the promotion of educational, extension, and co-operative services not directly related to cotton were rather neglected.

standards of production efficiency. These standards of husbandry, although imposed from above, seem to have not weakened, but instead strengthened, the economic and technical performance of family-type farming in the land reform areas of Egypt.[8]

With all our faith in democratic methods and goals and in the efficiency of individual incentives and initiative, we must recognize the fact that the transition from traditional prescientific farming by illiterate, poor, under-privileged and economically very vulnerable farmers cannot come about simply by giving them a piece of land in fee-simple ownership, with a little technical advice thrown in, and letting them sink or swim. Production organization always requires some socio-economic disciplinary framework, and if major changes in production methods and organization are required, the disciplinary framework must be changed accordingly. The discipline formerly imposed by tribal chiefs, landlords, and moneylenders must be replaced by a discipline established almost necessarily under government auspices, through tenure and other institutional arrangements which will not only induce the required changes in production organization, but will do so in the economic interest of the farmers and with the largest possible opportunities for farmers to learn, participate, and assume more and more responsibilities as entrepreneurs and citizens.

Family-Type Farming in a Co-operative Setting

As the Russian Kolkhoze can serve as a prototype of a modern large-scale collective farm, and the Sudanese Gezira of a large-scale family-type farming combination, the Israeli Moshav can serve as a prototype of modern family-type farming in a co-operative setting. It, too, has a far-flung relevance throughout the agrarian world.

The typical Moshav in Israel is a community of individual family-type farmers supported by a strong multipurpose co-operative organization. The farmer is an independent entrepreneur as far as the internal management of his farm is concerned. In his external relations, he is a member of the Moshav, a community organization patterned along co-operative lines. Most of the marketing, of selling farm products and buying production goods, he does through co-operatives. In addition, machinery use, communal pasture management, vocational schools and extension services, credit, consumer goods, and various cultural and recreational services are often provided co-operatively. The distribution of land and irrigation water, through nominally in state ownership, is controlled by the Moshav.[9]

Recent studies indicate that in over-all production efficiency the family-type farms in the Moshavim is fully as high as in the large-scale Kibuzim.[10]

The significance of this type of tenure and production organization lies in the fact that it demonstrates the efficacy of co-operatives in providing the same or similar economies of scale to family-type farms as are inherent in large-scale farming. It also seems to be preferred by the farmers, especially the younger generation, as most of the new settlements in re-

---

[8] Sayed Marei, Agrarian Reform in Egypt (Cairo, 1957). See especially Parts IV and VIII.

[9] Emanuel Labes, Handbook of the Moshav - An Introduction to Israel's Cooperative Farm Village (Third Edition, Department of the Jewish Agency Jerusalem, January 1961).

[10] Yehuda Lowe, Kibbutz and Moshav in Israel - An Economic Appraisal Based on Two Case-Studies, 1956/57 (Ministry of Agriculture, Israel, August, 1958), mimeographed.

cent years have been of the Moshav type. One Kibutz in the Lachish Region recently transformed itself into a Moshav.

In most parts of the underdeveloped world, the very poorly educated farmers do not have the experience, traditional self-discipline and sense of civic responsibility required for effective multipurpose co-operatives. Hence, they will need a good deal of assistance in organizing, financing and managing co-operative services. Co-operative managers and technicians and clerical staff must be trained, usually by people coming from outside the community. This is not easy. But we should keep in mind that this is just as essential a requisite for establishing large-scale farming. If the creation of effective co-operatives should require, at least in the beginning, some compulsory means such as mandatory membership and the compliance with certain standards of husbandry, the degree of compulsion as well as its kind will be much smaller and less restrictive to the individual than would be involved in setting up large-scale farms.

In many cases, it might be possible to adapt traditional local institutional arrangements to the needs of modern co-operative functions. For instance, where tribal or village councils have traditionally assigned land to individual families, as in many parts of Africa and some of the Indonesian Islands, a broadening of the representation on these councils and assistance to them for bringing about necessary consolidation of holdings, redistributions of land, soil conservation practices, and other standards of husbandry, might well prove to be much more effective than a sweeping transfer of land ownership from the tribe or village to individual farmers. Human beings, as well as production systems, require some form of social organization and individual and co-operative discipline in order to prosper.

Co-operative organizations in developing countries are essential to accelerate progress on family-type farms. But they will have to be promoted and initially managed or supervised, under some governmental or quasi-governmental auspices, even at the risk of expanded bureaucratic control. The alternative is too slow a rate of progress and perpetuation of the more insidious, less visible, but more restrictive control of local landlords, merchants, and moneylenders. It is, after all, an outstanding characteristic of modern democratic governments in the newly developing countries that they are more responsive to the aspirations of farmers, are more under public scrutiny than are the present wealthy rural gentry. The principle that needs constant stressing in promoting co-operative organization through government is to assure the most intensive participation of farmers possible, the systematic provision for training local people in the management of co-operatives and in the duties of the members, and the transfer of co-operative management to membership control within a reasonable period of time. In this process, several countries have made remarkable progress, such as India and Egypt.

Systematic research in the newly developing countries where vigorous programs for promoting co-operatives in conjunction with agrarian reforms are under way would be very useful. Such studies should focus on those institutional arrangements which affect primarily the tenure conditions of the family-type farmer, his incentives and motivations, his opportunities for managerial functions, and consequently his over-all production performance on the one hand, and income position and social status on the other.

Supervised Credit - A Key Government Service

It is not enough to educate and give technical advice to the millions of small farmers. They need credit to follow almost any technical advice on increasing their production efficiency, be it through improved seed, fertilizer, pesticides, livestock expansion, land improvement, machinery use and many other means. This requires production credit and on terms farmers can afford without incurring what appears to them as dangerous risks. It requires technical advice and supervision in the use of the credit, that is a combination of farm planning and budgeting of loan repayment with financing of specific farm practices. The security for such loans should not be the land, nor even the crop in a strict Western sense of banking procedure. It should be expected income increase resulting from the improved farm practice. Commercial or agricultural banks, under normal procedures, cannot offer such loans on their own in sufficient quantity and with the necessary managerial advice and technical supervision. It is clearly the government's responsibility to organize either directly or through the medium of specialised departments of agricultural banks, supervised credit programs for the masses of small farmers.

Here, again, the tenure aspect is important. Supervised credit should be given to the cultivators, not the landlord or the employer of farm labor. This means that the expected increase from the use of the credit must be received by the farmer, if he is to do the work and repay the loan. If half of the crop increase is siphoned off by the landlord in rent or by the local moneylender for accumulated debts, the farmer will have little or no incentive to use the credit. This, along with several other good reasons, points to the need of freezing rents in absolute terms, either in kind (standing rent) or in cash (fixed cash rent). Research on this problem, in the context of existing local conditions, is urgently needed.

The Land Ownership Issue

Individual "fee-simple" or nearly absolute ownership of agricultural land with its many economic, financial, and market connotations is a highly specialized type of ownership which played an important role only in the Western countries for the last one hundred years or so. In the rest of the world, ownership of agricultural land typically has quite a different character and is vested with a strong group or public interest in its use, disposal, and revenue yielding aspects. Except in the immediate vicinity of urban centers and in a few regions of highly capitalized modern farming in Latin America and Africa, agricultural land has never been a commodity readily transferable in a commercial market and commonly used as a collateral for credit, certainly not by the millions of small family-type farmers throughout Asia, Africa, and Latin America.

There are no signs, that agricultural land will become such a readily marketable commercial commodity. Even in countries where land reforms have distributed expropriated lands to cultivators, the state has usually retained certain controls over various aspects such as succession and inheritance of holdings, restrictions on subdivision or size of holdings, mortgaging, sale and purchase of land, and other provisions concerning its use and disposal. In many countries, agricultural land is not taxed at all, and the boundaries of individual ownership units and the allocation of

the various "sticks in the bundle of property" to different persons or legal
entities are only vaguely defined.

Agricultural progress in the newly developing countries does not require nearly absolute individual ownership in agricultural land, with freely
negotiable titles. In fact, a strong trend in this direction could easily retard progress, as it would tend to entrench the power of the traditional
wealthy, be they tribal chiefs or landlords or plantation owners or moneylenders, and to encourage concentration of ownership in areas where it is
now widely dispersed. Both tendencies would work against progress. This
is a crucial issue today in Africa where "alienation of tribal lands" for
granting individual property in land is widely debated.[11]

Nor do I believe that complete state ownership involving direct and detailed government control over use and management of land would be in the
interest of economic and social development. I do not see any strong tendencies toward such direct state ownership and management of agricultural
land.

Instead, there is a growing awareness that modern governments cannot
evade the responsibility of exercising some control over the distribution of
land among farmers, over succession, inheritance, subdivision and size
ceilings, and over certain misuses of land leading to severe erosion or
salinity of soil. These types of control do not conflict with the aspirations
of the small farmers who want to be owners in the sense of usufructuary
and permanent occupancy rights on the land they now cultivate or that is
assigned to them in land reform or settlement projects. To them, land
ownership means security of occupancy and freedom from the whims of a
landlord and the burden of excessive rents, and an opportunity to reap the
full reward of their efforts; it does not mean the right to mortgage or sell
the land, because they have always lived in fear of the moneylender and
have looked to the land for their livelihood and source of security and potential wealth.

This means, that the changes in the allocation of land to individual
farmers will become more a matter of planned rationing on the basis of
need and production requirements than of free market transactions or inheritance processes. It also means that security for credit must be found
elsewhere and not in land as a collateral, and that land values will be
determined by imputation and administrative procedures rather than in a
commercial land market. I can see no serious disadvantages in this trend,
and quite a few advantages, with respect to economic and social progress.

Research must be directed toward providing good rationing methods of
land allocation and land valuation systems for ownership or rental payments and tax purposes without recourse to land market prices.

In the immediate context of tribal ownership as it exists in many
African countries, for example, it might often be possible to redistribute
farm lands according to the requirements of better types of farming under
customary tribal methods of land allocation with few legal difficulties and
delays. Where this can be done, the boundaries of individual holdings
should be registered and given more permanent legal status only after re-

---

[11] Report of the Working Party on African Land Tenure 1957-58, Colony and Protectorate of Kenya,
Nairobi, 1958. This informative report states that "it has been proved in many countries that the
surest way to deprive a peasant of his land is to give him a secure title and make it freely negotiable".
(paragraph 101, p. 45) In Africa one hears often the saying of a Nigerian Chief: "Land belongs to a
vast family of which many are dead, a few are living, and countless numbers are still unborn."

allocation has taken its course and has proven its adequacy. Even after such a cadastral registration of individual holdings has been completed, provisions should be made for future adjustments in the size and layout of holdings through exchange at imputed land values and according to production and family income requirements. For these adjustments in the size and layout of holdings, appropriate credit arrangements must be made to fit the specific purpose of agricultural development and the repayment ability of the farmers.

These problems receive increasing attention in land reform and settlement schemes in many countries. But sufficient knowledge and reliable research findings are lacking almost everywhere, and consequently the decisions reached on these ownership and tenure conditions are often arbitrary and too much governed by immediate political and administrative expediency. Here, again, studies specifically designed to solve these problems would be most useful.

The tenure structures now in the making probably will have various mixtures of State, group and individual controls, with a wide spectrum from individual family farms under near-absolute ownership to large-scale state farms. But most farms will emerge in the range of family farms within strong co-operative organizations and partially collectivized farms with individual family farm or small garden allotments. The functions of the present landlords will be assumed partly by the cultivators, especially the internal management functions, and partly by co-operatives and government services, such as capital and credit supplies, technical assistance and marketing. In none of these forms of agricultural land tenure will individual free disposal of land in a commercial land market play a significant role. This, in a broad sketch, is the shape of things to come, as I see it, in the agrarian structure of the newly developing countries.

LAND RESOURCES DEVELOPMENT

The other major land economics issue in the newly-developing countries is the improvement and more effective use of their land resources. Modern technology, transport and communications, and the gamut of western economic and social institutions are forcing a revolutionary reappraisal of the use capabilities of the basic land, water, grazing, and forestry resources of these countries. Present land use patterns are much out of line with potential use opportunities in vast areas. To improve land use patterns and develop land resources for higher production levels, investment of labor and capital in land amelioration, and changes in institutional arrangements and organizational methods are needed.

It is useful to think about these problems in terms of an analogy with industrial development. Agriculture, like industry, requires for its development an adequate infrastructure of roads, communications, schools, storage and marketing facilities, and other public and communal services. Moreover, permanent improvement of the land's productive capacity, in the form of land clearing, drainage, irrigation, levelling or terracing, deep plowing, fencing, etc., corresponds to the building of factories and installation of permanent machinery and equipment. Quantitatively, the amount of investment required for an adequate level of infrastructural

facilities per person employed in agriculture is higher than in industry due
to the spatial dispersement of agriculture, while the amount of investment
required for permanent land improvements is lower than in industry.
Agriculture has been notoriously at a disadvantage compared with industry
on both counts, and especially so in the underdeveloped world. There are
many causes for this relative disadvantage most of which are of an institutional and socio-political nature, and some of which must be overcome if
agricultural progress is to be accelerated.

Infrastructural Requirements

Transport, communications, electricity, education, and health facilities for the bulk of the agricultural areas in the underdeveloped world -
and even in many of the backward rural areas in Western highly developed
countries - are woefully inadequate. In area development surveys, minimum adequate standards for these facilities should be determined, and
programs devised to provide them as rapidly as possible. This requires
research.
One of the basic economic characteristics of infrastructural investments is that their cost is distributed over a large proportion or the total
of the area's population, either completely or partially irrespective of the
extent to which individuals use the facilities. An individual tax payer bears
his share of the investment cost of public schools whether he uses them or
not, of public health services whether he needs them or not. Even the
costs of such public utilities as electricity, telephone, gas, for which the
users pay directly, reflect current operating costs rather than first investment costs. For instance, the rates do not vary according to the distance of the user from the central supply station and in many cases various
forms of government aid are provided to make these services accessible
to most people. In any case, these infrastructural facilities and services
are distributed over a sufficiently large population to keep whatever rates
are charged directly for their use low enough to be in reach of most of the
people. If such rates do not cover the costs, the government carries the
difference by way of subventions. This principle should be extended generally to include the rural areas.
Land economics research is needed to determine reasonable minimum
adequate requirements for the major infrastructural facilities and services
of old agricultural areas as well as for areas planned for new development
and settlement. These minimum adequate requirements for an area should
be determined according to the type of land use, crop and livestock systems, farm sizes, and population density expected to prevail in the near
future or being planned for in development programs. This means that
land use surveys, appraisals of land use capabilities, and land use planning
for area development should include the facts and considerations necessary
to determine the nature and scope of such minimum infrastructural requirements. These will, of course, be quite different for an area used
primarily for extensive dryland farming than for one used for intensive
irrigation, just to give an example.
In developing such infrastructural standards, we will have to strike a
practical balance between the technically desirable goals and what might be
actually achieved in a given area over a feasible time schedule within the
planning horizon. In most of the underdeveloped regions, a simple trans-

fer of western standards is not appropriate. It is more realistic to tie
such standards to those prevailing in the more advanced areas of the country or a major region. For instance, for such general communal facilities
as schools, roads, communications, and health, the standards for rural
areas might be derived from the actual conditions prevailing in larger towns
or the capital of the region or country.

Research is also needed in the planning and programing of infrastructural investments in such areas. The land economist should work with
public service administrators and fiscal experts in determining what is
administratively and financially feasible, keeping in mind, however, that
existing administration and fiscal devices may have to be changed to permit an accelerated rate of economic development in the rural areas. In
this respect, perhaps the most crucial issue is to find ways by which the
investment costs of infrastructural facilities for a new or neglected rural
area could be absorbed into the financial structure of the province or nation as a whole and thereby dispersed over a much larger part of the
population, instead of burdening the direct users in the area with the total
cost which in most cases they would not be able to pay, at least for quite
a number of years to come. This means nothing more than applying the
principle of infrastructural cost allocation now generally accepted in urban
areas or highly developed regions to rural and underdeveloped agricultural
areas as well. This is a basic prerequisite for agricultural land resources development and accelerated economic progress in underdeveloped regions.

Investment in Land Improvement and Development

Investment in permanent land improvements, such as irrigation systems, land clearing, swamp reclamation terracing and other erosion
control, soil and water conservation structures, pasture improvement and
livestock watering places, reforestation, fencing and construction of various farm buildings needed for efficient farm production and storage, is
analogous to investment in the expansion and technical improvement of
industrial factories and machinery. Largely due to institutional and socio-
political reasons, investment funds have been very much harder to secure
for such land improvements than for industrial purposes. The result has
been chronic starvation for land development capital in most of the agricultural regions in the underdeveloped world, and even in some regions of
the industrially developed world.

Land economics research has much to contribute in determining the
nature and amount of development capital which would be economically and
socially feasible, or even necessary, to invest in improving the productive
capacity of land resources. There are vast areas of land where the profitable application of modern production techniques is severely limited because
present land characteristics hamper full utilization of such improved techniques. For instance, fertilizer and better seeds yield uncertain and often
discouraging results on poorly drained or droughty land, or on eroding hill
sides. Yet it is feasible in many areas to modify these land characteristics so as to improve the basic productivity of these land resources by
drainage, irrigation, terracing or other erosion control measures. For
this, certain amounts and kind of capital are required, along with some
new organizational and administrative arrangements, and these are peculiarly difficult to come by in typical backward agricultural areas.

There are many reasons for this dearth of land development capital.[12]
Here, I only want to stress that over-all scarcity of capital is not one of
these reasons. We only have to remind ourselves of all the conspicuous
and unproductive capital investment usually associated with urban, commercial and industrial development, even in underdeveloped countries,
taking such forms as filling station palaces, speed highways with small
traffic loads, sumptuous office buildings of banks and commercial and
industrial companies, duplication of many sorts of retail, advertising and
other commercial services way beyond economically justifiable limits, etc.

Moreover, in the longer-term perspective of a dynamic economy, the
demand for capital is by far the most important determinant of capital formation. If the potential justifiable demand for land development capital
could be activated, there is ample evidence that it could be met without
reducing the availability of capital now in effective demand, that is without
slowing down capital investment in the nonagricultural sectors of the economy. This assumes, of course, that international financial and trade
arrangements continue to be improved and expanded to more nearly meet
the needs of the underdeveloped world, an objective which is equally in the
interest of the industrialized part of the world.

Land development capital will have to come mainly from public sources.
Private investors are overwhelmingly city-and industry-orientated. Even
wealthy landowners usually invest their incomes from agriculture in urban
real estate and industrial assets rather than in agricultural land development. This places the responsibility of land development planning and
financing mainly into the hands of the government. Apart from determining the most promising kinds and amounts of capital needed for land
development, the land economist should also contribute to finding ways of
securing the required investment funds. He is especially qualified to determine the limits of repayment ability of farms and other direct land
users, with respect to amounts, time period, conditions of debt obligations,
methods of assessment, and collection of payments. In many cases, part
of the investment cost in land improvement and development might best be
met by government subventions, since they are bound to generate a series
of indirect and secondary benefits accruing to nonagricultural sectors of
the economy. All these problems offer a great challenge to land economics research in the developing countries.

Organizational Aspects of Land Development

Developing countries are notoriously short of foreign exchange, unless
they happen to have large oil or other mineral resources whose exploitation is already in full swing. In many cases, however, the capital requirements for land improvement have only a small foreign exchange component
as compared to capital requirements in industry. A major part of investment needs can be provided by the local labor force, which is often characterized by a high degree of at least seasonal, and often year-round
underemployment, and by locally available materials. For instance, the
construction of irrigation and drainage systems can utilize large amounts
of local labor and materials and often requires only modest amounts of

---

[12]Rainer Schickele, Agricultural Policy (New York: McGraw-Hill, 1954), ch. 9, "The Agricultural Lag." Also, Rainer Schickele, "Resettlement Problems and Policies", Netherlands Journal
of Agricultural Science, Vol. 5, No. 4, November 1957.

imported capital goods. What is primarily required is the motivation, mobilization and organization of local labor forces, and of domestic administrative and financial resources. For instance, under the "Food for Development" program which is now taking shape, a good part of land development cost might be met by the use of surplus food for feeding the workers on such projects.[13]

Beyond this, technical assistance from foreign experts is required. Such technical assistance, however, is becoming more readily available as a result of the rapid expansion of technical assistance programs under the auspices of FAO and other United Nations agencies and bilateral aid. The United Nations Special Fund, through its pre-investment survey and demonstration projects, is bound to lead to an accelerated rate of land development activities.

It is not enough to improve the productive capacity of land resources. It is equally important to organize their utilization in accordance with their increased capacity. This requires changes in systems and intensity of farming in land tenure conditions and farm size distributions. Often, new technical and administrative services are needed, such as irrigation districts to control the distribution of irrigation water and advise farmers on water requirements of various crops during the growing season and on prevention of soil salinity, or land use and watershed management districts to improve land use patterns, establish soil and water conservation measures, and control erosion and flood hazards.

Several other organizational measures have already been mentioned, such as extension service, co-operatives, and supervised credit which are essential in bringing land development projects to full fruition.

All these issues fall squarely into the scope of land economics. There is a serious urgency for land economics research directed at solving these complex and crucial problems in the developing countries. There is hardly a country among them, in which systematic and sustained research in these fields is being carried on. There are probably two main reasons for this: one, that land economics is a relative new discipline which has barely expanded beyond the borders of the U.S.A. and Canada; and two, that governments in the newly-developing countries associate research almost exclusively with the natural sciences and industrial technology, and are unaware of the benefits they could derive from well-oriented and competently conducted research on these land economics problems.

RESEARCH APPROACHES

Some Methodological Comments

I have outlined two major groups of issues in land economics facing the agricultural sectors in the newly developing countries. Since the research needed is eminently of the problem-solving type, we must be clear about the nature of the problems. What are the obstacles in present institutional arrangements inhibiting farmers' motivations, incentives, and opportuni-

---

[13]Food and Agriculture Organization of the United Nations, Development Through Food - A Strategy for Surplus Utilization (Rome, 1961), pp. 79-86. and Uses of Agricultural Surpluses to Finance Economic Development in Under-Developed Countries - A Pilot Study in India (Rome, June 1955).

ties to improve their production performance, living standards and social status? What changes in economic and institutional arrangements can be made that will promote land resources development and rural infrastructural investments so urgently needed for better production performance, higher living levels, and more active participation of farmers in community affairs?

The traditional tools of neoclassical economic analysis are not sufficient for studies of this kind. It is not a question of manipulating quantities or prices of one or a few goods as independent variables, to see what happens to prices or quantities of these same or a few other goods as dependent variables, keeping all other relevant factors constant, including institutional arrangements, income distribution, technology and consumer preferences and what not. The nature of the problems demands that, instead, we manipulate specific key institutional arrangements as independent variables, to see what happens to farmers' incentives and production performance as dependent variables, with quantities of certain key resources assumed available for certain time spans as parametric constants, and with the ultimate goal of keeping all resources fully employed under conditions of advancing technology and organizational efficacy. The mathematical terms are used here merely as a rough analogy, since obviously mathematical methods are not suited for dealing with the problems.

It is very important for research workers to ponder about the appropriateness of their analytical tools to the nature of the data and the problems they deal with. The methodological approach just outlined means that:

(1) ceteris paribus conditions are greatly relaxed and refer only to certain broad aspects of social structures and value systems and empirically feasible rates of change over time;

(2) often it is not necessary nor desirable to isolate the effect of one single factor upon aggregate outcome; instead, the effect of alternative patterns or collections of factors upon the outcome is the purpose of the inquiry;

(3) some of the key factors are qualitative relationships or conditions or characteristics not measurable on a continuous scale of homogeneous quantitative units, and

(4) the quantitative aspects involved, such as production, income, etc., are often best treated in terms of directional changes (e.g. more or less) and in relevant orders of magnitude rather than in exact amounts.

The focus of inquiry is: What is the result of a certain change in various institutional patterns and collections of resources and services likely to be on the total outcome, and which changes are likely to affect the total outcome most favorably with respect to production, income, and welfare? These policy goals are taken to converge toward the superior end of creating an agrarian structure which facilitates acceleration of farmers' production performance through promoting land resources development and infrastructural investment, and generating appropriate motivations, incentives, and opportunities for developing production skills, managerial functions and civic participation, rights and responsibilities.

The researcher must divest himself from some preconceived notions which economists have taken over from the physical sciences without sufficient scrutiny of their appropriateness. For instance, correlation analysis, production functions, linear programing, input-output matrixes and similar statistical-mathematical devices are not the only analytical methods which yield useful and reliable results. In fact, for studies of economic policy and processes of economic development, the limits of methodological appropriateness of these analytical tools are much narrower than is commonly assumed. Their main role is to describe what happens in the quantitative aspects of production and consumption processes, and thereby furnish important raw materials for studies of economic policy and development processes. Nonclassical analysis cannot alone and by itself solve specific policy and development problems, but must become part, and sometimes a rather subordinate part, of other analytical methods such as analogy and deductive inference and comparative case studies and Gestalt-theoretical concepts which are indispensible for problem-solving research in the crucial aspects of economic policy and economic development.

Let me elaborate this point. Since the advent of electronic computers it has become possible to handle a larger number of independent variables and to deal with various sets of parametric constants (such as transformation rates and production coefficients). True, this permits manipulation of more variables and relaxation of ceteris paribus conditions. But there are always some key elements in developmental processes of which a mathematical model cannot take adequate account. Some of the relationships between variables (which must be quantitatively measurable by empirical-statistical observations) are not "functional" in a mathematical sense, since they are subject to changes in motivations, behavior, and actions and reactions on the part of persons with volitions and choices in their attitudes and purposes concerning their actions. Just to indicate the kind of things I have in mind, I refer to the rather awkward and not very successful attempts in mathematically formulating oligopolistic models designed to represent really quite simple bargaining-power situations. Another more pedestrian example would be the case where a given combination of labor and capital resources, expressed in quantitative terms, can produce widely different volumes of output depending on a number of factors not measurable in quantitative units such as morale, team spirit, incentives, spatial arrangement of equipment and various organizational and external servicing devices. Yet, all these qualitative factors are objectively observable, describable, classifiable, can be manipulated and controlled; in other words they are data amenable to analytical treatment and to scientific inquiry in the sense of social science.

Another example of limitation in the usefulness of neoclassical theory is the concept of a single-value solution. In the framework of social science methodology directed at solving problems of economic development and policy, the notion that there is only one maximum national product, one optimum combination of resources, one highest profit position is untenable either on theoretical or empirical grounds, and can lead to dangerously wrong conclusions, if applied to economic policy recommendations. The common retreat behind the "ceteris paribus" defense is no better than an ostrich's head-in-the-sand or a Maginot Line in a rocket and atomic age.

People want to improve their economic position, and there are many different combinations of increased goods and services, each of which would be considered decidedly better than the present one. There is no single-value solution to the problem of "maximizing the national product", or "optimizing an aggregate consumption pattern," if for no other reasons than the two very simple ones: (1) that many individual goods are substitutable within fairly wide limits in their utility to consumers, and (2) that populations are very heterogeneous as to their preferences. For instance, combination A might be somewhat more to the liking of the richer, B to the poorer sections of the population, or to the younger and older, or men and women, or rural and urban groups. But all of them would be better off with either A or B, and this is the most relevant point.

The obvious conclusion is that searching for a single-value solution to problems of economic development, of resource allocation and aggregate production increase is basically inappropriate to research in economic development. A concept of multiple solutions, instead, is not only more realistic, but also rests on much firmer theoretical foundations. The focus of research, therefore, should shift from determining, for instance, "the best" pattern of resource allocation (necessarily based upon present or forecast price relationships, which in itself is a questionable ground to stand on), to determining a number of alternative resource allocations leading to roughly similar rates of economic growth. It then becomes a matter of social, organizational, administrative, political, or even common sense negotiating considerations to decide which of them can be most readily attained and is most feasible under the particular circumstances of the various countries. The choice will rarely, if ever, be determined by the absolute size of the imputed values of the resultant national products, but by the feasibility of the various policy measures and institutional arrangements necessary to bring about one or the other pattern of resource allocation, each one distinctly superior to the present.

These considerations are of prime importance for the task of designing research programs in land economics as well as in other fields dealing with problems of accelerating economic development.

The Role of Comparative Case Studies

The kind of land economics research most needed in newly developing countries, in the light of these methodological considerations, should not be based on mass statistical data of the census or enumerative type, but on a sophisticated use of case studies in the widest sense. Comparative case studies are for the social sciences the counterpart of laboratory tests in the physical sciences. The case studies yield the factual information concerning the relevant aspects, qualitative and quantitative, of the problem, and make it possible to predict the effect of contemplated changes on the total outcome.

Analysis and conclusions are based upon analogy and deductive inference, transferring relationships, events, etc., from one case to another with appropriate adjustments for important differences in certain qualitative and quantitative aspects between these cases. If competently carried out, the level of reliability even of the quantitative aspects of the conclusions from comparative case studies is likely to be, for most practical purposes, as high or higher than that of conclusions based on statistical correlation or production function analyses of complex economic factors.

Methodological development and refinement of the comparative case study approach has been sorely neglected in economic analysis. Land economics research in the underdeveloped countries offers a great opportunity to improve these analytical tools and demonstrate their value in policy and program formulation and in the understanding of economic development processes.

In the United States, the field where this method has been most successfully developed is farm planning and budgeting. In its simplest form, the
structure and production organization of a given farm is ascertained, and
various experiences and relationships concerning production observed in
other cases are introduced into a forward-looking farm plan and budget, on
the basis of which production and management decisions are made. In
farm management extension, supervised credit programs of the Farmers
Home Administration, and Soil Conservation Service programs, this farm
planning and budgeting approach has proven extremely useful and a reliable guide for managerial decisions. The problem to be solved in these
studies is, of course, much simpler than the problems of tenure and
settlement programs in underdeveloped areas. But the method needed in
the latter is basically similar.

For instance, to appraise the effect of a change in institutional arrangement on the motivation of farmers and their prospective change in increased
production efforts and improved farming practices, a typical farm can be
planned and budgeted under existing and proposed new institutional arrangements, by the transfer, with appropriate modifications, of observed experience from cases with institutional arrangements similar to those proposed.

Often, such studies cannot be confined to a particular area or country,
because certain promising institutional arrangements are nonexistent in the
area. One must find cases where comparable institutions (not necessarily
identical ones) do exist to appraise their effect on incentives and production
performance.

This approach is in principle the most direct and useful one for research that is designed to determine which set of changes in institutional
arrangements is most likely to bring forth the desired results.

A crucial step in this research method is the selection of cases. All
cases should be "typical" in the sense of a certain set of characteristics,
but not necessarily in the sense of a modal concentration of statistical
occurrence. For instance, if we want to appraise the probable effect of
ownership transfer to tenants in a tenancy area, we must construct one or
more cases typical of the predominant tenant farms in the area and then
look for other cases, similar in most relevant respects, where ownership
has been transferred to tenants. For that, we may find only few farms in
the area, which are obviously atypical in the statistical sense. We even
may have to go outside the country to find them.

A "case" should rarely be one single farm or "observation unit", but
an average of a small number of them, all having approximatley the same
or similar relevant characteristics, and enough of them to abstract from
irrelevant but highly effective characteristics, such as exceptional managerial capacity or lack of capacity of the farmer, fortuitous circumstances
like local floods or wide differences in family size, or other peculiarities
not relevant to the study. At the other extreme, a "case" may include a
whole country, depending upon the problems to be analysed and solved.

The construction of "typical cases" is really a difficult problem. The
all-important point is that planning for development must not concern itself
primarily with describing the present average or modal situation (except,
of course, for benchwork purposes to determine the position from which
development starts), but must project quite different production processes
and desirable typical or modal situations which do not exist at present but
which constitute the goal toward which economic development is to progress.
For this reason, it is more relevant for planning and policy determination

to have a deep insight and realistic understanding of present atypical (rare) situations which if propagated promise to foster economic development and which should become typical (in the sense of modal concentrations) in ten or twenty years from now.

The selection of "relevant characteristics" is another important step. To use again our example, the question is not to isolate the effect of transfer of ownership per se, but to determine what other things may be needed to give full play to the production incentives created by the ownership transfer. If the new owner-cultivator, for instance, has no more, or even less, operating capital than he had as a tenant, his increased production incentives have no way to translate themselves into higher production performance. Hence, it is fruitless to isolate whatever effect we might ascribe to the single factor of ownership transfer. Obviously, that effect cannot materialize without certain corollary requirements such as capital, credit, and other things available to the former landlord.

One of the best sources of information is found in areas where projects are in progress, where something is happening, even if on a very small scale. Concurrent studies for the analysis and evaluation of projects in progress, with benchmarks of relevant characteristics at the beginning, and with periodic resurveys every two or three years, are extremely valuable. Yet, such studies are practically nonexistent. It is a great pity for these countries and their peoples to see such precious experience go to waste, while only a ridiculously small investment in such concurrent studies could bring tremendous dividends.

ORGANIZATION OF RESEARCH

What might be done to get some systematic research work in land economics started in the newly developing countries?

First, we need to set out a few major problems around which a research program could be orientated. There are not enough research workers and facilities available to tackle many problems at once. I would give high priority to studies in two broad fields: land tenure and settlement problems and land resources development problems. I would suggest starting with comparative case studies of carefully selected land reform and settlement projects (both on new land and on old land), for example, in Egypt, Iraq, selected areas in India, and selected settlement schemes in Indonesia, Latin America, and Africa. Some of these projects should have a strong component of investment in land development.

Second, we need an outline of research methods for such studies, a simple framework which assures a modicum of comparability of observations and results, but which is adaptable to a wide range of local conditions and can be elaborated according to the caliber of the researcher and the facilities at his disposal.

Third, we need a small central steering committee to give general guidance and supervision, and to make arrangements for comparative analyses of the various case studies between projects and countries, and their publication.

Fourth, we need a fellowship fund to get competent research workers on the job, at least one senior land economist for each project, with at least one assistant who speaks the local language fluently and is preferably a native of the respective country. The duration of each study should be at least one year and preferably two years.

Fifth, we need the co-operation of the respective government. It must assign one or more assistants to the researcher and arrange for local facilities, access to farmers, village leaders, and local officials. This will often not be easy to achieve. Still, since most of these projects are in one form or another under government auspices, its co-operation will be necessary.

These probably are the minimum needs for a systematic research program in this field. It is not a very ambitious program. One might well start with say three projects over a period of two years and come out with very useful results. This would involve a cost of around $100,000 per year.

The most important conditions of success would be the caliber of the senior research workers assigned to the field projects. It would be well to get them together for a few months before they go out, and to see to it that they remain in correspondence during the period of the study.

There would be no attempt at mass collection of statistical data, and hence no need for much clerical work. Emphasis would be on intensive field observation of farmers' behavior and reactions to certain changes, of the workings of old and new institutional arrangements, of various government services, of the role of local leadership of various types, and the effect of all these things on land use, production, income and social participation of farmers. A certain amount and kind of quantitative statistical data, of course, must be collected, some from farmers and other local sources, some from government agencies and other national bodies. For this, genuine interest and co-operation of local people and government officials will be most helpful.

Such studies cannot be conducted by graduate students of average or even good college records. They require mature land economists with much experience and keen insight into human behavior and the nature and role of institutional arrangements and policy measures. They must approach these land economic problems as broad-gauged social scientists and political economists rather than as statisticians, mathematicians, lawyers, or anthropologists. They should know enough about these related disciplines to draw upon them where needed, and in critical cases one or the other of these disciplines may have to be called upon through special consultants. But the focus of these studies should not be blurred by a host of details about a large number of related aspects too complex and divergent to be manageable within the scope and purpose of these studies.

Each study should be primarily the result of the mature and creative mind of one man who has set out to accomplish a manageable, limited, but strategically important task, who has had sufficient time to observe and think through the relevant aspects of the problem, and who has had ample opportunity to consult with others, to receive stimulation and criticism. Only if approached and carried out in this spirit can such studies be of greatest scientific value and practical usefulness in charting the course of land policy in this critical period of economic development throughout the agrarian world.

PART II. THEORETICAL CONSIDERATIONS

7

Relevance of Production
Theory to Land Economics Research

by Walter G. Miller*

Land economics has been regarded as a special field of study only within relatively recent years. But many of the problems to which the early anticipators of modern production theory addressed themselves could today be referred to as land economics problems.[1] As a field of concentration, land economics is concerned primarily with the actual use of land resources and the institutions that govern their use. In contrast, production theory constitutes an abstract representation of production as a process or an economic activity.[2] It focuses on the organization of re- sources, on the functional relationships between these resources and the goods or services they yield, and on the behavior of the producers involved.

In a view of the fact that in most respects land is just another resource, the relevance of production theory to land economics should cause no particular concern. However, because assumptions such as those regard- ing technical relations and the institutional environment are necessary in developing the general theory of production, this general theory cannot be applied directly to the various circumstances within which production activities actually take place. The theory needs to be scrutinized and modified for specific applications, as in land economics, in which land use and the institutions that affect it are the center of interest.

The main question with which we are concerned here is the extent to

---

[1]The determination of rent, for example, was a central issue in the evolution of the marginal productivity theory of distribution, which is the same as the widely accepted theory of production.

[2]By production is meant all the processes or activities of "combining and coordinating materials and forces in the creation of some valuable good or service." Sune Carlson, A Study on the Pure Theory of Production (London: P. S. King and Son, Ltd., 1939), p. 1.

---

*WALTER G. MILLER is an agricultural economist with the Economic Research Service, United States Department of Agriculture. Born in Jamaica, West Indies, in 1919, he received his B.S. and M.S. from the University of California, his Ph.D. from Iowa State University. Since 1955 he has been engaged in land tenure and production economics research.

which production theory can contribute to analysis of land economics problems. Presumably, some land economics problems are more amenable than others to conceptual or empirical analysis based on production theory. Then, too, the theory may have serious weaknesses when attempts are made to apply it to real situations. An attempt is made here to point out the usefulness of the theory as an analytical frame of reference.

In the ensuing discussion, elements of the production and land economics problem are stated first. Next, the fundamental features of production theory are reviewed and the theory is oriented to the analysis of land economics problems. Finally, some of the limitations of the theory are summarized.

THE PRODUCTION AND THE LAND ECONOMICS PROBLEM

From the viewpoint of land use, the problems of production and of land economics are identical in many respects. Within all productive units -- firms, industries, regions, or countries -- land plays a vital or even an indispensable role as a productive agent. Therefore, practically all major and long-run decisions pertaining to production involve the use of land. Conversely, land use decisions affect the kind, quality, and amount of goods or services that are produced or made available.

The widely accepted theoretical treatment of production in current economic analysis deals simultaneously with the allocation of land and other resources among their various uses, and the distribution of the returns among those resources. Accordingly, the problem of how factors of production are used is resolved along with the problem of how much they are rewarded.[3] This dual role of production and distribution theory should make the theory relevant in land economics research because the problems involved have been classified, coincidentally, as problems of land utilization and of property rights.

For purposes of this discussion, however, license is taken to depart slightly from this classification. It seems more convenient analytically to consider land economics as dealing with problems in the use of land and calling for analyses pertaining to questions (subsets of problems) of resource allocation, development, and control.[4] This subclassification of problems is preferred because land utilization questions often stem from the nature and distribution of property rights in land. Also, the questions of resource allocation and development, although not always distinct, often require separate decisions and different types of analysis.[5]

---

[3]See for example: Edwin Cannan, A History on the Theories of Production and Distribution in English Political Economy, 1776-1848 (Ed. 3., London: P. S. King and Son, Ltd., 1924). George J. Stigler, Production and Distribution Theories (New York: The Macmillan Co. 1948). American Economic Association, Readings in the Theory of Income Distribution (Philadelphia, Toronto: The Blakiston Co., 1946), especially pages 103-97, "Production Function and Marginal Productivity."

[4]Many land economists are also directly involved with questions of water utilization, and justifiably so because water is so closely related to land. However, no special attention is given to water here; attention is largely given to land as space. For an introductory treatment of production theory with respect to water use, consult Earl O. Heady and John F. Timmons, "Economic Framework for Planning Efficient Use of Water Resources" in John F. Timmons, et. al., editors, Iowa's Water Resources (Ames: Iowa State College Press, 1956), pp. 47-61. See also, Warren S. Gramm, "Limitations of the Theory of the Firm to Water Resource Analysis," Land Economics, Vol. 34, No. 2, (May 1958) pp. 113-21.

[5]Another important subset of questions may be called the "conservation" questions. But these are neither independent of, or parallel with, the questions of allocation or development, which are "means" through which conservation may be accomplished. That is, the solution of problems in conservation may call for reallocation of land between uses, or development, or both.

Land utilization problems continue or reappear because of the competing and changing demands for land in its various uses and the relatively fixed total supply of land. Solution of these problems may call for reallocation of land between uses and users, development, and changes in institutions. Analysis of land utilization then requires consideration of the following: the purely physical possibilities and the quantity of land resources available to productive units; the selection of the purposes to be served by land; the economic criteria by which available land resources are to be exploited to achieve the desired purposes of land use; and the fashioning of the institutions that will direct the use of land along lines consistent with the economic criteria accepted. It should be recognized however, that these economic criteria may well be shaped by the institutional enviornment and that in the management of land resources, the criteria, guidelines, or standards adopted are sometimes determined politically.

The physical possibilities (production functions) and institutions are ordinarily considered as given in solutions based on production theory. The solutions deal largely with the allocation problem, which is concerned with the direction in which resources are channeled. It deals only implicitly with the development problem, which involves changes in the production functions themselves through permanent investments in land.[6] A complete and rigorous analysis of land use, however, should recognize production functions and property institutions as variables rather than as constants or constraints. A basic assumption either implied or expressed in economic studies is that all lands should be put to their highest and best use. To achieve this objective, all facets of the land utilization problem -- allocation, development, and control -- need to be considered and evaluated.

Questions as to the use of land necessarily arise at different levels. They arise, in the very broad sense, from the viewpoint of a country;[7] and in the narrow sense, from the viewpoint of individual producers or resource users. At all levels, the principles for land use should remain the same, even if differences occur as to what is being maximized. Land economics is concerned more with the broad social problems of land utilization, but it is concerned also and inevitably, with resource use by individual users. This is true because the institutions pertaining to land affect the way in which these resources are handled by individuals.

In this attempt to relate production theory to land economics, specific problems are not considered. Also, the variations in controls through such institutions as ownership, leasing, taxation, and zoning are treated only in a very general way.

THE ESSENCE AND IMPLICATIONS OF PRODUCTION THEORY

Production theory, as generally accepted today, has been shaped by the concept of the firm as a maximizing unit operating in an enterprise economy, and by the marginal productivity theory of distribution. Hence,

---

[6] In some instances, the specific problem may be concerned with avoiding negative changes in the production possibilities; that is, to prevent "deterioration" or "depletion", which may be reflected in the production functions or may even cause land to shift to a "lower" use.

[7] Cf. S. V. Ciriacy-Wantrup, "Conceptual Problems in Projecting the Demand for Land and Water" in Modern Land Policy (Urbana: University of Illinois Press, 1960), pp. 41-67.

production is treated most frequently as a part of the theory of the firm. The principles have been extended, however, to such other "productive units" as industries, regions, or countries. Essentially, the theory attempts to explain how land and other resources are used, and how these resources should be allocated in order to maximize some end.[8] For this reason, the theory is sometimes referred to, perhaps appropriately, as a theory of resource allocation. The pure theory of production rests heavily upon the assumptions that production functions exist, that relative market prices are appropriate choice criteria for allocating resources, and that a producer seeks to maximize the difference between his receipts and his expenditures. The discussion that follows focuses on the concept of a production function and on the criteria for allocating resources.

Production Functions

The production function is probably the most fundamental of all the concepts used in connection with modern production theory. This relation, which supposedly represents the output of a commodity as a mathematical function of the quantities of the various productive factors that go into producing it, has been stretched in economic analysis to include numerous types of input-output relations, physical and otherwise.[9] Then, too, it seems to be usual to refer to the production function for "what is produced" (minerals, livestock, crops, etc), as well as to the function for a particular "productive factor" (labor, land, etc). Accordingly, different perspectives are taken of production functions. From one perspective, attention is focused on the product; from the other, attention is focused on the respective factors. Thus reference is frequently made to the production function for land or for each of the other factors involved. The basic mathematical relations, however, are the same regardless of the perspective.[10]

Conceptually, production functions vary as to their shape and parameters. Hence, both theoretically and empirically, the characteristics of these functions have long been a matter of interest and concern. Agricultural land in particular has occupied a prominent place in the various expositions of production relationships. For land economics, however, interest must necessarily be widened to embrace the characteristics of the functions for all the processes or activities in which land is a productive agent.

From the product viewpoint, production functions will vary according

---

[8] The end, which is sometimes referred to as the "objective function," is usually assumed to be "profits" for the firm. The theory of the firm has therefore been derided at times as a theory of profit maximization, and as such it cannot be applied to all "units" that produce goods or services. In this discussion, the implications of the theory for firm analysis are de-emphasized, as land economics is concerned more with the broader questions of production.

[9] For different senses in which the concept of production functions has been used, see as examples: G. G. F. Simkin, "Aggregate Production Functions," Economic Record, Vol. 31, No. 60, (May 1955), pp. 32-39; Ralph Hawtrey, "Production Functions and Land -- A New Approach," Economic Journal, Vol. 70, No. 277 (March 1960), pp. 114-24; Earl O. Heady and John L. Dillon, Agricultural Production Functions (Ames: Iowa State University Press, 1961); Joan Robinson, "The Production and the Theory of Captial," Review of Economic Studies, Vol. 21, No. 55 (1953-54), pp. 81-106.

[10] From the product viewpoint, the production function may be represented by the equation from a multiple regression in which all factors are explanatory variables. From the factor viewpoint, the concept is analogous to the equation with only one factor as the explanatory variable. Therefore, this depends upon the function for the product because the effects of all the co-ordinate factors are incorporated in a constant for the intercept of the equation.

to the quality of the factors. At one extreme, land of a certain quality may produce nothing if an attempt is made to put it in certain uses. The production function does not exist in such uses because the quality of land is not adaptable to them. The same land, however, may be very well adapted to other uses. Thus for a given quality of land, the production function varies according to the use to which the land is put; and different production functions are obtained for a given product from lands of differing quality.

From the factor viewpoint, the production function for a particular factor depends also upon the qualities or quantities of the other co-ordinate factors.[11] Hence the production functions for land may be expected to differ, at least in their positions, if not in their other characteristics, according to the quantities and qualities of the other factors used in combination with it. Correspondingly, the functions for other factors applied to land must necessarily be conditioned by the quality and quantity of land. Thus, by implication, whenever reference is made to the marginal product of land, the quantity and quality of the resources combined with land need to be recognized or specified.

It would seem, however, that true production functions with ascertainable input-output transformation coefficients may be reasonably expected only in agriculture or other "extractive" industries. Special problems arise with respect to identifying and measuring the output (the dependent variable for the production function) when land is used for such purposes as recreation and transportation. Production functions, if they are ascertainable in these instances, clearly cannot be expressed in physical terms. In addition, homogeneity, or standardization of input, which is required for production functions can hardly be preserved for some land uses, because each piece of land differs technically from each other piece, at least so far as site is concerned. For these various reasons, production functions in some land uses are so far purely imaginary constructs.

Even when the production function associated with a land use is determinable, the distribution of the total product that is attributable to the respective productive factors, although conceptually possible, causes some uneasiness empirically. This is particularly true for situations in which the productive factors may be complements, as are land and labor in the construction of buildings, or for situations in which capital is sunk into land for productive purposes. In such instances, formidable difficulties would be encountered in attempts to derive the respective contributions of each factor--their transformation coefficients into products-- as suggested by the definition of a production function. Despite these conceptual and technical difficulties, the assumption as to production functions is basic to the reasoning in production theory.

Production Efficiency

The concept of efficiency, although ambiguous in some respects, represents an important concept in production theory,[12] as do production

---

[11] The better quality or greater quantity of the "fixed" factors will cause changes in the position of the functions for the "variable" factor so far as the intercepts of the functions are changed. The differences, if any, in the transformation (production) coefficients that may be generated by differences in the quality of the co-ordinate factors is however debatable.

[12] Cf. Margaret Hall and Christopher Winsten, "The Ambiguous Notion of Efficiency," Economic Journal, Vol. 69, No. 273 (March 1959), pp. 71-87.

functions. Economic efficiency pertains to the overall input-output relation associated with a particular organization of resources. Accordingly,
the concept is relative in this context as one pattern of resource organization and use may be more or less efficient than another. Production
theory is oriented to achievement of the highest level of efficiency in
resource use, referred to as optimum.[13]

Efficiency as a guide to resource allocation is achieved if three conditions are satisfied for a productive unit.[14] These conditions are regarded as the criteria for allocating resources among competing uses and may
be restated as follows:

(1) The maximum-valve-product criterion by which one product
(land use) may be increased at the expense of another at margin and by which an optimum combination of products (uses)
from a set of resources is achieved.

(2) The minimum-cost criterion by which productive agents, including land, are substituted one for another and by which an
optimum combination of factors for a given total output is
achieved.

(3) The optimum-output criterion by which a product and a productive factor are simultaneously increased or decreased and
by which an optimum scale or most profitable level of output
is established.[15]

In an attempt to fit these criteria into a framework for land utilization analysis, the term "land use" is suggested as synonymous with the
term "product." A particular product can be identified with a particular
land use. That is, if land is used for grazing, the product is forage. If
it is used for buildings, the product is building space, and so on. As
customarily assumed, the adjustments involved are timeless. The
necessary conditions to be achieved are therefore static. So far, only a
static theory of production has been developed and applied to any extent.

Optimization, Equilibrium, and Applicability of Concepts

The three criteria together are regarded as necessary and sufficient
for maximizing the "net returns" from production. But given the production functions, the prices of products and factors (revenues and costs),
such a statement is a mathematical truism. Also, when the criteria are
met within a productive unit, production may be said to be at an optimum
or in equilibrium. It should follow that if land is a factor in the productive
activities, by implication, land utilization also should be in equilibrium if
the conditions are satisfied for the productive unit. But it is fairly well
recognized that equilibrium is never actually attained, particularly for

---

[13]For some situations, more than one optimum may actually be found.

[14]These conditions are stated in different ways in the various textbooks and other economic
publications. See as examples: Kenneth E. Boulding, Economic Analysis (New York: Harper and
Brothers Publishers, 1941), Chapter 31; Carlson, op. cit.; J. R. Hicks, Value and Capital (2d ed.;
Oxford: The Clarendon Press 1946), Chapter 6; Richard H. Leftwich, The Price System and
Resource Allocation (New York: Holt, Rinehart and Winsten, 1955), Chapters 7 and 15; Alfred W.
Stonier and Douglas C. Hague, A Textbook of Economic Theory (London: Longmans, Green and Co.,
1953), Chapters 5, 10, 15, and 16.

[15]This third criterion, of course, is not independent of the other two criteria.

aggregated productive units in a dynamic economy.[16]   The concept of equilibrium is of interest, however, as an ideal situation; and it is of methodological value.[17]

Underlying the necessary and sufficient conditions for achieving an optimum is the assumption that production functions of a certain form exist.   It has been suggested, however, that the indeterminacy of the production functions or transformation coefficients for some land uses automatically limits the application of the theory.   In addition, the uncertainties as to the true form of the production function, the possibility of variations in the objectives of different producers, and the fact that production theory has not been satisfactorily tested against conditions in the real world, tend to leave doubts that the theory is useful for predictive purposes.   It has been suggested "that socalled production theory is close to mere speculation."[18]   The theory, however, may be modified and extended and thus may contribute to the development of operational hypotheses and to the selection and organization of variables in land utilization for purposes of research.

To direct our thinking in the discussion that follows, two pivotal questions are raised on the applicability of the concepts and reasoning in production theory with respect to land economics research.   First, in what ways does the theory provide tools for analyzing problems in land economics?   Second, to what extent can the theory, or any part of it, be applied to land economic research calling for empirical determination and quantification?

ALLOCATION AND DEVELOPMENT IN LAND UTILIZATION

The reallocation of land between its alternative uses is a continuous problem brought about by the pressures of economic forces.   Then, too, major capital outlays for permanent investments in land are sometimes necessary in the process of land use adjustment.   Whenever such permanent investment in land is a prerequisite to the allocation or reallocation of land, the development and the allocation problems merge.   Thus separation of the problems of allocation and development may be valid only at a certain level of abstraction.   For allocation, the central issue is the distribution of land of given possibilities between its alternative uses or the selection of the various uses to which such land should be allocated.   For the development problem, the issue is how and in what ways the possibilities of a given area should be changed.   Each change in the production possibilities reflecting changes in the production functions may provide new opportunities for reallocation.

---

[16]Consult: Leftwich, op. cit., Chapter 17; F. Machlup, "Equilibrium and Disequilibrium: Misplaced Concreteness and Disguised Politics," Economic Journal, Vol. 68, No. 269 (March 1958), pp. 1-24

[17]It may be mentioned at this point that the concept of equilibrium has also been adopted in location theory to apply to land use. Cf. Edgar S. Dunn, "The Equilibrium of Land-Use Patterns in Agriculture," Southern Economic Journal, Vol. 21, No. 2 (October 1954), pp. 173-87; Walter Isard, "A General Location Principle of an Optimum Space Economy," Econometrica, Vol. 20, No. 3 (July 1952), pp. 406-30.

[18]A. N. Halter and H. H. Jack, "Toward a Philosophy of Science for Agricultural Economic Research," Journal of Farm Economics, Vol. 43, No. 1 (February 1961), p. 95.

Evaluating the Production Functions

In analyzing either allocation or development problems, the concept of production functions should become useful in evaluating the relative productivity of land. As production functions are said to reflect the physical possibilities of land in its various uses, such a function becomes a necessary condition for employing land in any particular use. These functions are therefore useful as "planning" functions,[19] and some uses of land may be automatically ruled out on the basis of this physical criterion alone.

It cannot be too greatly emphasized that a production function assumes a given state of arts (technology). Hence the functions are changeable; they change over time to the extent that technology changes. Also, at a given instant, the different techniques available (for example, the methods of applying fertilizers) may yield different functions. The techniques adopted and their costs then become important variables in evaluating production functions.

Comparative analysis of production functions in meaningful only in these situations: First, the physical characteristics of land as a productive agent are similar and the uses to which land may be put differ; or second, the physical characteristics differ but the contemplated or actual uses are the same. In short, comparison of production functions makes sense only if either the characteristics or the uses of the land are held constant.[20] Both conditions may affect the form and parameters of the production functions. In effect, what we would have is a "matrix" of production functions.

In land utilization studies, it may become necessary to hold the land characteristics constant if the specific problem involves the allocation of marginal land between exclusive alternative uses. Production functions with land quality as a constant are implied in determinations of "optimum" combinations of products (land uses). Failure to recognize the significance of homogeneity of land for the purposes of deriving the related production possibility functions with their marginal rates of substitution may well be misleading. "Production possibility functions" are meaningless, and probably useless, if the qualities of the resources used for the alternative purposes (products) under investigation are not the same.

The analysis of production functions should be useful also in problems involving multiple use of a given area of land, assuming that there is a production function for each use. These functions also may be scrutinized for relevance in any attempt to order land according to its highest and best uses subject to the restraint that the value of other productive agents are held comparable in each use.

Consideration of production functions in which the land uses are held the same but the quality of the lands differ should become a useful first step in evaluating the relative economic productivity of land in a given location. Land uses could be arrayed according to the production func-

---

[19] Schumpeter suggests that "the full logical meaning of the concept of production functions reveals itself only if we think of them as planning functions in a world of blueprints...," Joseph A. Schumpeter, History of Economic Analysis (New York: Oxford University Press, 1954), p. 1031.

[20] It is true that various levels of "aggregation" may be employed both as to "uses" and "land characteristics"; but it is known that the greater the level of aggregation the greater the amount of useful information that is lost, and the further removed are the results from the original and true meaning of a production function.

tions and some use or uses would probably be eliminated because of the low level of the productivity of the land in these uses. Determination of production functions, if possible, also would provide a basis for evaluating the "comparative advantages" of land uses and, hence, the most economic use for land in various locations.

Considering the Efficiency Criteria

The maximum-value-product criterion requires the values of the respective marginal products from a resource to be equal. Or, the rate at which one product substitutes for another at the margin is equal to the inverse of the ratio of product prices. With particular reference to land, the criterion would require that land be allocated or reallocated between its respective uses so that the values of the marginal product in each of its respective uses are equal. This condition implicitly assumes that the value of the nonland productive factors remains the same in each use. Ignoring the problems pertaining to the technical production relationships (the production functions), the substitutability of uses is important when the problems of land allocation between uses are considered. Here, also, the concept of "opportunity cost" is implicit, as one land use is expanded at the expense of another in arriving at a different pattern of allocation.

The reallocation of land between its competing uses is an everyday problem. Within agriculture, a choice of crops is necessary. This holds true also for land on the margins of grazing and agriculture and for agriculture versus urban-commercial-industrial uses. This criterion is therefore of special significance in evaluating shifts of land between alternative uses. These shifts are called for by changes in consumer demands.

When "choices" involve such uses as transportation, recreation, or military purposes, the principles of substitution are applied with greater difficulty. As previously intimated, "returns" from these uses defy measurement and, in addition, the price mechanism may not provide the appropriate choice criteria. There are no competitive forces to induce action by public planning agents to maximize returns or minimize costs as do private agents.[21] Nevertheless, the notion of "opportunity costs" or "sacrifices" implicit in the maximum value-product criterion can provide guidelines for public decisions in these instances.

This criterion may then be regarded as a useful guide for allocating land between various uses. The guide it provides is less useful for resolving the development questions, which may be equally as, or even more, important than the allocation questions. In applying this criterion, the production possibilities and the resources are considered as given. They are constraints . In handling the development problems, these possibilities must necessarily be regarded as variables if land utilization in its totality is to be considered.

The minimum-cost criterion for combining productive agents is inherently more applicable to analysis of development problems because developmental activities essentially involve a recombination of capital and land. In such recombinations, however, land is regarded as fixed, and variations occur only in capital. Hence no substitution actually takes place in terms of capital for land, and the associated product increases rather than

---

[21] Cf. Roland N. McKean, Efficiency in Government Through Systems Analysis (New York: John Wiley and Sons, Inc., 1958), Chapters I and II.

remains constant, as assumed under the minimum-cost criterion. There is a change in the proportions of factors without substitution.

To obtain the lowest possible costs, productive factors, including land, must be substituted for each other at the margin so that the rate at which one factor substitutes for the other is equal to the inverse of their respective price ratios. This means also that the ratios of the marginal products of the factor to the prices of the factors must be equal not only for a given land use but for all uses. Accordingly, the minimum-cost criterion may give direction to the way in which land should be combined with other resources in making long-run adjustments consistent with the least possible total outlay for a given level of production derived from the use of land. This criterion is therefore relevant to appraisal of the distribution of land between its owners and users in terms of minimum sizes for economic units.

Another implication of the minimum cost criterion is that land and other productive agents may be very highly interdependent in productive processes through the characteristic of factor substitution. This relationship suggests that optimum use of land cannot be accomplished by considering land alone in either a long- or a short-run analysis.[22] The productive agents that may be substituted for land in the creation of any good or service must be considered as well.

Intuitively, of course, other factors can be substituted for land only up to certain limits. In some instances, and for some range, the other factors may be complements to, rather than substitutes for, land. In other instances, land may be completely independent in its use. A main reason for special interest in land as a productive agent is its indispensability in addition to its relative immobility, and the social institutions that usually affect its utilization.[23]

The optimum-output criterion, which is the same as the marginal-revenue-equals-marginal-cost criterion, sets the limit to which the use of resources should be extended in any particular line. The validity of the criterion, however, is based upon whether the assumption of diminishing returns holds. It becomes relevant if the resources to be varied are unlimited and there is a possibility of extending their use beyond the theoretical optimum, a determination based on mathematical logic.

This criterion is useful in defining the degree of intensity to which other resources should be applied to land. It has been adopted accordingly, in the theoretical analysis of watershed-improvement programs, the details of which are not elaborated upon here.[24] Some attention needs to be given, however, to the kind of changes that occur in the production function because of the investments that are sunk in the land. Conversely,

---

[22] For problems of land utilization, the long run refers to the situation in which all allocations or reallocations of land between its various uses are possible. In the short run, the land is committed to certain uses, and the remaining questions are concerned with the other productive agents that are to be applied to it.

[23] Hawtrey, op. cit., has attempted to show why land should be treated differently in production functions. His arguments and conclusions seem to rest, however, upon his concept and definition of a production function.

[24] See for example: Inter-Agency Committee on Water Resources, Proposed Practices for Economic Analysis of River Basin Projects (Washington: U. S. Government Printing Office, May 1958); John F. Timmons, "Economic Framework for Watershed Development," Journal of Farm Economics, Vol. 34, No. 5 (December 1954), pp. 1170-83.

if land is regarded as a variable input, then the limit to which it should be used in combination with the other resources that are fixed, particularly management, is also set by this criterion for resource allocation.

Obtaining Optimum Solutions: Some Limitations

Admittedly, it would be very nice if optimum and equilibrium patterns of land utilization could be obtained or determined; but the obstacles are formidable. The actual determination of optimum production for any economic unit and, hence, optimum land utilization, depends significantly upon whether the production functions can be specified for each land use and whether the variables involved can be identified and measured. Little or no empirical validity has been given to the form and characteristics of the production functions or surfaces for land uses other than agriculture. This situation poses a limitation to estimates of optimum land utilization based on production theory as it has been developed. The other major limitation to the empirical determinations of optimum, as already suggested, is the valuation of such land services as recreation, military, and transportation services.

In addition, the reallocation and development of land is subject to forces that cause continual changes in the "optima." These forces or disturbances that are of economic significance include changes in the wants and preferences of consumers, in technology, and in the level and distribution of income, as well as shifts and growth in populations. For these reasons, the optima for land use are constantly changing and the concept of equilibrium is of relevance only as a methodological device.

At the micro level of analysis, optimum utilization plans in the theoretical sense may be determined under specific assumptions. On the larger levels of aggregation, such determinations become increasingly difficult, and in these instances, the theory of production becomes useful only to the extent that it can aid in understanding the functional relationships and the variables that may be involved in land utilization. Land utilization in the broad sense is more appropriately a problem for general rather than partial analysis because major decisions concerning land uses can have far-reaching effects in several parts or sectors of the economy. Production theory is applicable only to a part of this total picture. In land utilization analysis at the higher levels of aggregation, the constants of production theory become variables and the price relatives that are exogenous variables become endogenous. Changes in the price relationships may be generated by changes in land utilization itself.

With particular reference to development, production theory, although useful in evaluating the extent to which capital should be reasonably applied, has limitations because it provides essentially static tools of analysis. But some account can be taken of time by dating and discounting output and input. Much more needs to be done, however, in formulating a more unified theory of production and investment, which is necessary in evaluating development problems. Investment analysis is equally, and perhaps more, important than production analysis for decisions pertaining to land development. In addition, the changes that may occur in production possibilities, as reflected in the parameters of the production functions, through various kinds and degrees of development activities are still open to conceptual and empirical studies.

PROPERTY RIGHTS AND CONTROL IN LAND UTILIZATION

Even if the rules for optimum land utilization are correct, considerable difficulty would be encountered in applying such rules. These
difficulties stem from the institution of private property in land and the
associated independence and decentralization in land use decisions. Thus,
because of differences in individual values, and the problem of interpersonal comparisons, optimum solutions for land use that cover a number
of different ownership tracts may not be consistent with the objectives of
some or all of the individuals considered separately. In these circumstances, the pure theory of production needs to be supplemented by a
theory of "welfare economics."

At the same time, the price mechanism might fail to direct allocation
and development of land if the property-related institutions surrounding
land were to serve as impediments. The movement of land from lower to
higher uses may be retarded by the ways in which these institutions are
fashioned. Under our exchange economy, a productive unit bases its
plans on the relations between the prices of the products and the prices of
the factors of production. This is what is decisive in guiding production.
In this way, each planning agent controls in its own sphere a fraction of
the economic activities, and the activities as a whole are governed by the
price system, subject to institutional constraints. Among the constraints
that directly affect land utilization are government ownership and management of land, leasing, taxation, zoning, credit, and so forth.[25]

In analyzing the effects of property-related institutions on land utilization -- in terms of allocation, development, or both -- the criteria for
using land optimally may serve as "norms." Departures from these
norms may be associated with the functioning of a particular feature of an
institution under scrutiny. Thus the effects of property-related institutions may be analyzed in terms of the criteria for efficiency in land
utilization. In this context, the theory becomes "normative" in the sense
that the criteria are assumed as the immediate ends that "ought to be
achieved" in the allocation or development of land resources.

Empirically, the analysis of these institutions in this way is fairly
straightforward, provided the optimum can be reasonably estimated and
other land use patterns, "with" and "without" particular features of an
institution, are ascertainable also. The analysis of some leasing problems are usually cast within this framework, but the same could be done
for problems in credit, taxation, zoning, or other institutions that affect
the distribution of land between users or the uses to which land is put.
Production theory cannot be used, however, to determine the overall
efficacy of any institutional arrangements. The effects considered are in
terms of the assumed norms.

Because of the way in which the property institutions operate, the
optimum "land utilization plan" for individual resource owners or users
may not coincide with a plan that is considered socially desirable. In
these instances, property institutions may be said to distort the optimum.
Supposedly, a reasonable function of the institutions should be to avoid

---

[25] Cf. U. S. Department of Agriculture, Land: The 1958 Yearbook of Agriculture (Washington: U. S. Government Printing Office, 1958), pp. 278-314, "Rights, Ownership and Tenure"; H. W. Hannah and N. G. P. Krausz, "The Role of Law in the Development of Land Resources," Modern Land Policy (Urbana: University of Illinois Press, 1960), pp. 325-36.

distortions of this type. Property-related institutions may impede improvement in land utilization patterns if they are (1) insecure or indefinite, (2) inflexible, and (3) inequitable in terms of income and cost
distribution.

Private utilization plans for resources tend to be more efficient if
the institutions are not subject to erratic changes over time. If the
expectations are for drastic changes unfavorable to the income position of
a resource user, the tendency will be toward using resources in a way
that is inconsistent with the optimum for an extended period of time. The
objective of land utilization is thus virtually distorted -- short-time gains
are emphasized in preference to long-time gains. Production theory may
be applied to show the differences in net gains stemming from the expectation of unfavorable changes in any particular institution.

The expected duration of occupancy, whether through owning or
leasing, may also materially affect the land use decisions and plans if the
expectation is limited or uncertain. Again, an attempt may be made to
maximize the immediate gains because of the restraint inherent in the
limited time of occupancy. Heavily encumbered owners in depressed
times or renters with uncertain expectations of occupancy are similarly
insecure. Hence they may adopt plans that they would not adopt in more
secure circumstances.

The feature of "indefiniteness" in property rights in particularly
relevant to land used for recreational and wildlife purposes and to the use
of water resources. The "product" of the land used for recreational or
wildlife purposes may have no "definite" owner. Similarly, water as a
land resource creates special problems of establishing proprietorship.
The indefiniteness of rights to the use or enjoyment of land resources may
cause departures from socially desirable plans if the uses are not
appropriately controlled.

Insecurity of property rights should be distinguished from inflexibility
to avoid ambiguities. Essentially, insecurity refers to situations stemming from uncertainty as to the distribution of the kind and quantity of
rights in land. Inflexibility, on the other hand, refers to the resistance
of the property-derived institutions to make needed adjustments to cope
with social and economic needs as they change over time. The inflexibility
(or rigidity) of such institutions as leasing, taxation, credit, and zoning
may serve as restraints to the continual readjustments that are called for
in land utilization. On the other hand, these institutions may serve to
facilitate the changes needed in land utilization.

When rigidity in the ways in which the rights to land are distributed
retard adjustments, the principles of production may be applied to discover whether the institutions cause departures from the "ideal" patterns
in land utilization and the extent to which a superior pattern of land utilization in terms of the efficiency criteria could be achieved with changes in
these institutions. Rigidity of institutions may fail to provide the owners
and users of land resources with the incentive to use them in a way consistent with maximum social welfare.

The claims to the returns from land use are distributed between public and private individuals, on the one hand, and among private individuals,
on the other. "Inequities" may stem from the distribution of these claims
to the land returns if the distribution is not functionally related to the

incidence of the costs or sacrifices incurred to obtain them. [26] Problems in associating the returns with costs because of property rights distribution may occur because of leasing or credit arrangements, because of the legal boundaries of land property, and because of the flow over time of the net returns from land utilization practices.

The set of problems concerned with leasing and credit arrangements and economic efficiency involving land utilization has been covered extensively elsewhere. [27] Even though the emphasis has so far been directed toward agricultural production, the logic used may be applied also to analyzing inefficiencies that may occur in other types of major land uses because of inequities stemming from the interpersonal disassociation of the returns and costs connected with land utilization. As such, the economic principles of production may be applied to analysis of leasing or credit arrangements as restraints or as factors conducive to achievement of the objective of land uses in addition to agriculture.

Land utilization may be adversely affected also because of the private boundaries of ownership, use, and control of land. Efficiency in the use of land in one location and under a certain ownership may need investments in land in another location that is under a different ownership. Conversely, the expenditures in one location may yield a large part of its returns in another location owned by someone else to whom the benefits derived would accrue. Because of this spatial aspect of landownership and control, practices consistent with optimum land utilization may be deterred if private adjustments are left purely to the price mechanism.

Nor, if landownership is monopolized, is there any guarantee that the way in which the land will be used will be in line with the criteria for maximization through the competitive price system. The implicit assumption is that, under competitive conditions, the price mechanism tends to force land into its most desirable uses. Under other market conditions, allocation of land between its various uses need not be consistent with the tastes and preferences of consumers.

A SUMMARY

The main purpose of this paper was to apply some of the fundamental concepts of modern production theory to problems of land economics. In this treatment, land economics has been regarded as an applied phase of economics with special interest in land as a productive agent of goods and services. Production theory, in contrast, has been defined as an abstract representation of a productive activity or process.

For the framework of production theory, the problems in land economics are considered to constitute a set of problems that may be

---

[26] So-called "inequities" regarding property rights also are treated as problems of interpersonal disassociation of returns and costs or problems of imbalances of property rights. The term "inequities" is used here arbitrarily, recognizing that in some instances it can be "value-loaded."

[27] See as examples: Rainer Schickele, "Effect of Tenure Systems on Agricultural Efficiency," Journal of Farm Economics, Vol. 23, No. 1 (February 1941), pp. 185-207; D. Gale Johnson, "Resource Allocation Under Share Contracts," Journal of Political Economy, Vol. 58, No. 2, (April 1950), pp. 111-23; Earl O. Heady, Economics of Agricultural Production and Resource Use (New York: Prentice-Hall, 1952), Chapters 20-22; S. V. Ciriacy-Wantrup, Resource Conservation: Economics and Policies (Berkeley, Los Angeles: University of California Press, 1952), Chapters 12-13.

conveniently divided into three subsets: the allocation problem, the development problem, and the control problem. The problems of allocation and development of course, are highly interwoven, and their practical solutions depend considerably upon the controls that are exercised through the institutions surrounding land.

The main concepts in production theory that were reviewed are the production function, production efficiency, and optimization. An attempt was made to apply these concepts to studies in land economics.

It was suggested that production theory rests heavily upon the assumption of production functions, and that examination and comparisons of these functions could provide a very useful first step in many land use studies. It was also intimated, however, that if this theory is to be applied to land economic research generally, production functions or transformation coefficients should be ascertainable for land in all its various uses. But the form of production relationships for land in its different uses has not been clearly defined, tested, or quantified. For some land uses, production functions may not be even ascertainable in the crudest forms. They are purely imaginary constructs. In addition, it is possible only conceptually to derive true transformation coefficients or true marginal products for land even for products that are tangible and measurable.

Accordingly, although production functions are the main building blocks of production theory, they are of more methodological than operational value for analysis of land uses generally. These functions may be of practical significance only in special instances. Much more needs to be done, basically, in terms of specifying and finding the true form of production functions and the role of land in its different uses.

Despite the difficulties and limitations in identifying, measuring, and isolating all the variables and functional relationships called for by production theory, the theory is useful in land economic research. It can contribute to the formulation of operational hypotheses, to the selection of the variables involved in the allocation and development of land resources, and to the organization and direction of the analyses that are required. In particular, the criteria for efficiency are relevant to the choice of land uses, particularly for marginal lands. They also provide principles for combining land with other productive agents.

Caution must be exercised, however, in attempts to determine optimum solutions based on production theory, and more seriously, to apply the solutions. The validity of the theory has not been satisfactorily tested; and, therefore, it has no productive record. For reasons other than those inherent in the production functions, the determination of optimum land utilization, although conceptually sound, is virtually impossible except for micro-productive units under restrictive assumptions. The difficulties stem from the premise that land utilization is more a problem for general dynamic analysis rather than it is a problem for partial static analysis with which production theory deals. Then too, in regional analyses, the objectives and values of individual resource owners and users may not be consistent with an over-all regional optimum for land use.

Production theory may be applied in land economics also to the extent that it provides "normative goals." In dealing exclusively with the problems of allocation and development, the efficiency criteria may serve as guidelines for organizing resources. With respect to the problem of con-

trol and property rights, the distributive aspects of the theory may provide the basis for distributing the returns from productive efforts between
those who hold rights or claims to the income from land or the resources
used in combination with land.

In addition, the effects of particular institutional arrangements may
be evaluated in terms of the efficiency criteria. The practical application,
however, depends, upon whether the patterns of land utilization "with"
and "without" particular institutions as constraints can be estimated or
imputed. Institutional effects, defined in terms of the efficiency criteria
in resource use, may be detected, empirically at least, at the micro-
levels of analysis.

8

Land and Rent in Welfare Economics

by M. Mason Gaffney*

In the classical **synthesis**, human welfare and land rent were two parts of an integrated philosophy. As Smith, Mill, Marshall, and especially Ricardo scan us from their present eyries they must note with shock two virtually separate disciplines tagged "land economics" and "welfare economics." The first has come to connote Wisconsin Institutionalism with its skepticism of marginal analysis, its emphasis on evolution, its earthy pragmatism and inductive reasoning. The second designates a rarefied a priori Scholasticism that proceeds from sanitary postulates through tangencies and equations to anything from sweeping reforms to nagging doubts about the value of any economics. The division of the two constitutes an indefensible compartmentalization of thought, and the writer does not favor either over the other. Rather he suggests some paths toward reintegration.

The two subdisciplines contrast in a number of ways. Welfare economics tends to emphasize static optimality, with only perfunctory obeisance to the passage of time; land economics deals with long-run intertemporal changes. Welfare economics is generally spaceless, also, while space is the essence of land economics. Land economists have been impatient of theory to the verge of anti-intellectualism, while welfare economists exhibit more patience than most of their readers in spinning subtleties which, instead of being means to human welfare, sometimes

*M. MASON GAFFNEY has been associate professor and professor of agricultural economics at the University of Missouri since 1958. Born in New York in 1923, he did his undergraduate work at Reed College, and obtained his Ph.D. from the University of California. He has been an instructor at the University of Oregon, an assistant professor at North Carolina State College, and a Ford Foundation fellow. One of his interests is land rent, a matter which he treats in this chapter.

Author's Note: To Thomas Crocker, Research Assistant sans pareil, my thanks for many valuable contributions; to Dean Elmer Kiehl, my thanks for fostering an environment favorable to basic research; to Marion Clawson, my thanks for gently prodding me into finishing this chapter; to all three, my thanks for tolerance of my heterodoxy, and absolution from responsibility for it.

seem to become the ends of their lucubrations. As to policy, land economists are probably too easily pleased, asking only to see movement in economical directions; welfare economists are often implacable, spurning mere "piecemeal" optimizing, pointing ever upwards and outwards to ideal and universal Platonic prototypes. Land economists are the more eclectic for they do read the welfare literature, which in its turn, however, yields no evidence that any pure welfare theorist since Pigou knew a shred of land economics.

As an earthbound land economist levitates through the pure welfare literature he sees much to admire: the rigor; the elegant marginalism; the normative pursuit of the general welfare; the suppression of subjective bias; the boldness with policy. He wishes he saw more of those in his own subdiscipline. But he also finds it a long way between drinks, and he wonders what earthlings can survive in these arid and vertiginous altitudes. He does not insist that all economists have met payrolls, but those who declaim on so humanistic a subject as welfare should exhibit some sign that they bleed when cut and weep when wounded. Between the Platonic peaks and the deeps of life and sin there must lie a temperate zone where the universals of theory come to bear on more humid human problems. Probably the greatest reciprocal contribution of land and welfare economics is to balance one another and keep within that temperate zone, where indeed we already see the tracks of Regan, Chryst, Margolis, Tolley, Clawson, Krutilla, Eckstein, Renshaw, Hirshleifer, Milliman, and others, who commendably defy subclassification: they are economists.

Welfare economics has a signal contribution for land economics in its normative outlook. Land economists are prone to accept the institutions they emphasize as ultimate constraints, fixed with the stars in their courses. They cast themselves, with notable exceptions, in the subsidiary role of commentators scribbling in the margins of history, annotating the ineluctable. Dulled by the gross wastes their profession keeps disclosing they grow uncritical.

Welfare economists are more delicately attuned, more imperious, and in an important sense more realistic. They look through and beyond institutional constraints to the ultimate goals of human organization. They assert the status of those ultimates over mere institutions, evaluate institutions accordingly, consign to perdition those found wanting, and rise on their hind legs with bold new gadgets such as social dividends, lump-sum capacity taxes, or open-ended stock issues to enhance the general welfare.

To accompany this attitude they supply an analytical apparatus on which land economists often rely who do render normative judgments. The apparatus may grow unwieldy with all the armor it has clad to fend off cynics and spoilers, but deep inside we still find a simple working rule, The Rule, the equimarginal principle, and many qualifications to temper it.

The obvious contribution of land economics to welfare economics is an element of reality, a wealth of experience, a feel for human possibilities. Welfare economics has a surplus of empty boxes, which land economics is peculiarly competent to fill.

But ironically the prime contribution of land to welfare economics is a higher degree of generality. For all its ecumenical purport, most of the "pure" welfare economics is both spaceless and timeless. It is all very well to abstract from localisms, but space and time are absolute universals. It is welfare economics that preaches against "piecemeal" optimizing. Economizing at dimensionless points in space and time is piecemealism beyond sufferance. Space and time are the very stuff of land economics, and if it contributed nothing else to welfare economics that would be enough to fill several of those empty boxes.

Consider consumer surplus. In land economics that attaches not to free-floating individuals, but specific lands. If Connecticut commuters, for example, put more aggregate value on the New Haven Railroad than that unhappy bankrupt can collect at the ticket window, the surplus finds its way into Connecticut land prices. If California irrigators derive from water supramarginal benefits above the price, that surplus imputes to lands under the ditch.

Consider external economics. Their most general cause is spatial proximity, and land economics copes with them, both technological and pecuniary, constantly. Every irrigation development affects ground water levels and local trade. Urban buildings affect their neighbors' views, share their transport-utility lines and taxes, and pull customers to or away from them. A basic way to render external economies internal is to acquire more land, whereby one evolves from an atomistic parcel-holder to a competitor of the local government and democracy, which in turn maintains itself and the viability of atomistic landholdings, by judicious manipulation of external economies related to land.

Consider the welfare economist's problem of interdependencies. Again, these most often entail spatial proximity. Land economists have grappled for decades with problems of co-ordinating and synchronizing complementary public and private contributions to the interdependent land settlement process, both urban and rural.

Consider the welfare economist's specifications for an ideal tax, a lump-sum "capacity-tax" based on latent potentialities, uncontingent on actual economic behavior, without distortion or excess burden. Having given the specifications, welfare economists are at a curious loss to identify a suitable base, yet land not only affords a theoretical base of the requisite properties, but is so taxed and has been for centuries where-ever assessments are based, as the law now directs in most American jurisdictions, on site potentialities regardless of current use.

Last, consider the welfare economist's problem of identifying de-creasing cost operations, determining marginal costs, and meeting the deficits implicit in marginal cost pricing. The prototype of decreasing cost operations is the transport of utility service over a network within a fixed perimeter. Hotelling, recall, was discussing the general welfare in relation to problems of taxation and of railway and public utility rates. Dupuit was concerned with Ponts et Chaussées. The consumer surplus generated was clearly imputed to the rental value of lands served, where it could be measured and whence recaptured by lump-sum land-capacity taxes to meet the deficits of marginal cost pricing. [1]

Since Hotelling, welfare economists, in their praiseworthy pursuit of generality, have abstracted his principle from its earthy genesis until the material referents are lost and the box emptied. But returned from the abstrusities of Laputa to the terra firma of Swift's admirable Houyhnhnms, the box is full of relevant experience with municipal transit,

---

[1] Harold Hotelling, "The General Welfare in Relation to Problems of Taxation and of Railway and Utility Rates," Econometrica, July 1938, pp. 242-69, p. 256, and "The Relation of Prices to Marginal Costs in an Optimum System," Econometrica, April 1939, pp. 151-55.

144

irrigation districts, cheap power, et hoc genus omne. The "subsidy"
which offends many conservative economists[2] is seen to be not properly
a subsidy at all, not a redistribution from "other industries" or regions,
but a means of extracting supramarginal surplus windfalls from specific
beneficiaries by the approved capacity-tax method. Distributionally, it
bears the earmarks of a charge on gainers usable to compensate losers ---
again an ideal of welfare economics.

Those, then, are some reciprocal potential contributions of land and
welfare economics which we now proceed to develop. First we define
ground rent and differentiate it from other distributive shares. Second,
we treat the role of ground rent as an economic constraint on the posses-
sion of land, both in space and time, by atomistic individual landholders.
Last, we treat the role of ground rent as a guide to land development by
transport-utility networks.

GROUND RENT AND OTHER DISTRIBUTIVE SHARES: SIMILARITIES AND DIFFERENCES

The concepts of land and ground rent have suffered a terrible mauling
in recent decades. The new conventional wisdom has it that ground rent
is only one of many rents, and land is scarcely worth distinguishing from
other resources, if indeed it can be.

This is not the place for technical analysis of the imputation of ground
rent. I have tried elsewhere to show how ground rent may be segregated
from depletion and depreciation charges and from income of depletable
virgin fertility and old improvements.[3] In general it is my position that
the ground[4] has salvage value and a future opportunity cost where old improvements do not, so land is valued from the future and old improvements
residually. In the same work I treat the traditional quibbles about "made"
land, underground improvements, soil exhaustion, substitutability by
capital, and Venus de Milo, none of which need detain us here.

This is the place to point up the importance for welfare economics of
land's unique qualities: natural origin; fixed location; extension; permanence;[5] fixed aggregate supply.

Fixed location is the quality that lets land serve as the measure and
trap for localized consumer surpluses and external economies. Labor and
capital immigrate to share local windfalls to their kind, and in due time
compete them away entirely. Benefits to local land are rather imputed
away in higher rents. Institutional barriers may preserve local benefits
to local monopolies of labor or capital, but then the windfall imputes to the
monopoly, not to labor and capital as such. The obstacle to land immigration is physical, inherent in the resource itself, and the windfall imputes
to land as such, whose local monopoly is granted by Nature.

---

[2] For example, Howard S. Ellis and William Fellner, "External Economies and Diseconomies,"
The American Economic Review, September 1943, pp. 493-511.

[3] Mason Gaffney, "Ground Rent and the Allocation of Land among Firms," Proceedings, 1961
Land Economics Seminar, North Central Land Tenure Research Committee, to be published 1962.

[4] By "ground" I purport something more than "site" but less than "land" as the term is usually
used. Ground is site plus permanent geological matrix, but excluding that much of virgin fertility
which it is economical to deplete. In general the difference is small relative to other economic
magnitudes, and in the present work "ground" and "land" are interchangeable.

[5] This excludes from the present discussion geological funds which are depleted by use.

Fixed location is also the key to land's unique relation to the inter-dependency question. Water service that opens up new lands, for example, requires the complementation of sewers, houses for customers, and ultimately the whole complex of transport-utility lines that make a finished community. The water service requires these complements not just anywhere but serving the same lands. The services achieve necessary scale economies by finding many customers not just anywhere, but compactly grouped in space.

The importance to welfare economics of land's natural origin and permanence is in the unique suitability those qualities give land as the base of a lump-sum "capacity-tax," a neutral nondistorting tax not contingent on man's creating the tax base by storage or saving, not avoidable by consuming or removing it. The only contingency is that the landholder retain title, but a financial flight from land titles removes no square foot from the supply. Ad valorem land taxes are simply capitalized into lower land prices and the net outcome is to substitute a tax burden for an interest burden, explicit or implicit. Insofar as that shift would cause reallocation of the fixed supply it is by the removal of a distortion --- unequal access to credit --- and not (assuming accurate assessment) by the imposition of a new distortion.

Natural origin and permanence of ground give it a unique place in the distributional ethic. Ground rent as private income is without functional rationale, as generations of economists have duly, if discreetly, noted. It neither elicits the supply nor preserves it. It only serves to allocate it to the high bidder, but this function is so badly distorted by speculation in anticipated increments to the market price of infinite future rents, as almost any city planner will document, that there is reason to believe public rent collection through heavy lump-sum ad valorem capacity taxes could serve the allocative function better.

When, however, we claim uniqueness of the ground in its fixity of supply we run afoul of the new conventional wisdom which preaches a blurring of such discriminations. Some leading arguments are these: man can increase the land supply; rent is one of many differentials; Roger Maris can earn more slugging than soda-jerking; labor supply is wage-inelastic; capital formation is interest-inelastic. Let us entertain them in order.

When urban economists speak of increasing land supply they apparently have in mind such operations as extending expressways and sewer mains, bringing new lands into the urban sphere. Farm economists who speak of "elastic" land supplies in turn have in mind reclamation and clearing. Cities may take land from orchardists, they from pig-farmers, who push on wheat-farmers. Wheat-farmers push on cattlemen, they on sheepmen, they on forestry, recreation, and the Indians, but none of that, as the displaced persons keep reminding us, creates new land. It intensifies the use of land formed when the Earth was young.

Similarly we intensify the use of labor when it grows relatively dear, and of capital. We do not describe that as creating new labor and capital, although over some range it substitutes for such creation. But in addition we actually do spawn new people, and store up net new capital. There is the difference.

The idea that rent means "differential" is I believe a case of confounding the incidental with the essential. The concept of rent arose to help explain why men should pay for something Nature supplied gratis, courtesy of the house. Its expositors, following Ricardo, have taken note that lands differ in quality per acre and command different rents per acre. Some writers have siezed upon that difference as the essence of rent, but it is a secondary aspect.[6] Rent arises because land is scarce relative to demand and would arise in that circumstance if land were uniform.

The public celebrity analogy projects a resemblance between ground rent, a payment without the function of eliciting supply, and the income of theatrical and athletic stars who allegedly enjoy their work, are good for little else, and would work as much for less money. The analogy falls on two counts.

First, the alleged rental component of the star's income is indefinable. It is supposed to be the excess of his star income over his opportunity cost. Expositors describe that best alternative as remote and illrewarded: BB as a scrubwoman, Roger Maris as a teacher. Thus they make most of star-income a rent. But the alternatives are arbitrary and the rent is rubber. There is a whole range of closer alternatives, and what is rent and what is not depends entirely on the one specified, until we have Roger playing for another team, and Brigitte for another audience, near their present fees, and their rent vanishes into earned income.

Second, ground rent is a macro-economic concept, that is it applies to the whole class of land incomes without reference to allocation among different industries or uses. It would obtain if all land and labor were homogeneous and produced but one commodity. It is distinguished from wages by the curse of Adam that labor toward suppertime grows irksome, and at all times represents a sacrifice of pleasant diversions. Wages in general serve the necessary function of enticing man from leisure. Rent in general evokes no supply response: the Creator never sees it.

If the remolders of terms and issues must describe celebrity income as "rent" let them at least spare the original term uncorrupted, and the language unimpoverished, by qualifying their concept as "micro-rent" or "transfer-rent." Then their readers could divine that land income is double-rent, macro and micro. The block at 34th and 5th Avenue, that is, that sustains the Empire State Building, is not only given freely by Nature, like true love without demand for requitement or threat of removal, but also might be a potato patch. And so its million-dollar yearly ground income is 100% rent and also 99.99%, double-damned to damn Brigitte once. No doubt we are all poor sinners, as the micro-rent concept intimates, who if we got what we deserve wouldn't get much. But among economic sinners, the ground rent collector holds a unique pre-eminence.

Those who regard wages as a form of rent have another string to their bow, however. They note that incomes are higher today than in 1900 but hours are shorter. Post hoc ergo propter hoc: pay them more and they work less. The argument of the road gang boss has been commandeered by the modern Cameralist. Wages do not elicit labor; labor is perversely elastic to wage rates.

The argument might be neater if ceteris were paribus. Over sixty years many things have changed. Today among other new things we have steeply progressive income tax rates, more accumulated wealth, longer subsidized schooling, big unions, seniority and tenure, reduced interprofessional wage differentials, social security, Freud, protection from

---

[6]Indeed, the area unit is an arbitrary one within which to define quality and supramarginal ranking. Low-valued acres may in some extensive uses produce more per man than high-yielding ones, be higher above the margin and slower to go out of use when costs rise or prices fall.

immigration, and Miltown to bank the inner fires of workmanship, and it is a violent assumption to attribute all our modern otiosity to high wage rates. But is long-run response really relevant at all? Insofar as higher wages over time are responsible for reducing hours it is by helping us accumulate the wherewithal to put a higher price on leisure. The price we put on our leisure is not a function of the wage of our marginal efforts at a given moment, but of the wages we got yesterday and expect tomorrow, our property income, government checks, and a variety of things. The money we get for working from 4 to 5 P.M. on Friday, December 22, 1961 is necessary to elicit the supply under the conditions of that moment. In that sense wages are functional where ground rent is not.

The new conventional wisdom also has it that we save and create capital more or less by reflex, so that interest[7] is a rent, too. It would be presumptuous in a few words to sum up decades of debate around and about this topic, but the lagging rate of capital formation in the United States during three decades of the new wisdom at least gives us license to wonder if the last word was spoken when the rentier was consigned to euthanasia. A land economist suspects that interest rates do affect capital formation, if not directly then through their effect on asset values and especially land values, with their high interest-elasticity. High land values, the result of low interest rates, satisfy without benefit of real capital formation their holders' demand for assets and so tend to weaken saving.

It also seems obvious, land values or not, that at zero interest we could live by borrowing indefinitely and would give up not only saving but our jobs and all unpleasantness, deprivation, and restraint whatsoever. The Gesellniks can hardly dodge that dilemma by pleading credit rationing, for at the end of the credit line lies capital scarcity and an interest rate. Zero interest is clearly a fantasy in which we would run through the accumulations of centuries in a few glorious days. As Natura non facit saltum, it is plausible to suppose that near approaches toward zero interest would likewise tend to discourage capital formation.

In a closed economy the effects of farther approaches toward zero interest would make interesting debating. But as a practical matter the issue is seldom so drawn. Taxing jurisdictions are defined as specific land areas, from which capital will flee for light and transient causes, while you can tax the very all out of the land and never a square foot will rise up and walk out of town.

In summary, when we speak of "rent" we mean an income share that appertains specifically to land and which is likened to other distributive shares only by specious analogies which never should have risen above the dignity of debaters' ruses.

GROUND RENT AS A CONSTRAINT ON LAND USE
BY ATOMISTIC PARCELHOLDERS

Ground rent is a "surplus," we have maintained, differentiated from other distributive shares in lacking the function of eliciting the aggregate supply.

---

[7] I personally prefer "profit" to denote the net return on stored capital realized ex post, reserving "interest" as the price of money reflecting ex ante anticipations. But this is not the place to open that box and I here use "interest" in the classical sense.

But factor payments serve two functions. Besides calling forth the
aggregate supply they ration it among competing demands. Rent serves
the second function quite as much as do other shares. "Rent," wrote
Ely and Wehrwein, "acts as the 'sorter' and 'arranger' of this pattern
(of land use)." Rent pre-empts the choicest sites for uses that most need
their advantages, and ranks land uses in order of rent-paying capacity.
The body of lore called "location theory" advanced by Thünen, Weber,
Lösch, Hoover, Dunn, Isard, and others elaborates at length on this
principle, so that the allocative function of rent is not only received but
embellished doctrine.

The systematic and comprehensive welfare economist, however, must
feel that land and location economists have not fully established the
economic rationale of rent in a quantitative sense. They have rationalized
the qualitative function of ranking land uses, but have slighted the quantitative function of arbitrating the margins between landholdings: just how
much land should each firm occupy, and at what intensity? They have
given us no demonstration that the rent of central sites serves optimally
to constrain landholders from expanding and thereby imposing private
and social costs on utilities and peripheral land users who must traverse
their holdings. They have generally been content to accept private transport-utility costs as equal to social costs, even though that is conspicuously
untrue, and have asked no very deep questions about the nature of social
transport costs, nor therefore about the effect of land occupancy on those
costs.

The geo-welfare economist would note with approval that location
theorists demonstrate that individuals with greater demands on transport
tend to locate centrally, thereby tending to minimize transport costs, at
least the part paid by individuals. That is important information. But
transport costs also vary with the over-all intensity of land use. If all
land users, preserving their ordinal ranking, were to double their landholdings, they would much increase the miles they, their supplies,
customers, and products had to travel, and very likely the social costs per
mile as well. [8]

Clearly, an important function of rent is to constrain such extension,
to the end of minimizing aggregate transport costs and maximizing productive linkages. Clearly, too, this is one of the more interesting
questions in an era of rapidly increasing per capita space use, both urban
and rural. But it is a question on which the geo-welfare economist finds
precious little guidance. Transportation economics has yet to be integrated with land and location economics.

The interrelations are rather extended. For example, suppose it
be true that at urban fringes, private transport-utility costs are less
than social costs. That would first, obviously, open up excess peripheral
lands. But that in turn would relax rental constraints on intramarginal
lands, and reduce intensities there below economical levels. This in its
turn would disperse population wider, and impose more transport costs
on the society that underwrites them. The burdens imposed by uneconomical transport rates are not simply the obvious short run misuse of sunk
social overhead, but the long run thinning of land settlement, the relocation of population, with demands for further extension of subsidized

---

[8]Hoover's and Dunn's assumption of decreasing costs per mile refers only to private costs in
trucking. Social overhead costs are another matter--unit costs rise as trade territory density
declines.

transport facilities. Those are the extended interactions of land use and transport-utility rates that a geo-welfare economist would want worked out explicitly.

Rent as a Constraint on Spatial Extension

Let us begin with the atomistic individual landholder and define the positive expansive force within, against which the constraint of external opportunity cost must contend at every margin. Rent is too crude a term for this kind of quantitative analysis – rent is an average concept, and we need a marginal one. If rent from an integral land-using operation is the average net product per acre, the outthrusting force is not that, but the marginal net product, which we can call "marginal rent," which may be higher or lower than the average depending on whether the operation is too small or too large. While that may seem obvious to any marginalist economist, it has not to my knowledge been explicitly developed in the literature, and certainly its implications are widely flouted. Let us then develop the concept of marginal rent.

To proceed step by step, first abstract from scale by assuming constant returns. Let us also at first abstract from the transport question and discuss simple adjacent farmholdings on homogeneous soil and without significant location differences. That leads directly to some interesting welfare conclusions about equilibria at the margins between adjacent landholdings.

In Figure 1 we signalize the assumption of constant returns by plotting on the abscissa not land alone, but the ratio of land to complementary inputs. The two solid curves represent per acre figures: Average Gross Revenue per acre (AGR); and Average Complementary Costs per acre

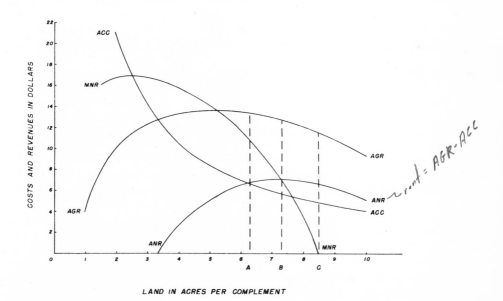

Figure 1. Complementary costs, revenues, and derived average and marginal net products of land with assumed constant returns to scale.

(ACC). The ACC curve is a rectangular hyperbola.[9] AGR behaves as any conventional average product curve, showing the result of varying proportions on output. Note that "average" here means "per acre," and not "per unit of output."

The vertical span between AGR and ACC, their difference, is Average Net Revenue (ANR), or rent, which is also graphed separately (dash line). ANR, of course, peaks farther to the right than AGR peaks. Note the characteristic lenticular form of the area between the AGR and ACC curves. It is a form we will meet several times.

The most interesting curve is the last, Marginal Net Revenue (MNR), or marginal rent, and the most interesting thing about it for the present analysis is the contrast it draws between two firms, one of which is a little too intensive (at A), and the other of which is a little too extensive (at C). The average net value of land is the same to each, and if that were our sharpest tool we would be at a loss to choose between them, and to allocate marginal acres between them. But we would probably give the acres to C because it is very much the fashion these days to applaud lower costs per acre and overlook output per acre, and that would be exactly wrong because the marginal rent, the proper arbiter of boundaries, is much higher for A.

The curves of Figure 1 do not exaggerate how quickly marginal rent falls with a slight decline of average rent. Table 1 is a numerical example of such a relationship. Marginal rent falls from 15 down to minus 3 while average rent barely changes.

Table 1: Relations of average and marginal gross and net revenues with declining intensity of land use

(1) Land (Acres Per Complement)	(2) Gross Revenue (GR)	(3) Average Gross Revenue (AGR) (2)÷(1)	(4) Marginal Gross Revenue (MGR)*	(5) Comple- mentary Costs (CC)	(6) Average Comple- mentary Costs (ACC) (5)÷(1)	(7) Net Revenue (NR) (2)−(5)	(8) Average Net Revenue (ANR) (7)÷(1)	(9) Marginal Net Revenue (MNR)*
			4					4
1	4	4.0		42	42.0	−38	−38.0	
			16					16
2	20	10.0		42	21.0	−22	−11.0	
			17					17
3	37	12.3		42	14.0	−5	−1.7	
			16					16
4	53	13.3		42	10.5	11	2.8	
			15					15
5	68	13.6		42	8.4	26	5.2	
			13					13
6	81	13.5		42	7.0	39	6.5	
			10					10
7	91	13.0		42	6.0	49	7.0	
			6					6
8	97	12.1		42	5.3	55	6.9	
			0					0
9	97	10.8		42	4.7	55	6.1	
			−3					−3
10	94	9.4		42	4.2	52	5.2	

*MGR and MNR are here identical, because Marginal Complementary Costs (MCC) are zero, throughout.
MGR and MNR are tabulated between rows because they represent changes between the defined values of Gross Revenue.

[9]Determined by the definition of the abscissa, of which it is the reciprocal.

The implication of all that is that, insofar as our analysis comprehends the relevant considerations, adjacent users of similar land for similar purposes should be drawn by the rental constraint toward comparable intensities, with due allowance for differences of managerial energy and skill. We cannot rationalize the extensive use of valuable land by citing lower costs per acre, higher output per man, and that sort of thing. The relevant driving force is the marginal rent of land and it is, given the rein, a strict taskmaster.

But need we limit the conclusion to land used "for similar purposes?" I think not. Let the ACC curve of Figure 1 be an envelope type curve, representing not just the best adjustment to different intensities of producing one product, but the best adjustment of products to each intensity as well. Adjust the other curves, all measured in the economist's universal ruler, to the new definition of ACC. Their positions and curvatures will change, but not their basic shapes nor critical intersections, nor the conclusion they impose on us. Of two uses yielding the same rent per acre, the more intensive should, in a perfect market, acquire marginal lands from the less until the intensities are equal.

The observation of extensive land uses persisting in central places on valuable sites has seemed to call for rationalizations, such as those of Ely and Wehrwein. But it is also possible that these are evidences of badly distorted markets. I do not believe that a meticulous geo-welfare economist would give the standard apologetics very long shrift. He would even find the assumption of managerial differences stretched beyond capacity. He would insist that a perfect market should achieve an equimarginal balance at the fence lines: that the outthrusting force of operator A should be the marginal rent of land to him, and the opportunity cost surrounding and constraining him should be the marginal rent of land to his neighbors, like C. He would have to deplore the failure of most land economists to apply such a standard in their judgments and comparisons.

Rent as a Constraint on Scale

Or is it just that he doesn't yet understand the marvels of large-scale production? Let us now drop the assumption of constant returns to scale, retaining yet however the homogeneous soil, and locational indifference. The analysis changes surprisingly little, so long as we limit it to atomistic individual landholders who do not capture many of their own external economies. Land, to the atomistic landholder, is much more divisible than labor or buildings or machinery, so that scale economies are almost synonymous with spreading the overhead of large capital and labor inputs over more land. Thus the scale question can be analyzed as a variation of the intensity theme. The necessary adaptations are in Figure 2.

Figure 2 differs from Figure 1 in these ways: the abscissa is now simply acres, instead of acres per complement; ACC is no longer a rectangular hyperbola but is appreciably flatter, being an envelope representing optimal adjustment in all respects to increased acreage, of which adjustments reduced intensity is only one;[10] MNR is no longer identical with MGR but lesser, because MCC are now positive (in Figure 1 they were zero;) MNR intersects AGR to the left of the latter's peak, or not

---

[10]When scale economies spring from landholders' entrapping their own external economies, the ACC curve may rise over some range. But ANR still traces a lenticular figure, so that comparable conclusions emerge.

152

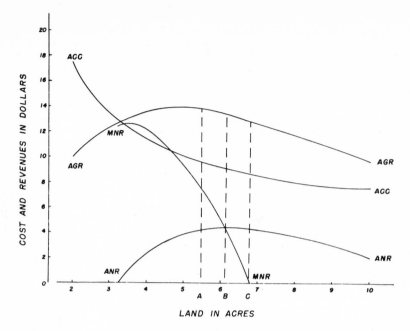

Figure 2. Costs, revenues, and derived average and marginal net products of land with increase of scale.

at all; and AGR peaks nearer the peak of ANR, at least relatively so, because of the flatness of ACC, and AGR (which is easy to measure) becomes more nearly normative.[11]

The essential lenticular shape of the ANR curve is still with us; likewise the normative value of its peak, its intersection with MNR, which now represents optimal scale as well as intensity.

As before, the most interesting curve is MNR, and this time it draws a pointed contrast between the firm at A which is a little too small, and another at C which is a little too large. Their average rents (ANR) are the same. But the marginal rent curve (MNR), which the geo-welfare economist insists on, reminds us that in private as in public welfare economics it is not good practice to let the supramarginal parts of an operation carry the submarginal. There are substantial social gains from transferring marginal acres from the too-large firm to the too-small, so long as the latter remains viable.

In its long love affair with scale economies, the profession of agricultural economics has tended to overlook such nagging marginal considerations. It has leaned heavily on that falling ACC curve to the neglect of the others. Geo-welfare economists have a mission to bring equimarginalism into the picture. We have come to imagine small farmers as weak and inferior, to be preserved, if at all, only for sentimental, military, or "sociological" reasons. But in terms of the marginal revenue productivity of additional lands for their cramped holdings, overmanned, overimproved, and perhaps overequipped relative to their land base, some of them must be as ravening wolves. Just what keeps those wolves behind fences should make an interesting study in market imperfections.

---

[11]It is worth signalizing the implications of the last point. The great emphasis of production economists on minimizing costs per acre may be misleading. If we must emphasize a single criterion of good combination of inputs, maximum output per acre (AGR) comes closer to the norm.

The scale question now appears as an aspect of the intensity question.[12] Rent is more than a constraint on "extensity" abstracted from scale. In the process it assumes a key role as an absolute limit on scale, because it is one cost that does not decrease with scale. That is most obvious in the short run: as one expands his landholding he presses on his neighbors and meets increasing costs per acre. In the long run the cost of homogeneous land is constant, while the cost of land within finite distributive networks tends, as we see later, to increase.

By contrast, there are definite economies in larger buildings, larger rooms, larger machines, and so on. One doubles the floor space of a house, for example, without doubling the building cost. The role of rent as a constraint on scale is well exemplified by observing the evolution of autos and trucks, which are partly exempted from the constraint thanks to public underwriting of progressively wider and straighter streets and highways, and vehicle taxes based on criteria other than space occupancy. As the roads widen and straighten the vehicles widen and lengthen, and if they were publicly garaged, too, might eventually approach the dimensions of yachts and railroad cars. When they have to pay for the space they pre-empt, or when traffic congestion applies a constraint, they shrink again.[13]

Another aspect of land's special role in limiting scale economies is that the MCC required to integrate fringe lands with a firm's operating center include rising internal transportation costs. The essence of a firm's individuality, and hence of scale economies it may realize, is its integral organic nature centered about some nucleus like a farmstead. Land added to a firm is marginal not just in quantity, but in location relative to the nucleus. Increasing internal transportation costs result from both longer lines and, after some point, overcongestion at the nucleus. The TNEC Fetterites and others have pointed to analogous diseconomies in the administrative nexus, but the geo-welfare economist need not reason by analogy. The long lines and congested centers are physical facts.

And so the landholder adding an acre to his operation must discount its net product for remoteness in space, just as he does future net products for remoteness in time. But whereas we swim through time together, we occupy different points in space, and one man's remoteness is another man's proximity. As A encroaches on B, therefore, the MNR of land falls to A, but rises to B, constraining the encroachment and limiting economies of scale.

Yet a third way in which rent serves to constrain scale of firms is by penalizing the lavish use of land-time that characterizes large-scale operations. Large scale of capital inputs is associated, as a rule, with durability, and the economy depends on spreading initial costs over a long period. Annual rent, an inexorable function of time, is a serious brake on

[12]One could also interpret the risk question as a variation of the intensity theme, but space limitation precludes that here.

[13]In the example, road space, although partly a human product, is made analogous to bare land, which is entirely a natural product. I do not allege that road space is generally synonymous with land -- only analogous, in the particular example, and in the short run. In the long run, streets and roads and highways may be widened, and in that process the unique role of rent as a constraint on scale is manifest in the contrast between rural roads, where land is a minor cost, and downtown streets, where land is the major cost. Widening rural roads, we meet decreasing costs per foot of width; widening city streets, we meet sharply rising costs, as the street clips off the fronts of small and valuable lots.

154

all such grand conceptions. We proceed next to chrono-welfare economics: the role of rent as a constraint on extension in time.

Rent as a Constraint on Temporal Extension

Extension in space, with fixed complementary inputs, obviously makes land use less intense by spreading the fixed or indivisible inputs over more land. It is a little less obvious, but equally important, that one reaches a similar end by spreading fixed inputs over more land-time. One does this by letting buildings depreciate and yet survive over many years at low values unrenewed, thus encroaching on the time-margin of land use.

The primary constraint on this temporal extension is again rent, which the chrono-welfare economist views as part of the marginal cost of time. Rent as an opportunity cost puts land uses under pressure not just from all sides but from the future. Rent is not the only marginal cost of time--all costs have a time vector. But rent behaves in time as in space, that is it holds up inexorably at fixed or rising levels as one approaches the margins of decision where other costs as a rule taper off.

The usual capital input occupying land depreciates and obsolesces with time and has little, no, or negative salvage value toward its senility. Without rent, old buildings would almost never be demolished. On a base of zero any return is infinite. Along Park Avenue today a sound 30-story building has just fallen to the wreckers' ball to release the site for a larger modern improvement. The same building in St. Louis, or another part of Manhattan, would survive another half-century; in Aberdeen, S. D., perhaps two centuries; in Malta Bend, Mo., until it fell of its own weight, for it could always be used for storing grain, or old equipment, and ultimately for disposing of junk. There is always a use, however humble, for an old building. If the site beneath has no salvage value there is no limit to economic life but sheer physical collapse.

This function of rent is known to urban land economists, and ably expounded by Ratcliffe, but somehow it has never found its way into the main body of production economics which has tended to remain not only spaceless but timeless. Open almost any tome on cost analysis or price or production economics and you will see the axes labeled "Input A" or "Output B" with no reference to the time unit assumed, or the method of annualizing fixed costs. It is to the credit of Boulding that he has made the effort to apply marginal analysis to time economics, but he has concluded--I believe mistakenly--that marginal analysis there breaks down.[14] Literature on capital theory has tended to neglect both marginal analysis and the role of ground rent. I hope I am not preaching to the converted, therefore, in expanding on the role of rent as a temporal constraint.

The rental constraint on time-extension operates more specifically as follows. Let us adopt Terborgh's expressive wording and describe old and new rivals for a site as "defenders" and "challengers." The time to salvage an old site arrives when the defender's current annual income net of operating costs falls below the top challenger's anticipated annualized

---

[14]Kenneth Boulding, Economic Analysis (3rd edition) (New York: Harper & Brothers, 1955), Chapter 39. For a criticism see Mason Gaffney, "Concepts of Financial Maturity of Timber," A. E. Info. Series No. 62 (Raleigh: North Carolina State College, 1957 and 1960), pp. 45-52. See also p. 54, which seeks a reconciliation -- it is not alleged that Boulding is entirely wrong, by any means.

rent net of all costs. Note that we are biased for the defender because
its capital costs are already sunk and nonsalvageable, so in the marginal
comparison we deduct no charge on sunk capital, neither depreciation,
obsolescence, nor interest. What's done is done and historical costs are
irrelevant even if embodied in outstanding debt.

The challenger's annualized net rent is a more difficult concept.
Since the challenger is typically not another firm but another land use
contemplated by the same firm we have little excuse to assume this rent
has been correctly determined "externally." We will have to compute it
ourselves.

A new use usually entails heavy initial costs, compensated by revenues
tapering off over many future years until the next challenger succeeds to
the site. The entire cycle of investment and liquidation is an indivisible
unit that must be evaluated as a whole.

The challenger's rent must be an average of its performance over
time. A simple mean will not do, however, for in addition to the quantities
of costs and revenues, we must consider their distribution in time. A
"time-average" is necessary. This is found by annualizing all costs and
revenues--for brevity let us henceforth say simply "net revenues."
Annualizing a quantity of given time-position, n, means finding the amount,
call it a, which if received as a constant annual sum from now to n
would be of equal present value with the said quantity received once at n.

Net revenues in the terminal year, t, are annualized by the following
standard formula:

$$a = \frac{i \, R_t}{(1 + i)^t - 1} \tag{1}$$

where R is net revenue, i is the relevant interest rate, and t is the
terminal age of the improvement.

Net revenues in any other year, n, are annualized by compounding
them forward to the terminal year, t, before applying the annualizing
operations of equation (1). Thus the complete annualizing formula is:

$$a = \frac{i \, \Sigma \, R_n \, (1 + i)^{t-n}}{(1 + i)^t - 1} \tag{2}$$

It only remains to select the value for t that maximizes a, which one may
do in a number of ways.

It reassures one's faith in marginal analysis to note that one way of
doing so is to find the year when $R_n = a$, that is when the marginal revenue
of time (R_n) equals the marginal cost of time (a). In the first years of
heavy initial costs the values of R_1, R_2, and so on may be less than a, and
ordinarily will be even less than zero as the initial costs are counted as
negative revenues. That is inevitable in the nature of long-term improvements. But toward the later years any value of R_n which fell below the
running time-average, a, established by preceding years, and not representing a new investment to be requited by later revenues, would lower
the time-average of the whole and call for demolition and renewal.

Which is also to say that in time analysis, as in space analysis, and
as in the timeless-spaceless abstract analysis on which economists still

nourish their young, a marginal revenue intersects the corresponding average revenue function where the latter is a maximum.

The accelerated replacement constrained by rent is a form of intensification of land use, as one would expect from the operation of a land constraint. Without the constraint the individual's motivation would be to squeeze the last drop of income from the initial inputs by spreading them over as much land-time as they would endure, thus minimizing the time-average of his costs without regard to the time-average of his revenues.

The intensity that the time-constraint encourages is of a sort that is not necessarily obvious if we should observe the static ratio of land to improvement at any given point of time. Intensity over time takes the form of faster turnover of improvements, rather than heavier initial improvements. Rent as a spatial constraint, it is true, prompts heavier initial improvements, but rent as a temporal constraint, chopping off the last years of each cycle, puts a premium rather on quick recoverability of capital, on flexibility and speedy replacement. Rent penalizes the ponderous and the monumental, and so has a tempering influence on initial costs. Its influence is rather toward maximizing volume of business, the joint product of capital times turnover. It is worth emphasizing that this rapid turnover of a nation's capital is a major factor tending to enhance employment opportunities for labor. [15] Conversely, all factors that weaken the operation of rent as a time-constraint tend thereby to reduce employment opportunities.

This influence of rent is pervasive, affecting not only buildings but the daily use of rooms, floors, and shelf space. Rent is no less the executioner of the creaking lathe and the stale bread than of the firetrap apartment and the tired orchard. A high-rent economy is one that economizes on land-time by introducing a note of urgency into all phases of life.

Rent is not, however, entirely the enemy of quality, substance and durability. It is an optimizing force that abhors extremes. While it does not let the minimization of time-average costs dominate decisions to the extent of overlooking time-average revenues, neither does it the opposite. It rather strikes a golden mean, maximizing the excess of time-average revenues over time-average costs.

In Equation (2) we submerged this relationship by combining revenues and costs in one inscrutable expression, R_n. Let us now express them separately and observe graphically a typical interplay of the time-averages of costs and revenues with increasing life of improvements (Figure 3).

Here we see the now familiar lenticular shape of average net revenue (ANR), manifesting the same general principle as in Figures 1 and 2, only here applied to spreading fixed costs over time instead of space. The rental constraint precludes indefinite rightward drift because the slight decline of time-average costs is offset by the sharper decline of time-average revenues. The rental constraint does not however drive us clear back to the maximum of time-average revenues at A, for there time-average costs are too high. It drives us rather to B, where the curves are parallel and farthest apart, and time-average rent is a maximum.

The systematic chrono-welfare economist would now want to explore many more dimensions of this analysis and fill in many missing details. He would want to trace the behavior of the challenger's <u>marginal</u> net

---

[15]Cf. Knut Wicksell, <u>Lectures on Political Economy</u>, Vol. I, <u>General Theory</u>, trans. E. Classen (New York: The Macmillan Company, 1934), pp. 127 ff.

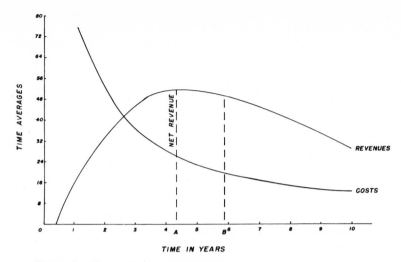

Figure 3. Time-averages of costs and revenues over building life.

product of land-time and assure himself that it equalled average net product at the latter's peak. He would want to trace out optimal intertemporal
marginal arbitration when the challenger's future was constricted by an
impending higher use so that his average net product could not be maxi-
mized--and he would discover he could improve a good deal on the "ripen-
ing-cost" apologetics of R. T. Ely. He would want to adapt his analysis
to land uses like stock-feeding in which the capital appreciates over time--
there he would discover the German forester Martin Faustmann to have
anticipated him by over a century. But in this wide survey we must leave
the question here.

Rent as an Expression of Traversal Costs

Our geo-chrono-welfare economist is now equipped, albeit crudely,
for an excursion into transport costs and their relation to land use.
Rent serves to constrain excessive pre-emption of space generally,
but most particularly of space that others must traverse. It is a most
important principle for the layout and rating of transport-utility networks
that the force of the constraint equal the increased traversal costs imposed by extension of land occupancy. While that may appear a welfare
truism, it has not to my knowledge been formally expounded, and its
policy implications are widely ignored both in practice and theory.
Let us suppose a row of five plots, equal in all qualities save location,
running uphill from a common source of free water, S. A Water District
serves them from a common pipeline, delivering to the uphill corner of
each plot. Pipe capacity fits demand all along the line, declining after
each outlet gate, in the likeness of an untelescoped telescope, but with
enough excess capacity to permit a small adjustment.
Water is free at the source but not at the outlets. Service at each
outlet is priced optimally to cover marginal costs, in a graduated manner
we detail later. Now it is enough to note the water users feel the full
social costs, exemplified by pumping, so that each successive user pays
a higher rate.

In Figure 4 the capacity needed for each plot is represented by a line running from its service outlet to the water source, S. The plots are designated in ascending order, A, B, C, D, and N. N is the marginal plot, and as our curtain rises it is dry-farmed.

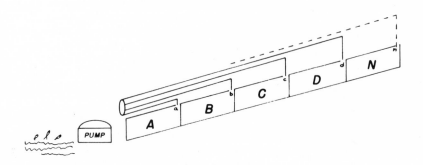

Figure 4. Schematic diagram of water service to hillside parcels.

In order for each plotholder to justify his tenure, both total and marginal, in the court of welfare economics, he must impute a marginal rent to the land as great as the traversal costs he imposes on landholders above, all of whom his presence pushes one slot uphill and who must pay for lifting water past his entire holding.

Let us concentrate on the margin between A and B. It is now affected by more complex factors than in our earlier example where location was unimportant. The outthrusting force of A is still the marginal rent he imputes, but B's resistance is tempered by his higher water rates, because he can encroach on C whose land is cheaper, or move to N. B has in fact a large family of interesting alternatives to scan, but for an introduction, the basic forces are exhibited by supposing A to buy plot B outright, and B to skip up to plot N. We now make that supposition.

When B leapfrogs over C and D to plot N he leaves C and D virtually unaffected, so the costs imposed on society are largely summarized in the costs felt by B. That is encouraging, for it suggests that B will·require of A a price for plot B, or any slice thereof, equalling the social costs of his total or partial move uphill. Such a price would constrain A optimally.

The costs imposed on B are those of acquiring land at N, hopefully at the price of its marginal rent without water; the cost of lifting water past plots C, D, and N; and the loss of producer surplus on the water that he took at plot B but now thinks submarginal at the higher pumping cost.

It is encouraging, too, further to note that the additional pumping costs imposed on B equal the sum of everyone's cost of traversing the land onto which A has expanded. That is, B's cost of pumping one supply past three plots, (C, D, and N,) represented by the dash line in Figure 4, equals the cost of pumping three supplies, for B, C, and D, past one plot (B.) Thus the new transport costs imposed on society are the costs of traversing A's new territory. The removal of B to plot N gives the same result as though A's expansion had simply boosted B, C, and D uphill in order.

So far, then, it seems that market rents can be accurate constraints guiding social economy of central space whose extension imposes traversal costs on outsiders.

To be sure the elegant geo-chrono-welfare economist would be aghast at the crudeness of our model. He would resolve to do a monograph embellishing the finer points at an early opportunity and lay no claims of accuracy until that was done.

But he would also note the futility of piecemeal optimizing. The normative welfare implications of our pumping model depend utterly on the assumption that privately felt transport costs equal social costs, and the fact is they do not. Where is there a water service that graduates rates with pump lifts? I know of none. Postage-stamp and capricious pricing are the rules in transport and utilities.

The location theorists have been content to spin out elaborate detailed models of lacy geometry on the assumption that private transport costs equal social costs, and that is their privilege. But it seems a poor allocation of their scarce time and abundant talents when not only is the assumption untrue, but no welfare theorist seems to be telling us what normative rate structures would look like. There is also an economy of economists, and our geo-chrono-welfare economist would wonder if he shouldn't rather go back to where Hotelling left us and develop a welfare pricing for transport and utilities as a framework within which to economize on land.

He would note that if B can get water at plot N and beyond as cheaply as at plot B, little restrains B from ranging and roaming gaily up the hillside, heedless of the costs underwritten by society. Looking back toward the valley, that release of constraint would cause B to sell plot B too cheaply, and relieve A of a proper constraint to economize on valley lands. If the valley lands --- here made analogous to central city lands --- had already, as in actual history, been intensively improved before the release of constraint, A would make his adjustment in the temporal margin of land use, reducing intensity over time by letting improvements age without renewal. Demolition is another name for salvaging land, and if land is made too cheap, renewal comes too slowly.

One reason some of the worst slums are found in American cities, of all places, is the same reason we have some of the world's worst-used soils, and some of the sloppiest camping manners: rather than renew we migrate. We have had that nearly-empty frontier, and a series of races to get out their firstest with the mostest, which seemed to justify the whole uneconomic process. We have subsidized one after another new form of transportation, spreading thin the ground rent that otherwise would have concentrated about the older centers and mandated their intensive renewal. The result has been careless exploitation at the fringes, and stagnation at the cores. Periodically, the process has brought on stagnation at the fringes, also, as rents have collapsed following bursts of overexpansion. Low rents, recall, mean low constraints on the temporal extension of land uses, hence a freezing of capital turnover, and reduced employment of labor.

And so our geo-chrono-welfare economist's train of thought leads him back to one of the great figures of welfare economics, Hotelling, who initiated a goodly share of marginal-costing and all that, back in 1938, by inquiring into criteria for setting railway and utility rates. He now sees that question as integrally related to a normative economy of land.

THE ROLE OF GROUND RENT IN PLANNING OPTIMAL TRANSPORT-UTILITY NETWORKS

We now rise above the viewpoint of the atomistic individual land-holder, to whom rent is an external constraint, and adopt the vantage of the municipality, or utility, or large land company -- very large, that is -- which is presiding over the layout of a transport-utility network to service large numbers of atomistic plots. This latter activity is land "development," as distinct from the "improvement" of individual plots. It differs from mere improvement among other ways in this, that development creates rents on the atomistic parcels served, which parcels capture consumer surpluses and external economies from transport-utility networks. Municipalities and large landholders can recapture these spillovers, the one by taxation and the other by ownership, and use them to help finance development and to optimize rate structures along the guidelines of welfare economics. Let us assume a municipality in charge of development, dedicated to practice an art we will call enlightened Ricardian Cameralism, in the light of the best geo-chrono-welfare economics. What policies should it adopt for distributing water from a single free source?

To begin, it would mince no words quibbling whether to apply Lerner's Rule. The logic is inescapable. Price should be equated to marginal cost in every possible dimension, until the point where the cost of fiddling with prices exceeds the gains. No enlightened individual land manager would deny himself the gains of internal equimarginalism, and the enlightened Ricardian Cameralist can do no less.

We may abstract from and defer the short-run question by noting that a planner should aim roughly toward building and sizing so as to equate long-run marginal costs with the time-average of short-run marginal costs over project life --- a straightforward application of chrono-equimarginalism. There will be an early developmental stage of excess capacity, with short-run costs below long-run costs, and a terminal stage of the opposite. Here we discuss simply long-run marginal costs.

We must not be taken in by a specious sort of "increasing cost" that appears when we lengthen the pipelines to serve more lands. That is not a true increasing cost because the product is not homogeneous. "The product" we are supplying is not water -- that, recall, was assumed free at the source -- but transportation. We are producing place utilities. As we carry water farther, costs per gallon rise because the gallons are carried farther.

The homogeneous gallon is that delivered to one outlet. There, we increase the product by delivering more to one buyer at one place. And there we find decreasing costs, long-run costs, among other reasons because the cross-section of our pipe grows with the product of the radius times the circumference.

The Ricardian Cameralist is therefore selling not one product in increasing costs, but many products each in decreasing costs. He requires not one indiscriminate rate for the whole, but a graduated structure rising with distance from the source. Once having freed himself from the fallacy of regarding his product as homogeneous, he can allocate costs to each outlet individually, and marginal-cost pricing comes into its own.

First, note another problem we can solve jointly with the marginal cost pricing problem. Each outlet represents not just an individual product but an individual market, a perfect bilateral monopoly. Society protects the buyer from the seller, after a fashion, by regulating rates, but nothing protects the seller from the non-buyer, the landholder who does not choose to participate, although the physical nature of space gives the seller no choice but to make service available and to invest money in capacity traversing the holding. Ricardian Cameralism will give the seller an equipoise.

Now the Ricardian Cameralist sets a water rate equalling marginal cost as allocated to the individual outlet. The resulting deficit he covers by a lump-sum land-capacity tax on the land served from that outlet. The tax is a price paid for having water service made available -- an insurance premium if nothing else -- and a means of collecting consumer surplus. The landholder is compensated by getting water transported at low marginal-cost rates, with the net social gains thereby effected, and by the great economy of a compact distributive network. He loses the option of keeping his land out of the system, a welfare question we return to later.

The problem of allocating pipe costs to individual outlets is straightforward. Each section of pipe may be conceived as a large sleeve telescoped full of smaller sleeves. One sleeve is cast off after the pipe reaches each outlet, until the last outlet is reached by a simple, narrow, empty sleeve, the core of the pipe. A complete sleeve-length running clear back to the source, is allocated to each outlet.

In computing marginal cost the outermost sleeve does multiple duty, being allocated to each outlet. It is generally the cheapest sleeve per unit capacity, although the big trunks near the source will in a large system exhaust their scale economies. The allocation of total costs among individual parcels does present some complications, but as it is a less critical question we will not dwell on those here. It is certain, however, that the outermost sleeve should be allocated to the outermost parcel of land, for there we have the marginal decision to make: how far to extend service. That we take up now.

Marginal cost pricing is commonly criticized for providing no test of whether an operation is economical overall. It is a strength of Ricardian Cameralism to supply such a test, for each extension of a system and of course thereby for the whole. Our sculptor is pressing us for a decision where to locate his bust to the ancient god Terminus. How do we calculate an answer?

We have given the peripheral landholder shabby treatment so far, at least by his lights. We have let rates increase roughly with distance from the source, and actually somewhat faster because, although we allocate him the cheap outermost sleeve all the way, toward the end of the line that sleeve is at or near the expensive inner core. We are not following the common practice of letting the profitable center of the system carry the margins. The peripheries are segregated and must stand on their own feet, receiving only those economies inherent in the large-scale distribution system in which they participate.

It is therefore with a clear conscience that the Ricardian Cameralist resorts to the ultimate weapons of marginal cost pricing to justify extending service. Indeed he can do no other, for he will not have exhausted the last economy inherent in his position until he has done so.

He has already deployed his penultimate weapons: marginal cost pricing itself; and allocating the outermost sleeve to the outermost parcel. He has one other, usually reserved for sick railroads and submarginal reclamation schemes, but which actually should be marshalled to pinpoint

the margins of every distributive network. The ultimate weapon is this:
he measures and recaptures every last shred of consumer surplus and
external economy created by water service --- his yardstick is a land
assessment and his reaper is a lump-sum ad valorem tax --- and applies
it to cover the deficits of marginal cost pricing. He proceeds outwards
until the surplus which he creates and reaps just covers the deficit. Thus
far and no further. There we raise the bust to Terminus, the ancient
god of boundaries. Thus we determine the total supply of land within our
system.

At the termini we can be certain to find costs decreasing more steeply
than further in, because a larger proportion of the sleeves allocated to
the terminal parcel will be near the core. The Ricardian Cameralist
must expect, therefore, to have relatively greater need of the land tax
toward the termini, even though marginal costs and water rates are abso-
lutely higher there. Figure 5 exemplifies the penultimate situation and
makes the points graphically.

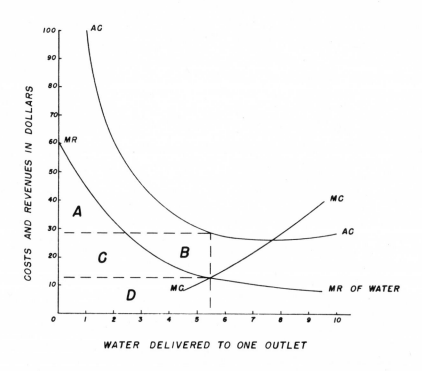

Figure 5. Costs and revenues of water service to a penultimate outlet.

As we proceed outwards along the water pipe, the AC curve, which
represents costs allocated to just one outlet, rises bodily. Demand is
here synonymous with the marginal net revenue of water applied to the
land. Total benefits are the area C + D + A. Total costs are C + D + B.
It is economical to extend service until area B waxes to equal or exceed
area A, which in turn wanes as the AC curve ascends.

In terms of deficits and taxes, the deficit is C + B. Consumer sur-

plus, captured in land rent, is C + A. The lump-sum land tax can cover
the deficit and still leave some rent unrecaptured so long as A outmeasures
B.

It is geometrically obvious that as the AC schedule ascends, and we
approach the terminal outlet, the intersection of MC and MR drifts left-
ward, beneath ever steeper reaches of AC, where costs are decreasing
more rapidly, where the net social gains from marginal cost pricing are
greater, and where, as we said, relative reliance on the lump-sum land
tax must be greater.

Having pushed Ricardian Cameralism to its spatial limit, let us again
don the chrono-welfare hat and return to the short-run vs. long-run
question. When a system is new it should generally be overbuilt, antici-
pating increased demand. In those early years even the central parcels
may exhibit the marginalistic traits shown in Figure 5, even though the
time-average outcome is to be supramarginal. In those early marginal
years, of course, price should be set to equal short-run marginal cost,
which will be low, and the heavy deficits met by land-capacity taxes,
which also serve as mandatory injunctions on landholders to accelerate
improvement, thereby synchronizing interdependent investments. Thus
at the temporal as at the spatial margins of the system the Ricardian
element of Cameralism assumes greater importance.

There, then, are the bare bones of a transport-utility rate structure
wherein social transport costs would be privately felt, and it would make
sense to economize carefully on atomistic land parcels by geo-chrono-
welfare principles. It is a system in which rent plays a central role, and
which would in turn profoundly alter the present pattern of rents, were it
applied.

The proposed system departs radically from present practice. Now,
instead of subsidizing decreasing cost distributive operations we relin-
quish them to the publicans as tax-collecting machines, setting rates to
cover not only average costs but the city deficit as well. With decreasing
costs, and elastic demand, the excess burden from this form of indirect
taxation, especially at the centers of the systems, is awful to contemplate.

Now, instead of graduating rates with distance we maintain postage-
stamp rates over wide areas, letting surpluses from the center under-
write extensions into no-one-knows how deeply submarginal outlands. In
respect to city streets we may temper the felony with gas taxes, but we
compound it with taxes on vertical transportation, and indeed all manner
of intensification, in private buildings, doubling the bias against the
underfilled third dimension. The predictable result of taxes on downtown
buildings and subsidies to capricious horizontal extensions is the checker-
boarding and leapfrogging that we get.

Why do we subject ourselves to those hardships? Certainly not because you and I are the first who ever noticed that transport costs increase
with distance; and lump-sum land taxes have been imposed in some measure throughout recorded history. The counterforces to Ricardian
Cameralism fall also within the scope of welfare economics, and of them
I would dwell on three most prominent: freedom of choice; economies of
aggregate social scale; and the conflict of distributive equity with allocative efficiency.

As to freedom of choice, it strikes many people that to charge a
landholder for transport-utility service whether he wants it or not is to
bereave him of a dimension of freedom in choice, and reduce his welfare.

The view is specious, but I believe must yield to deeper values.

For one, whatever increases the community's net product increases the individual's free choice, quantitatively of course, and doubtless qualitatively as well. To permit holdout landholders to disrupt the spatial integrity of the community is to permit a distance-barrier among all citizens, a barrier to the linkages in space that give richness and reality to the abstract freedom of choice. There is not a wide range of alternatives in an isolated homestead at the end of a mud road.

For another, hyper-individualistic welfare economics may have undersold the value of the freedom of men to act in concert. Man is a social animal, after all, and to allow one or a few holdouts to veto group projects and frustrate neighborly co-operation may be carrying a good thing too far. It certainly implies an interpersonal comparison in which the holdouts' freedom to say "No" is ranked above the majority's freedom to act as a community.

Last, the alleged loss of freedom is based on an implicit indivisibility, the identification of particular men with particular parcels of ground. But there is certainly no welfare postulate more basic than that man is the measure of all things; and an option denied to a square of land does not deny it to the man. He is not a serf, to the glebe adscript, but a free agent, master of his fate in society with many alternatives including other squares of land. In a word, people can move around. We complicate social problems needlessly if we impute the immobility of land to the men who own it.

Once the man is loosed from the matrix we see that Ricardian Cameralism would compensate for the loss of veto power by adding a new dimension to free choice. Today we can choose different quantities at a given price; then we could choose the price as well, by choosing the location: low rates in the center, high at the fringe, and a full spectrum in between. Let the individual choose freely just which combination of lump-sum land charge and variable use-rate best suits him. Today we impose a dull uniformity on all sites, epitomized in the grid system and postage-stamp pricing, in a crude gesture toward some pre-monetary barter concept of distributive equity, with every man's plot made as good as his neighbor's; Ricardian Cameralism would differentiate sites, fully exploiting and accentuating the natural advantages of the center, leaving the extreme peripheries for the misanthrope. To secede from co-operative society is certainly every man's inalienable right, and worth protecting, but not, please, right in the middle of it.

Now let us entertain the second counterforce to Ricardian Cameralism, the economies to aggregate social scale. Ricardian Cameralism may appear to be an introverted and short-sighted policy. Cheap subsidized peripheral transport, as today, helps to widen markets and so open the way for scale economies at the center. That is a point from which our examples abstracted by assuming water free at the source. But it is no problem now to price water at the source, before it enters our pipe price system, which is only a means of pricing transport. If there are scale economies at the source they can be optimally encouraged by marginal-cost pricing. There is no magic in scale economies that exempts them from comparison with other values in the price balance, and it would be folly, it is folly, to enshrine them as national idols and sacrifice net welfare to them.

But the hyper-scale economist looks beyond the present. If his city,

his utility company, his region, his agency, his nation doesn't stake
claim to untapped peripheral resources now, preclusively, some other
empire-builder may sneak out there first. While we aren't quite sure
what we want with the territories today, we certainly don't want those
other fellows taking over and discrediting all the lies we tell about the
destinies of our crossroads and its merchantable real estate, our corporation and its public shares, etc.

So to secure those figments of future economies we acquiesce in
otherwise uneconomical transport-utility extensions. In the process we
sacrifice true present economies in scale of distribution lines serving
compact populations, economies that come from broadening or thickening
rather than lengthening lines, economies of a sort to put most modern
American cities in at once both the stages of increasing returns to scale
but negative returns to more space.

As to the hopeful future economies, it is now some 100 miles across
what passes for the city of Los Angeles, to cite an extreme example, with
precious few possibilities of true economic sharing of common costs
between extremes, and two-thirds of the downtown sterilized by the space
demands of the insolent chariots. The New York Regional Planning
Authority recently estimated a need for $50 billion in the next 25 years
for transport-utilities to reintegrate the fragments of what used to be New
York City. It is noble to sacrifice the present for posterity, but it is
stupid to sacrifice both to an illusion, which we may have let get a little
out of hand, just as our daddies did before us on several immemorial
occasions.

It would seem wiser for most cities, and analogous distributive organisms, to grow compactly, at peace with their neighbors, and when the
time came to break out of the shell and integrate with other organisms to
the end of widening markets and achieving scale economies, to do so at
the wholesale and trunk-line level, proceeding in order and the fullness of
time toward complete integration. That would present its problems, to be
sure; but the alternative is the interurban mess we have today.

Finally, there is the conflict of allocative efficiency with distributive
equity, and there is a counter-dominant to sunder the social fabric indeed.
By this point I trust no reader remains unapprised that the distribution of
utility services in space has an important bearing on that other kind of
distribution -- of income, of wealth, hence ultimately of that other kind of
utility of which the welfare economists write. Setting rates, locating lines
and terminals here instead of there, those are key activities that make or
break the value of lands, and the men who hold their titles.

Ricardian Cameralism, as sketched out thus far, appears to favor the
center over the circumference. It charges the outer landholder not only a
higher use-rate but a higher lump-sum tax as well, thus abusing him
thrice: initially he received lands less favored by Nature, from those
lotteries of Fate we call history and patrimony; next we would raise his
utility rates; and then, instead of compensation, on his groaning back we
heap the bulk of municipal taxes! But that is insufferable. It not only
overburdens the outlanders, it cuts off their escape routes and throws
them back on the mercies of the inner few, mercies not always tender.
Clearly we have developed only a partial philosophy and must think farther.

Terminus, the god of boundaries, has not found favor in American
history because so often he appeared as an agent of the inner interests, the
Establishment, a sort of sheep dog hounding us to the clipping houses. It

is curious that economists who, since discovering monopoly 30 years ago
have defined it into every jar and carton on our shelves, have given so few
words to the most transcendent and entrenched monopoly of all, that community of interest of important local landholders organized openly and
aboveboard as city councils and county boards and state legislatures. But
the outsiders, although they may not have known a cet. par. from a mut.
mut., have maintained a healthy skepticism of the Establishment, and
American history is a series of successful revolts against overcontain-
ment. George III sculpted Terminus on the Appalachian Trail, the Procla-
mation Line, and reaped The Revolution. Hamilton tried the Ohio River
line but got Jefferson and Louisiana. The Whigs tried again and got old
Hickory and the canal boom. The southern Democrats tried once more
and got Oregon, Lincoln, transcontinental railroads, the Homestead and
Morrill Acts, and all the rest. Downtown has tried and reaped the shopping center. The Budget Bureau tries but cannot contain the Reclamation
and Flood Control Associations. You cannot hold the American people
behind fences. Negative containment policies do not work, and we wouldn't
like them if they did.

The inner few, therefore, seeing the limits of power, have accommodated the demand for admission and expansion as befits shrewd cartel
managers. They are custodians of a surplus, a potential social dividend,
which we have called ground rent. They need a formula to distribute it
among their retainers, and they have used for this the atomistic land
parcel, a quota in the cartel, with postage-stamp utility rates a means
toward a crude communion, a species of distributive equity, among members. The institution of property in land ceases to be a means toward
efficient allocation of a resource and becomes (perhaps it always has
been) a means to maintain a viable political structure. I do not belittle
the achievement. It is worth some sacrifice.

How might Ricardian Cameralism resolve the problem and reconcile
distributive equity with allocative efficiency? The answer clearly lies in
levying on those central rents. The containment effected by graduated
transport-utility rates would multiply those rents over present levels, and
we could with clear consciences go after them on the welfare principle of
taxing the gains of winners to compensate losers. We could use the same
lump-sum land-capacity tax already described, which would have the important bonus of converting a large share of the landholder's implicit rent,
a soft and easy-going sort of constraint, into an explicit cash obligation,
a regular fixed charge, which would increase the leverage of the remaining
net rent and so whet his incentives remarkably.

The question next arises, which Ricardian Cameralist should collect
those central rents? The local distributive organism has already been
adequately financed from the charges levied as constraints on peripheral
parcelholders. Here is a pleasant sort of dilemma, and the obvious
answer is that the central surpluses are the proper preserve of state or
federal government. From the larger view, indeed, the analogy is almost
perfect between the State-local relationship and the local-individual relationship. To the State, presiding over trunk highways, power pools,
natural gas lines, interregional canals, and the like, the local distributive
organism is an atomistic parcel, a cell surrounding a nucleus, with
marginal rents declining toward the peripheries, just as in the individual
parcel, and for perfectly analogous reasons: growing internal transport
costs.

The ground rents generated at the centers of these local organisms are but the reflection of natural location advantage, in the larger scheme of things, plus the artificial enhancements of natural advantages constituted by the trunk distribution lines that link the cells in the nexus of the regional, national, and world superorganisms. Ricardian Cameralism in the larger sense would simply entail applying at the regional and national levels the same principles already worked out at the local. We might then discover that an increasing population can live quite comfortably on no more lands than we presently pre-empt, but a good deal less.

And so the geo-chrono-welfare economist, who began by joshing welfare economists for dreaming of unattainable Platonic prototypes, culminates with a model that will strike some readers as farther-out than any scheme yet hatched by the Cam or the Thames. Yet, so rough and ready a monarch as William the Norman was able to apportion his feudal levies among his vassals by the capacity of their lands, and produce in the Domesday Books a tolerably useful national cadaster. Not long ago most American States levied directly on every lot and acre, and few would deny today that State Boards of Equalization assess land more truly than their local counterparts. Even without any Ricardian Cameralism, the Federal Bureau of Internal Revenue today must check the market value of every parcel when it changes hands by sale, gift, or death, and while that is the thousandth part of its present impossible task, it is virtually the whole of the Ricardian system. As to overambitiousness, the Ricardian system can be writ small as well as large, approached gradually as well as abruptly, applied piecemeal as well as whole.

I do not believe the barrier to Ricardian Cameralism, therefore, lies in any complexity or remoteness, but only in the minds and customs of men. Western man has now been pushing back frontiers, and running away from problems behind him, for some 1500 years, and the realization has not quite fully broken that the world is round and finite. Without question the world offers still more frontiers where, with the usual elbowing and throat-slitting, we could expand beachheads, but to what avail? Manifest Destiny has already stretched us thin from sea to shining sea; world resources may be tapped through trade. With the problem of atomic survival now uppermost, today's challenge is rather to demonstrate that a free economy can prosper without forever thrusting outward to encroach on its neighbors; that it can reorient a vigorous people's aggressions into heightening and deepening our capital and culture on the land we already have. Too, we are challenged to find better modes of balancing and reconciling the legitimate claims of society and individuals, of socialism and free enterprise. Toward those ends the land economist and the welfare economist, severally and jointly, can offer society more plausible alternatives than those it now faces so distraughtly.

9

The Contribution of
Institutional Economics Analysis
to Land Problems Research

by Kenneth H. Parsons*

We are concerned in this essay with the contributions of institutional economics analysis to land problems research-but not with the whole array of either. We shall limit our discussion to the public aspects of land problems - the issues of public policy and administration; and we shall accept Commons' formulation of institutional economics for the terms of reference in this aspect of the inquiry. This selective emphasis is made in the interest of both brevity and relevance. By so defining the inquiry, the task becomes reduced to more manageable proportions. Also land economics as a field of specialization derives much of its justification and usefulness from the fact that this public approach has enabled students to deal effectively with the public issues in resource policy and control.

Commons' formulation of institutional analysis was designed to understand and help modify the economy as a social organization in an age of concerted action and economic power. Furthermore in his approach to economic analysis he strove always to supplement, not to supplant, the more traditional, individualistic and mechanistic approaches to economic analysis. Commons viewed the economy primarily as a social organization - as a system of organized activity. Within this system the economic

*KENNETH H. PARSONS has been professor of agricultural economics at the University of Wisconsin since 1936. Born in Indiana in 1903, he received a B.A. from Butler University, did graduate study at the University of Chicago, and received his Ph.D. from the University of Wisconsin. Employed by various federal agencies such as Farm Board, Resettlement Administration, and Bureau of Agricultural Economics in the early 1930's, he then turned to teaching and research at Wisconsin. He has been consultant to a number of national and international organizations in recent years and has travelled widely around the world. He is the best contemporary representative of the Wisconsin tradition of institutional economics, the subject of this chapter.

Author's Note: The paper is an almost completely revised version of the one prepared for the seminar held at The University of Nebraska in June 1961. I have benefited a great deal in this revision from the comments of Professors C. W. Loomer, Peter Dorner, and Don Kanel, as well as the comments from the Nebraska discussions.

functions of transformation and exchange take place - but the functions are organized differently according to the nature of the (including) system of human relations, which is commonly referred to as the social framework. But it is not a framework in a "given" sense in Commons' view but is rather a part of an inclusive changing process. This follows from the fact that Commons was interested in more than proportionality and efficiency. He was concerned basically with development and public policy - with a central interest in how the structure of the economy changes as an economy develops from the traditional handicraft agricultural system to a market economy, characterized by investment, economic power, industrialization, and concerted action.

Commons' analysis leads him to view the economy (and other organizations) as an array of going concerns, which have the common (formal) structural characteristics of working rules which define the terms upon which participation in the concerns is experienced, with transactions as the meeting place of the different social sciences. Accepting man as a volitional being, Commons came to accept the principle of willing participation as the leading principle of social organization. His acceptance of the necessity for authority, so exercised as to create order and assure (even coerce) performance, led him to concentrate upon the working rules and the sanctions by which they were enforced. The state in this view is distinguished from other going concerns principally by the sanctions of sovereignty - ultimately the legitimate use of violence (arrest, imprisonment, etc.). Creative function in the design of the structure of the economy is exercised at the point where working rules are invented, or discovered, and generalized. It is such working rules, enforced by the appropriate sanction, which restrain, liberate, and expand individual action.[1] Thus Commons approaches behavior from the perspective of the working rules which channel and direct action.

I

We are concerned with the public aspects of land problems, in which the public is viewed as the state. The public point of view is general and comprehensive, in contrast with the private and particular, but the meaning of the public is to be understood not in terms of itself alone, but in relation to the private. The public, in the view accepted here, is what one might call the creative reconciliation and harmonizing of less extensive interests. In one of Dewey's phrases, "the perception of consequences which are projected in important ways beyond the persons and associations directly concerned in them is the source of the public.[2] Commons has more explicitly stated the interrelationships of public and private in the thesis that: "The question always is, not, What is a private purpose over against a public purpose? but Is the private purpose also a public purpose, or merely a private purpose. Will the behavior of the person benefited prove to be, in the direction of that benefit, also a public benefit?"[3]

---

[1] John R. Commons, Institutional Economics (New York: The Macmillan Company, 1934), p. 73.

[2] John Dewey, The Public and Its Problems (New York: Holt, 1937), p. 89.

[3] John R. Commons, Legal Foundations of Capitalism (New York: The Macmillan Company, 1924), pp. 326-27.

One implication of these conceptions of the public is that the term has different meanings, if used to refer to different kinds of economic organization, according to the degree of emphasis upon opportunity, individual initiative, freedom, incentives, etc. Although we shall endeavor in later portions of this essay to comment briefly on land problems in other types of economic systems, we shall be concerned initially with problems on the American scene, and can work within the accepted distinctions of public and private.

We may note here, however, that economic systems differ in the way they organize human behavior for the similar purposes of providing the commodity and service basis for a civilization. In general terms, public policies in a "free" society center upon designing and putting into effect working rules which are intended to lead to the functioning of an economy by major reliance upon the voluntary acts of participants. Authoritarian societies concentrate primarily upon the planning of specific performance, and rely on general rules principally as directive administrative means of rationing. Stated differently, one of the critical differences between economic systems is the degree to which they rely upon the "market" as the allocator of resources. This problem is formulated by Commons as being a matter of variable preproportions between authorized transactions and authoritative transactions - according to whether the transactions are between parties deemed equal before the law - the bargaining transactions of the market place - or whether the parties stand in a superior-inferior relationship, as in the rationing transaction of industrial government or the managerial transaction of plant operations. [4]

It is also of significance here that public policies for and programs of economic adjustment in America are executed on a gradual or incremental basis. This is what is meant by a progressive rather than a revolutionary approach to public policy. The gradual or progressive approach accepts the economy as a functioning going concern and concentrates upon modifications which are intended to change it in significant details without destroying the functioning concern itself. Although there are tremendous problems of getting a modern economic concern going in the newly developing countries (to which we shall return later), in contemporary America public policies are essentially incremental and this helps to set the problems of analysis - for land economics as well as more generally. [5]

Specialization in land economics in America as a professional field has occurred in this century. The national economy was a vigorous going concern by this time, and land economics - according to our understanding of the matter - developed as a field of study primarily to deal with pressing public problems of conservation, patterns of land use, irrigation developments, decadent areas of rural settlement, and so on. In this emphasis the students of land economics are working in a policy continuum toward land which runs back over the whole history of the Anglo-American economy. The principal manifestation of that policy was, of course, the national land policy of the United States with the emphasis upon private ownership of land as far as feasible.

Although much is made in America of national policies which are intended to encourage and strengthen the family farm - and they are both numer-

---

[4]As in the discussion of Public Purpose, <u>Legal Foundations</u>, at p. 313.

[5]For discussion of the significance of incrementation in policy analysis, see the works of C. E. Lindblom, including "Policy Analysis," <u>American Economic Review</u>, June 1938, pp. 298-312.

ous and significant - the basic proposition of land policy and tenure policy of the United States is undoubtedly that of the salability and free alienation of land. Anyone can buy land who has the means and can find a willing seller. The family farm has established itself and survives in this contest, principally because it is an efficient way of organizing a farm. Most of our public assistance to family farms is intended to offset the disadvantages for small-scale, rural agricultural entrepreneurs which are inherent in an urban-oriented, large-scale business and industrial economy. Within this principle of nondiscriminatory market freedom in the alienation of land, people who keep a farm in the family generation after generation do so by means of family planning and financial management.

Thus, the special emphasis in this century upon land economics as a field of professional specialization combines an interpretation of the historic establishment in land policy with a study of ways of modifying this policy to meet the needs of our times. There is thus something of a tension or a shifting equilibrium in the way in which freedom of contract and alienation of land is confined, supplemented, or modified by the land use controls which the new age of increasing populations and urbanization requires. Consequently there is a common principle running through most of the public problems to which land economists address themselves of the inadequacy of private choices and freedom of contract and land markets as the means of public administration of land use. This same kind of limitations and deficiencies is forcing land economics research into urban renewal, recreational land uses, water utilization, and regional planning. In all these areas there is the central problem of how to protect the public interest in land use, of which one major question is that of the public interest in privately-owned land.[6] A brief review of American history may put these issues into clearer perspective.

The American economy, especially the agricultural economy, was given shape by the transplantation and adaptation of British institutions to a virgin continent by persons dedicated to equality of opportunity - "life, liberty and the pursuit of happiness." Since the natives were pushed aside, the institutions "took-over" and virtually shaped the social structure. This occurred at the time when rationalistic liberalism was at its height in England. Consequently freedom of contract, the free alienation of land, and eventually the market-oriented system of private enterprise were encouraged as a matter of principle.[7]

But land has marked peculiarities as a commodity. As in all other commodities the economists' interest is in uses, not physical properties; but the physical characteristics affect the uses. This cluster of interrelated characteristics has given land (broadly defined) a peculiarly strategic place in the welfare and survival of a people. Consequently after the first round of enthusiastic exploitation of natural resources was finished in the United States, thoughtful people began to see that special arrangements were necessary, if the land (including water and minerals) and timber resources were to serve the national welfare over the long range. In the ac-

---

[6]For statements of the fundamental issues see: John R. Commons, Legal Foundations, Chapter IX, Public Purpose, especially pp. 326-27; R. J. Penn, in Land Problems and Policies, edited by Murray and Timmons (Ames, Iowa, 1950); Johnson, Timmons, and Howenstine, "Rural Public Works," Parts I and II, Journal of Land and Public Utility Economics, Vol. XXIII, Nos. 1 and 2, February and May 1947, pp. 12-21, 132-41.

[7]See Willard Hurst, Law and the Conditions of Freedom in Nineteenth Century U.S. (Madison: University of Wisconsin Press, 1956).

tion along this line of establishing procedures for protecting the public interest in land, it was necessary to modify in countless ways the procedural
and administrative aspects of the "market" in land, largely through the
devices of land use regulations.

The public interest in privately-owned land has been exercised historically, through the police powers of government and taxation, these being
primarily attributes of state governments and their subdivisions. Increasingly, in this century the public interest in privately-owned land has been
expressed through public expenditures which affect directly the value and
usefulness of land; these include farm to market highways, as well as other
public facilities. More recently the federal government has instituted payments to private owners of agricultural land for the purposes of encouraging conservation practices.

Through taxation, mostly by local governments, and especially by
improvement districts, the annual charges upon agricultural land in the
vicinities of cities readily become so heavy as to force land from agricultural to a higher economic use.

The most diversified method of land use regulation is, however,
through the exercise of the police powers, through zoning and related regulations. Characteristically in this country the regulations limit the possible array of uses of land, modifying the nature of the substantial interests
in land - i.e. permitting only specified uses of particular tracts of land.
With minor exceptions, such as limits on the ownership of agricultural
land by corporations in some states, there are no restrictions either on
who may own land or in what quantities. Under this type of regulation, the
sovereign power of government is used as a sanction for enforcing limits
within which both private enjoyments and the authorized transactions by
free market negotiation take place. These authoritative limits are stipu-
lated in various ways, but a common one is for the governing body of the
local government to be granted the sovereign authority to determine, and
therefore change, the zones of permissible uses of land.

The regulations on land ownership in the underdeveloped countries
seem to have a different orientation. The ownership of land may be reserved for nationals. Also there are many instances in which ownership of
agricultural land is restricted to self-cultivators, or a ceiling is placed
upon the area that one person may own. Such regulations limit entry into
the land market as well as the substance of what is bought and sold as land.

II.

Looking to the future, and outward onto the world scene, the nature
of the research problem in the public-institutional aspects of land economics may be classified in two separable but interdependent categories:
(a) the evaluation of existing institutions and (b) the creation of new
institutions.

The evaluation of existing institutions as a problem in research is
frequently formulated as that of estimating the "effects" of specified rules
or procedures - such as studies of the effect of tenure arrangement upon
the efficiency of farm organization and optimizing resource allocation - or
upon conservation practices. In similar fashion the effectiveness of zoning
regulations, the private ownership of recreational land, or the public
ownership of grazing land may also be studied. Two implications of this

kind of research may be noted: (a) the study of the "effects" of specified institutions blends directly and necessarily into an evaluation of the institution - simply because effects can be studied only on a selective basis; and (b) the study of effects consequently leads directly to suggestions for modification of institutions. At this point the evaluation of institutions blends into the problem of creating new institutions.

The creation of new economic institutions, or the modification of existing institutions, entails an additional and entirely different order of research problems than is encountered in estimating or evaluating the effects upon resource use of existing institutions; for, institutions have careers of their own and must be developed in relation to an inner logic or principle which relates the new institutions to the functioning economy and society, the functioning going concern.

In America during this century there have been a great number of major innovations in economic institutions. For the economy as a whole, there is the whole array of control programs in agriculture, embracing acreage allotments, market quotas and federal market orders; each of these programs operates as limits to private decisions and alters the relative attractiveness of alternatives. The Social Security program, particularly the provisions for Old Age and Survivors Insurance was an imaginative projection of retirement and social insurance programs from previously established procedures and practices, which innovations included a plan of financing jointly by the worker and the employer as a tax upon particular employment rather than the general public, the extension of insurance into new problems, especially for the care of widows and dependents, and above all of insurance and retirement benefits as a matter of right of participation. Similarly in the realm of land-use controls, soil conservation districts have been added to an already long list of special improvement district organizations - for irrigation, drainage, etc.

An obvious common feature of all these innovations is that they represent extensions from previous practices through changing somewhat the public arrangements under which private economic activity is carried out - such as the terms of access to markets, and the conditions of employment, or the range of permissible private discretion in land use.

One requirement which institutional innovations must meet in the American system is the test of constitutionality; of not depriving a person of life, liberty, or property without due process of law. Consequently administrative procedures through which policy innovations are carried out must meet not only the particularly economic objectives such as price stabilization, labor standards or land use requirements, but the procedures must meet the juridical tests of constitutionality. Consequently no innovation in public procedures, i.e. institutions, is secure until the practice has been accepted by the high courts.

III.

This American practice of judicial review is the culmination, or apex, of a vast complex of legislative, administrative, and judicial arrangements for determining and protecting the public point of view. It is probably as objective and as impartial as any system yet designed to create security of expectations out of uncertainty, conflict, and potential mutuality - and

Professor Commons understood these processes in a superlatively profound way.

In America we can take this system of honoring public purposes for granted in our imaginative projections of institutional innovations - for we must honor it - but this is not true everywhere. In the new developing countries the very nature and existence of the public is itself an issue. Consequently, if the fruits of economic research upon the public aspects of land use problems are to be put into effect, it may well be necessary to consider the question of how a "public" viewpoint is created procedurally as well as how institutional innovations may be fruitfully and securely projected. We can do no more here than merely point to a few issues.

The first question to be considered by research into the process of creating or modifying institutions for directing the activities of land use and occupancy in newly developing countries, would seem to be that concerning the source of the raw materials for the working rules or procedures. The method of projecting a new procedure, or modifying an old one must be imaginative and creative. Consequently the question can be restated to inquire upon what should a disciplined imagination be turned, to meet the requirements of the case. Although this question probably cannot be answered categorically, the principal differences in approach appear to be according to whose experience is taken as the source of insights.

To the extent that the experience of the people of the area is taken as the source of insights to be expanded and generalized in an economy newly developing from traditional forms, the research problem evidently centers upon a selective analysis of social practices, or customs, of the people with a view to finding social procedures which can be built upon. The development of laws out of customs, by the common-law method, represents the essence of this approach. Professor Commons has shown in Legal Foundations of Capitalism how this approach was developed in the Anglo-American tradition, in the formalization of the law of landlord and tenant, of creditor and debtor, and of employer and employee, among others.

This searching of the customs or social practices of a people for elementary rules which can be extended and strengthened is somewhat alien to the habits of thought of much of contemporary economic analyses. An opposite and alternative approach may very well commend itself - namely that of bringing in policies, laws, and business procedures from another culture and a different legal system. For one thing, the derivation of tough serviceable economic practices and institutions out of traditional and customary behavior is a difficult task; it requires deep insight into and intimate knowledge of a culture and society such as foreigners are rarely able to achieve. Also there is a widespread view, supported by both the Marxian and Veblenian analyses, that customs and related economic institutions merely inhibit technology and retard growth. This negative and deprecatory view toward customs has probably been reinforced in recent years by the widespread use by economists of commodity-economic-models as stipulating the requirements to be met as criteria for policy proposals. Also, quite beyond the direct advice and influence of professional economists, very strong influences have been operative in the less developed areas of the world to bring their economic systems into deep reciprocal involvements with the world economy of markets and trade. The necessities for public order and security of expectations in market transactions and creditor-debtor arrangements have pushed the business law and practices of western countries into the traditional economies of the less developed countries. As the influence of such transactions permeated the economies, the more rigorously developed systems of law and practice have come to serve as a model both by direct colonial administration and by the conduct of commerce.

But however one interprets or explains the fact, one encounters attempts in the newly developing areas of the world to transplant institutions, including systems of tenure, from the outside. Thus one finds Americans advocating owner-cultivatorship; the British (at least prior to the Report of the East African Commission of 1953-55) favoring long-term leases; the Israelis recommending their variety of co-operative farms; and the communists pushing the collectivization of agriculture.

When one considers how deeply dependent the survival of a people is upon the land tenure and debt-incurring practices in the traditional agricultural economies of the underdeveloped world, the conclusion seems virtually necessary that ways must be found to build onto and modernize traditional practices and not merely attempt to replace these practices by imported procedures. More technically, the inquiry and research problem appears to be twofold: sorting out practices of land occupancy and use as some kind of "singulars," and then integrating these elementary practices into new systems. The logic and principles of systematization can come from the outside.

An interesting contrast is provided between the analyses of J. S. Furnival and John R. Commons on this issue. In his Colonial Policy and Practice, and elsewhere, Furnival shows how the introduction of western law and business practices into Asia by the colonial powers led to great social disorganization despite the deeply constructive and liberal views of the British civil servants who administered the systems of law giving and justice. Commons, working in an entirely different context, shows in Legal Foundations how the institutions of property and business practice basic to the liberal views were actually derived out of the customs of farmers and guildsmen of England. Stated in more general terms, Commons demonstrates through historical analysis how economic theory and economic institutions have the same roots in problems resolved. The increased investment in physical capital necessarily involved the future more deeply into the present, thus requiring a degree of control over future events, which in turn required not only the formulation of customs into the more precise and more powerful common law but also required the development of equity law (as well as statute law) in order that acts might be controlled before they occurred. The law of landlord and tenant, the invention of the negotiability of promises, and the sale of debts: all these adjustments in procedures were forced by the struggles for survival, commercial gain, and military power. The rudimentary ideas of a market, of contracts, and of fair competition were all implicit in the practices of the guilds; the expansion of population, the emergence of citizenship, the accumulation of wealth, the efficiency of specialization and market sales led step by step to the devising of procedures which first permitted, then liberated and expanded the very division of labor with market specialization upon which the modern western economies have been built.

Commons traces out the resolution of the theretofore conflict between authority and interdependence in the emergence of property in land out of the previous array of personal services, dues, and status positions in feudalism.[8] He formulates what we may call a relationship of "practical

---

[8]Especially in Legal Foundations of Capitalism, Chapter VI, The Rent Bargain: Feudalism and Use Value.

necessity" between, or among, sovereignty, liberty, and opportunity. The liberty of persons and the opportunity to use and enjoy things and the fruits of one's labor according to one's own volition, were secured by measures which limited the exercise of arbitrary power by the king. When behavior in these areas of liberty and opportunity was systematized according to the customs of the people, the common law approach was put into effect; from liberty came the citizenship of the people; and relative to opportunity there were devised the laws of property, especially for land use and occupancy. There thus developed the three interrelated functions of sovereignty, property, and citizenship. Each limits the other. Property rights and citizenship were made possible by the restrictions imposed upon the previously unlimited prerogatives of the monarchs of England in a series of achievements by "freemen" running over the centuries from Magna Charta, 1215, to the Act of Settlement of 1700. As Commons interprets these centuries of turmoil and revolution, the outcome was the acceptance by the monarch of limits upon the exercise of royal power and prerogative, which created a zone of secure possible action by "freemen" by the assurance that the prerogative powers would not be exercised arbitrarily. This curbing of arbitrary authority created a zone where the will of at least some of the people was free. From this "indefinite residuum," "this orbit where the will is free," to use Commons' phrases[9] - came the phenomenon of property in land and rent. The curbing of the arbitrary powers of the monarch was forced by the achievement of rudimentary rights of citizenship - first by the landlords by the challenge of armed might, later by the business men through the sharing in the constitutional exercise of sovereignty[10], and still later was extended to all persons by universal suffrage. The prerogatives of the absolute monarch were reduced to the constitutional exercise of sovereignty out of the necessities of interdependence, which necessities were recognized in the behavior of successive classes of people contributing their willing participation to the economy of the realm.

Although Commons' analysis is basically of British experience, it is referred to here as an instance of a method - a method of deriving serviceable economic institutions out of the customary behavior of a people. As a research project in the institutional basis of land economics problems, this kind of inquiry would seem to have very great value in the newly developing countries. It is, we judge, a valuable and effective method, but not sufficient unto itself. There is an obvious need for systematizing concepts of law and procedure in order to provide generality and even deep validity.

The emphasis in this comment throughout has been on the public aspects of institutional analysis. Consequently to the above suggestions on possible lines of inquiry on the creation of institutions, we need to add a comment on making the distinctions of public and private in the process of development. A public point of view is essential for any set of institutions for directing the activities of land use and occupancy, since security of expectations in such matters requires that the rules be dependable over long periods of time and throughout the realm. In Commons' analysis, the public point of view emerges from the judicial function in the settlement of disputes.

---

[9]Legal Foundations, op. cit., p. 221.

[10]Ibid., pp. 104-5.

"Our analysis of a transaction has shown there is always a third party to every transaction, the judge who decides or is expected to decide every dispute upon the principle of the common rule applicable to all similar transactions... This judge, however, necessarily takes a public point of view, since his decisions must conform to what other judges have decided in similar disputes and to what the customs or laws of the community authorize and support. In applying the common rule he is conforming to public purpose. Hence the public point of view is inherent in every transaction, and just as much so in primitive society as in a credit economy." [11]

The rudiments of the distinctions between public and private, are most likely to be found, as Commons has suggested, in the group practices of even primitive people. As is well known, councils of village elders have assembled from time immemorial in the villages of Asia, and elsewhere, to settle the disputes which arose among the people regarding rights in land, etc., and to dispense justice. It would seem to be a most worthy research to inquire systematically into the ways in which these traditional practices have fared in recent centuries under the impact of colonial administration and the intrusion of laws and practices from the more technically advanced countries. Our impression is that these traditional procedures were largely ignored, if not suppressed.

A recent visitor to Russia has commented brilliantly upon the consequences of the lack of clear-cut distinctions between public and private, observing: "The Regime compels him [the "citizen"] to think exclusively in public terms: he in self defence reacts by thinking of government and society almost entirely in private terms." [12]

Peasants and elite alike in many underdeveloped countries are trapped in traditional societies where they can think only in personal and "private" terms because there are no general procedures for establishing the zones where the collective will must prevail, set off by limits which define the dependable zones of privacy and personal discretion. It is in the nature of the struggle for survival under such conditions, that the rules by which land is occupied and used should become among the first in which clear-cut distinctions should be made by dependable rules between public and private.

IV.

In conclusion and as a general orientation for the argument of the essay, three issues may be noted. First, the specialization in land economics in America has grown out of a public need to supplement the operation of land markets and resolve problems of land use and occupancy by designing institutions which supplemented the market. In this respect, professional work in land economics is a part of a larger movement in economics, which might be called the economics of public administration, which now includes such diverse fields of public action as the regulation of public utilities, the administrative determination of fair trade practices and labor standards, and the regulation of product markets under federal orders. This type of administrative economic function evidently differs from the more inclusive type of economic stabilization through monetary and fiscal policy programs

---

[11] Ibid., p. 242.

[12] Richard Pipes, "The Public Mood," Harpers Magazine, May 1961, p. 108, in Symposium on the Mood of the Russian People.

in that the administrative decisions come to a focus upon specific localized problems.

Economic analysis directed toward the administrative determination of permissible limits of specific choices and market behavior all emphasize the procedural or institutional aspect of economic organization, as well as the substantive outcome of the expected performance. Whereas it is possible in production economics, and even welfare economics, to focus upon the commodity flow of inputs and outputs, upon the transformation of resources into useful things, and arrive at significant conclusions about the production processes, as one approaches the economic problems of direct administration of the order dealt with in land economics, this type of marginal analysis is useful primarily as formulating the conditions or requirements which policy and administration should meet if resources are to be used efficiently. It is the attempt to go beyond this level of performance and embrace analytically and co-ordinately both the procedural activity and the substantive outcome in economic affairs which has led to the development of what has come to be called institutional economics, at least in formulations of Commons and as operative in land economics.

One of the critical links between the procedural and substantive approaches to economics is the phenomenon of property and property rights, in a market-opportunity oriented economy. In no area of specialization is this more central than in land economics.

It is this attempt to comprehend the procedural aspects of economic affairs, co-ordinately with the analysis of the substantive flow of commodities and services that pushes institutional analysis in the direction of collaboration among the social science disciplines. This follows from the fact, in our judgment, that the common ground of all the social sciences is the activity of man, which acts are organized into systematic concerns, or social organizations, by rules which guide and limit conduct. In this administrative-institutional field of emphasis, economists and lawyers are likely to find the most common ground, because they are both concerned with the activities of man in the processes of commodity production and exchange. The interests of lawyers, in terms of principle, are procedural. The interest of production economists is substantive. The attempt to develop an institutional formulation of economics which co-ordinates analytically the two - procedure and substance - through an institutional economics has been born of the necessity in America of supplementing freedom of contract and alienation by procedures which modified the substance of liberty and property according to due process of law.

10

Synthesis and Differentiation
of Economic Theories

by Howard W. Ottoson*

The assignment represented in this chapter is the consideration of the similarities and the differences in the frameworks of economic theory which have been covered in the three preceding chapters. A note of clarification is appropriate at this point.

The chapters by Miller and Gaffney stem from the same conceptual roots, those of neo-classical, production-distribution economics, or in the words of Boulding, commodity economics.[1] Miller has surveyed the applications of production economic theory to problems of land economics. In doing so he has paid particular attention to the limitations of production theory in the research process. Gaffney has dealt with land as a distributive mechanism, including the process by which values become imbedded in land, and the implications of private versus public rent collecting! Both Miller and Gaffney have dealt with institutions as well as "pure theory." Miller has suggested the incorporation of variable institutional arrangements into the setting of efficiency analysis in order to measure the effect of these institutions.

On the other hand Parsons starts from the framework of institutionalism, and more specifically, the institutionalism of John R. Commons. However, he has reached well over the boundaries of production-distribution economics and has emphasized the complementary relations between the two.

The discussion which follows will be concerned with the differences, similarities, and complementarities between production-welfare economics

---

[1] Kenneth Boulding, The Skills of an Economist (Cleveland: Howard Allen, Inc. 1958), Chapter 12.

---

*HOWARD W. OTTOSON has been professor and chairman of the Department of Agricultural Economics, University of Nebraska, since 1956. Born in Minnesota in 1920, he obtained his B.S. and M.S. from the University of Minnesota and his Ph.D. from Iowa State University. After some experience as a graduate instructor and with the Bank for Cooperatives, he located at Nebraska. He has worked primarily in the area of production economics, including both land economics and farm management.

on the one hand, and the institutional framework outlined by Parsons on the other.[2] Some repetition is inevitable. It will be noted also that the author has not been particularly conscientious about keeping within the bounds of land economics.

INSTITUTIONAL VERSUS PRODUCTION-DISTRIBUTION ECONOMICS

It is possible to exaggerate apparent points of argument between institutional and commodity economics; zealous proponents of either have sometimes inferred a measure of "rightness" and "practicality" to one, while attributing comparable frivolity and impracticality to the other. Thus the statement by Boulding: "Institutionalism in economics may be regarded as a premature attempt at synthesis of the social sciences, an attempt to synthesize bad economics, bad sociology, and bad anthropology in a medium of subconscious emotional bias."[3] On the other hand a sympathetic analysis of institutional economics versus what he calls "orthodox" economics was made in response to discussions at the land tenure workshop at Columbia, Missouri, in 1956, by Sargent, who is trained in institutional economics.[4]

Perhaps some of the arguments have arisen because of excess zeal on the part of students in the respective theoretical fields, for whom the particular conceptual areas still hold certain magical qualities, and for whom the newness has not yet worn off! Others are more fundamental and are related to the definition of what constitutes an appropriate research problem, and what is legitimate, worthwhile research.

It may be useful to summarize at this point some important features of the two bodies of theory of particular relevance to land economics, as interpreted from representative literature of both, in terse form. An attempt has been made to organize the summary as a series of fairly parallel characteristics from the two theoretical fields. It is recognized that in some cases the comparisons are "forced," and not entirely satisfying. Also, somewhat unintentionally production economics has been dealt with more completely than distribution and welfare economics in the first column.

Production-Distribution Economics	Institutional Economics
Deals with functional relationships between resources, between resources and products, and between products, in the processes of production, distribution, and consumption.	Deals with human behavior, human organization, and human relations of all kinds including courts, laws and administrative customs.

---

[2]Other kinds of interesting comparisons of systems of economic thought could make a similar comparison between an aggregative system of theory, such as that of Keynes, and institutional economics.

[3]Kenneth Boulding, A Reconstruction of Economics (New York: John Wiley & Sons, Inc., 1950), p. 5.

[4]Frederic O. Sargent. "A Methodological Schism in Agricultural Economics." Canadian Journal of Agricultural Economics, Vol. VIII, No. 2 (1960), pp. 45-52.

Production-Distribution
Economics (cont.)

Assumes technical relations between resources and products, and utilizes them directly in analysis. Technological advances change these technical relations, but are usually considered outside the scope of tradition analysis.

Not intrinsically interested in details of technical relations. One institutional school (The neo-Veblen school of Texas) regards technological advance, including tools, machines, materials, and instrumental knowledge of all kinds as the principal variable indicative of social progress. It suggests that technological developments outstrip institutional organization, and social progress is slowed by this conflict. Institutional patterns tend to be rigid.

Assumes preferences-priorities--registered by people for economic goods and services as given and sometimes considered outside the scope of analytical attention. In fact some writers have inferred that economists are indifferent to ends. In recent years, however, considerable attention has been given to trying to understand more about the goals and values of people. The notion of bargaining is introduced in the monopoly models, but is not recognized explicitly in the competitive model.

Emphasizes that values rise from the particular cultural and organizational setting of the society. As institutions change, so do values. However, definitions of values are hard to come by, and they need further study. But in pragmatic fashion we can still try to help people get what they want, say the institutionalists; compromises between groups at the point of a transaction may result in net benefits in the absence of knowing more about fundamental values. The emphasis by Commons on bargaining at the point of a transaction is somewhat distinctive.

Tends to assume institutional relations; takes them for granted, and intuitively accepts them as given, as for example the family, private property, the corporation, capitalism, and the nature of supply and demand. However, effort has been given to the posing of institutional arrangements as well as technical possibilities as variables (as for example the great attention which has been given in land economics to leasing arrangements, and variations in these arrangements). The "firm" is the primary maximizing unit in pro-

Our institutions are growing, changing things. They have evolved out of others which have existed in the past, and we will in turn change them into other forms. In fact the notions of technology can be applied to institutions also, namely, that they can be changed for the betterment of society. Institutionalists are inclined to look at the whole economy--private and public--as a bundle of institutions. Economics is the study of the structures and functioning of these institutions, particularly from the standpoint of human re-

Production-Distribution Economics (cont.)

duction, being an entity exercising managerial independence. Under the free competitive model the pursuit by firms of their own self-interest results in the greatest welfare for the society. (In this connection Alexander Pope is appropriate: "thus God and Nature formed the general frame and bade self-love and social be the same"!) This model has been altered, however, to the imperfectly competitive model, and the monopolistic one in recognition of different degrees to which the assumptions of the free competitive model do not hold in our society.

Rests on the efficiency criterion, which assumes that people prefer more to less, and can make rational choices. These choices are registered through the market mechanism. Older work in the area of welfare economics, in which interpersonal comparisons of utility were assumed, has been displaced by ordinal definitions of welfare, however. Under the latter it is necessary not to get a person to indicate how much utility an additional quantity of a commodity represents, but rather to indicate that he prefers, or is indifferent to, one combination or the other. [6]

Efficiency for the firm involves the maximization of returns. Other values besides those registered in monetary terms are recognized, but are sometimes troublesome to handle analytically. For example, the nonagricultural uses of land, such as recreation,

Institutional Economics (cont.)

lations as they affect the provision of material goods and services for the satisfaction of human wants. These institutions are not all readily defined nor are they mutually exclusive. Their purpose, in the words of Commons, is "collective action in control, liberation, and expansion of individual action". [5] As suggested by Parsons there is a marginalism in the notion of modifying institutional structure which is somewhat parallel to the marginalism of production theory.

Rests on procedural criteria--justice, freedom, equal access to opportunity, and assumes that cause-effect relations involving these effects can be established. Stresses that many values are not registered in the market clearly, if at all, suggests that not all goods and services can be converted into dollar values.

There is no specific condition for efficiency in the institutionalist concept which is parallel to the efficiency notion of classical economics. Institutionalism has in it an inductive property, one of "let's see how it works," of emphasis on observation and judg-

---

[5] John R. Commons, Institutional Economics, (New York: The MacMillan Company, 1934), p. 5.

[6] M. W. Reder, Studies in the Theory of Welfare Economics (New York: Columbia University Press), pp. 18-19.

pose questions of measurement of both physical product and value. In analytically parallel fashion, efficiency for the consuming unit involves the acquiring of the collection of goods and services which maximize welfare, or satisfactions. The concept of efficiency is expanded to include an industry of producing firms, or a group of consuming units.[7] The human resource is treated as a commodity in analysis; qualitative aspects of labor and management, such as pride, morale, etc., have not been dealt with adequately. Production economists have had much difficulty in trying to measure labor and management and even understanding what the latter is. The difficulties in measuring labor have complicated the estimation of marginal productivity of other factors.[8] Most analysis has been static; that is, the values taken by variables at a given point in time are dependent only upon the values taken by other variables at that point in time. Dynamic analysis, where values of variables depend upon previous behavior of the system, characterizes much work with respect to business cycles.[9] In production economics the mathematical technique of dynamic programing has been used recently to undertake dynamic analysis in the Hicksian sense, that is, by intro-

ment. There is in it an emphasis on history (e.g., German Historical School) and on philosophy. There is doubt on the part of some institutionalists (but not Commons) that man is by nature equipped to make rational choices, or that he is permitted to do so. His institutions can push him around, and coerce him, says Veblen; consumers do not always rule. Institutionalists say that our economic system is not a "natural order of things," but rather an evolutionary phenomenon stemming heavily from our mercantilist heritage and Anglo-Saxon law. Thus it is not automatically transferable to other cultures. Commons emphasized compromise, and reasonable solutions to conflicts. There is an implication of efficiency in getting as many conflicts solved as possible. Veblen stresses the workmanship instinct of labor, as opposed to the pecuniary motivations assumed by commodity theory. Commons stresses the relations between people and their institutional arrangements, and those between one group and another, and particularly their conflicts. Governments are one type of group, albeit more powerful, and more apt to be neutral. Labor is the real focus in institutional economics, and the notion that organization affects labor's energy and

---

[7]M. W. Reder, op. cit., Chapter I.

[8]For an interesting and realistic discussion in which conventional theory is used as hypotheses to explain the contribution of people to economic growth as related to investments in the personal assets of people, see Theodore W. Schultz, "Investment in Human Capital," The American Economic Review, Vol. LI, No. 1 (March 1961), pp. 1-17. Research attention has recently been given to the management factor in the Interstate Managerial Survey carried on in seven states of the north central region. See David H. Bryne and Glenn L. Johnson, "A Partial Evaluation of Static Theory from Results of the Interstate Managerial Survey," Journal of Farm Economics, Vol. XL, No. 2 (May 1958), pp. 458-69.

[9]W. J. Baumol, Economic Dyamics (London: Macmillan and Company 1951), Chapter 7; and R. G. D. Allen, Mathematical Economics (London: Macmillan and Company, 1957), Chapter 1.

Production-Distribution
Economics (cont.)

Institutional Economics (cont.)

ducing time through dated variables. 10

creativity. The commodity aspects
of labor are only secondary. The
problems of statics and dynamics
are not comparable since institutionalism does not embrace a
basic mathematically consistent
static equilibrium theory. There
is no notion of the ideal state, or
deviations from a physically tangible norm.

Tends to regard institutions,
including price-making institutions (markets) and institutions of
control and finance as "limita-
tional," inferring that if the "obstacles are removed" economic
improvements will take place. In
the absence of other consideration
it is desirable to have as much
freedom as possible in the private
sector.

Institutions (including business
organization and practice) can be
barriers; Commons also suggests
that they can be positive vari-
ables--in other words, a type of
new technologies--releasing new
possibilities for improving welfare.
As positive forces requiring
ingenuity to devise and operate,
they deal not only with resources,
but also with efficiency in decision-
making, and with democratic values.

Relies on related technological
disciplines, as well as social
disciplines such as psychology and
sociology.

Relies on closely related
social disciplines of political
science, group psychology, sociology, and law.

The production-distribution
model has in it inherent mechanisms to bring the system to an
equilbrium. It is recognized that
various disturbances upset the
system continually, but the equilibrium concept is still operationally
useful.

Does not recognize any notion
of equilibrium; the only normal
thing in the world is change. The
best we can hope to do is to study
the courses of action which man
can take in controlling and improving his environment, and try
to provide him with more knowledge with which to do so. A type
of equilibrium is present in institutional arrangements in that they
tend to be interrelated and slow
to change. Often the "forces"
supporting change are not strong
enough to overcome those supporting established arrangements.

---

10 James S. Plaxico, "Dynamic Programming and Management Strategies in the Great Plains"
Management Strategies in Great Plains Farming, Nebraska Agr. Exp. Misc. Pub. 7, Great Plains
Agricultural Council Publication 19, August 1961. See also Laurel B. Loftsgard and Earl O. Heady,
"Application of Dynamic Programming Models for Optimal Farm and Home Plans," Journal of Farm
Economics, Vol. 41, No. 1 (February 1959), pp. 51-62.

THE ROLE OF THEORY IN RESEARCH

Theory versus Hypotheses

Part of the arguments between those who subscribe to production distribution economic theory and those who follow the paths of the institutionalists arise in the confusion about the questions "What is theory"? and "What is a hypothesis"? The answer to the first is not simple, and one finds that a great deal of philosophical attention has been given to it. [11] However, theory is usually assumed to have a mathematical character, and to be in the nature of an if-then proposition. A theory which is logically tight is self-evident in and of itself. Its truth or falsity must be determined outside of the logic, in other words, on the basis of the truth or falsity of the assumptions from which it is generated. However, beyond its being a chain of logic, it seems reasonable to suppose that economic theory has assumed the role it has because of its attributes of reality, or more precisely that its assumptions are reasonably realistic. There is no denying the usefulness of demand theory, or of the principle of diminishing marginal returns, to economists, and there is no need to cite literature to verify this fact. However, Halter suggests that too little attention has been paid to the underlying assumptions of our traditional theory, that they are assumed to be known "by intuition," that they are "self-obvious" or known by any "rational" or "competent" mind. [12] He suggests that the burden of proof still rests with those who take this position. Further, there have been others who, without pausing to rationalize the underlying assumptions, have followed theoretical logic directly through to policy conclusions, under the premise that, in the absence of evidence, empirically valid prescriptions can be deducted from theory, as the next best alternative.

In contrast to the Austrians who have viewed economics as a "pure" (mathematical) science, most economists are properly conscious of the empirical underpinnings of economic theory. As Wiener suggests, "Any useful logic must concern itself with ideas with a fringe of vagueness and a Truth which is a matter of degree. A Logic which ignores the actual history of ideas and limitations of human faculty is a logic in vacuo, and is useless." [13] However, at its best, theory must be viewed as an abstraction of the world, and not an adequate explanation of it. This is not unique in our field alone. For example quoting again the Wiener article:

> Von Neuman has shown that .... the indeterminacy of the world is genuine and fundamental. There are no clean-cut laws of motion which enable us to predict the momentum and position of the world at future times in terms of any observable dates whatever at the present time. In other words, while it is possible to give an account of the world in terms of our observations which themselves disturb our world, this account has only

---

[11]For a recent, interesting discussion of the subject of theory in Agricultural Economics see A. N. Halter and H. H. Jack. "Toward a Philosophy of Science for Agricultural Economics Research " Journal of Farm Economics, Vol. XLIII, No. 1 (February 1961), pp. 83-95.

[12]Ibid. The writers are referring to statements from Frank H. Knight, "What is Truth in Economics," Journal of Political Economy, Vol. 480 (February 1940), p. 5.

[13]Norbert Wiener, "The Role of the Observer," Philosophy of Science, Vol. 3 (July 1936), pp. 307-19.

186

statistical validity, and cannot be brought closer by the precision of any chain of observations. Thus physics, the most exact of all sciences, has had to have a thorough logical housecleaning. We no longer conceive the laws of physics to apply to some mystical world of reality behind our observations and instruments; they merely constitute an intelligible statement of the manner in which our observations and the readings of our instruments hang together. About any proposition of physics we must ask: does it enable us to predict the results of actual or possible experiment. If it does, it stands or falls with this experiment; if not, it has no meaning whatever. Physics is merely a coherent way of describing the readings of physical instruments.[14]

The logic of our normal thinking, in which universals exist, but have no perfectly clear-cut outlines, and in which the growth of universals is real, and not a mere fictitious account of our perception of eternal verities is inductive logic. Deductive logic and canons of pure introspection only exist as ideal limiting cases of inductive logic.

When I want an auxiliary function to do a definite job, I try one after another, finding the first too big here, the second too small there, until by the grace of luck and familiarity with the habits of the species, I come an exact fit. Nine-tenths of the possibilities are eliminated on the basis of a general feeling for the situation before it comes to a matter of any real deductive logic whatever. The tenth suggestion slips into place in a way which convinces an old hand that there is something in it--it resolves the difficulties at just the right points, but not so readily as to excite suspicions of a sheer blunder.[15]

Even if the above is overdrawn for emphasis it illustrates the empiricism which is characteristic of many modern philosophers. Where does this lead us? It is the suggestion of the writer that there is an important difference between theory as such and what may be called an operational hypothesis. Theory will contribute to, but probably will not constitute an operational hypothesis. Its large role is that of serving as a source of ideas in research. In considering this notion we must start with the definition of the problem situation. The operational hypothesis is designed specifically to cope with the uncertainties of the problem situation, and to expose knowledge about cause and effect relations which are operative or which can be made operative in the problem situation. From what stuff is the operational hypothesis formed? It is based on casual observation, previous work, deductive logic thought to be empirically descriptive, and judgment. It will be tailored to the sorts of fragmentary evidence which may constitute all the knowledge that is available; it may even be conditioned by the size of one's budget. It will be a work of art in the best sense of the word, in that it will be a direct result of the perceptive power, imagination, persistence, and knowledge of the research worker. It will reflect the worker's opinion of the expected nature of relationships, on the kinds of evidence necessary, and on the

---

[14]Norbert Wiener, op. cit., pp. 311-12.

[15]Norbert Wiener, op. cit., pp. 315-16.

degree of probability necessary to support or reject the hypothesis.[16]

The operational hypothesis will be a model of a very small part of a very large and complicated world. Wold suggests that "... an integrated theory is like an iceberg, and the small part visible above water is the hypothesis that is specified in the analysis of given data; a self-contained experiment makes explicit use only of the visible part, but with observational data the hypothesis testing will often draw material from the part of the iceberg which is submerged. [17]

In view of the above qualifications one might even be suspicious of the notion that objectivity is a sufficient condition for uniformity of results between two research men, even under ideal conditions. Two men, with the same access to theory, and working on the same problem in economics will not necessarily come out with precisely the same answers, in view of the subjective nature of hypothesis formulation and testing. [18]

What does the preceding somewhat labored discussion have to do with arguments between "traditionalists" and "institutionalist"? Simply this: The productive research man will not be interested in particular theory per se when he is at the stage of problem formulation. However, as he cuts and pieces together his model, his operational hypothesis, he will draw on relevant segments of theory as appropriate. His concern may be primarily resource oriented, or organization oriented, or both. His knowledge of theory may suggest the form of a useful relationship to him, or he might alter the "shape" of it considerably for purposes of his analysis. He will of course be interested in the results of similar hypotheses tested by others. [19]

The Role of Institutionalism

Another source of quarrels in the land economics family between institutionalists and production-distribution economists probably lies in the uncertainty about the place of institutionalism in the world of theory. Can institutional economics be considered a type of running mate for production-distribution theory, whose company the production-distributionist can either accept or reject? Or, is it a question of how many parts of institutionalism to mix in the batter? These questions miss the nature of institutionalism--what it is and what it is not.

We would suggest that institutionalism is not a theory in the same sense as production theory. It does not include a logically framed set of propositions; its assumptions are vague, and at times one is tempted to

---

[16]"The slightly juvenile conception of the cold-blooded, emotionless, passive scientist mirroring the world perfectly in the highly polished lenses of his steel rimmed glasses,--this stereotype--is no longer, if it ever was, adequate". From Richard Rudner, "The Scientist qua Scientist Makes Value Judgments," Philosophy of Science, Vol. 20, No. 1 (January 1953), pp. 1-6.

[17]Herman Wold. "Casual Inference from Observational Data," Journal of the Royal Statistical Society, Series A. (General), Vol. 119, Part I (1956).

[18]The term operational hypothesis as used here is probably synonomous with the term "model" used by Boulding. (See Kenneth Boulding, op. cit., p. 16) Halter used the term "scientific theory" for the same purpose, and suggests three necessary conditions if the theory is to be in accord with the empiricist viewpoint: (1) the statements of a theory must be in part, and usually in the main, synthetic a posteriori statements; (truth based on experience) (2) it should be genuinely descriptive and explanatory; (3) it will stand or fall on the basis of empirical tests. (Halter and Jack, op. cit., p. 92.)

[19]The reader will have recognized by now that the terms "theory" and "hypothesis" are being used in specialized fashion in this discussion.

suggest that its theoretical models are even more vague. What, then, is it? It would seem that institutionalism is an approach, a philosophy, rather than a theory. By nature it is an integrative philosophy, drawing on several theoretical roots. We must recognize, with Boulding, that the psychological contribution of some institutionalists may have been of no greater merit than that which they in turn have attributed to Bentham and others. Other institutionalists have been awed by the great number of variables which operate in the world and have ended up with a sense of frustration because they tried to grasp too many handles at once. Institutionalists seem to rely more heavily on intuition than production-distribution economists, partly due to the complexity of the problems which they define.

Viewing it objectively, institutionalism as a field would seem to draw on political science for insights and hypotheses on the organization of political groups, and the administrative relations between people. It draws similarly on sociology for insights on the group relations between people; it stresses psychology for explanations of why people behave in the ways (not always rational) in which they do. It looks to law for the specification of the legal institutions which bound and direct the activities of man. It refers us to history for perspective, particularly with respect to change. And so, we as economists have been chided by the institutionalists in various ways. We have been challenged to re-examine the philosophical basis for the assumptions underlying our analysis, and the theoretical models which we use. [20] We have been asked whether it is really feasible to seek "ideal" solutions in our analysis, or whether rather we can only chip away piece by piece at problems involving "felt" difficulties in order that the circumstances giving rise to problem situations can be alleviated, or in order that people can make choices more effectively. Our psychological assumptions have been taken to task, and research work by psychologists has indicated some basis for complaint. [21] We have been encouraged to become aware of history, although historical analysis has not yet been accepted as having quite the same degree of sophistication as other analytical approaches. We have encouraged political scientists to become interested in the political and administrative aspects of economic problems. [22] We have seen the great interest in co-operative work between lawyers and economists, and have also discovered that co-operation was not a magic wand which could be brandished to bring forth integrated work automatically. [23] The "family farm" concept has figured in arguments between the efficiency-minded and the institutionally-oriented; perhaps intellectual progress is represented in the difference between the present day concept and that of twenty years ago. And more recently has been the interest in organization, and the

[20]See Carl M. Bogholt, "The Value Judgment and Land Tenure Research," Proceedings of the Land Tenure Workshop, University of Missouri, 1956, p. 133.

[21]George Katona, Psychological Analysis of Economic Behaviour (New York: McGraw Hill 1951). Katona shakes the underpinnings of what Keynes called a "fundamental psychological law" about the relation between income and saving.

[22]W. Robert Parks, "Political and Administrative Guide-lines in Developing Public Agricultural Policies," Journal of Farm Economics, Vol. XXXIII, No. 2 (May 1951), pp. 157-68; and Charles Hardin, The Politics of Agriculture (Glencoe, Illinois: Free Press, 1952).

[23]John F. Timmons, "Integrating Law and Economics in Analyzing Agricultural Land Use Problems," Journal of Farm Economics, Vol. XXXVII, No. 5 (December 1955), pp. 1126-1142.

concern with organization structure and communication in administrative entities. [24]

Thus, the major theoretical contribution of the institutionalists has been their pragmatic prodding, rather than distinct theoretical formulations. We probably have to retreat from too dogmatic a statement on this, however. Veblen's "Theory of the Leisure Class" or his "Instinct of Workmanship" are specific formulations, as in a different sense is Commons' "transactions." However, I would question any suggestion that the institutional analysis of Commons reaches an ultimate generalization of economic system referred to as Communism, Capitalism, Feudalism, as being so broad as to be without meaning. But an important contribution of institutionalism is the synthesis into which it forces itself by virture of its pragmatic approach. (Synthesis is not unique to institutionalism, of course.) Commons did not view institutional economics as a substitute system. Rather, he said the "The problem now is not to create a different kind of economics--'institutional economics'--divorced from preceding schools, but how to give to collective action, in all its varieties, its due place throughout economic theory."[25]

What is Synthesis of Economic Theory?

> There was a dachshund once, so long
> He hadn't any notion
> How long it took to notify
> His tail of his emotion.
>
> And so it happened, while his eyes
> Were filled with woe and sadness
> His little tail went wagging on
> Because of previous gladness.[26]

Webster defines synthesis as the combination of separate elements into a complex whole. Several meanings of the term may be applied to land economics analysis.

A first meaning might refer to research. It does not seem possible to synthesize economic theories in the sense that we can take production theory and institutional theory and come out with a hybrid with green hair and blue eyes. Theories are logically derived relations generating from specific assumptions. However, as we have suggested, there is a difference between theory and hypothesis. A set to operational hypotheses in a research problem may embody theoretical fragments from several subject-matter areas. These hypotheses are to be tested, and either accepted or rejected. They can include the effects of specific institutions on resource allocation, for example, or the effect of one institutional change on another institutional arrangement, or the outcome of resource transformation in terms of an economic product. The degree of synthesis

---

[24]Kenneth Boulding, op. cit., Chapter III. See also Herbert A. Simon, Models of Man (New York: John Wiley and Sons, 1955).

[25]As quoted in John S. Gambs and Sidney Wertimer, Jr., Economics and Man (Homewood, Illinois; Richard D. Irwin, Inc., 1959), p. 198.

[26]From Glenn Negley, The Organization of Knowledge (New York: Prentice Hall, Inc., 1942), p. 62.

represented in the operational hypothesis will depend on the way in which a problem situation is defined, and on the particular relations which are deemed to be important.

This is the eclectic approach. Eclecticism is not the compromising or hybridization of differing conceptual fields of thought; rather, it is the selection of interesting elements from these fields where they appear useful to the purposes of the research worker.

A second meaning of synthesis relates to training of research workers. Here synthesis becomes a matter of understanding, of being able to go from production theory to economic history, to psychology, to law, and to seek out the conceptual fragments, the tools, which will be useful in explaining the particular bits of phenomena with which we are concerned. This is difficult, as we know from experience. It is demanding enough to become qualified and to stay qualified in the field of one's choice, without trying to master others even closely allied. However, the differences between fields are sometimes exaggerated. For example, the various social sciences are not different because they deal with different kinds of subject matter, fundamentally; they are different aspects of the same subject matter, and different vocabularies for describing them. In order to take advantage of the efficiencies of specialization, workers from two related fields can work together on a research problem, as for example, a lawyer and an economist. However, placing a lawyer and an economist side by side does not automatically insure a synthesized product. Until each of them, or at least one of them, can feel somewhat familiar with the other man's field, and visualize the important relations between variables in that area, little communication, and consequently little synthesis may take place.

A third application of synthesis is policy-making, or policy-advising. The bridge between inaction and action is knowledge, and synthesis is involved in the placement of the girders, the design of the braces, and in the mixture of sand and cement in the mortar. A policy advisor must be familiar with the various fields in which his problems are framed. His boss will not appreciate it if too many times the worker crosses himself with the qualification "Everything else being equal," or "assuming free competition." In policy implementation the parts of dog must move together!

Again, synthesis is an art; it is a matter of judgment, and breadth of knowledge. The art of being able to utilize theoretical frameworks in creating effective hypotheses, of being able to assemble the evidence with which to test them, and of being able to translate the results into significant and interesting findings has its own qualities of rarity and beauty.

Land economists may justifiably reserve for themselves a measure of pride at having achieved some success in integrating into their work insights from many related disciplines. With the expanding commitment which our nation is making concerning the economic progress of many other countries, land economists are likely to be called on in increasing measure to play roles which will represent mixtures of research, education, and policy-advising. As such, they are going to be forced to act as generalists, to be synthesizers of knowledge.

SYNTHESIS ILLUSTRATED

Research on Land Easements

A research situation from land economics is presented below to illustrate the idea of synthesis. This is followed by some consideration of the implications of synthesis for economic development problems.

The project described is one in which the author is involved in very small measure. It is entitled "The Land Easement Device as a Means of Resource Adjustment." It is not introduced here because it is held to be a model project, or because there are interesting results available, but because it illustrates rather aptly the way theoretical concepts from several disciplines become amalgamated in one research undertaking. The situation is briefly as follows: The land easement device, whereby the federal government might buy easements in perpetuity on the rights for specified uses of certain farm land, has been proposed as a means whereby desirable shifts in land use might be encouraged, and whereby long-run adjustments of labor and certain types of capital in agriculture might also be accomplished, in the interest of production reduction.

The basic objective of the research is to determine whether this proposal is a feasible means of satisfying the policy objectives which have been suggested for it. Obviously, this objective is too general to tell one much. It has to be broken down into component parts which imply more directly the kinds of evidence that might be useful when a decision is finally made concerning policy. It is obvious that the economic implications of several types would be important in a consideration of this proposal. However, other types of questions which might be loosely called institutional questions are also likely to be important to a decision. Below are the components into which this problem might be broken down, with an indication of the type of relationship or data implied in each.

1. Legal framework. The decision-maker would want to know whether the federal government can legally acquire and hold the type of use-easements described, and if so, by what powers? Could the easement be released and under what conditions? These questions require the posing of the organizational arrangement in a legal setting and would involve inferences from statutes and from court cases relating to the powers of the federal and state governments.

2. Program organization and administration. The matter of federal, state, and local organization for the program is implied. Obviously there are several organizational alternatives, each with its individual strengths, weaknesses, and administrative efficiency. The administrative processes required by the specific program would affect the organization. Consideration would be given to the nature of existing program structure, and the possibility of using existing administrative framework. Such things as the physical measurement of easements, records, and enforcement have both organizational and legal implications. Local responsibility and local acceptance are terms which imply additional analytical attention.

   This topic implies the insights of political science. However, like the rest, it cannot finally be left in isolation. The economics objectives which are proposed will bear on the nature of the administrative organization; likewise the organizational and operational feasibilities will condition the economic effect. Both would be created by this program, and each would affect the other.

3. <u>Supply of and demand for easements.</u> Questions of measurement occur immediately. How is supply measured? In acres? In bushels? The basic relation in which we are interested from the supply side is the number of units of the "commodity" made available for purchase at various prices. Several related variables underlie the supply concept; these include types of crops, types of soils, sizes of soil areas, size of farm, and other resources besides those associated with land, such as machinery and livestock which will affect the nature of supply response. The type of tenure will also affect the supply of easements. This area is a complicated one involving particularly the conceptual insights of a production economist.

   The demand side is represented in the magnitude of the program which is posed from outside the problem itself. The number of acres of specified types of land for which a change in use is desired may already be specified; or the primary objective may be a reduction in feed production of specified amount. Finally, aggregate effects may not be specified, in which case different levels represent alternative choices which the society will eventually have to make.

4. <u>Consequences associated with tenure arrangements.</u> On the one hand the tenure arrangements will channel the aggregate economic effects of the program; on the other hand, the program, as a variable, will affect these arrangements. Questions of dissociation of costs and returns occur. On rented farms the basic rights would be purchased from landlords, but some consequences would be borne by tenants. What are the issues of equity here? What arrangements will be equitable, as well as efficient? What will happen to land values, and to the security of credit agencies which have lent funds on the basis of land? What changes in credit arrangement might be called for? The tenure specialist would be expected to contribute intellectually to this facet.

5. <u>Consequences in the nonfarm sector of farm communities.</u> Several complicated questions come to mind: What will be the effects of the program on the volume of business flow, and more fundamentally on employment? What of the demand for public services--schools, roads, power, government? What will happen to public revenues with which these services are financed? What are the welfare and equity aspects of these questions?

6. <u>The aggregate consequences.</u> The research topic which we posed is rapidly getting out of hand, but assuming a national program, or at least a regional program, several aggregative aspects would challenge an economist who concerns himself with these matters. What would be the effect of the program on the labor factor in farming? Specifically what kinds of farm people would be affected by the program, and over what time periods? What are the implications to education, and to the labor market? What about capital in farming? What are the implications to credit arrangements? What are the consequences to supplies of agricultural products, and to their prices?

   In the fairly simple problem which has been posed we have ranged from the individual family and farm to the region and the nation. We have looked to several species of economists, as well as members of other social disciplines for insights. A change in one type of variable has implications for other variables. The **circular aspects** or relationships has been illustrated. If we twist the dog's tail, or prick him with a pin, he will growl, or at least eye us reproachfully, given enough time. He might even bite, thus completing the circuit.

All of the sectors mentioned are relevant to the kinds of decisions involved in the instituting of this new type of land use adjustment program.

Synthesis in Economic Development

Problems of economic development are not unique to the so-called underdeveloped countries of the world. Probably no country is uninterested in economic development, and least of all the United States, despite the material level which it has attained. However, typical references to the term visualize the large number of countries in the world with levels of national income per capita at exceedingly low levels, say $50, $100, $200, or $300 per capita. Of course, the dollar values are simply symbols of very low levels of physical welfare.

Economic development in concept infers synthesis of economic theories. What is economic development? It is a process which focuses on growth, on rise in per capita real incomes. We are interested in such things as the rates of change, the stability or instability of these rates, and in the lengths of the periods over which rapid rates of growth are sustained. We are also interested in the sequence of expansion in production and factor use, with the interaction over time between producers, consumers, and investors in interrelated sectors of the economy. Any causal factor which may affect growth is of interest, and consequently any theoretical tool which may explain a particular phenomenon contributing to growth is relevant. Further, in most developing countries today there is a sense of urgency, of the need to have everything happen at once; thus we have the concept of "balanced growth," the simultaneous expansion of a number of sectors of production. In the eyes of the policy-makers, at least, there may be a willingness to change institutions which is greater than that of more advanced countries. In the eyes of common people there may also be a pressure to overthrow certain established institutions, although certain institutions may also be remarkably stable. In fact, in developed economies the tradition and momentum of economic advance may have weakened traditional institutions and created a favorable environment for the creation of new ones. On the other hand, in the less developed countries, the absence of economic advance creates a motivation for the maintenance of status, rather than for achieving it, and a reliance on institutions to preserve the status quo.

What are some of the characteristics of underdeveloped countries of particular interest to a land economist? Some are listed below:

1. Low per capita income,
2. High proportion of people on the land,
3. Disguised unemployment among agricultural workers,
4. Low amounts of non-land capital per head in agriculture,
5. Overpopulation in rural areas,
6. Small and fragmented holdings of land, encouraged by systems of inheritance,
7. Importance of the family and the village as institutional forms, and the regulation by tradition, including religion, of much of the social and economic activity,

8. Poor credit facilities, with very high interest rates,
9. Soil erosion,
10. A tendency to push crop yields to the physical limit, although the yields may be low,
11. Low levels of education,
12. A high degree of labor immobility,
13. Land sometimes owned communally or tribally rather than individually,
14. Little entrepreneurial activity--risk-taking and innovation-- of the kind known in developed countries,
15. High rentals on rented land.

What theoretical tools does an economist apply in a research situation while working in an underdeveloped country? The suggestion is occasionally made that the economics of western countries do not "fit" in underdeveloped countries. However, most writers on economic development seem to contradict this idea; for example Bauer and Yamey state that "There are no special economic theories or methods of analysis fashioned uniquely for the study of the underdeveloped world. But while the tools of analysis are of wide relevance, in a study of underdeveloped countries the situations to which they must be applied vary greatly".[27] However, "The economist, although equipped with versatile general purpose tools, must proceed with caution in the way in which he uses them and in the identification of the relevant data in a situation or problem to which he is applying them." Bauer and Yamey go on to suggest that:

> Whether the direction and content of economic activity are determined primarily by the market mechanism or by government directives, the functioning of the economics system is profoundly influenced by the institutional framework, within which it takes place; and, in turn, the framework is necessarily affected by government action. The establishment of institutions suitable for the efficient operation of the economic system does not necessarily emerge from the operation of the system itself. For example, the market cannot be expected to bring about a suitable law of property or the institution of limited liability. Changed conditions may render obsolete existing institutions and the economic endeavor of individuals and firms may be frustrated unless the institutional structure is consciously and appropriately reshaped.[28]

Synthesis and its relevance can be illustrated in an underdevelopment situation by a simple example; assume a general problem situation posed by the interest of policy-makers in country X in increasing the production of agricultural products through expanded use of fertilizer. In pursuit of this interest, questions have been raised concerning degree, results, and organization of policy. On first glance this does not seem to be a prob-

---

[27]Peter T. Bauer and Basil S. Yamey. The Economics of Underdeveloped Countries (Chicago: The University of Chicago Press, 1957), pp. 8-9. See also Benjamin Higgins, Economic Development (New York: W. W. Norton & Co., Inc., 1959); and W. Arthur Lewis, The Theory of Economic Growth (Homewood, Illinois: Richard D. Irwin, Inc., 1955).

[28]Bauer and Yamey, op. cit. p. 142.

lem which would customarily be labeled land economics. However, there are important land economics questions involved, as well as questions relating to other disciplines. Let us consider it first at the local level of the village or tribe.

One aspect of the fertilizer problem which would obviously need early consideration would be the related technical practices, including planting rates, water use (in case irrigation were available), tillage practices, and equipment. The relation of fertilizer use to these technologies, and the effect of these technologies on fertilizer response would call for the knowledge of the agronomist and the engineer.

A corollary question posed by this technological complex concerns education. What kinds of training, such as short courses and demonstrations, would be most effective in introducing these technologies to the village? What kinds of technicians and teachers would be necessary for the dissemination of this knowledge? Where would they come from?

Another technological question would relate to the productivity potential of the fertilizer input when injected into the village economy, in other words, the regional input-output relation? What does this mean in value terms, assuming the appropriate accompanying shifts in resource combinations and levels of other resources? (We shall refer to the market valuation problem posed by this question later.)

The village or tribal culture may be a mysterious and frustrating phenomenon to an impatient economist who has concluded that fertilizer appears to offer interesting prospects for enhancement of productivity of village resources. It may be sinful to use chemicals. Or, the local medicine man may have some time-honored device such as a rag on a stick which is firmly imbedded in farming practice as insurance against crop failure. Someone is going to have to delve into the complexities of the local religion and mores. Are there facets in the local beliefs which can be turned to the advantage of fertilizer? By what means can the medicine man or priest be converted from an antagonist to an ally? Will education of the people reduce any inhibiting effect of these prior beliefs? Another type of value problem is represented here -- cultural tradition versus increased productivity.

The extended family--the cultural privilege by which even distant relatives share in new economic gains by an individual--may be an equally serious problem which may partially explain the backward sloping supply curve suggested as a characteristic of underdeveloped society by some writers. What are the quantitative aspects of this, that is, how much prosperity, if any, can an individual risk before his in-laws move in on him? What happens if the majority of farmers in the village share in the prosperity? Are there any social solutions which might alleviate the effects of the extended family tradition?

The tenure system can pose several questions related to the use of a new resource like fertilizer. What effect, if any, will fragmented hold-ings have on the use of more fertilizer, in view of the accompanying technologies? Fertilizer by itself may not involve any economies of scale but some of the other technologies which accompany it may. Who holds title to the land--individual farmers, resident landlords, absentee land-lords, or the whole village? How will this affect fertilizer use? What cost-sharing arrangements can be worked out, and what will be their impact? Who will apply the fertilizer, and who will get the gains?

Closely related will be the credit system. What are the present debt levels of the tenant or the owner-operators, and how does this affect the level of fertilizer use? Do the villagers have untapped credit available in quantities necessary to finance additional fertilizer, and accompanying technologies? Perhaps alternative credit organizations need to be explored, such as co-operative societies, governmental agencies, or governmentally regulated and sponsored private programs? Each will "cost"; each will have its own effects.

The matter of market prices was inferred previously. How much of the total agricultural product has been exported previously from the community, and what are the factors affecting the quantity moving out? Is there an efficient market system available through which to move additional product, or will one have to be created? Are the values now reflected in the local market place reflective of the social "values" which may be placed on increased food production at the national level? Several institutional devices such as co-operative marketing organizations, state marketing agencies, or governmental supervision may be considered as alternatives where the present market system is not efficient.

The above are some of the considerations which would be important at the local level to anyone who is trying to make more knowledge available to policy-makers on the subject of fertilizer use. There are still other questions which will need attention from the aggregative standpoint. The primary information of interest to the minister of agriculture would be what fertilizer use would mean in terms of the increase in food production for the country as a whole. The national economic planning agency would also wish to consider the impact of this increased food when distributed in alternative ways through the economy of the country. It might also be interested in the quantity of labor which might be released in a given period by the incorporation of fertilizer in agriculture, and would already be considering alternatives uses for the labor in both the private and public sectors. Where will the fertilizer come from? Will it be imported, thus requiring foreign exchange? Or will it be produced by plants as yet unbuilt, and which may require exchange for the importation of equipment and technical assistance?

This example illustrates the complexity of the questions posed by the introduction of even a simple resource into the economy of an underdeveloped country. Synthesis as far as research is concerned will be forced by the nature of the questions asked by policy-makers working with a sense of urgency to promote growth in all sectors.

CONCLUSION

Many other examples could be cited to illustrate the complementarity between various conceptual fields in research. Most research workers engage in synthesis, whether intentionally or intuitively. It cannot be forced, or prescribed; rather it is apt to occur naturally as a function of one's knowledge about the causal relations involved in the problem at hand.

The eclectic approach emphasizes the need for objectivity regarding theory; a research worker with a strong ideological bias toward a particular field of theory is not apt to regard either his own framework, or others, in completely detached fashion. The eclectic approach infers the ability to regard an interesting explanation of social phenomena unemotionally, it involves intellectual curiosity, a profound desire to see what "makes things tick," a readiness to ask naive questions and to discard one explanation in favor of another.

PART III. PROCEDURAL FRAMEWORK

11

Interdisciplinary Approaches to Land Economics Research

by Glenn L. Johnson*

Land economics solves problems - it deals with economic problems associated with land. If problem-solving were not involved, land economics would probably be only economics, specialized to deal with one factor of production, land, and interdisciplinary discussions would have little relevance.

Land economics is and has been problem oriented, however, and problems do not respect academic organization charts and the subcategories of abstract classifications found in man-made concepts of his academic endeavors. Typically, problems are interdisciplinary requiring knowledge from several different academic disciplines for both definition and solution.[1] Further, the required range of interdisciplinary activity includes both the normative and the factual or descriptive disciplines. Problems involving only factual or normative knowledge are mainly academic and occur when (1) the pure positivist is choosing among hypotheses concerning the nature of reality[2] and (2) the pure normativist is addressing himself to questions of goodness and/or badness. In the solution of practical problems purely factual and purely normative questions are ordinarily

---

[1] Glenn L. Johnson, "Some Reflections on the Nature of Managerial Problems," A Study of Managerial Processes of Midwestern Farmers, ed. by Johnson, et al. (Ames: Iowa University Press, 1961).

[2] Statistical estimation and prediction can be viewed as choosing among all possible alternative hypotheses.

---

*GLENN L. JOHNSON has been professor of agricultural economics at Michigan State University since 1952. Born in Minnesota in 1918, he obtained his B.S. from the University of Illinois, his M.A. from Michigan State University, and his Ph.D. from The University of Chicago. After four years with the Bureau of Agricultural Economics and an equal period with the University of Kentucky, he went to his present location. He has done extended advanced study, including a period abroad. His main interest is in general agricultural economics, including production economics where he has conducted special researches. He is or has served as, a consultant to the U.S.D.A., T.V.A., State Department and the Norwegian Agricultural Economics Research Institute at the Universities of California (Berkeley) and Manchester.

subquestions (problems?) involved in solving the practical problem of bringing about a reconciliation between reality and some system of normative concepts.

Defining and solving practical problems may require three different kinds of factual knowledge: (1) descriptions of present conditions; (2) descriptions of the consequences (generally future) of alternative actions - the "if ..., then ..." statements of science and (3) descriptions of what will happen (predictions) regardless of what is done.

It should be understood, without stating it, that factual knowledge involves functional relationships among events as well as the events themselves.

In addition, defining and solving practical problems requires criteria (normative concepts). For instance, descriptive concepts examined in view of a normative concept may indicate that reality involves less goodness than it could or more badness than it could. Predictions and the "if ..., then..." statements of science may indicate that reality can be changed or will change. The problem is to select one of the alternative changes as best -- as the right thing to do.

Selecting the right[3] involves finding an appropriate compromise among the "goods" and "bads" involved in view of what is, of what will be regardless, and of what can be, if so-and-so is done. Thus, solving as contrasted to defining a problem involves information about alternative decision methods and arrangements (institutions). Still further information is required on how to use a particular decision-making method or arrangement such as, for example, a free enterprise economy, a democratic political system, or the French legal structure.

The range of required interdisciplinary work may cover any or all of the factual and normative disciplines.

A further complicating factor arises from the roles played by various philosophic points of view about the nature of inquiry and man and society. Some points of view serve to limit inquiry to the factual to the exclusion of normative disciplines, thus placing limitations on the range of interdisciplinary activity. Others would limit inquiry to the normative to the exclusion of the positive disciplines thus placing a different set of limitations on the range of interdisciplinary activities.

Differing philosophic conceptions about the nature of man and society place similar restrictions on research. Following Plato, Hegel, and Marx, man is sometimes regarded as a component part of groups deriving what significance he has from the roles he plays in such groups. Conversely, Hobbes, Locke, Rousseau, Kant, Bentham, and J.S. Mill regard man primarily as an individual who may be (at times) a building block in groups which he creates to serve the simple sum of his individualistic purposes. Obviously, the combination of these views of man and society followed in land economics research alters the pattern of interdisciplinary activity which will be followed in solving land economic problems.

In this chapter, three broad streams in American agricultural thought will be discussed. These streams of thought profoundly influence the interdisciplinary character of agricultural economic research. Then, the author's relationship to these streams of thought and his interdisciplinary experience will be examined. After this, an examination will be present-

---

[3]C. I. Lewis, The Ground and Nature of the Right (New York: Columbia University Press, 1955).

ed of how various philosophies and disciplines (both factual and normative) have contributed to the solution of three problems involving land. The problems to be examined originated in connection with: (1) the T.V.A. and the activities of Cap Edmonds, a local western Kentucky farm leader; (2) the operation of the burley tobacco price support and production control program; and (3) the pickle-producing industry of Michigan.

The examination of these three cases will lead to conclusions about the relevance of different philosophic positions and their implications for interdisciplinary research. These conclusions will lead to further conclusions about doing, organizing, and training for land economic research.

THREE STREAMS IN AMERICAN AGRICULTURAL ECONOMIC THOUGHT

To understand land economics research in 1961, requires perspective with respect to at least three streams of agricultural economic thought. One of these is the rationalistic stream which came into U.S. agricultural economics from the classical and neoclassical economists via such men as Carver and Taylor. The second stream has origins in the Baconian positivism of the physical sciences and in statistics; it came into the discipline via George Warren (including his numerous disciplines) and Pearson.[4] The third stream was pragmatic, originating with Pierce, Dewey, and Veblen,[5] who furnished raw materials for Commons' institutionalism which was carried throughout the profession by Wehrwein, Hobson, and others.

The positivistic and statistical stream of farm management made a place for agricultural economists among the positivistic, but not too well-trained, physical scientists of the agricultural colleges. As this work was also instrumental in winning financial support from the public for farm management and, later, agricultural economics, we owe it a special debt of gratitude. The particular line of positivism found in Cornellian farm management, like positivism elsewhere, encountered rationalism with its demand for the use of theory (logic). The particular form of rationalism encountered was the classical and neoclassical stream of economic thought.[6]

This stream was also normative in the Marshall-Pigou sense. As such, it conflicted with the Cornellian stream on two counts, it was theoretical and it was normative. It is also important to note that the Pareto-Hicks contributions softened the normativism of the neoclassicists to that of "modern welfare economics." Except for its classical and modern emphasis on welfare (the normative), the new stream might be labeled logically positivistic. After the 1940's members of the new stream tended to concede the absence of interpersonally valid utility measures and to accept the positivistic argument that normative knowledge is subjective

[4]Karl Pearson, The Grammar of Science (London: Adam and Charles Black, 1900).

[5]Some of the connections between institutionalism are found in John R. Commons, Institutional Economics - Its Place in Political Economy (London: Macmillan & Co., Ltd., 1934), pp. 154-55, "we therefore ... follow more closely the pragmaticism of Dewey," and p. 647, "Herein it is Dewey's psychology which most nearly fits the case." Also see footnote 6, Chapter 9, this book for further references.

[6]Glenn L. Johnson, "Agricultural Economics, Production Economics and the Field of Farm Management," Journal of Farm Economics, Vol. 39, May 1957, pp. 441f.

and beyond the realm of science. This new stream remains problem oriented however and requires criteria both to define and solve problems. The result is that values are taken as given and to be maximized generally within abstract systems which eliminate non-Pareto better changes. It seems appropriate to characterize this stream, which includes much of the formal work of Black and Heady, as <u>conditionally normative</u>.[7]

The pragmatic stream of institutional economics which included the early Wisconsin land economists was less systematically empirical than the positivistic stream which included Cornellian farm management and land economics. It was also problem oriented and cosmopolitan with respect to both factual and normative disciplines.[8] Members of both the pragmatic, institutionalist land economic (Wisconsinian) school and the positivistic farm management and land economic (Cornellian) schools shared a common distrust of classical and neoclassical economics (English and Austrian); the difference, however, was that the positivists tended to distrust <u>all</u> theory as nonempirical and a source of bias whereas the pragmatist distrusted this particular body of theory. Probably the difference with respect to study of the normative was more fundamental, though less emphasized in academic discussions, than the difference with respect to theory.[9]

The institutional stream like the rationalist stream from neoclassical economic thought also encountered positivistic (including statistical) influences from Cornellian land economists. By the late 1920's the positivistic and pragmatic schools of land economics were in conflict.[10]

In 1939 John Dewey published his <u>Logic, The Theory of Inquiry</u>. This book expressed the implications of Dewey's pragmatic philosophy of value for science and furnished a basis for extending the institutionalist school's philosophy of science. Salter accepted Dewey's philosophic position on science and rejected the positivism of the Cornellian land economists.

Though Salter's (Dewey's) position on scientific method is similar to that dubbed conditional normativism earlier in this paper in that both deal with <u>both</u> factual and normative concepts, there is a fundamental difference between the two. This difference has escaped many quite close observers even though it has maintained a gulf between such important research organizations as the North Central Farm Management Research Committee (which has tended to be conditionally normative) and the North Central Land Tenure Committee (which has tended to be institutional and pragmatic in the Dewey-Salter sense.)[11] The difference is that the <u>conditional normatives take ends or norms as given</u> whereas the <u>pragmatic institutionalists treat them as variables in the special sense that the values of means and ends are regarded as interdependent.</u> Dewey argues that it is ludicrous to assume one fixed while studying the consequences of varying the

---

[7]Glenn L. Johnson, "Values in Farm Management," <u>British Journal of Agricultural Economics</u>, Vol. 14, June 1960, pp. 13f.

[8]<u>Ibid.</u>, pp. 19f.

[9]<u>Ibid.</u>, pp. 29f.

[10]L. A. Salter, <u>A Critical Review of Research in Land Economics</u> (Minneapolis: The University of Minnesota Press, 1948), pp. 39f.

[11]See Rainer Schickele, "Theories Concerning Land Tenure," <u>Journal of Farm Economics</u>, Vol. 34, 1952, pp. 734f. for a contrast between conditional normativism and institutionalism and an attempt to merge the two.

other.[12] In a recent chapter,[13] Parsons has done much to clarify (1) the essential dependence of institutional land economics on Dewey's pragmatic philosophy of values[14] and (2) the difference between institutionalism and conditional normativism.[15]

THE AUTHOR'S INTERDISCIPLINARY EXPERIENCE

I presume that my past experience with interdisciplinary research is a reason for giving me this assignment. This experience is of interest as it illustrates how philosophic positions determine approaches to interdisciplinary work. Much of my own earlier interdisciplinary research work on practical problems was conditionally normative. Such work drove me across academic boundaries into agronomy, animal husbandry, sociology, psychology, etc., in search of factual but not normative knowledge.[16] Some of this work has been individualistic but much has been of a team nature. If, in doing this practical research, I had been following Salter's research methodology in the pragmatic tradition of Wisconsin institutionalism, I would have freely crossed still more academic boundaries into the humanities in search of the normative. As it turned out, I was forced across these same boundaries by problems encountered in studying both managerial theory and theory of the firm. In both areas, I have encountered problems which are not entirely amenable to positivistic (including logical), conditionally normativistic, or pragmatic philosophies of inquiry.

The manager makes decisions in an uncertain world. In doing so, he has to set specifications for choice as well as specifications for concluding that his initial specifications are met. Such specifications depend on his value system.[17] Irresponsible managers often tolerate loose specifications for choice - the result is rapid decisions which keep their resources fully employed in endeavors so risky that they tend to lose their businesses. "Casper Milquetoast" managers, on the other hand, set their specifications so high they seldom make any decisions and, hence, leave their resources idle while they suffer for lack of income. Obviously, a managerial theory which could do something other than ignore values (as positivism demands) or assume them (as conditionally normativism demands) would be an improvement.[18] On the other hand, not all problems seem as complex as

---

[12] John Dewey, "The Continuum of Ends-Means," republished in Ethical Theories, edited by A. I. Melden (New York: Prentice-Hall, Inc., 1950), pp. 360f.

[13] Kenneth Parsons, "The Value Problem in Agricultural Policy," Agricultural Adjustment Problems in a Growing Society (Ames: Iowa State University Press, 1958).

[14] For an earlier statement of this dependence, see Kenneth Parsons, "The Logic Foundations of Economic Research," Journal of Farm Economics, Vol. 31, 1949, pp. 656f. and John R. Commons, op. cit., pp. 154-55 and p. 647.

[15] Glenn L. Johnson, op. cit., "Values in Farm Management." Also see D. Gale Johnson, "Resource Efficiency and Policy," Journal of Farm Economics, Vol. 32, 1950, pp. 123f.

[16] References to TVA, Dairy Husbandry, and IMS books.

[17] Richard Rudner, "The Scientist qua Scientist Makes Value Judgements," Philosophy of Science, Vol. 20, pp. 1f.

[18] "The Labour Utilization Problem in European and American Agriculture," W. E. Heath Memorial Lecture published in Journal of Agricultural Economics, June 1960; "Some Basic Problems for Economists and Statisticians Arising from U.S. Agricultural Policies," Manchester Statistical Society, November 1959.

problems are envisioned to be by the pragmatists.

In the theory of the firm, problems of imperfect knowledge and asset fixity can impose capital losses which are non-Pareto better.[19] Evaluation of these losses in policy research requires a formal structure going beyond modern welfare economics into direct consideration of normative matters. The author's most recent direct experience with these losses in connection with policy issues involves an evaluation of U.S. agricultural production and price support programs done for the Committee on Economic Development.

My excursion into the humanities in search of methodology originates with purely academic as well as with practical problems. This excursion has included courses in philosophic value theory, ethics, and the philosophy of science. It has also included a sabbatic leave period of intensive reading in England with guidance from Professor John Wisdom of Trinity College, Cambridge University. I am currently on sabbatic leave with Rockefeller Foundation support for further investigation of this area. In fact, this paper can be regarded as part of that investigation.

APPROACHES TO THREE PROBLEMS

TVA With Special Emphasis on the Activities of Cap Edmonds

In the early thirties, the situation in the Tennessee Valley was characterized by the presence of a governmentally owned, World War I, nitrogen fixation plant useful for producing either munitions or fertilizer; a river which subjected towns and cities along itself, the lower Ohio, and the lower Mississippi to disasterous floods; a river which did not provide many opportunities for commercial navigation; underdeveloped phosphate and coal resources: and a population of disadvantaged people living, for the most part, on poor, small farms with meager know-how, capital, and access to improve technology and without substantial local employment opportunities. All of this existed in a nation characterized by extreme unemployment and economic depression.

The "goods" to be sought included utilization of the existing nitrogen plant, flood protection, employment opportunities, navigation facilities, farm technology and electricity. Some of these goods were competitive. Others were complementary.

The facts needed were available from many disciplines: engineering, physics, meteorology, hydrology, agronomy, economics, political science and sociology.

When the TVA experience is reviewed in the broad sweep of time, it is evident that the philosophies behind all three broad streams of agricultural economic thinking were useful.

In some instances, the facts spoke for themselves. There were the available plant and the floods. The earth had coal and phosphate. Detailed description of these resources was useful, and a form (at least) of positivism had a clear contribution to make. It was worthwhile acquiring the facts, not because a specific problem required them for its solution, but

---

[19]Glenn L. Johnson, "Supply Function - Some Facts and Notions," Agricultural Adjustment Problems in a Growing Society, Ed. E. O. Heady, et al. (Ames: Iowa State University Press, 1958), pp. 75f.

because the facts were useful in general -- almost for their own sake. Failures to specify problems were of little consequence in such instances. The avoidance of purpose did not materially affect ability to solve problems.

In other instances, problems could be posed and solved in terms of normative concepts which were not subject to substantial change as a result of the process of defining and solving the problem. In these instances, the perceived goodness or badness of a situation, condition, or item did not appear to change as a result of defining the problem. The "goodness" of flood control was a case in point. It could be accepted as a given. The questions then involved factual estimates of the consequences of alternative actions. How much flood control would be attained at its value "at the margin" were open questions but not the "goodness" of flood control.

This is also quite different from saying that new normative concepts of what always had had value were produced in solving the problem.

There were also instances in which the values of means and ends appeared to be interdependent in the Dewey sense that "the value of an objective as an attained end is a value of something which is being an end, an outcome, stands in relation to the means of which it is the consequence. "[20] Examples include the value of being identified with the dams, lakes, and spirit of TVA.

These values are commonly observed among TVA employees and the population of the area. These did not exist before the TVA experiment got under way as a solution to prior problems. Another example involves the ethics of means of making decisions. Major normative questions arose involving the "goodness" and "badness" of governmental versus private control over investment decisions; the result of attempting to answer such normative questions was a change in the importance (value) which various groups and individuals attach to each of the two means of reaching decisions.

Included in the Tennessee Valley are seven counties in Western Kentucky. The land in these counties is of medium to poor quality. It was badly in need of liming, fertilizing, and other advanced practices. Marketing, credit, and other institutional facilities did not supply the area with the services required for the needed improvements in the region's agriculture. When the TVA dam which impounded the present, 100-mile long, Kentucky Lake was built, much limestone was quarried. This limestone was graded with the screenings being rejected to pile up on the bottom of the future lake.

Cap Edmonds, a farm leader in the area, knew of the need for limestone in Kentucky's "Valley Counties." He also knew of the value of more commercial services and of the value of more technical training. The screenings were available for the hauling. He organized a co-operative to haul and spread screenings. Edmonds knew that capital was needed in order to get more than screenings. He arranged for the co-operative to make a profit on each load of free screenings. The resultant accumulation of profits became the capital base for the Valley Counties co-operative. In time, the Valley Counties co-operative obtained and distributed fertilizers from the old World War I plant as well as from the phosphate deposits of the valley and from the new nitrogen fixing plants built to provide still more explosives for World War II. From here on, it was but a few logical steps to expand the co-operative to provide many of the remaining needed services.

---

[20] John Dewey, op. cit., p. 361.

Edmonds also took advantage of the TVA's legislative mandate to educate with respect to fertilizer use. Eventually two associate county agents were assigned to work in the Valley Counties with financial support from TVA. One was a specialist in agronomy, the other a farm management expert.

The Valley Counties now had two new institutional arrangements - the co-operative and the associate agents - both concerned with land problems. As the co-operative grew to provide a wider range of services and as the educational efforts of the associate county agents became effective, several of the initial problems of the area were solved.

As far as I can see, Edmonds' philosophic approach was conditionally normative at times and/or both positivistic and normative at other times. His training, however, was not such that he was consciously anything in these respects. It appears that he either accepted the goods and bads as obvious or deduced them. There is little evidence that he regarded the values of ends and means to be inextricably interdependent. Edmonds simply found or assumed answers to both factual and normative questions in trying to see what actions were appropriate. His common sense insisted that people who talked to him on either factual or normative matters "knew what they were talking about" -- in short, their normative and factual concepts had to be clear and understandable. Further, they had to "hold together" -- to be logically consistent. When concepts did not lead to workable conclusions, they had to be overhauled.

The Operation of the Burley Tobacco Price Support and Production Control Programs

Starting in 1933, a great number of problems concerning the burley industry were faced and handled in the development of the present burley tobacco price support and production control programs. Some of these problems involved: (1) the level at which the burley prices should be supported, (2) how (acreage allotments) the right to grow tobacco would be distributed among large, small, and new growers and by areas, (3) appropriate penalties for nonco-operators, (4) the expansion of production (and acreage) to meet the increasing demands accompanying World War II, (5) how prices were to be supported, (6) the means of securing price, economic, and social stability and, finally, (7) the distribution of voting powers among producers within the program.

In the period after 1933, legislators, administrators, and farm leaders, with the advice of economists, evolved the burley control programs now in existence. The historic situations would not have been conceived as problematic were it not for concepts regarding the goodness of income, productive efficiency, freedom, democratic voting processes, equality, price stability, and lawfulness. In designing the price support and production control programs and in bringing about modification therein, many compromises had to be reached among these "goods" with the giving up of any of them regarded as "bad."

The extent of possible compromises depended upon the situation which existed, the ability of leaders and administrators and legislators to conceive of alternatives which would produce different consequences and on what was going to happen irregardless of what legislators, administrators, and leaders did. The history of the burley tobacco control programs as

revealed in the Kentucky Bulletin 580 <u>Burley Tobacco Control Programs -</u>
<u>Their Over-all Effect on Production and Prices in 1933 to 1950</u> indicates
that in many instances the values attained were independent of the process
of obtaining them. The value of income and freedom seem to be little
different after almost 30 years of experience with the control programs.
Both were sought and both sometimes sacrificed in ascertaining right
actions. This history also indicates that the value of certain ends was
discovered in the process of obtaining them; this, however, is something
different than having the values which were to be discovered change in the
fundamental way in the process of studying the problems. There seems to
be no clear-cut instance in which the value structure, itself, changed as a
consequence of the process of trying to solve the problem. Values were
"discovered" or rediscovered, yes, but not changed.

On many occasions in the evolution of the present price support and
production controls for burley, the amount of one good which legislators,
leaders, and administrators were willing to give up in order to attain
another good changed.

Such changes occurred with the famous Hoosac Mills decision which
invalidated substantial parts of the AAA Act of 1933. Once the alternatives
opened to legislators and administrators were limited by those decisions,
the compromises which could be reached among the goods and bads were
different than they had been before the amount of one good which <u>could</u> not
be sacrificed to attain another was changed. The history of the burley
tobacco production control and price support programs indicates clearly
that the point of compromise changed. It does not indicate at all clearly
that the value structures being compromised themselves changed.

The processes whereby compromises were reached among the goods
and bads in view of what was possible were sometimes those followed by
economists in locating optima and sometimes those used by politicians in
political decision-making.

While it would be difficult to argue that the solutions reached for the
various burley problems have always been right, it is equally difficult to
attribute failure to the employment of any of the diverse philosophies
involved.

Problems in the Pickle-Producing Industry of Michigan

In 1958, various groups became concerned with the earnings of Mexican nationals being brought to Michigan to pick pickles. The interested
parties included the State Department, which had responsibility for negotiating with the Mexican government concerning the general conditions under
which Mexican nationals are brought into the United States. In addition,
the U. S. Department of Labor was interested in the earnings of Mexican
nationals as a result of some pressures from labor unions for the prevention of competition for domestic employment. The pickle processors were
also interested in the problem for, obviously, the ability of farmers to
deliver pickles to the processors was directly related to their ability to
acquire Mexican nationals at relatively low wage rates. Pickle producers
also had a keen interest in the arrangements for importing Mexican
nationals and in arrangements for paying them. Last and probably least
insofar as power to influence the situation was the Mexican national himself who, it is reputed, often paid bribes to his own governmental

officials for the privilege of coming to the United States to work at wage
rates deplored by most Americans.

As a result of the various pressures which existed in 1958, representatives of the National Pickle Packers Association and of the National
Pickle Growers Association devised a formula for paying Mexican nationals
for picking the 1959 crop. It was generally recognized in designing this
formula that earnings for Mexican nationals were low on fields with poor
yields. The new formula for paying nationals, therefore, provided for a
payment of one half of the crop to Mexican nationals who worked in fields
producing more than a minimum yield of 120 bushels per acre. When
yields fell below 120 bushels the proportion of the crop going to the Mexican nationals who picked it increased proportionally.

In the spring of 1959 the Agricultural Economics Department of M.S.U.
was asked to evaluate the operation of the new formula in the summer of
1959. Feelings ran high. The representatives of the U.S. Department of
Labor refused to furnish lists of farmers employing Mexican nationals to
M.S.U. researchers. Apparently there was some conviction that M.S.U.
researchers had "sold out" to the National Pickle Growers and National
Pickle Packers Associations. In some localities, farmers were equally
suspicious of M.S.U. researchers. In fact, a grower organization with
the title of Michigan Pickling Cucumber Grower Association was created
to take over some of the functions of the National Pickle Growers Association which some regarded as a captive organization of the National
Pickle Processors Association. County agents helping in the organization
of the Michigan Pickling Cucumber Association were referred to as "tax
paid rabble rousers" by some processors. The approach of M.S.U. researchers was twofold. They attempted to describe the situation existing
in 1959 and to predict what the future would hold both with and without
industrywide actions. In addition, the entire summer was spent trying to
sort out and understand the various values which motivated interested
parties to take the positions which they took.

The factual investigation involved a sample of 83 farmers employing
1100 nationals. These nationals worked about 160,000 hours and picked
about 270,000 bushels of pickles in the summer of 1958. The pickles,
worth $190,000, were marketed through 25 receiving stations belonging
to 15 different companies, 13 of which were members of the National
Pickle Growers Association and 14 of which were members of the National
Pickle Packers Association.

The normative investigation was less formal. Repeated meetings were
held with executives of the National Pickle Growers and National Pickle
Packers Associations to ascertain and understand the values represented
by these two organizations. In addition, all meetings held with growers
whether by the National Pickle Growers Association or by the new Michigan Pickling Cucumber Growers Association were attended by at least
one M.S.U. researcher. Still further, the opinions of both growers and
Mexican nationals were obtained in the survey work. Each of the 83 growers was interviewed. Four Spanish-speaking interviewers carried out
intensive interviews with 300 of the Mexican nationals working on the
sample farms.

As the summer progressed and information of both a factual and normative nature accumulated, the picture clarified. It became clear that
situations which did not permit Mexican nationals to earn as much as 90
cents an hour for their work were also unprofitable to farmers. It also

became clear that the 1958 worker yield-return formula, with its emphasis on physical yields, encouraged dishonesty on the part of farmers and the operators of the receiving stations.

When it became clear that a farmer's field would not yield 120 bushels of pickles distributed according to the usual size distribution, it was a fairly simple matter to leave the pickles in the field until they became large and unusable. When harvested these large, unusable pickles raised the total <u>physical</u> yield above 120 bushels and kept payments to Mexican nationals at the 50 per cent of the crop level. After being delivered to the receiving stations, these large pickles were hauled in some instances out into fields and spread with manure spreaders. During the summer, the industry rediscovered the value of honesty as a result of their experience with this situation.

They also discovered that the growers who did not produce yields much above 120 bushels per acre were not making any money and were, in fact, receiving less per hour for their own labor than the Mexican nationals they employed. It became rather obvious that the worker yield-return formula had to be changed from a physical yield to a dollar yield basis. It also became obvious that the problems created by low yields for the industry in its relationships with the labor unions, the U. S. Department of Labor, the State Department, and Mexico were such that low yields should be eliminated. This conclusion had major consequences for land use.

It was recommended that the worker yield return formula be converted to a dollar basis with the breaking point at $115 per acre. It was also recommended that an educational program be carried out by both the National Pickle Packers Association and M.S.U. to: (1) show and demonstrate to farmers the consequences of low yields and to show them how to increase yields or (2) encourage producers with low yields to get out of the industry if unable to increase their yields. In addition, many packers undoubtedly concluded that they should re-examine their contracting procedures so as to eliminate contracts with growers who could not produce large yields.

As a result of having these recommendations put into effect by the U. S. Department of Labor and by the National Pickle Packers and Pickle Growers Associations, pickle production has been withdrawn from land marginal to pickle production. In 1960, it was rather difficult to find low-yielding pickle fields in Michigan. From 1958 to 1959 the average yield of pickles in Michigan increased substantially as a result of the elimination of low-yielding fields and farms. Many growers who originally resisted formulas which penalized owners of low-yielding fields have now either increased their yields or withdrawn from production.

SOME CONCLUSIONS

I. An examination of solutions reached by society to three broad problematic situations involving the use of land (1) in the Tennessee Valley, (2) for the production of burley tobacco, and (3) for the production of pickles in Michigan reveals:

    A. Philosophies and approaches which confine inquiry to factual matters would not have permitted all of the solutions which were reached.

    B. Pragmatic institutionalism, with its insistence on the interdependence of the values of means and ends, would have been more complicated than required to reach some of the solutions reached, though this philosophy and approach appeared appropriate in other instances.

C. Some of the solutions reached appear to have been based almost entirely on the results of normative inquiry. The same is true for most positivistic inquiry.

D. The solutions reached are difficult to criticize as wrong because an inappropriate approach was used in reaching them.

II. Paragraph I above indicates that conditional normativism, pragmatic institutionalism, and positivism are individually too restrictive to serve as a universal approach to economic problems involving land. Yet each appears to have a place. None appears to have enough capacity to handle purely normative questions, pragmatic institutionalism coming the closest but tending to be restrictive in some instances and unduly complicated (because it treats the values of means and end as interdependent) in others. Maintenance of flexibility to shift among approaches (including what might be called pure or outright normativism) appears desirable. This, of course, amounts to the adoption of a more general approach capable of subsuming each of the above approaches under it as special cases.

III. The elements of the general approach mentioned in II would include:

A. A willingness to address research efforts to answering specific factual questions pertaining to present and future states of land, people, institutions, markets, technology, etc., independently of the process of answering questions of B below.

B. A willingness to address research efforts to answering specific questions about "goodness" and "badness" independently of the process of answering questions in A above.

C. A willingness to do both A and B above on the assumption that the answers and processes may be mutually dependent.

D. A willingness to seek solutions to problems on the basis of factual and normative concepts secured by any of A, B, and C above.

IV. With respect to interdisciplinary approaches, the philosophic approach suggested in III indicates:

A. That interdisciplinary work may not always be needed in solving land economic problems.

B. That interdisciplinary work will often be required among (1) the factual disciplines such as agronomy, agricultural engineering, sanitary engineering, dairy husbandry, sociology, psychology; (2) the normative disciplines such as ethics, theology; (3) the decision-making disciplines (such as economics, law, and political science) which are concerned with the determination of "right actions" in a wide range of problem areas including the problem of forming new institutional arrangements; and (4) factual and normative disciplines simultaneously under the assumption that the values of ends and means are interdependent.

V. The interdisciplinary work required can be organized on, around, and by either an individual or a team.

A. To do such work, an individual need not master all of the relevant disciplines. Freed of restricting philosophic positions, aware of range of factual and normative, cognizant of the availability of private and public decision-making methods and institutions, and finally, able to use these decision-making facilities, even an individual researcher can contribute to the solution of complex interdisciplinary problems.

B. When such work is undertaken by a research team, it places requirements on both the individual members and on the team as a whole. As a totality the team must be similar to the individual described above - freed of philosophic restrictions, aware of the required interdisciplinary range of data, cognizant of public and private decision-making facilities and the use of such methods and facilities. Individual members of teams need not meet all the requirements for the team or for the individual who is "doing it alone." A positivistic team member may be a highly productive specialist, provided he doesn't impose his philosophy on the entire team thereby destroying its ability to define and solve problems. Similar conclusions apply to other restrictive philosophic positions on the nature of man. In addition, to the advantages and dangers of philosophic specializations, the team approach also involves the advantages and dangers of disciplinary specialization by individual members.

In addition to the dangers of philosophic and disciplinary specialization the team approach encounters intra-team administrative problems often aggravated by drawing team members from different academic departments in a college, different colleges in a university, different universities, both universities and government, both public and private organizations, different private organizations, different governmental agencies, and even different countries and governments, in the case of international land economics research.

12

Selection of Analytical Procedures

by Gene Wunderlich and W. L. Gibson, Jr.*

Progress in land economics research depends partly upon the selection of efficient analytical procedures. But selecting the appropriate procedure is seldom easy because often research problems are complex, research resources are limited, and various methods to some extent are interchangeable. Moreover, some economists have not arrived at complete agreement philosophically on what constitutes a problem -- to say nothing of how to solve it. Nevertheless, the researcher must decide upon the procedure he will use. A basis for making this decision is the burden of this chapter.

As viewed here, an analytical procedure means the method of analysis used to determine whether data affirm or reject a hypothesis. The method of analysis must do two things: (1) identify the association between variables and (2) measure the association or relationship. To accomplish this, the researcher must know how to adapt and use the methods available to him.[1] Although various methods are to some degree substitutes, selection of the more appropriate one will increase the reliability and usefulness of the analysis.

The purpose of this chapter is to assist the researcher to select the

---

[1] The development of new methods is an important phase of any science but it lies outside the scope of this chapter.

---

*GENE WUNDERLICH has been an agricultural economist with the Economic Research Service of the United States Department of Agriculture since 1955. Born in North Dakota in 1928, he received his B.S. from the University of that state and his M.S. from Iowa State University. After a year at Bombay University in India, he completed his Ph.D. degree at Iowa State University, and then joined the Economic Research Service, where his special field of interest has been land tenure.

W. L. GIBSON, Jr. has been connected with Virginia Polytechnic Institute since 1934. Advancing steadily through the academic ranks from a beginning position as instructor, he has been professor since 1947. Born in Virginia in 1910, he received his B.S and M.S. degrees from Virginia Polytechnic Institute and the Ph.D. degree from the University of Virginia; one year of graduate study was at the University of Wisconsin. He has been particularly concerned with land and water use problems of his state and the South generally

method of analysis best suited to the problem under study, consistent with
the resources available. Discussion is included of research problems
and scientific method, some key elements of the reasoning of research,
criteria useful in selecting a research procedure, important features of
several classes of analytical techniques, and land economics as science
and as technology. The chapter is limited to land economics as a positive science concerned with analytical "why" problems. Discussion of
technological "how to" problems is omitted except briefly in the last
section.

PROBLEMS AND THE SCIENTIFIC METHOD

The function of science is to identify and solve problems. Science
begins by observing a connection between facts not previously associated.
It proceeds from observation to theory by induction and thence to hypotheses by deduction. Hypotheses, in turn, are tested against additional
observations (data) derived either from controlled experiments or from
observed experiences as they occur in the real world. The process of
going from fact to theory, to hypotheses, thence to test the hypotheses is
the essence of science, and the analytical procedure chosen for this
process identifies and measures the association or relationship between
and among phenomena.

A problem is a framework for identifying the evidence needed to explain a situation or given phenomenon. It is a question posed for solution
and so precisely stated that it has an answer which can be validly related
to experience.

First indications of a problem often are mere expressions of doubt or
uncertainty regarding relationships among phenomena. These doubts may
come directly as a researcher notices discrepancies between observed
occurrences and previously accepted explanations, while pursuing his
studies. For example, Parsons' attention to the tenure situation in eastern Wisconsin, where few farmers were tenants, arose from his observation that the farms had a higher total value per farm than farms in
southwestern Wisconsin where the tenancy rate was relatively high.[2]
Also, indications of problems may be transmitted to the researcher by
others -- farmers, professional staff members of program agencies,
legislators, administrators, or other consumers of the results of research. The work on father-son farm agreements in Virginia arose from
a request from a farmer for information on alternative business organizations under which he could gradually transfer the farm business to a son
who desired to farm but had relatively little capital with which to get a
start on a farming career. Recent requests for studies of the economic
impacts of highway improvements on land values and land use, with
particular reference to equity in the allocation of the costs of highway
improvement, are an example of a research problem arising from
legislators and transmitted to the researcher.

First observations usually differ greatly from well-defined problems.[3]

[2]K.H. Parsons and E. O. Waples, Keeping the Farm in the Family, Wisconsin Agricultural
Experiment Station Research Bulletin 157 (Madison, September 1945).

[3]Herein lies the futility of much so-called administrative research, when those in charge become
impatient with the researcher who wishes to spend the necessary time in the vital stage of determining what the research problem really is.

The researcher must look for the strategic factors that underlie the situation observed, so that he can state the exact nature of the problem. At the risk of oversimplification, let us assume that a researcher observes that many farms in a given area of highly productive farmland have dilapidated buildings and unsheltered machinery. He is uncertain as to the cause of such conditions. He depends upon his store of knowledge to direct him to his first evidence. Eventually, he discovers two strategic conditions about the farms and the farm people -- the farms are operated by tenants and the number of farms available for renting each year is fewer than the number of tenants desiring to rent farms. An examination of the leasing arrangements discloses annual leases without provisions to compensate for unexhausted improvements. The strategic situation -- the problem -- is insecurity of tenure, an institutional barrier to investments in housing and machinery shelters.

When a problem has been clearly identified, critical elements can be isolated, and a theory can be formed. This theory will be an abstraction; in other words, it need not describe the real world in detail. It will, however, provide adequate explanations or predictions; and the measure of its adequacy will be a valid test.

THE REASONING OF RESEARCH[4]

Scientific method, as generally understood among social and other scientists, consists of two prime components: (1) the construction of a "theory" and (2) the verification of hypotheses. The function of the theory[5] is to reduce a problem to a valid explanation of interrelationships between elements in the problem. The theory contains the premises, the

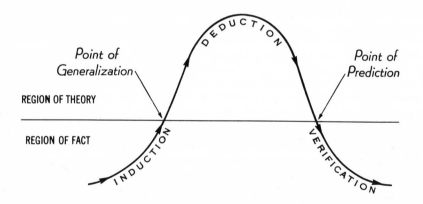

[4]The following references are useful: Morris Cohen and Ernest Nagel, An Introduction to Logic and the Scientific Method (New York: Harcourt, Brace and Co., 1934), Chapters 1-3, 5, 10, 11; John G. Kemeny, A Philosopher Looks at Science (Princeton: Von Nostrand, 1959); Kemeny, Snell and Thompson, Introduction to Finite Mathematics (Englewood Cliffs: Prentice Hall, 1956), Chapter 1; Hans Reichenbach, The Rise of Scientific Philosophy (Berkeley: University of California Press, 1953); F.S.C. Northrup, Logic of the Sciences and the Humanities (New York: Meridian Press, 1959).

[5]Theory is commonly used in three related senses: (1) a concise, often mathematical, statement (more often called a model) bringing together the critical elements of a set of propositions into hypotheses; (2) the whole of an analysis including assumptions, model, hypotheses, and tests; and (3) a body of generalized propositions relating to a broad class of phenomena (e.g., "economic" theory, "price" theory). "Theory" is used here in the sense of (2).

deduced chain of relationships, and the conclusion. The function of verification is to check the specific hypotheses against experience either to reject them or to add to the weight of evidence in their favor.

The scientific method moves between the region of theory (abstraction, generalization) and the region of fact.[6] Schemata, such as the one on page 212, show this relationship.

The scientific method is, in a sense, a process of alternating between reason and facts.[7]

Inference,[8] the Chain of Reasoning

A scientific theory is a chain of reasoning that often contains many links. These links, or premises, must be so stated and so arranged that the theory is internally consistent.

Most of the problems in land economics, and hence the theories that "solve" the problems, can be arranged in a hypothetical form; i.e., on an "If A, then B" basis. The land economist may look to the hypothetical syllogism for an idealized form around which to build his problem; e.g.:

(1) If A is B, C is D
(2) A is B
(3) .'. C is D

Examples of the correct and incorrect use of this idealized form might be as follows:

Valid (1) if price supports are capitalized into land values, land values are high
     (2) price supports are capitalized into land values
     (3) .'. land values are high

Not valid (1) if price supports are capitalized into land values, land values are high
     (2) land values are high
     (3) .'. price supports are capitalized into land values

A basic, or necessary, condition in a valid chain of reasoning is that each link (or premise) must hold a particular relationship to the other links with which it connects. This relationship -- the logical form of a theory -- is not, however, sufficient to demonstrate the "truth" of a proposition. For a really adequate theory, truth of the actual content of the premises must be demonstrable in experience.

Premises

Each theory in land economics research contains a number of explicit and implicit premises. The critical (controversial) premises are usually explicit -- or, at least, they should be if the researcher wants to maximize comprehension or minimize misunderstanding of his theory. Many premises are so commonly used and generally agreed upon, however,

---

[6]The theory-fact cycle takes place in a discipline as a whole, as well as in the analysis of a particular problem.

[7]The steps of this procedure are detailed by Marshall Harris in Chapter 13.

[8]Classes of propositions in land economics are discussed in greater detail elsewhere in this volume by John F. Timmons and Glenn L. Johnson. Technically, we are concerned almost exclusively with a posteriori synthetic propositions; i.e., with propositions whose validity cannot be analytically established by their word content and can be determined only after they are related to facts.

214

that they remain implicit. For example, land economists, as they apply economics to land problems, use many of the assumptions of economics about human behavior, such as independence of decision-making units, a preference for "more" over "less," substitutability and diminishing effectiveness of means to accomplish ends.

In studying the relationship of specified factors, an important, and often implicit, premise is that all things other than those specified in the theory remain the same. Land economists, whose levels of aggregation often include whole regions and nations, can have trouble with the assumption that all factors, other than those specified as variable, are constant. Furthermore, when the unit of observation is a whole country or a large area, the assumption of smooth and symmetrical distributions required for some empirical tests is questionable. A description of the stages of economic growth, for example, may be interesting and useful but, in fact, too few countries have existed to make any generalization about a distribution of countries.[9]

Interdisciplinary research requires special attention to premises because many of the implicit assumptions of one discipline are not contained in its connubial discipline. Constants in one discipline may be critical variables in another, and so interdisciplinary research problems contain more explicit premises and are more complex.

Hypotheses

The prime function of the hypothesis is to predict (explain) facts (factual relationships). The hypothesis, in order to be called one, must be so stated that it can be related to fact through verification; i.e., tested empirically and rejected or accepted. Because hypotheses are tentative solutions or answers, they must be in the form of declarative assertions, not interrogatives nor imperatives. These assertions, if they are to be scientifically useful, cannot be irrelevant to the problem or untestable. Neither should these assertions be trite, in the sense of testing something that is not crucial to the theory. In the words of Friedman: "A hypothesis is important if it explains much by little, that is, if it abstracts the common and crucial elements from the mass of complex and detailed circumstances . . ."[10]

Fully stated, the hypothesis is not only a tentative explanation of the phenomena under study, it is a framework of tests needed for acceptance or rejection. The hypothesis contains the basis for selecting, organizing, and analyzing data, and the limits of certainty required to avoid its rejection. The standards of acceptance or rejection must always be established before the hypothesis is verified. If, after the verification, a new hypothesis is suggested by the facts used in the test, such new hypothesis cannot be satisfactorily tested with the facts from which it was obtained. All alternative hypotheses must be listed before the facts are introduced in the verification.

---

[9]For examining economic growth, one may be limited to case studies and the intuitional device of analogy. For an interesting article on the limitations of development theory for economic policy, see: John H. Adler, "Some Policy Problems in Economic Development," Economic Development and Cultural Change, Vol. 9, No. 2 (January 1961).

[10]Milton Friedman, Essays in Positive Economics (Chicago: University of Chicago Press, 1953), p. 14.

Quite often a problem is of sufficient size and complexity that verification of several hypotheses is necessary. In such instances, the separate hypotheses must be logically related to the larger problem.[11]

FACTORS CONDITIONING THE SELECTION OF
RESEARCH PROCEDURE

A process of selection presupposes some basis for ordering, preferring, and choosing. Just so, the choice of a research method assumes some criteria or standards. In their early phases at least, many problems can be so treated that alternative methods for empiricizing can be used. How does the researcher decide when to use a case study, a regression analysis, or any of the other devices available to him?

Research, as we have confined it to the scientific method, is a process of relating a theory to facts. Analytical techniques or procedures, therefore, will be conditioned by (1) the problem from which, or about which, a theory is formed and (2) the available or obtainable facts. The discussion in this section, then, will treat separately the attributes of problems and conditions of facts that will influence the choice of a research technique or combination of techniques.

The Problem

From the standpoint of the steps of research, as detailed in another chapter, the problem can be regarded as the prime determinant of method. "A problem well put is half solved" because a clear statement of all important features of the problem permits the analyst to select a means of solving it. A well-stated question also will indicate the kind of answer desired; suggest similar problems on which previous research provides clues to tentative answers; indicate the relative importance of universality of the answer; and imply the level of precision required.

The state of knowledge about a problem is revealed by its subject matter. The specialist's or expert's day-to-day familiarity with a subject may provide immediate insight into methods. Perhaps the problem is well known, and a ready-made solution is available. Or a new problem may suggest some exploratory studies using some simple descriptive or a few nonparametric statistical tests. Still another problem may be a particular aspect of an otherwise well-analyzed subject, and an elegant statistical model may be required to treat a particular implication. The literature of research in the economics of water resources indicates, for example, a substantial growth of the state of knowledge in a relatively short time. Part of this rapid progress is due to the state of economic knowledge about other resources.

The universality or specificity of a problem may indicate its relative importance and so help to determine the extent to which a solution will be pursued. How general are the inferences of the research? Is the

---

[11]Friedman's concept of a hypothesis seems to transcend separable components and tests. The difference seems minor because, if a "Big Hypothesis" must be tested indirectly through a series of lesser assertions, the same rules of verification apply. In a multiple regression, for example, each of the partial regression coefficients is separately "tested" as to its significance in the context of the entire model, itself a Big Hypothesis of relationship between and among a set of variables.

phenomenon under study so uncommon that its explanation adds little to
the sum total of knowledge? Because of their pervasiveness, explanations
of gravity or light become quite significant. Identifications of the source
of a telephone call may be unimportant except to the person called.

The precision required of the results of an analysis may affect also
the research procedure used. Identification of a few of the major factors
associated with a problem may be enough in some circumstances. In other
circumstances, very precise measurement of a degree of interrelationship
may be required.

Methods of analysis can be determined by the form of answer required. Some problems require answers showing order of sequence;
others require answers indicating arrays of importance by a certain
scale; still others require numerical measures of relationship. Many
problems in land economics call for answers that show the most probable
consequences of specified alternative actions taken in specified circumstances.

The use to which the findings will be put is closely related to the
precision requirement. Usually, the person who encourages the initiation
of the research can best specify use of the results. Great detail with
minute precision may be required by an analyst specializing in a subject matter. Rough generalization may be adequate for someone interested in a broad policy matter.

Problems generated by experts in a discipline tend to be more
specific, more precisely stated -- often they are "thought" problems.
The problem presented by the nonexpert is more likely to be a difficulty
in accomplishing some goal which may not be clear to him; often these
are "action" problems.

Time and resource limitations frequently impinge upon analytical
procedures. Most research is subject to the number and capacity of available personnel, and to limited funds. Most research is subject also to
over-all time limitations within which analysis must be completed or
abandoned and to the sequence of phases of study. For example, a different technique of analysis may be used on a preliminary study than is used
on the principal study.

The Facts

The selection of a research procedure is conditioned also by the form,
amount, and availability of facts with which to test the hypothesis. A
research procedure can be as good as, but not better than, the data it
uses. The two basic qualifications of facts to be used in verifying a
hypothesis are, of course, relevancy and accuracy. Beyond these basic
requirements, however, such factors as the scope, form, precision,
homogeneity, and accessibility will have a bearing on the choice of an
analytical procedure.

The quantity and range of reliable information will prescribe the
scope of a study. Particularly is this true of historical data where the
opportunity to collect supplementary information is foreclosed by time.
Many agricultural series, for example, extend back only to 1880.
Similarly, data from intensive studies are often available only for a small
geographic area. Data from personal interviews are often limited by the
memory of the interviewee.

Careful researchers are chary about projecting beyond the scope of available information. A regression equation, for example, may predict quite accurately within the range of given observations and yet be unsuitable for estimates outside the given observations.

Not all information is quantitative. Many historical and descriptive studies make use of qualitative data. When information cannot be measured on a numerical scale, ordinal measures can sometimes be used to determine a specific relationship; e.g., as in rank correlation. Quantitative information can be transformed into qualitative information more frequently than the reverse. Many of the institutional problems of land economics require methods to deal with phenomena about which information is qualitative. These institutional problems may well be treated by methods that are not conventional in economics.

Social science, including land economics, uses both attribute and measurement data. There is little the researcher can do to specify which of these types of data he will use because it depends upon the phenomenon under study. The researcher may effect research economies by making adjustments in analysis or transforming data to accommodate differences in type of data. Such transformations, however, generally go from measurement to attribute and not vice versa -- a fact that might be remembered by data-collecting services.

In an empirical procedure, precision in data is desirable but it must sometimes be weighed against availability of research resources. When data are extremely costly to collect, compile, or manipulate, a less elaborate model with simple tests may be devised. It might be better to solve some land policy or program problems by judgment than to obtain, at great cost, information so imprecise that it is no better than a judgment.

Procedures designed to avoid bias [12] do not ordinarily involve great cost. Except in planning an empirical design, very few additional resources may be needed to eliminate or reduce bias.

The degree of homogeneity of a population under study will affect not only the intensity of the analysis but the procedure. If all watersheds were alike, for example, an intensive study of one would be sufficient to infer various relationships about all watersheds in the country. The case study is the obvious research answer to perfectly homogeneous populations. Most land economics problems, however, face stubbornly variable facts. Grouping, stratification, geographic delineation, and similar organizational devices can help the researcher eliminate some of the effects of a heterogeneous population. If little is known about the population, exploratory studies may aid in developing groups or strata.

Analyses are affected by the availability of ready-made data. [13] Ideally, the researcher would like to reach for a volume of information and find exactly what he needs, and in the form he needs, to test his hypotheses. Particularly in the phenomena of land economics is this ideal unlikely to be realized. If primary data must be obtained, greater flexi-

---

[12]Bias is used in the sense of deviation of an expected value of an estimate from the true (population) value.

[13]Economists often experience considerable difficulty in securing reliable data for testing their hypotheses. Secondary data from established statistical and primary data collected for other purposes often do not provide quantitative measures of the specific variables. Intricate models and techniques of analysis are in no sense a substitute for deficiency in data.

bility in analytical procedures is possible. However, this advantage may be lost if limited resources are used to collect rather than analyze data.

Availability of secondary data can do much to promote the advance of a discipline. [14] Availability, however, goes beyond collection, and many improvements in land economics data could be made by the systematic compiling and cataloguing [15] of data already collected.

RESEARCH PROCEDURES -- THE TOOLS OF ANALYSIS

The purpose of any of the research techniques described below is to relate a simple, comprehensible model to experience, with valid tests, to see whether behavior is explained or predicted. In the statement of a theory or design of an experiment to suit a particular problem, these techniques may sometimes complement one another; at other times, if research resources are very limited, they may substitute for one another. From the standpoint of the entire discipline of land economics, however, these devices complement and supplement one another.

Historical

All data are both past and present. Our analyses require some record, including our own memory and that of others, to supply the past events which we examine now in terms of a present question. In one sense, then, all empirical science is historical.

But all history is not necessarily scientific. If a historical study produces a set of sequential facts without using them to test a hypothesized pattern, then the study probably does not warrant the name "science" or "analysis." Certainly, the Aristotelian view that history studies the unique and nonrecurrent would omit the "historical method" as an analytical procedure in this chapter.

However, most modern historians no longer visualize history as simple inscription of facts; facts are selected and, therefore, a science [of history] is necessary ". . . the main problem [of history] is not so much to fill in the many gaps in our factual knowledge as to make sense out of the vast deal we do know. For a historical fact never speaks for itself. [16]

To the extent that a historical study is analytical, it requires a theory. A theory, in turn, presupposes an isolation of a special class of phenomena. Thus, as science, there are many histories -- a history of agricultural settlement, a history of statistics, a history of economic growth, and so forth. Although history cannot universally be called a science, it can be used as an analytical tool in a social science -- and is

---

[14]Philip M. Raup, "Structural Changes in Agriculture and Research Data Needs," Journal of Farm Economics, Vol. 41, No. 5 (December 1959), pp. 1480-91. M. R. Benedict and G. M. Kuznets, "Better Basic Data for Agriculture: Some Possible Approaches," Journal of Farm Economics, Vol. 40, No. 2 (May 1958), pp. 208-22.

[15]For examples, see Karl Gertel, Water: Uses, Supplies, Projections -- An Introduction to Terms and Reference Sources [mimeo] (Washington: U.S. Department of Agriculture, FED-ERS, 1961); U. S. Department of Agriculture and U.S. Department of Commerce, A Graphic Summary of Farm Tenure, and A Graphic Summary of Land Utilization (1957); and H. H. Wooten and J. R. Anderson, Major Uses of Land in the United States, Summary for 1954, U.S. Department of Agriculture Agricultural Information Bulletin No. 168 (1957).

[16]Herbert J. Muller, The Uses of the Past (New York: Oxford University Press, 1952), p. 29.

here so regarded. History is concerned more with the identification of important events or conditions than with measurement. Generally, sequence of these events is a critical feature. Determining the relative importance[17] of events or conditions is often the main problem in a historical analysis.

Land economics as a discipline is faced with many problems for which historical analysis is suitable. Many analyses of the problems of settlement in the developing areas could be aided by attention to historical analyses whose models range from the monumental sweep of F. Jackson Turner's "safety valve" thesis and W. P. Webb's single innovation ideas of "six-shooter and barbed wire" to intricate studies of the origins of tenure by A. N. Chandler and M. Harris.[18] Historical studies can contribute substantially to understanding the processes of development and growth.

Under what conditions is a historical procedure useful? If the problem under study is strongly involved with processes, changes, or variables subject to the influence of time or sequence; if verification of the hypothesis depends upon a sequence of events; if facts are not easily quantifiable; then a historical study may be useful. The historical analysis usually emphasizes identification rather than measurement. It is similar to the descriptive study but depends more upon the sequence of events.[19] The historical study may include statistical time series[20] but does not emphasize quantification.

Descriptive[21]

As an analytical procedure, the status of description (often known also as "mere description") is uncertain. Latter-day Baconians will emphasize the need for starting a study with a complete description while their Cartesian counterparts will stress a priori notions from which a search for data, if necessary, begins. If analysis is defined broadly to include a problem setting and situation, then description will be part of, but not a procedure for, analysis. The function of a description is largely to identify the characteristics of a problem to be analyzed.

Description alone may be useful in portraying the total environment within which the specific problem under study is found. Because events

[17]Ernest Nagel has described five useful meanings of "more important." These meanings depend on relative variability and frequency, relative effects, crucialness, and inclusiveness. Ernest Nagel, "The Logic of Historical Analysis," reprinted from Scientific Monthly in H. Feigl and M. Brodbeck, Readings in the Philosophy of Science (New York: Appleton-Century-Crofts, 1953), pp. 698-99.

[18]Frederick Jackson Turner, The Frontier in American History (New York: Henry Holt and Co., 1921). Walter Prescott Webb, The Great Plains (New York: Grossett and Dunlap, reprinted from New York: Ginn and Co., 1931). A. N. Chandler, Land Title Origins, A Tale of Force and Fraud (New York: Robert Schalkenbach Foundation, 1945). Marshall Harris, Origin of the Land Tenure System in the United States (Ames: Iowa State Press, 1954.)

[19]For two studies making excellent use of historical analysis see: F. J. Marschner, Land Use and Its Patterns in the United States, U.S. Department of Agriculture, Agriculture Handbook No. 153 (Washington, 1959); and F. J. Marschner, Boundaries and Records, U.S. Department of Agriculture ARS Unnumbered Series (Washington, 1960).

[20]See, for instance, F. Maier, S. Maitland, and G. Bowles, The Tenure Status of Farmworkers in the United States, U.S. Department of Agriculture Technical Bulletin No. 1217 (Washington, 1960).

[21]Salter does not call "qualitative description" a method as he does case, historical, analogical, etc., but by listing it with equal status in his series of methods he implies that it is a method. L.A. Salter, A Critical Review of Research in Land Economics (Minneapolis: University of Minnesota Press, 1948) p. 72.

and circumstances cannot be described in all their detail, however, some
selection of facts must take place. Thus some criterion or basis of
selection of facts is at least implicit in a description if it is to be of any
analytical use.

Some forms of descriptive studies incorporate numerical data and
are thus quantitative. The numerical data may be (1) related to specific
questions and (2) organized to show relationships. These descriptive
studies begin to approach statistical analyses. They may differ, in fact,
only by the type of inferences which relate a sample to a larger population.

A thorough description of the problem environment is often an important aspect of an analysis. However, description alone does not substitute
for analysis; land economists, who are often faced with social problems
containing intricate details, are sometimes in danger of describing without explicitly demonstrating relationships.

> Often descriptive projects are undertaken without clear-cut
> objectives ... . Such studies proceed on the assumption that
> no definite plan of analysis is needed; that any great collection
> of facts should reveal significant conclusions. The result is a
> hodge podge of unrelated statistics that defy interpretation or
> analysis. [22]

To the extent that relationships are identified and generalized through
induction, description will be useful in analysis. If, however, information
is collected with no view to patterns nor inferences, a description earns
the modifier "mere."

The Case Study

The case study has been widely accepted as a teaching technique, but
in the past, its use in social science research created much controversy.
This difference of opinion arose primarily because use of the case study
tended to result in only description of selected properties of the cases
studied rather than in an analysis of formulated problems and hypotheses.
Yet valuable case studies have been made,[23] and an evaluation of this
procedure rests upon whether it meets the requirements of scientific
inquiry.

The usefulness of the case method in research depends upon whether
the number of observations on one or several units is large enough to permit the formulation of theories and the testing of hypotheses. Evidential
materials derived from a single case or several cases may advance an
analysis from observation to theory particularly when little is known
about the phenomenon under study.

Economic problems often involve a determination of why a particular
situation is as it is; why the results produced by a going concern are
precisely what they are; and how the various elements of an individual

---

[22] Max M. Tharp, "A Reappraisal of Farm Tenure Research," Land Economics, Vol. 24, No. 4
(November 1948), p. 321.

[23] For examples see: J. S. Davis, Wheat and the AAA (Washington: The Brookings Institution,
1935); P.O. Foss, Politics and Grass (Seattle: University of Washington Press, 1960); and Hugh A.
Johnson and Jeanne Davis, Private Outdoor Recreation Facilities (Washington: Outdoor Recreation
Resources Review Commission, 1961).

situation fit together exactly as they do. These are broad problems and their solutions require analyses of many variables and of interactions among those variables. For example, an intensive study of the contractual arrangements of one broiler contractor could determine the effect of vertical integration upon farm tenure within the chosen case. However, generalizing about other integrated operations would be difficult without information about the relationship to other arrangements. This difficulty of generalizing the conclusions drawn, together with the problem of how objectively to select the case studied, places rather serious limitations on the use of the case method in research. As Salter said: "It will but rarely be true that analysis of a single case . . . will suffice for a full inquiry. There have to be as many cases as there are combinations of strategic means-ends factors for a full analysis of a problem."[24]

The Experimental Method[25]

A scientist conducts research to determine the relationships among phenomena. Any method he uses must control or eliminate, so far as possible, the effect of all variables except those under study. In the experimental method, the scientist designs an experiment which when conducted allows him to observe the relationships between variables under the conditions necessary to test his hypothesis. The experiment is a physical activity whereby selected variables are controlled to observe consequences.

The experimental method has received little attention in social science research because social phenomena generally cannot be manipulated without influencing the relationships studied. Brunk and others[26] working in field of marketing have given considerable study to this problem of improving data, and they have contributed greatly to a better understanding of how agricultural economists can use experimental design techniques for improvement of marketing research. The authors know of no studies in which these techniques were used in analyzing land economic problems.[27] However, it seems possible that investigations along similar lines warrant consideration. For example, the Farm Credit Administration might co-operate with one of the Federal Land Banks in an experimental study to determine the extent to which the terms of mortgage obligations -- size of annual payments, rigidity of the repayment plan, and interest rates -- result in less than optimum resource organizations. Another example might be experimental pricing of recreation facilities by commercial and public organizations.

---

[24] L. A. Salter, Jr., A Critical Review of Research in Land Economics (Minneapolis: The University of Minnesota Press, 1948), p. 71.

[25] A broad interpretation of "experiment" would include mathematical manipulation or organization of observations and could then mean any analysis. The term "experimental method" is used here to mean inquiry conducted under conditions in which objects and events are manipulated by the investigator; that is, in which the investigator can affect the events to be observed. Ackoff lucidly discusses a number of definitions in research, such as "experiment," "research," and "design." R. L. Ackoff, The Design of Social Research (University of Chicago Press, 1953), pp. 2-5.

[26] Max E. Brunk, "Use of Experimental Design in Marketing Research," Journal of Farm Economics, Vol. 40, No. 5 (December 1958).

[27] The experiment by the U.S. Department of Agriculture of the open-bid market under the Acreage Reserve Program in selected areas was, in a sense, an "experiment." The effects of such programs are seldom isolated from other uncontrolled, or uncontrollable, forces.

Statistical[28]
_____

Two common features of statistical techniques are the precise statements that can be made about the relation of a sample to a specified population, and the assumptions that are made about the similarity of the population under study to various mathematical distributions. Some measure of reliability thus can be placed on tests of hypotheses.

Correlation and regression analyses assist the land economist in determining how changes in one variable are related to changes in other variables.

Regression analysis describes the form of the relationship between variables. When only one predictor variable (x) is involved, a simple regression equation of $Y = a + bX$ may describe the relationship. However, economic relationships are generally complex and explanation of changes in a given phenomenon often requires consideration of several variables. Thus, a multiple regression equation of some form like $Y = a + b_1 X_1 + b_2 X_2 + \ldots + b_n X_n$ is required for a meaningful analysis. In this form, an assumption must be made that the effects of the predictor variables $(X_1, X_2 \ldots X_n)$ on the dependent variable (Y) are separate, distinct, and additive. The regression coefficient (b) provides a measure of the average change in the dependent variable for a given unit change in the predictor variable. The regression equation provides a technique both for predicting a value of a dependent variable and measuring the effect of a single predictor variable.[29]

Correlation measures the degree of association between variables. It is simply the combined regression of Y on X and the regression of X on Y. Except as a measure of goodness of fit of a regression (R^2), correlation, as such, has limited use in land economics problems.

Regression analysis is perhaps the most powerful and flexible technique available to land economists for a study of problems when functional relationships between variables exist.[30] It has been used more widely in price analysis and farm management studies than in land economics. But when sample data can be summarized in regression coefficients and tests of hypotheses can be expressed in terms of significant differences between populations, regression warrants even more consideration than it has received.[31] Similarly, when tests of hypotheses involve an explanation of phenomena as they exist within a given population,

_____

[28] The word "statistics" is commonly used in the sense of (1) numerical data and (2) estimates of the parameters of a population. In this chapter, the word has the second meaning.

[29] See Maier-Hedrick-Gibson, The Sale Value of Flue-Cured Tobacco Allotments, Virginia Polytechnic Institute Technical Bulletin No. 148 (Blacksburg, April 1960). Multiple regression equations were used to determine the sale value of an acre of flue-cured tobacco allotment independent of the land and buildings associated with it. Although the partial regression coefficients for other variables used in explaining the sale value of tobacco farms and the coefficient of multiple determination were of interest, the study was primarily concerned with the partial regression coefficient for an acre of tobacco allotment.

[30] Partial and curvilinear correlations are omitted here. An example of a complex application of regression to a land tenure problem is given in W. G. Miller, W. E. Chryst, and H. W. Ottoson, Relative Efficiencies of Farm Tenure Classes in Intrafirm Resource Allocation, Iowa Agricultural Experiment Station Research Bulletin No. 461 (Ames: November 1958). For discussion of methodology see also Walter G. Miller, "Comparative Efficiency of Farm Tenure Classes in the Combination of Resources," Agricultural Economics Research, Vol. 11, No. 1 (1959), pp. 6-16.

[31] For a discussion of the suitability of regression and test of significance procedures for analysis of problems of this nature, see, F. H. Wiegmann, "Use of Regression and Test Procedures," Journal of Farm Economics, Vol. 36, No. 4 (November 1954).

regression offers the researcher an efficient and refined way of analyzing
his data.

Regression is feasible when the dependent variable reduces easily to
a single value such as a price. As a consequence, one of the more common uses of the regression technique is in predicting land values. [32]
More complex phenomena that can only be measured by several dimensions -- for example, a type of tenure arrangement -- do not yield easily
to regression analysis; that is, unless all dimensions can be reduced to a
single index.

Some dangers regarding the use of regression in the solution of
economic problems should be mentioned. First, intercorrelation between
predictor variables often exists, and this results in unstable partial
regression coefficients with large standard errors and in illogical signs
for the coefficient of the weaker variable. [33] If the research worker is
primarily interested in estimating the dependent variable, this problem
is of little concern to him because he can combine the interrelated variables as an interaction variable. When the regression coefficient is of
primary importance, such intercorrelation can become a perplexing
problem. Second, when errors of measurement of the values of a predictor variable are randomly distributed with a mean of zero, such errors
will tend to bias estimates of this variable's regression coefficient toward
zero. [34] Third, correlation does not mean causation. Numerous examples have been shown where high correlations were obtained between
variables that were nothing more than spurious relationships. Coefficients
of correlation can be as easily computed on inaccurate data as on accurate
data and on nonsensical series as on sensible series.

Variability tests, such as Analysis of Variance (ANOVA), and the t
tests, are a family of statistical techniques designed to test parametric
differences between and among various classes and subclasses. Included
in this family of techniques are the simple t tests and the slightly more
elaborate analyses of variance. [35] Like regression and correlation, these
tests use measurement data rather than attribute data. [36]

In essence, these methods determine significant differences between
two or more averages. Significant differences are those that cannot be
accounted for by normal variation, except with specified infrequency, as
in 1 or 5 per cent of all possible samples. The t test is used to test
differences between two means, or more than two means, two at a time.

---

[32] Two examples of more recent works: Ed Renshaw, "Are Land Prices Too High: A Note on Be-
havior in the Land Market," Journal of Farm Economics, Vol. 39, No. 2 (May 1957), pp. 505-10.
Dale M. Hoover, "A Study of Land Prices in the United States, 1911-1958," Ph.D. Dissertation,
University of Chicago (1960).

A discussion of "correlation analysis" of historical interest from the standpoint of land econom-
ics research is contained in Advisory Committee on Economics and Social Research of Social
Science Research Council, Research Method and Procedure in Agricultural Economics [mimeo]
(Washington, 1928), pp. 219-98. This report was prepared by a subcommittee of John D. Black,
Chairman, L. C. Gray, E. G. Nourse, and H. R. Tolley.

[33] See K. A. Fox and J. F. Cooney, Jr., Effects of Intercorrelation upon Multiple Correlation and
Regression Measures, U. S. Department of Agriculture (Washington, April 1954).

[34] See R. J. Foote, Analytical Tools for Studying Demand and Price Structure, U. S. Department
of Agriculture Handbook No. 146 (Washington, 1958).

[35] Some interesting examples of the use of t and other statistical tests are contained in Wallace
Aanderud, "Farm Consolidation in Barnes County from 1955 to 1958", M.S. Thesis [mimeo]
(Fargo: North Dakota State University, 1960).

[36] Regression is simply an elaborate form of ANOVA. As such, many of the data requirements
are the same for both, although they test different types of hypotheses.

ANOVA is used to test differences simultaneously in more than two categories.

In ANOVA, the differences in means of the various classes are tested indirectly by a ratio of variances, F. This is possible because the ratio of variance of a combined group to the variance of its subgroups increases as differences in the subgroup means increase.

In contrast to regression, variability tests such as t and ANOVA, do not show relationship. These tests simply show that groups of phenomena do, or do not, differ by amounts more than can be accounted for by chance, and could, or could not, be considered as coming from the same universe. ANOVA, t, and other variability tests, in contrast to nonparametric tests, depend upon a normal distribution. If a normal distribution of the characteristics under study cannot reasonably be assumed, perhaps the researcher should use an easier but less efficient nonparametric test.

In economics, as well as other social sciences, phenomena can often be grouped. Variability tests are useful in making inferences about measured differences between these groups. These variability tests take many forms and have wide flexibility under controlled, semicontrolled, and uncontrolled conditions. During the hypothesis-formulating stage of research, t tests are often useful in scanning facts and in making preliminary tests.

Variability tests appear to have been little used in land economics, or in economics generally for that matter. The reason for the limited use of ANOVA probably stems from (1) the nature of economic problems, (2) the calculation required, and (3) the data needed.

Economics as a predictive science has emphasized functional relationships, and ANOVA merely indicates whether a relationship might exist, saying nothing about the kind of relationship.

ANOVA is not much easier to calculate than its equivalent regression, and a normal distribution of the test characteristic must be assumed.

The high quality and quantity requirements of data to make effective use of this technique are enough to recommend regression, with which relationships can be specified in form and measured in intensity. The time, financial, and professional resources required to collect primary data for ANOVA can be more effectively used on regression analysis. Not all secondary data, however, permit regression and under such circumstances, the researcher might use ANOVA.

The nonparametric tests, such as the chi-square independence and rank correlation, do not depend upon assumption of a normally distributed characteristic of the population under study.[37] The nonparametric tests often are easily computed. Inferences are straightforward, if not elaborate.

If, in a series of observations, two characteristics cannot be measured but each can be arrayed, a rank correlation test of their ordinal differences can be made. No assumptions of a normal distribution of the characteristic need be made. In general, rank correlation is best suited to relatively small numbers of observations.

For tests such as chi-square independence, attribute data are used. Observations are classified as either having, or not having, the characteristic studied. These tests make inefficient use of measurement

---

[37]To test the normality of a distribution, the chi-square goodness of fit test may be applied. This test also is relatively simple.

data that are converted to attribute information. Regression, for example, indicates the kind and degree of relationship between two or more variables. But chi-square can tell us only whether two variables are, or are not, related. If information is available to show the form and degree of relationship between two variables, it might seem foolish to test only if there were, or were not, a relationship. However, preliminary analysis might well employ some of the simpler nonparametric methods in preparing for, or precluding, more elaborate techniques.

Thus an important function of our simple nonparametric tests may be exploratory analysis. In pilot studies in which subject matter, not methodology, is undergoing a shakedown, one of several nonparametric tests may be useful. Similarly, side issues of the study under way may be probed with a nonparametric test for further analysis.

Activity Analysis

Activity analysis, especially as linear programing, received a great deal of attention in farm management and marketing research during the last decade. However, land economists have been somewhat less enthusiastic about its usefulness as a technique of analysis in studies of either land utilization or land tenure.[38]

Linear programing, as a technique of analysis, is primarily useful in the study of problems where the objective is to maximize a given end with scarce resources.[39] It is essentially a normative technique, a decision-making device for determining what ought to be done as opposed to an explanation of what is. What should be done to maximize a selected objective, given limited resources (restrictions) along with known technical coefficients (input-output and price data) and alternative ways of accomplishing ends (processes), is the type of question for programing solution. The proper selection of alternative processes, the accuracy of

---

[38]W. D. Toussaint has shown that the technique is useful in analysis of certain tenure problems, and he suggests that land economists give greater consideration to linear programing in the selection of procedures for their studies. See "Two Empirical Techniques Applicable to Land Tenure Research: Linear Programming and Single Equation Models," Journal of Farm Economics, Vol. 37, No. 5 (December 1955). Also see E. N. Castle, "Programming Structures in Watershed Development, "Economics of Watershed Planning (Ames: Iowa State University Press, 1960), for a discussion of linear programing as an aid in watershed planning; and George A. Pavelis, Howard P. Johnson, William D. Shrader, and John F. Timmons, Methodology of Programming Small Watershed Development, Iowa Agricultural Experiment Station Research Bulletin No. 493 (April 1961). F. D. Aigner utilized the technique in determining the marginal value product of an additional acre of flue-cured tobacco on two sizes of farms for comparison with estimates of the sale value of an acre of tobacco allotment independent of the land and buildings associated with it -- F. D. Aigner, "The Capitalized Income to an Additional Acre of Flue-Cured Tobacco Compared to the Sale Price of Tobacco Allotment, Pittsylvania County, Virginia," M.S. Thesis, Virginia Polytechnic Institute (Blacksburg, September 1960).

[39]Budgeting has been used widely in analyzing normative economic problems. In some respects, it is simpler than linear programing. If, however, the problem under study involves a large number of alternatives, the mechanics of calculation can be burdensome. The main deficiency of budgeting technique is its inadequacy conclusively to determine an optimum. It is a technique for determining only whether one combination of resources is superior to another, or at most, to several other combinations.

Budgeting estimates possible changes in costs and returns resulting from selected changes in the use of production resources. In research, the technique has been used primarily to analyze modal cases or firms. In some studies, both the quantities and kinds of fixed resources have varied significantly, while in other studies, fixed resources were held constant with variable resources applied through a range of application. The latter approach is perhaps more analytical and avoids confounding the results with complementary utilization of other resources.

For a discussion of this technique see I. F. Fellows, Editor, Budgeting, Storrs, (Connecticut) Agricultural Experiment Station Bulletin No. 357 (August 1960).

input-output and price data, and the precise determination of typical resource situations, are of critical importance in the use of the technique, but this is true also for other techniques. When the problem involves the allocation of resources, the returns from which will be received at some future time, the accuracy of output data, especially price data, may become somewhat unreliable. Furthermore, the future returns should be discounted to present values and this involves determining a proper discounting rate, a difficult problem indeed. Perhaps the greatest difficulty lies in reducing the number of feasible alternative processes to a manageable number.

There are numerous land utilization and tenure problems to which linear programing is adapted. Toussaint, [40] for example, utilized it to show differences in optimum enterprise combinations when a multiple-unit farm was planned with and without regard to separate landlord and tenant enterprises. In addition, he suggests its application in the determination of relative efficiencies of tenancy and encumbered owner-operatorship. De Benedictis and Timmons used linear programing to show differences in optimum farm plans resulting from differences among owner-operatorship and various leasing arrangements.[41] These are examples to indicate one type within a wide range of problems in which a group of limited resources must be shared among a number of competing uses.

Improving Research Techniques

In the long run, the tools of research are built because they are needed for a particular use. Literature in factor analysis, game theory, and organization analysis is suggestive, but land economics has not been visibly moved by them. Modifications and adaptations in these and other procedures, however, may be expected, and researchers in land economics may benefit from them.

A discussion of available techniques is necessarily partial because research procedures and their applications are continually being revised. [42] Many of the new tools will be developed by specialists in theory -- mathematicians, econometricians, and economists. Many also will be developed by researchers in applied economics. The strength of research in a discipline such as land economics will depend upon the close relationship between tool using and tool building.

The strength of land economics research will depend also upon keeping the problems before the procedure. If, as Professor Raup says, ". . . we tend to develop our concepts of problems in terms of data or a measurement device at hand,"[43] some of the perspective needed for useful tool building will be lost. Methodological studies are needed. But does a methodological analysis really test the efficacy of a technique, or is it merely a semantic maneuver to fit a problem to an interesting technique? If a technique is really being evaluated, presumably it will be compared with an alternative.

---

[40]W. D. Toussaint, op. cit., page 32.

[41]Michele De Benedictis and John F. Timmons, Identification and Measurement of Inefficiencies in Leasing Systems, Iowa Agricultural Experiment Station Research Bulletin No. 490 (Ames, 1961).

[42]"A scientific approach is undogmatic . . . it is not only paradoxical to adopt a dogmatic attitude -- it is almost suicidal." Irwin D. J. Bross, "Statistical Dogma: A Challenge," The American Statistician, Vol. 15, No. 3 (June 1961), p. 14.

[43]Philip M. Raup, op. cit., page 1491.

Perhaps no greater need exists in land economics research today than the need for devices to analyze the processes of development and growth. First there are the problems of so-called "resource development," which are essentially problems of transforming a resource into a more productive resource. Second, there are even more complex problems involving the processes of institutional transformations. Increased attention to organizational analysis in general economics may portend some useful developments in land tenure research.

The interdisciplinary character of many land economics problems presents the researcher with unique challenges and opportunities to tap the other sciences. Interdisciplinary research, however, only emphasizes the need for basic principles in methodology.

LAND ECONOMICS [44] AS SCIENCE AND TECHNOLOGY

Land economics as a social science, concerned with analysis and prediction, may be distinguished from land economics as a technology, concerned with physical or social engineering. [45] Both of these aspects of the field of land economics are so important, so much a part of the discipline, that neither can be ignored. In discussing tools of analysis, however, it is well to keep them separated, and the scope of this chapter is limited to the science of land economics. [46]

Although land economics qua science follows the same form as any other science, the subject matter of land economics will probably determine the alternatives of procedure open to the researcher. For example, land economics is intimately concerned with many problems involving changes and processes. Therefore, resource development and conservation, [47] concentration of control, and institutional change are problem areas in which procedures designed to analyze static problems may be weak. Furthermore, land economics includes problems involving rather large aggregations of resources, so that questions of social as well as individual welfare must be answered. Welfare transfers between and among groups and individuals often cannot be ignored. Analyses of land economics problems cannot always accept the same independence of, or linear relationships between, critical variables that are assumed in many economic studies. Land economics crosses into other social and physical sciences, thus compounding the problems of methodology.

Land economics qua technology provides or constructs the means to accomplish certain ends. The ends may be the best use of a forest or

---

[44]For an early separation of the various fields of investigation within land economics research that is still useful, see Report of Committee Appointed by the Secretary of Agriculture "to consider the Subject of Land Economics," U.S. Department of Agriculture Circular 138 (June 1919), A recent outline of the Aspects of Land Economics is contained in Land and Water Research Activities, [mimeo] (Washington: U.S. Department of Agriculture, ERS-FED, 1961), and in Chapter 14 of this volume by Harry A. Steele.

[45]Engineering is the practical application of knowledge, "arranging, managing, or carrying through by skillful or artful contrivance."

[46]Land economics as a technology is more adequately treated in the Land Economics Institute's Modern Land Policy (Urbana: University of Illinois Press, 1960), especially Charles M. Hardin's "Political Planning: Possibilities, Limitations, and Aberrations," and Mark M. Regan's "Implementing Land Resources Policy."

[47]See, for example, S. V. Ciriacy-Wantrup, "Conservation and Resource Programming," Land Economics, Vol. 37, No. 2 (May 1961), pp. 105-11

river basin, the most efficient lease, or the best location for a road or park. The means are physical or institutional devices each of which can be implemented, adapted, or combined with other devices. The technologist may well depend upon the scientist to predict the consequences of using a means to accomplish an end in a specified environment. However, a great many actions are engineered without direct recourse to an analysis,[48] or they are based on previous research so that no new analysis is necessary.

Land economics as a science can be useful to land economics as a technology. If both the relationship among premises and the verification of predicted consequences are critical elements in a social engineering problem, such a problem has a scientific aspect and the methods discussed here are applicable. However, resolving conflicts and soothing felt difficulties without generalization, deduction, and verification belong to the arts of arbitration and pacification and extend beyond the capabilities of methods treated in this chapter.

Land economics, as a science, is a process for producing valid inferences and verified hypotheses. To expect more from a science is to place on it a burden greater than available methods are designed to carry, and neither the progress of research methodology nor the value of research findings are enhanced by exuberant researchers of indulgent planners who equate an advance of knowledge with a scheme for action.

---

[48]Mark M. Regan, for example, comments: "Only a fraction of one percent of the expenditures for resource conservation and development is devoted to research." Mark M. Regan, op. cit., page 272.

13

Steps in Carrying Out
Formal Research Projects

by Marshall Harris*

The preceding papers have laid a broad, multifaceted foundation for
the execution of formal research projects in land economics. In light of
these essays, the research may be concerned, either separately or con-
jointly, with land use and land tenure -- the two general subject-matter
areas into which land economics may be divided. The research under
consideration is not confined to the problems of agricultural land. It may
encompass, among others, recreational land, the growing edge of sprawl-
ing cities, the more fully developed rural-urban fringe, city and regional
planning, and land for public use, for instance, highways, forest lands
(both public and private), publicly held grazing lands, and Indian reserva-
tions. In short, all land and water resources and all institutional arrangements for their use and control are encompassed within the concept of land
economics research as presented here.

The research may be cast in either the positive or the normative conceptual framework. It may be approached from the viewpoint of production,
distribution, welfare, or other economic theory and concepts, including
the analytical framework posited by the institutionalists. In some research,
a combination of the various viewpoints might be combined. An added
dimension, with which we have had only limited experience, is interdisciplinary research involving various disciplines and subdisciplines of social
science; for example, legal-economic research. The potential analytical
procedures, as presented, are limited only by the constructive imagination
of the researcher. They are neither confined to nor limited by the present
state of social science or by the mechanical devices with which scientific
data may be processed.

---

*MARSHALL HARRIS holds a joint appointment as agricultural economist in the Eco-
nomic Research Service, United States Department of Agriculture, and as research professor at the State University of Iowa. Born in Kentucky in 1903, he received his B.S. from
the University of Kentucky, his M.S. and Ph.D. from the University of Illinois. He has
been connected with his present federal agency and its predecessors since the early 1930's.
He has made many studies in land economics, particularly on land tenure and land
institutions.

Thus, the framework within which this paper is cast is without theoretical limit, except by the scientific method and the imagination of man, as applied to social science. The focus of attention is land economics. I observe a tendency, but only a tendency, toward emphasis on agricultural land. Obviously dangling before the speaker is enough rope with which to hang himself, and my impression is that the noose is already formed. This is both an enviable and an unenviable position. The urge is to accept fully the freedom offered, to refrain from effectively disciplining the imagination, and to wander over the entire intellectual landscape presented in the previous essays, picking out the most interesting spots on which to pause for a few comments before rushing to a greener pasture, a shadier brook, or a more craggy mountain that lies beyond.

This temptation has been overcome, I hope. The plan of this chapter is to outline in a highly, and perhaps a rigid, schematic form the proposed steps to be followed in formal land economics research, as visualized by previous essays. In this presentation, I do not recommend that the proposed steps be taken seriatim, with one completed before the researcher goes on to the next step. The suggestion is made that in carrying out a project, the researcher should work back and forth from one step to another, making adjustments here and there in previously taken steps as greater insight is gained during conceptualization throughout the planning and execution processes.

The presentation is focused on economics -- not all of social science -- and the illustrations are largely agricultural. A tendency to document or amplify the presentation from the subdiscipline of land tenure, rather than from that of land use, the other half of the land economics dichotomy may be observed. The ideas are based more on the normative than on the positive approach. Thus, the orientation is largely, but not exclusively, problem-solving, purposeful-action research, rather than either knowledge or the scientific ordering of what is -- what relationships exist in the real world, and what might be predicted as man accelerates the making of adjustments and the acceptance of innovations in the environment in which he engages in economic activity. Emphasis is also more on "applied" than on "basic" research.

The viewpoint is held that positivistic research does not yield directly alternative lines of remedial action. Nor is basic research designed to furnish results to guide immediate, purposeful action, whereas the end product of normative research is remedial action and applied research carries a connotation of immediacy.

The general flavor of the presentation, as judged from the assignment, is "do-it-this-way" -- a kind of step-by-step set of instructions so familiar to those who undertake do-it-yourself projects around their homes. This perspective seemed to be dictated by the subject-matter assignment and its place on the agenda of the symposium. However, the analogy is used because it fits so poorly; it may make the point clear because of contrast. The difference between following typical do-it-yourself instruction and using this essay in planning and executing a formal research project is this: The do-it-yourself outline is followed essentially without imaginative thinking or questioning. Whereas, if this presentation has any value, it is to assist in encouraging and organizing the constructive, imaginative thinking of the researcher chiefly in the conceptualization process, including particularly, the preparation of project statements for administrative use and the formulation of work plans to guide the researcher. It does not presume to tell you how to think; if you do not know how already, it may be that you do not belong in research. Rather, it is hoped that the contribution will be toward improvement of the thought processes that are undertaken throughout formal research projects in land economics. Research is an intellectual, as contrasted with a physical or mechanical, process, despite dependence on modern mechanical means of manipulating masses of statistical data. Thus, emphasis here is on the thought processes involved rather than the selection of analytical techniques and how to handle specific mechanical details. Even if not required, the suggestion is to write up a project statement and a work plan for your own benefit, and to keep them in constant revision as the study progresses.

With this general framework before us, we are now in position to evaluate and appropriate for our respective uses the proposed steps to be taken in carrying out formal land economics research projects. In order of presentation, the steps are:

A. Selecting the problem,
B. Stating the problem,
C. Thinking through the purposes,
D. Formulating the hypotheses,
E. Determining the evidence needed,
F. Assembling the evidence
G. Processing and analyzing the evidence, and
H. Presenting the results.

During the conceptualization of the study, the researcher will need frequently to reformulate previous steps. The term "step" is used in the sense of one of a series of actions or measures; as, the first step in an undertaking. What is visualized is a mental process -- thinking through the analysis in logical sequence. Although each step may be completed tentatively before going on to the next step, there will be much going back and forth among the several steps throughout the entire research activity, including not only the conceptualization of the study, that is, the formulation of the project statement, but the carrying out of the workplan that shows in detail how each operation is to be performed. Also, a research activity might not complete all of the steps; for example, it might stop with formulating the hypotheses.

Previously presented boundaries are assumed as given. Among the more important are: (1) land economics research encompasses all types of land and water uses and all types of tenure forms, (2) all types of land and water resources, including oil, minerals, air and climate, are within the purview of this chapter, (3) the approach may be either positive or normative, and basic or applied, (4) the viewpoint may be production, distribution, institutional, welfare economics, or other economic theory and concepts, and (5) other social science disciplines may be utilized whenever interdisciplinary research is considered appropriate.

A. SELECTING THE PROBLEM

Selection of the phenomenon to be studied is of crucial importance in the research process. Research cannot produce results beyond the limitations automatically imposed by the decision as to the specific problem (interpreted broadly) upon which scarce resources will be spent -- for instance, valuable limited time, exceptional intellectual capacity, and restricted financial support.

Regardless of the approach, this question needs to be raised: Will the proposed research solve a specific, definable problem, the resolution of which will add to the store of scientifically useful knowledge? The problem must be subject to testing, for it must be soluble. It may confront operating farmers, urban people, planning officials, or social scientists.

A problem comes from an observed gap in our store of knowledge. The observation might arise from the curiosity of the researcher. It may come from doubts and confusion about what to do. Or, it may be brought to the attention of the researcher by persons in need of specific information. In a positivistic sense, the scientific facts gained by the study of various phenomena, rather than a search for ultimate causes, may furnish indirectly the basis for the solution of observed problems. In a normative sense, the insight gained by the study of the differences between the present situation and stated norms furnish directly the basis for action.

If the selection process follows the normative thought pattern and the applied approach, the proposed phenomenon to be subjected to analysis would be evaluated in terms of these questions. Can the projected analysis be described accurately as problem-solving? Will the results point specifically to purposeful action? If it shows why the existing situation does not meet accepted policy goals or objectives and if it outlines alternative ways and analyzes the probable consequences of bringing the present situation up to acceptable standards, it is problem-solving and could lead to purposeful action.

If the selection follows the positive thought process and the basic research approach, a different order of questions would be raised. What is the situation in the real world? What relationships presently exist there? What relationship is the future likely to yield? As determined, the presentation emphasizes the former approach. Yet regardless of the approach, the analytical procedure, or the particular spot on the land economic spectrum upon which attention is focused, the ideas presented are generally applicable.

The problem to be solved and the action to be taken, or the analytical description of what condition exists and its meaning to society, should be among the most significant problems, actions, or descriptions recognized. Look for the most acute problems, or the most strategic gap in our knowledge -- those that represent the widest range between the present and the desired situation, either economically or knowledgewise. They may not be the problems on which the public spotlight is focused or about which the most noise is being made. Look through the superficial situation to the real shortcoming or the proximate cause of the difficulty. Seek out the basic maladjustment or the greatest lack of useful knowledge; eschew the apparent.

Select a problem on which the proposed action or the usefulness of the new information will be applicable over a wide geographic area or to many social scientists. This makes for economy of research. Parenthetically, it is suggested that economic researchers who are concerned with efficiency of production and maximization of satisfaction might well apply these criteria in selecting the research upon which they will work, whether with public or with private funds. The results of research should be applicable, ceteris paribus, to an area, whether geographic or intellectual, much larger than that included in the study. In some instances, the results might be useful throughout the nation or to all social science researchers. It is

well to attain balance between the magnitude of the area of applicability and
the urgency or acuteness of the phenomenon under investigation.

Preference might be given to research on which the needed evidence
can be assembled efficiently. Similarly, a project might be rejected because the evidence may cost more than the value of its results when compared with alternative studies. Also, if the undertaking is not in line
with the training and experience of the available staff, the data-collection
process may be unusually expensive. The cost might be judged to be too
high in light of existing budgetary limitations. Too frequently, we underestimate the cost of the study. Available personnel and their training and
preferences are important considerations. Tailor the research to fit your
men and money, not to fit readily available data.

In the process of selecting the problem, usually a project statement
is prepared. It may well include tentative ideas regarding the nature of
the problem, the objectives or purposes of the study, the general analytical approach, an estimate of the probable cost, and such matters. The
statement is prepared before the researcher is ready to outline the study
in detail. It is used administratively in weighing various research proposals. In most situations, a comprehensive workplan that encompasses the
various steps – from stating the problem to presenting the results – is
prepared after the problem has been selected. Its purpose is to guide the
research activity, and it should be adjusted as greater insight is gained,
particularly during the conceptualization process.

B. STATING THE PROBLEM

After a particular, definable subject-matter area or phenomenon has
been selected for study, the next step is to state concisely the specific
aspects that the researcher proposes to investigate. The statement of the
exact phenomenon to be studied is designed to guide the next phases of the
research. A general notion of the situation was visualized in its selection,
but this generalized picture is not sufficient. It is not concise, definitive,
specific, or clear-cut. It does not demand thinking in depth by the researcher.

Before the workplan for the project is finalized, search out and summarize all of the pertinent information on particular and similar situations.
Also, make detailed empirical observations, whenever such observations
are applicable and feasible. Think through all ramifications of the subject
to be investigated. Determine upon relevant scientific analytical theory.
Conceptualize the difficulty so far as possible. Test your ideas on qualified colleagues as to the intellectual gap you are trying to bridge.

Some of the questions that need to be answered in stating the problem
are: What is the exact nature of the difficulty? Are the parties involved
unclear as to their specific rights, duties, privileges, or responsibilities,
as to how to proceed to attain their purposes? Does something in the
situation prevent them from allocating their scarce resources to maximize
satisfactions, whether economic or otherwise? Are they unsure of how
to deal with unforeseen contingencies? Are they unaware of alternative
opportunities and approaches? Is the situation new and unfamiliar? Is it
the unknown that is causing the difficulty? Are customary ways of doing
things obstacles? Are new ways needed? How widespread is the difficulty?
In what respects is it most acute?

Turning to another aspect of stating the problem, study known and relevant facts before completing the final statement. What is known? Digest the content of related studies and the findings they have established. This will reduce the amount of work involved in later phases of the study. All research should be built upon extant knowledge gained through past studies. The proposition is this: Generally, if more time is spent on conceptualizing the job to be done, the quality of the results is improved and the cost of the study is minimized. Spending too much time in deciding exactly what is the core of the study is the exception. Not one case in which this was done has ever been brought to the writer's attention.

Another major criterion to follow in formulating the problem is to define it in light of accepted and pertinent social science principles -- theory, logic, and philosophy. This can best be accomplished by giving appropriate consideration to such items, inter alia, as the supply-demand situation, distribution of rights in resources, the allocation of resources, factor pricing, marginal analysis, institutional arrangements, and the greatest good for the greatest number. Pertinent theory would be used specifically in describing the difference between the existing situation and the results the researcher hopes to attain.

Theory needs to be used throughout the study, but it should not dictate the nature of the problem. The problem should not be fitted to receive theory; use the theory that fits the problem. Develop new theory, if necessary; use intuition, experience and empirical observation, along with theory, in problem formulation. Compare your feeling of the problem with what theory has to offer.

In a normative sense, the problem needs to be stated also in terms of anticipated types of remedial action, such as increasing farm ownership, adding greater security of occupancy for tenant farmers, improving production credit arrangements, and reducing excessive rental charges. It might be stated also in terms of the development, for research purposes, of a new tenure classification to replace the old full-owner, part-owner, manager, and tenant classification. In my opinion, the old system of classifying tenure has hampered research. It tends to conceal rather than reveal actual differences among farmers who have obtained management control over their resources via different means.

The statement of the problems should also contain a paragraph or more on the assumptions, presuppositions, and general viewpoints that guide the study. Frequently, the position of the researcher on minor premises and ideas taken for granted is relatively clear from the way the research is posed. But it needs to be stated explicitly. Implicit biases, if any, need to be made explicit. Any leaning of the mind toward a particular opinion or viewpoint needs to be explained. Value judgments need to be clearly stated. In this way, an advantage will be gained: The next steps in the progress of the study will be taken more easily and more effectively.

What is assumed in stating the problem? What previously formed beliefs are adhered to? What is accepted and believed that has not been proved? Let me illustrate the point by using a study of the production credit situation among tenants. It might be assumed (1) that tenancy will be important in the tenure system over a long period of time, (2) that existing production patterns will continue, or that new ones as indicated will take their place, (3) that specified price-cost relationships will hold in the forseeable future, (4) that legislation is a feasible means of adjusting relationships between creditors and debtors, (5) that credit should be furnished by private parties, co-operatives, public agencies, or a combination of the three, and (6) that the interest rate should not exceed a stated percentage or cost to government.

Formulate the statement of the research in such a way that its component parts and subparts will stand out clearly. Thus, an over-all, generalized statement of the proposed research is not sufficient; it cannot shed light on the necessary details. In many instances, refinement of the area of concern, or breaking it down into logical segments, will reveal not one but two or three separate, yet related, phenomena that should be studied. Their separate parts may differ sufficiently to call for different analytical approaches.

The problem statement should shed some light on the probable findings or alternative lines of remedial actions. However, the statement should not indicate a preference for any particular result. Neither should it be confined to one or two of the most obvious solutions. It should cover all lines of action on which evidence will be gathered and upon which some evaluation will be made as to probable consequences. It should shed some light, however tentative, on relationships that might be established by the study and on predictions as to their continuance under assumed circumstances. Inclusion of possible lines of remedial action and their probable consequences in the problem statement should: (1) Tend to further clarify the specific phenomenon to be investigated; and (2) help in formulating the hypotheses and in determining the evidence needed to test them. These purposes will be served by outlining a first approximation of relationships that are likely to be found and the degree of their predictability. State the problem in terms of measurable characteristics and attributes and in such a way that operationally feasible hypotheses will flow from the statement.

C. THINKING THROUGH THE PURPOSES

The next matter to claim the attention of the researcher is outlining the immediate and longtime purposes of the research. The purposes are included among the steps for two reasons: (1) To sharpen the thinking of the researcher as he takes the next steps in the research process, and (2) to give all interested parties a concise picture of what the research is designed to accomplish. The purposes are based in part on the formulation of the problem, but they are conditioned substantially by preliminary thinking on the hypotheses.

The purposes need to be specific, short and succinct. Long, involved, generalized statements usually become more descriptive than analytical and seldom point directly to attainable goals.

The purposes need to be broken down into their component parts so that each objective is kept separate and distinct. This will be of value in determining the evidence and processes needed to accomplish the desired goals. Although not necessarily cast in terms of possible lines of remedial action or predictions of future relationships, the purposes of a research undertaking need to be conditioned by one or more of the specific results that are anticipated. For example, the general policy objectives of a particular study might be confined to achieving "efficient utilization of resources," or to attaining "security of rights in land." A research project is seldom designed to encompass several unrelated purposes.

The statement will generally prove most useful if the purposes are formulated in terms of relationships between the various characteristics or attributes of the phenomenon under consideration. This is not always possible, particularly if the study is concerned with a situation about which little is known. But even such a research undertaking should be centered on specific attributes, characteristics, qualities, essential properties, traits, and features of the phenomenon being investigated. An attempt should be made to push the research to the place where relationships between variables, attributes, and characteristics can be measured in relatively precise quantities or stated as concisely as possible in qualitative terms. In stating the purposes, use cardinal rather than ordinal terms of measurement whenever feasible.

The purposes of research may contain one or more statements to indicate that the researcher purposes to suggest alternative lines of remedial action looking toward the attainment of specific adjustments or to specify relationships about which predictions of reasonable accuracy can be made. In this way, the purposes can be related to the statement of the problem. A mark of well-conceived research is the closeness and completeness of the integration of the problem and the purposes.

Thus, the researcher needs to look two ways simultaneously; he needs to be able to perceive both the problem and the hypotheses while deciding upon the purposes. Look back upon the problem statement in thinking through the purposes. This will make it possible to formulate both statements more specifically and to maintain the connection between them.

Looking to the next step, the purposes should foreshadow the hypotheses, not that the hypotheses flow directly from the purposes; they do not. The purposes-hypotheses relationship of normative research arises from these ideas: The generalized purpose of land economic research is to furnish better information upon which decisions can be made -- suggesting what alternatives may be better to follow in actual situations and indicating the probable outcome of each.

D. FORMULATING THE HYPOTHESES

In land economic research, as in other social science studies, an hypothesis is a statement of a proposition or principle to guide the investigation. Hypotheses can be formulated with various purposes in mind. Some may be designed to lay out the bounds or to fix the limits of the study. As such, they tend to be statements of what issues separate the problem under investigation from closely related problems. In essence, if stated concisely and followed rigorously, they will tend to prevent the research from wandering all over a whole series of closely related phenomena by sharpening the focus on one or two specific situations.

In large part, hypotheses are tentative statements of the relationships believed to exist. This is the most important phase of the conceptualization process, if any part of an integrated structure can be said to be more important than another. They may be descriptive, provisional, vaguely felt, or explanatory. Small errors in the hypotheses may result in exploring a few unnecessary side issues or missing a situation that is of importance. Errors in the relationships that are expected to be found may result in a faulty or partial picture of the real world as it actually functions.

Some hypotheses may be designed to provide a framework within which to test various lines of remedial action or the probability that existing relationships will continue in the future. These hypotheses should flow logically from the previous hypotheses. To any researcher who feels that research may stop with the establishment of relationships, these hypotheses would be superfluous.

Examine closely each hypothesis to determine whether or not it is well-grounded in logic and theory. If familiar with the particular situation, the researcher may determine what the problem is with only limited empirical observations. But when he begins to set up hypotheses, he must be meticulous. He must be as nearly right as possible, for the hypotheses tell him, so-to-speak, what evidence should be assembled, and what data should be gathered. State the hypotheses so as to give specific direction to the latter phases of the study. By and large, various items of evidence will be selected on the basis of their value in testing the stated hypotheses. The researcher may want to write out a whole series of hypotheses. These hypotheses will need to be worked over, revised, combined, and rephrased until they finally form as accurate hypothetical statements as possible of the relationships that will be found to exist in real life.

The next research step is the testing of these hypotheses, eliminating, revising, reconstructing, and adjusting them until they are accurate statements of the existing situation. In final analysis, research must carry the hypotheses through rigorous analytical techniques until they become accurate generalizations derived from reliable evidence. The results should be useful in solving the problems of society.

E. DETERMINING THE EVIDENCE NEEDED

Another crucial area of decision-making in land economics research is the selection of the evidence (data or whatever supplies the means of finding true relationships) needed to test the hypotheses. The potential quality of the study is determined largely by decisions regarding what evidence to assemble about the various hypotheses. The construction of the schedule or other framework on which to assemble the evidence involves a multitude of minor decisions. They are not recounted here. Suffice it to mention only the most important areas that should be kept in mind.

A major decision needs to be made at the time consideration is given to the evidence needed. This decision is concerned with whether to plan a statistical study involving many respondents, a case-method approach involving only a few interviews, or some other analytical procedure discussed in the preceding chapter. In the former, insight is gained through statistical measures and central tendencies of a relatively few relationships. The case method involves minute probing into many relationships, possibly with few statistical measures resulting. A case-study approach has distinct advantage under two circumstances: when little is known about the existing situation, the case-study approach may be needed as the first study to uncover probable relationships that should be subjected to statistical analyses. It is also useful when analysis in depth is needed to facilitate interpretation and understanding of existing (usually general) statistical evidence. Although in many areas, the trend is toward complete dependence on statistical studies, the case-study approach has much to offer, particularly in the early stages of development of a comprehensive research program on situations about which little is known. Decide which of the several analytical procedures will be used before outlining the evidence to be assembled.

Include only the evidence needed to test -- prove, disprove, or firm up -- the hypotheses. This is a matter of taking the hypotheses, one after another, and outlining the evidence needed on each. Do not adjust the hypotheses to fit available or easily obtainable data -- find the data necessary to test the hypotheses. Also, ask this question, Is the evidence as outlined, sufficient for reasonable proof? After evidence needed for proof of each hypothesis is listed, the next step is to eliminate duplicating or overlapping items of evidence.

The researcher will need to check back to determine whether the evidence as outlined covers all aspects of the situation and relationships subsumed under the hypotheses. A second check would be to determine whether the evidence is relevant to the hypotheses as stated. In working through this step of the study, the researcher might gain new insight into the total situation that would make it advisable to go back and adjust some aspects of the problem statement and possibly of the hypotheses. Conceptualization of all aspects of study may involve much reformation of previous steps.

Items of evidence may be added or adjusted from time to time as the study progresses, if necessary. If a field questionnaire is used, changing it after a number of interviews have been concluded is difficult and costly. It may be advisable, however, to adjust the schedule, even if a number of respondents must be interviewed a second time. In other instances, a substitute for the omitted evidence may be obtained from another source, for example, public records. Revising plans for gathering other types of evidence may be necessary. Try to finalize the evidence to be collected at the earliest possible stage in the process. Make it cover all aspects of the hypotheses. Gaps in the data are serious handicaps in the analytical process. Think through the process of evidence determination to the analytical step.

In outlining the evidence needed in light of the problem, the hypotheses, and the anticipated results, the researcher must visualize the statistical techniques that will be utilized and the analytical methods that will be employed. Resources should not be wasted in accumulating evidence that is not susceptible to analysis. Frequently, the researcher is overpowered by the acquisitive instinct. He is inclined to go out and collect much of the readily available data. Blind faith should not be placed in one's ability to organize the evidence once it is in the office. The facts never speak for themselves. The analysis depends upon the facts that are pertinent to the problem. Here, we are trying to determine what facts to gather. Later, we will consider how to handle these facts so they will reveal accurately existing relationships.

In selecting the evidence, think of the treatment, statistical or otherwise, to which it will be subjected. This takes considerable time and effort, but it will prove economical both in assembling and in processing the data. Try to select evidence that can be put into shape easily for statistical manipulation or other processes used in the analyses.

The researcher should also evaluate the availability and accessibility of each item of evidence that is needed to test each hypothesis. The basic question is: Can the evidence be obtained? Next, Is it accessible without unreasonable cost? The availability and accessibility of evidence depend upon many factors, particularly upon the nature of the phenomenon under investigation.

Usually, people and public agencies, and this is especially true of data needed in land economics research, do not keep adequate records over a period of time. Many of them keep no records at all. The detail of the information requested, therefore, must be in keeping with either the records that are generally available or the memory of the respondents. This is a matter of testing and judgment. Except for an occasional item, the data became less accurate as the time period to which they refer becomes more remote.

Field questionnaires used to assemble evidence need to be tested before they are put to final use. This testing should be done before the evidence needed is finally selected. The testing process needs to be carried out in the field, where conditions approximate those under which the actual interviewing will be made. Field testing, as part of the evidence–selection process, is undertaken only after the questionnaires have been put into the best possible condition in the office. Revise the questionnaire two or three times before asking anyone to review it. Then ask several colleagues in your own organization or elsewhere to do the reviewing. These general guides apply also to other types of evidence that might be obtained from public records, statistical or financial reports, or various sources of nonstatistical evidence.

Testing might involve use of the questionnaire or other devices for recording data, covering 10 or 12 respondents or other sources, or it might include a pilot (or miniature) study. All conditions need to be as nearly as possible like those to be experienced in the actual assembly of the evidence. Include a good cross-section of the sources from which the data will be gathered. Those who test the possibility of obtaining the desired evidence should be representative of those who will gather the final data. The time of year may be important; if so, plan the testing near the time when the data will be obtained. This is important, regardless of whether the data are to be gathered from private citizens, with or without records, or from public officials or records. The co-operation secured and the accuracy of the data obtained may well depend heavily upon determination of the proper time of year for the testing of the data-gathering process. Do not select data that cannot be obtained with reasonable completeness and accuracy. Use the same care, explanations, length of interview, questioning, and recording that will be used in the study.

Sometimes, especially in the case of a complicated study or inexperience with the particular type of problem or analysis, a pilot study is needed. This involves obtaining evidence from a considerable number of respondents or sources and then going through the processing and analyzing phases of the study. This type of testing gives a more accurate evaluation of the suggested evidence. It may be essential to the evidence-selecting step of the study. It is more costly and time-consuming, but it is superior to shorter means of determining the evidence needed. Pilot studies may need to be more widely used than is true at present in social science research. This may help the researcher on economic problems maintain a high degree of efficiency.

F. ASSEMBLING THE EVIDENCE

The next step in a formal land economic research project is to assemble the evidence. In actual practice, some consideration will have been given this item as the researcher has worked back and forth from one step to another in the conceptualization process. Although the data are usually obtained by interviews, some important studies might involve evidence obtained from other sources. Usually, interviewing is the most costly way of gathering data. Therefore, if more economical sources are available for some part of the evidence, the researcher should investigate them thoroughly. But he should remember that accuracy is usually more important than cost. The availability of data is considered in some detail later.

An important decision is concerned with the number of interviews needed and the sampling design to be used. Sampling may well be planned in consultation with a trained statistician who specializes in sampling. The number of cases (size of sample) will depend upon the nature of the data and the statistical treatment to be used. The adequacy of the sample can be determined only in light of the characteristics of the population to be sampled. When limited mass data are not available for the entire population, the job of sampling becomes hazardous, even for one highly qualified for the work. Suffice it to say that if the researcher is not well trained in statistics, he needs to obtain the advice and counsel of a statistician.

Before going to the field for the interviews (even those for testing the schedule), set down on paper a clear definition or statement of each term, class, unit, measure, and concept to be used during the interview. This may sound like an unnecessary precaution. It is done to assure so far as possible (1) that everyone working on the study will use exactly the same interpretations, (2) that the concepts will not change during the progress of the study, and (3) that those who depend upon the results of the study may be accurately informed of the interpretations and concepts.

After the definitions are agreed upon, make an effort to maintain the definitions throughout the progress of the study, whether during the interviews or the assembling and analyzing of the evidence. This is difficult. Interviewers may be influenced, quite unconsciously, to make slight variations from the original definitions, particularly if conditions differ somewhat from those anticipated. It is impossible to take care of these contingencies except by adhering rigidly to the original definitions, as set down, or to agree upon changes in the definitions.

The interviewers and others who assemble the data, if there are several, should consult frequently in the early stages of the work for the purpose of agreeing more precisely upon interpretation and for solving problems that were not anticipated in the original plans. It is not expected that any researcher, however experienced, can conceptualize so completely even a relatively simple study that no adjustments will need to be made during the assembling of the evidence. The key idea is that any adjustment in interpretations should be made immediately when the need arises and that everyone should begin at once to use the new interpretation.

Edit each questionnaire, each data sheet, or each piece of recorded evidence within a short time after it is taken. Errors can then be corrected by the gatherer of the data, or if necessary, the source of the evidence can again be consulted. Frequently, a crew leader is expected to edit all forms, schedules, and questionnaires. When this is not possible, the documents on which the evidence is recorded should be traded among the members of the crew so that no interviewer or worker is responsible for editing his own work. This editing should be undertaken, however, only after the worker has checked his own questionnaire and believes it to be complete and accurate.

Usually the evidence will be most useful if it can be reduced to quantitative terms. If reasonably possible, record the data on questionnaires or forms. When this is not possible, try to record the evidence in such a way that it can be manipulated readily in the office in light of the planned analytical process.

Frequently, the sequence of events is important. If so, the date on which each event took place should be obtained. For example, in obtaining the tenure-occupational history of a respondent, the schedule usually shows in chronological sequence the various tenure statuses and employment experiences of the respondent and the year in which each change occurred. From this raw evidence, one can work out not only the sequence but the amount of time spent in each situation.

Maximization of the usefulness of the evidence at this stage is largely a function of the data-gathering process. Major emphasis is on completion of the schedules in such a way that the evidence will be most useful for the purpose for which it was intended. High-quality enumerating will reduce the amount of work to be done on the schedules in the office, decrease the number of errors, and improve the quality of the evidence upon which the final analysis is based.

Written reports on impressions gained by the data gatherers during the interviewing and recording are needed. These reports may include general observations, but they should include specific and detailed comments on each item in the questionnaire or form about which the workers have a question or a suggestion. So far as possible, these reports would include comments on relationships and generalizations that such empirical observations may have inspired.

G. PROCESSING AND ANALYZING THE EVIDENCE

After the evidence has been gathered and all of the data is in the office, the next step is to evaluate the evidence. Edit each questionnaire and each form again and check in detail for internal consistency. An item-by-item checking of all questions and processes -- asking, answering, recording, and interpreting is needed. Completeness should be a goal. How much incompleteness will be tolerated before an observation is discarded is a matter of judgment. Internal inconsistencies need to be worked out or the inconsistent item eliminated.

Discard all untrustworthy evidence -- that which falls below an established standard. Whether the researcher needs to go back and check the data at the original source must be decided. Crucial items in this decision are: The effect of discarding a unit of observation on the number of cases desired, the magnitude of the errors, the significance of the items upon which errors are discovered, and the availability of time and funds with which to do the resurveying.

The normal urge is to get the data-processing machines running as soon as possible. The best advice is: Do not rush the final evidence-checking phase of the study. Size up the situation, check and double check the evidence, discard inaccurate data, and be sure that all evidence actually measures what is called for in the plans of the study. At this point, each decision has a high degree of finality. To make changes after the tabulations have been made usually is expensive. Get the data in the best possible shape before it is processed for use.

Make a final check of the proposed statistical and analytical procedures. The analytical methods should be adapted to all preceding aspects of the study, including assumptions, theory and logic, problems, purposes, and hypotheses, as adjusted. All changes need to be made before the evidence is subjected to statistical manipulation and analysis. Be sure that each hypothesis will be tested adequately by the proposed techniques. If a major weakness in methods should appear, this is the time to devise ways and means either of adjusting the analytical process or of securing additional data.

Examine the appropriateness of the statistical processes. A good question to ask is: Are the processes too refined for the evidence? If the evidence is in gross measure, use appropriate statistical processes. Compilation of percentages, averages, and such derived figures may be used for certain purposes and with data that are not susceptible to more refined statistical processes. Case-grouping procedures may be applicable to data to which typical cross-classification analysis is not applicable. Regressions, linear programing, and other analytical devices may be the basis for more refined analysis. Appropriate measures of dispersion, variance, and tests of central tendencies and significance should be used when needed. These are technical matters that demand precise statistical processes.

One important problem is classification. For example, in analyzing differences in the use and control of resources as between related and nonrelated tenants, do they in fact represent essentially different groups? Also, are the conventional tenancy groups, that is, classification of tenants on the basis of the kind of rent paid, the most appropriate classification? Another question, Are debt-ridden, heavily mortgaged owners to be put in the same classification as owners free of debt? Similarly, are part-owners all alike, even though, for example, some own 90 per cent while others rent 90 per cent of their land?

Another item of concern to the researcher is measurement. Many of the important characteristics, attributes, and variables in land economics have not been subjected to precise measurement. Difficulties with measurement impinge upon classification, for the two are related. Be sure that the measurement used describes as accurately as possible each observed item.

The general proposition is this: The procedure for processing the data should permit exacting means of classification and measurement in isolating and describing characteristics, attributes and variables, and finally in establishing relationships and in drawing generalizations. The best statistical processes cannot provide for accurate analysis of variables that are measured only crudely. The tendency is for poor classification and rough measurement to cover up rather than reveal relationships that actually exist.

Be sure that the procedures used in tracing relationships among the several variables are logical and meet acceptable statistical and analytical standards. The proposed process should be reviewed by competent colleagues. Theory, training, experience, and judgment are important, but they need to be complemented by adequate discussions with qualified

technicians. On a typical study, some of the evidence may not prove useful even for experienced personnel. Some statistical measures will be
derived and discarded. The basic idea is to reduce this wastage to a
minimum.

Integration of the various steps in carrying out the study is a mark of
good research. Relationships among variables are analyzed in terms of
the statement of the problem. State relationships so as to show their connection with the purposes of the study. The same principle holds true for
the hypotheses since many interesting relationships may have been uncovered. But they are most instructive and useful if they are related to
the particular study as planned. Unimportant, remotely related findings,
however interesting, will clutter up the study.

Make clear the connection between the evidence and the findings
(relationships and generalizations). Too often the researcher depends
upon an instinctive feeling or conviction, or upon intuition, for an important statement. He might well be right. But the report needs to show
clearly when dependence is upon the judgment of the researcher rather than
upon relationships established by the evidence.

In addition to these more or less formal testing procedures, make at
least one informal test of the results. Take a look at the real world. If
necessary, go back to the area (or the situation) from which the evidence
was originally assembled, look around, and talk with the people involved,
if possible. In this way, evaluate the relationships and generalizations to
see whether they seem logical and grounded in the experience of the people.

H. PRESENTING THE RESULTS

The interest and enthusiasm of the researcher may well wane when
the results of his efforts emerge in the analytical process. His curiosity
may have been satisfied. The findings are gratifying. He has finished
the course. But he cannot stop there. He must carry the results to all
interested parties, for a basic purpose of research is to furnish knowledge
to those who can use it.

Make a full presentation of the study. This need not be made in one
large report. It can be divided among particular interest groups. Some
reports may be made before the study is completed. For example, progress reports may be required by those who are responsible administratively. Also, the demand for the resulting information might require preliminary reporting, particularly on selected segments of the study. The
administrator may face pressures to show accomplishments to justify
financial support of the project.

A complete picture should be available for the serious student (possibly fellow researcher) who wants the entire story. Be sure to cover some-
where in the various reports these items: (a) How the problem was selected and why it was considered crucial, (b) a description of the central core
of the situation and its subparts, (c) the assumptions that were made, (d) the
purposes of the study, (e) the original hypotheses and perhaps such restatements of hypotheses as were made during the analytical process,
(f) the basic evidence used in testing the hypotheses, (g) how it was
assembled, including the sources from which it was obtained, (h) the methods used in processing and analyzing the evidence, (i) the results of the
study, including all aspects, (j) suggestions, if any, for further study,

(k) difficulties encountered in the study, including mistakes and shortcomings as well as accomplishments in regard to new methods and techniques, (1) limitations of the study, cautioning against uses for which it is not applicable, and (m) pertinent information about the research agency and the researcher. All of these areas need not be covered in each reporting of the study. But they should be available to a fellow researcher when needed. Negative results, as well as positive findings, should be included in the reporting.

The subject of how to write various types of reports is too large a one to be covered here. But a few ideas are presented. The reports should be complete, effectively written, and lucid. A good manual on writing will be of help, particularly to inexperienced writers or to any writer who experiences difficulty in reporting the results of his research. Have the report reviewed by several colleagues, then rewrite it -- again and again. Do not expect the first writing to be final. Three or four drafts are common, even for seasoned researchers. Start writing as early as possible to clarify the findings and to permit several revisions.

A part of the difficulty of reporting arises from the attempt to make one report serve all interested groups, which is seldom possible. The major report is addressed directly to the specific group or groups the study was planned to serve. It needs to be adapted to their status of knowledge. In many instances, narration can be supplemented by graphs, charts, tables, pictures, and similar visual aids. The reporting may be made, even for the audience for which the study was conducted, in two types of reports: (1) A fairly complex report for the leadership of the group, and (2) a rather simple, easy-to-read story for the general reader. Do not overlook such avenues of communication as radio, television, public addresses, discussion groups, and similar means of making information available to the public.

IN RETROSPECT

This chapter has not afforded an opportunity to delve into certain philosophical-theoretical aspects of carrying out a formal research project. The subject-matter area to be covered was too broad for anything more than "painting in a hurry with a broad brush." For example, there was an urge to dwell on the philosophy that undergirds the role of hypotheses in social science research. Also, the chapter would have seemed more complete if detailed comments could have been made on the many problems of processing and analyzing the evidence, of establishing relationships, and of drawing generalizations.

To deal effectively with many of these matters would require another paper, or perhaps a book. The literature on most of these areas is plentiful and presents various viewpoints. It can be utilized to fill in the detail. By and large, it seems adequate for most researchers.

I have tried to present a step-by-step process, albeit arbitrarily selected, for the carrying out of a formal research project in land economics. The chapter is designed more for the young, inexperienced researcher than for those with years of fruitful experience. If it helps, the mission will have been accomplished and the writer will have reached the maximization-of-satisfaction goal in the allocation of the scarce resources available to him for carrying out his assignment.

PART IV. PROGRAM AND ORGANIZATION

14

A Program of Land Economics
Research for the Next Decade

by Harry A. Steele*

The purpose of this chapter is to outline a workable program of land
economics research for the next few years. [1] It attempts to bring the
foregoing chapters on theory, techniques, and methods into focus on a
research program. The emphasis is on the content of a research program,
but related problems of organization, administration, and staff are
discussed briefly.

To be most useful in the decision-making process, research results
must be available at the strategic time. However, it takes years to plan
and carry out complicated research projects. A research program must
anticipate the problems that will be important in the future. A review of
past statements on research needs indicates that it is difficult to anticipate specific problems and circumstances. In fact, research oriented to
a current specific problem situation may have little value in solving other
specific problems at some future time. In outlining a research program,
a segment must be concentrated on data, methods, and analysis of the
trends and relationships that seem most likely to be important in the
future. Included in such a program should be research on relationships
that are significant to an understanding of economic behavior and which
may therefore be useful in solving future problems. Information flowing
from this segment of the program is likely to have more general applica-

[1] In preparing this chapter I have benefited by the suggestions of my associates in land economics
research. I want to especially acknowledge the assistance of Mark M. Regan.

*HARRY A. STEELE is chief of the Land and Water Economics Branch, Farm Econom-
ics Division, Economic Research Service, United States Department of Agriculture.
Born in South Dakota in 1909, he received his B.S. and M.S. degrees from the State
College of that state; later he did graduate study at the University of Wisconsin. Since
1934 he has done economic research on land and water resources for the federal government. He has had many staff assignments with special committees and commissions
investigating resource problems. He was stationed at Lincoln, Nebraska, for several
years before moving to Washington, D. C.

tion in the future than information from a research activity oriented to current problems.

How can a research administrator anticipate these future needs? To some extent, the needs can be anticipated from projections of trends and from calculations of probable future requirements and potentials. Through their contacts and specialized knowledge, research workers and program administrators may gain insight as to specific problem situations that are likely to arise. However, a research program must have broad coverage. Overconcentration on one area of work may carry a high risk of missing the important problems of the future.

This chapter will attempt to outline a framework program. It will not deal with specific research projects that might cut across parts of several of the elements included in the different parts of the program.

For this chapter, as well as elsewhere in the book. "land" includes soil, cover, water, minerals, and air, or in other words, the natural environment. Land economics is the economic discipline that deals with problems when some aspect of the use or institutional control of these natural resources is strategic or central to the solution.

Land economists may do research, service research, plan, or operate programs. Solutions to land economic problems often involve public action. Consequently, land economics is closely tied to policy and program decisions. The land economics research program should contribute to these decisions but must be kept independent from these other activities. This independence is necessary for objectivity in research, but more important is the necessity for a research program that looks beyond immediate program problems. Perhaps the best way to do this is to provide for definite staff arrangements for taking care of service and planning activities.

EMERGING PROBLEMS AND TRENDS [2]

As we look to the future, it is certain that our land, water, and forests will be used more intensively. We will be obliged to get along with about the area of land and amount of water that we now have, but population and related requirements will likely more than double in the next 50 years. Technological breakthroughs may change the picture by making sea water useful or poor land fertile, but these technologies usually require intensification of use through application of capital and better management to natural resources. Without radical changes in technology, some regions will reach a ceiling in their ability to support economic activity; other more favored regions will forge ahead. The beginning of these trends can be observed now. The effect of resource use and productivity on regional economic growth will become of strategic importance in national resource policy.

The large amounts of management and capital going into the production process may lead some persons to conclude that this makes land unimportant, or at least less important. Actually, of course, the capacity of land and watersheds to respond to management and capital investment, as well as their inherent productivity, will determine their value in the

---

[2]See the more detailed discussion in Chapter 1 "Future Land Use and Tenure Problems Requiring Research," by Marion Clawson.

future. Given a favorable climate and suitable material, it is possible to
make great improvements in land now by land-forming engineering, but
this is merely saying that this land had the capacity to absorb management and capital. In the same way, a water-management system may
make a productive area of a swamp or desert.

When we conclude that we can meet the requirements of a doubled or
tripled population in the next 50 years from our land and water resources,
we are saying that the use of our land and water resources will be intensified in similar proportions.

The land and water problems of the future will arise from these expanding long-term requirements; from the management of increasing
amounts of capital inputs; from increasing competition and shifts between
crops, grassland, forests, recreation, urban developments, and other
nonagricultural uses; from the institutional devices necessary to reach
the group managerial decisions to guide and control changes in the use of
land and water; and from the problem of balancing private interests with
the increased public interest that will attach to all resource use. The
problem of distribution of ownership and access to resources will continue to be an important phase of land economics studies.

RELATED PROBLEMS OF RESEARCH ORGANIZATION
AND ADMINISTRATION

While organization problems are treated in another chapter, a few
of them are so directly related to program content that they should be
mentioned here.[3]

Land economics research has developed over the last 40 years around
organizational units in the U.S. Department of Agriculture and the land-
grant colleges. The development of a group of economists whose principal interest is in land economics, the development of graduate training
programs in land economics, the establishment of land economics professors in all the major universities, the development of a national program of research through the U. S. Department of Agriculture, and the
emphasis on land economic studies in the research foundations have all
contributed to an atmosphere in which a meaningful program of research
can be organized and carried out.

Research staffs can be organized most effectively on continuous
lines of work. Organizing by disciplines allows specialists to develop in
various fields and provides for continuous recruiting and training of staff
and for knowledge to be passed more easily from one scientific generation
to the next.

A competent staff in any field of research cannot be obtained on the
open market. Such staffs must be developed over a period of years. The
success story of almost every outstanding research organization is the
ability of management to recognize and develop research competence.
Whether we are talking about a professor and his corps of advanced graduate students, a government agency, or a private research organization,
this generalization holds. This means that the organization must
facilitate the process of wise selection, training, and development of

---

[3]See Chapter 15, for a more detailed discussion of organization problems.

researchers. It must also reward achievement if the results of developing such a staff are not to be drained away by competing institutions. However, a good research institution will welcome some turnover in personnel. This is part of its function to provide competent land economists for key roles in other agencies. The development of a competent staff can come only in research organizations that have some degree of stability as to organizational structure and budgets. Nothing is quite as demoralizing as continued shifts in functions or budgets, accompanied by long periods of uncertainty as to the mission of the organization or even its very existence.

As has been pointed out in several previous chapters, research is an intellectual process that is best done by following generally accepted procedures. This involves a penetrating analysis and testing in advance of actually determining the research data to be collected and analyzed. The process requires considerable flexibility and freedom of action on the part of the researcher.

There is some conflict between the usual form of research administration and these recommended research procedures. There is some question as to whether the current research-project system in use in the land-grant colleges and the U.S. Department of Agriculture is flexible enough to allow the researcher the necessary freedom of action.

The project system and detailed work plans prepared by supervisors, often with little opportunity for firsthand information, could prevent a researcher from carrying out a penetrating economic inquiry. In actual practice, fortunately, these project statements are not always rigidly adhered to in carrying out the research. Another troublesome problem is the statistical and other clearances that are required. These are likely to prevent full inquiry into a problem, or, once clearances are obtained, they may create inflexibilities in research plans. It was this type of inflexibility in research administration and its consequences in data collection and analysis of which Salter was most critical in his review of land economics research.[4] State-supported and private research organizations are not directly affected by these federal rules. Often, however, they have their own inhibiting administrative regulations. The attention to basic and pioneering research in recent years is an effort to free the research worker from any inhibiting administrative restraints.[5]

A major factor in the development of land economics has been the regional land tenure committees. These committees, which are made up of land economists from state colleges, the USDA, and the Farm Foundation, have served an important purpose in furthering land economics research. Research workers with a common interest in land economics need to get together to discuss their work. At such meetings, researchers are forced to take stock of their progress. With his ideas, one research-

---

[4]Leonard A. Salter, Jr. A Critical Review of Research in Land Economics (Minneapolis: The University of Minnesota Press, 1948).

[5]Dr. B. T. Shaw, in a memorandum dated July 16, 1957, establishing the Pioneering Research Groups in the Agricultural Research Administration, stated: "Pioneering research laboratories shall be staffed with research scientists who have demonstrated their capacity to work productively and progressively in an 'atmosphere' where exploration into the unknown, without specific objectives, is a continuous undertaking." Scientists in these pioneering research groups "have only one concern - to advance the frontiers of knowledge." Dr. Shaw directed that the creation of the pioneering research groups should in no way prevent program researchers from engaging in basic research as a means of achieving objectives.

er stimulates another, and the group dynamics of a good seminar results in a stimulus far beyond the summation of individual contacts. Researchers have a tendency, however, to try to carry out research through this committee type of organization.

If the research effort is based on the judgment of informed experts, this approach may work very well. But experience with part-time, committee-operated research is not very good, and most regional committees long ago allocated their regional funds to the individual states for "contributing" projects, or hired full-time project leaders to carry out regional projects.

Researchers should not limit their participation to committees of fellow researchers. They should also mix with workers from other disciplines, policymakers, and the public. A researcher should occasionally try to make his research findings operational by consultation on some public issue. If he cannot translate his research findings into suggestions for an operational policy or program, it is likely that other people also will have trouble doing it. Often the land economist will find in an action program a good laboratory for study of his research problem. Contact with policymakers and the public will help to insure that real problems are selected for study. The researcher needs to be placed in the position of explaining his activities to the public and taking account of the response. It is only through this process that he will become aware of what others think and, in turn, perhaps form a more objective judgment of his own efforts. It is not often that there is any objective way of measuring the value of research efforts.

Various devices may be used to keep the research worker from becoming involved in the controversy that often surrounds important public issues. Special task forces or committees may be established which the research worker may serve. The possibilities of several alternative courses of action should be outlined and the consequences of each alternative action presented. The research worker should identify and understand the decision-making process involved in the situation so that his data on alternative courses of action will be most useful in that process.

RESEARCH APPROACHES IN A LONG-RANGE PROGRAM

A long-range research program must be built around a series of investigations which will establish fundamental relationships and provide the basis for problem-solving research. It is difficult to anticipate the exact nature of problems that will be important at some time in the future. However, an attempt must be made to anticipate the general nature of land economics problems so that the research on fundamental relationships will be of maximum usefulness. In conducting any one research project whose purpose is to solve a specific problem, several types of research approaches may be used. However, in outlining this long-range research program, the work on economic relationships will be discussed separately from direct problem-solving research.

The following outline will be used:[6]

---

[6]See Chapter 2, "Scope, Content, and Orientation of Land Economics Research Today," by Maurice M. Kelso, and Chapter 3, "Objectives, Purposes and Goals of Land Economics Research," by John F. Timmons for more detailed discussion of the framework of land economics.

A. Explanatory research
   1. Basic data - description of existing situations defined in terms (classes) significant to land economics prob- lem-solving - kinds of resources, patterns of uses, productivities, institutional structures, and patterns, etc.
   2. Functional analysis of the economic process so far as land resources and resource-centered institutions are central to the process -
      (a) Explanations of current situation and past trends;
      (b) Projections and predictions of these relationships.
B. Problem-solving research
   1. Guides to resource policy goals.
      (a) Positivistically as to what people's goals are;
      (b) Philosophically as to what people's goals should be;
      (c) Goals determined by legislative and administrative processes.
   2. Devising land policies and programs:
      (a) What manipulation of land-centered institutions or of human behavior will change the land resource situation toward the posited goals?
      (b) What are the probable impacts of alternative courses of action?

A RESEARCH PROGRAM [7]

Basic Data

Adequate basic data on the use, productivity, ownership, and control of land and water resources is essential to a land economics research

[7] There have been a large number of statements on needs for research on land, forest, and water resources. Some examples are:

Perspectives on Conservation--Essays on America's Natural Resources (based on the Resources for the Future Forum lectures of 1958), Henry Jarrett, ed. (Baltimore: Johns Hopkins Press, 1958);

Farm Foundation, Agricultural Land Tenure Research - Scope and Nature (Chicago: October 1955);

Facility Needs - Soil and Water Conservation Research, Senate Document No. 59, 86th Congress, 1st Session (Washington, 1959);

National Academy of Sciences—National Research Council, Final Report of the Advisory Committee on Weather Control, Vols. I and II (Washington, 1957);

Resources for the Future, Inc., A Report on Planning, Policy Making, and Research Activities of the U.S. Department of the Interior (Washington, 1961);

National Academy of Sciences—National Research Council, Present Needs for Research on the Use and Care of Natural Resources, Publication No. 288 (Washington, 1953);

National Academy of Sciences—National Research Council, Principles of Resource Conservation Policy with Some Applications to Soil and Water Resources, Publication No. 885 (Washington, 1961);

Forest Service, U.S. Department of Agriculture, Problem Analysis - Research in Forest Recreation (Washington, 1957);

Proceedings of the National Water Research Symposium, Senate Document No. 35, 87th Congress, 1st Session (Washington: U.S. Government Printing Office, 1961);

U.S. Department of Agriculture, Program for the National Forests, (a) Miscellaneous Publication 794 (Washington, April 1959) and (b) Estimates of Work Needed and Costs by States for the Short Term - initial 12 years (Washington, May 1959);

Soil and Water Problems and Research Needs of the West, Senate Document No. 98, 82nd Congress, 2nd Session (Washington, 1952);

Resources for the Future, Inc., The Nation Looks at Its Resources, Report of the Mid-Century Conference on Resources for the Future (Washington, 1954);

National Academy of Sciences—National Research Council, The Need for Basic Research with Respect to Renewable Natural Resources (Washington, 1957);

Preliminary Report - A Land and Water Resource Policy for the United States Department of Agriculture, National Conference on Land and People, January 15, 1962 (Washington, 1962);

Council of State Governments, State Administration of Water Resources (Chicago, 1957);

Water Resources Policy, Report of Presidential Advisory Committee on Water Resources Policy (Washington, 1955);

U.S. Department of Agriculture, Water Resources Research Needs, Senate Select Committee on National Water Resources Print No. 28 (Washington, 1960).

program. While data collection is not the primary function of the research staff, the availability and adequacy of data will greatly influence the success of research. Researchers must concern themselves with data compilation to the extent that they make known their needs to those responsible for data collection. Land economists are as interested in data on the physical and biological properties and relationships of resources as they are in legal, institutional, and economic aspects of the behavior of people. In a study of water rights, for example, data may be needed on legislation, court decisions, custom, administrative procedure, group and individual rights, rainfall, hydrology, competing uses, methods of increasing efficiency of water use, productivity in different uses, and many other factors. Unless, over the years, pertinent data are systematically collected, summarized, and preserved, research will be handicapped. It would be impracticable for a research worker to gather first-hand original data on all aspects of the problem for each research study.

With the developments in rapid data processing, it is now possible to consider uses of mass data that a few years ago would have been prohibitive. However, many problems in data compilation, storage, recovery, and analysis remain unsolved, and much remains to be done before researchers have the full potential of machines and basic data at their command.[8]

We should move in the direction of electronic processing and storage of basic data on resources and adapt retrieval and analyses systems to the needs of research activities. Researchers should be able to program out of the electronic storage files of basic data the information they need in the most useful form for analyzing their immediate research problem. Until we reach this stage, land economists will continue to be handicapped by the lack of data and will be unable to comprehend the vastness and complexities of the land and water resources with which they deal.

Some of the areas in which data collection could well be expanded and improved follow:

A. Resource situation inventories

1. Better data are needed on the present use of land and water resources. A complete enumeration of uses of all resources at periodic censuses and annual estimates based on sampling, airphotos, and secondary data would be valuable.

2. Data on current productivity could be assembled for "land classes" that have similar responses to management. Productivity should be indicated in different major uses (crop, grass, forest) and levels of management.

3. Land and water use hazards could be covered in special inventories. These hazards would include erosion, flood, drought, and pollution.

4. More usable data are needed on water resources covering quantities available related to quality characteristics, dependability of supply, development possibilities, and other pertinent characteristics.

5. An inventory should be made of strategic sites that may be needed for public purposes in the future for water-control reservoirs, parks, open spaces, highways, and other purposes.

---

[8]Committee on Government Operations, Documentation, Indexing, and Retrieval of Scientific Information, 86th Congress, 2nd Session, Senate Document No. 113, and 87th Congress, 1st Session, Senate Document No. 15.

B. Tenure situation inventories

1. Periodic inventories of land, water, and forest-resource use should include a classification of the ownership of these resources.

2. For each of the major use categories, data are needed on classification of tenure by degree of control and the type, amount, and value of resources controlled.

3. Data are needed on the characteristics of farm operators, on how farmers get started, and on how they leave farming.

4. Information is needed also on (a) characteristics and frequency of use of various legal instruments (deeds, contracts, leases, etc.) through which tenure control is exercised; and (b) the characteristics of the land-rental, sale, and credit markets.

C. Resource institutions inventories

1. More information is needed on legislation, court decisions, and administrative regulations governing land and water use. These data need to be compiled in relation to the public interest in the use of these resources. For example, data on legislation, court decisions, and administrative regulations relating to water rights and water use should be compiled for each of the 50 states.

2. Improved data are needed on the number, type, size, authorities, length of operating experience, and other characteristics of organizations and districts for resource management.

3. A compilation of information on state enabling legislation providing for local control and direction of land and water use and development would be valuable.

4. Data are needed on the extent, type, and form of local public regulation and direction of land and water use. For example, the use by local government of zoning, building regulation, sanitation, and pollution control.

Functional Analysis

In addition to basic data and descriptive analysis, an understanding is needed of the functional relationships between and among various economic and physical factors as a basis for problem-solving research. This functional analysis of the economic process - when land resources and resource-centered institutions are central to the process - forms the basis for predicting the economic consequences of alternative lines of action.

There are so many variations of economic activity that the number of possible studies in this category would seem to be almost unlimited. A careful selection would be necessary, and there would be need for periodic review of the selection. The following are illustrations of functional studies that might be carried on in a national program:

1. The value of land and water resources in various competing uses, both within and between various agricultural and nonagricultural uses. Emphasis would be on the marginal value of land or water in alternative uses. Such studies would be useful in policy considerations of the problems of allocating land and water among various uses.

2. Resource income and value relationships; including measures of income, factors determining income, and factors affecting the process by which income is converted into capital values. These findings might be

applied in land-value appraisal procedures for purchase and sale, taxation, credit, and public acquisition.

3. Effects of land-management practices on yields, sheet and gully erosion, and water runoff; appropriate management practices for various types of soil and rainfall conditions; and costs and returns from various resource-management practices.

4. Costs of land, forest, and water improvement and development measures, comparisons of costs of alternative measures for achieving comparable results by alternative means in the same and other areas, and costs of land and water use adjustments between major uses. Such studies would help to determine the feasibility of expanding or contracting land and water resources in different uses.

5. Relation of tenure to efficiency of use of land, forest, and water resources; including effects of various types of tenure and leasing arrangements on output, resource conservation, capital accumulation, and the combination of factors used in production.

6. The operation of different land-survey and title systems in relation to ownership and transfer costs.

7. Analysis of the operating experience of local resource district organizations; including available authorities, extent used, sources of revenues, types of expenses, method of assessing charges, revenues, and financial position. Such studies would help in devising local organizations for integrated land- and water-resource management.

8. Relation of resource institutions to the efficiency of resource use and to the distribution of resource holdings and income. Included would be the effects of such institutional arrangements as water rights, interstate compacts, zoning, forest-crop law, and land-use regulations.

9. Analysis of the incidence of benefits and costs of various types of government resource-development and production-control programs; included would be the extent of capitalization of benefits in land values and the effects on other productive factors, succeeding owners, consumers, and others.

10. Factors affecting access to opportunities for farm operation and ownership - capital requirements, comparison of costs of ownership with other forms of control, and experience with different means of achieving control.

11. Problems associated with expanding nonagricultural uses of rural land - urban expansion, rural industrialization, highway programs, and recreational uses.

12. Experience with part-time farming operations, including farm activities combined with either industrial work, forestry, recreation, retirement, or others.

13. The relation of ownership and use of natural resources to regional and national economic growth and the effect of resource development on economic activity.

14. Methods of combining physical data on soils, climate, slope, and erosion with relevant economic indicators such as land sales prices, rents, and calculated net returns. This would enable techniques to be worked out for classifying land in terms of present and potential productivity.

15. Basic economic evaluation of physical relationships and management techniques designed to alter these conditions. For example, development of techniques for analysis of drought probability, response

of crops on different soils to these moisture deficiencies, and economic returns from alternative water-management systems.

16. Studies of technological developments in the resource field that have a potential for increasing or decreasing future water supplies or improving their management, and the impact of such technological changes on future water use potentials.

Guides to Resource Policy Goals

Land and water resources are vital national assets. The policies that guide the use, ownership, management, conservation, and development of these resources have an important relation to economic development, to the strength of the nation, to the distribution of opportunity and income, and to the status of the nation in international affairs. Resource policy goals become interwoven with many other national considerations. To ascertain the goals of peoples, or to suggest what their goals might be, the researcher needs to consider many tangible as well as intangible values.

Many public and private decisions regarding resource use are irreversible. Action now may preclude future choice. Not only are some decisions irreversible, returns from resource investment occur over long periods of time, thus requiring projections of future conditions as a basis for current decisions.

Another factor that affects policy goals is the fixed location of resources. Many conflicts between resource users and between regional and national interests arise because of the fixed location of resources.

There are several phases of policy formulation. Some new directions and institutional arrangements need to be visualized. These new directions and arrangements need then to be tested to permit comparison of results that might be achieved from different policy and program approaches differing from those used in the past. A desirable policy might then be recommended based on criteria as to what is desirable and the findings of the studies.

This type of study cannot be carried out by the researcher alone. He needs criteria, goals, or guidelines with which to outline his studies. He cannot substitute his values for those of others who have the final decisions as to what needs to be done. This is a difficult phase of research because the researcher can hardly keep from becoming a proponent of some one policy choice. Some general areas of research are listed below:

1. Projections of resource potentials and requirements, alternative areas and sources of meeting needs, and consideration of alternatives for balancing production potentials and requirements. Consideration would be given to shifts in resource use, resource conservation requirements, and the scheduling of resource-development operations.

2. Desired patterns of distribution of ownership of land, forest, and water resources, including the possibilities and limitations of family farm operations, preferences to be granted groups and geographic areas, and cost-sharing and incidence policies. Attention would be given to the effect of distribution on political stability, economic growth, and national and individual security.

3. Research to determine the significance of multipurpose land, water, and forest-resource management and development in terms of national and regional welfare and to define the concepts and criteria of

benefits and costs of public resource development. Further study is
needed of the economic principles governing impacts on economic efficiency, income distribution, alternative methods of allocating joint
investments serving several purposes, and the sharing of program costs.
Techniques for evaluating the products and services resulting from
resource projects and the inputs required for these projects need further
study, especially the possibility of extending monetary measurements to
include project effects that do not find expression in market prices.

4. Improved procedures for formulating watershed and river-basin
projects. Such procedures should take account of the interrelation of
land, forest, and water resources in plans for development that jointly
provide for the purposes of flood control, erosion control, drainage, irrigation, and agricultural water supply. Improvements are needed in
methods for appraising each purpose separately. They are needed also in
application of methods such as mathematical programing for simultaneously determining the optimum scope of various purposes in project plans.

5. International resource policies and programs. This would include
research designed to outline policy goals to guide U.S. assistance to resource-development programs of other countries through augmenting
available capital resources, agricultural land reform, improvement of
credit, tax policies, etc.

Devising Land Policies and Programs

Once a general policy goal is agreed upon, there are many ways of
achieving such a goal. Often, controversy centers around these means
rather than the ultimate goal. For example, there is general agreement
on the goal of conservation but less agreement on the use of such alternate
means as education, technical and financial assistance, land-use regulation, taxation, or public purchase, in achieving the goal. Similarly, there
is agreement as to the desirability of comprehensive river-basin development but very little agreement on the type of organization under which
such development might best be achieved.

There is a continuing relation between goals and means, and no sharp
dividing line between them. Sometimes, the controversy over means in
reality reflects underlying controversy over goals.

It is in this area of means that the researcher can provide analysis
of great usefulness in public affairs. This is the area in which institutional, economic, and statistical analysis must merge. The researcher
needs to devise new institutional arrangements, make analyses of the
probable economic consequences of different institutional arrangements
in terms of desired goals, and test these analyses statistically with such
data as can be obtained.

It is the hope of researchers to be able to develop economic models
that will simulate the type of economic activity with which they are concerned and thus to be able to indicate the effects that various policies and
institutional arrangements might have on the economy. Major obstacles
seem to be econometric methods that simulate a dynamic economy
characterized by irreversible decisions and the lack of data that reflect
accurately the current and projected economic relationships involved.
Until we have such advanced methods, the economist who wishes to be
helpful in program development must do his best to improvise estimates
of the probable results of different courses of action.

1. Analysis of alternative types of measures likely to be effective in accomplishing policy goals.

2. Organizational arrangements for effectuating policy; including types and relationships between national, regional, state, and local organizations, and the functions and authorities appropriate for each level.

3. Studies of various processes to be applied by operational and administering agencies; including land and water resource planning and project and program formulation, management of program operations, and financial management of programs - including charges for services and assessments, means of modifying institutional obstacles, and reconciling conflicts of interest.

4. Explore legal and institutional innovations for the control of land use. With the increased public interest in the private use of land there is a need for new techniques of control. For example, such innovations as purchase of use rights to control and direct land use and the purchase of development rights to reserve open spaces in urban areas should be explored.

5. The conceptual construction of alternative legal systems of allocating control of water, and appraisal of the possible economic consequences of these alternative systems as indicated by the analysis of the relation between legal provisions and the use of water.

SUMMARY

The specific projects in a research program vary from time to time, depending upon current problems, the mission of the particular research organization, and available funds. Therefore, this chapter is an attempt at an outline of the framework of a research program in land economics rather than a list of specific projects.

The framework consists of basic data, analysis of economic relationship, policy goals, and means of implementing policy. Any one major research project might involve a combination of some elements of all these phases.

The land and water problems of the future will arise from expanding requirements, increasing capital inputs, and increasing competition between farm and nonfarm uses, and from the institutional devices necessary to reach the group managerial decisions that guide and control the use of land and water and that balance private interest with the increased public interest which in the future will attach to all resource use.

Some of the more urgent problems involving national policy questions are as follows:

We have about 640 million acres of potential cropland. Crop production potential will continue to outrun requirements for the foreseeable future. Land use adjustment programs are needed to shift cropland to other uses and to keep other potential cropland from being brought into uses as cropland. While all of our potential cropland is not needed at present, we do need to protect and conserve this land and use it in such a way that it will be available to meet future needs.

A large acreage of unsuitable land is still devoted to crop production. Programs are needed to get such lands shifted to more suitable uses.

There is need to adjust our land resources to changing requirements and technologies so that resources are put to use instead of lying idle. There is expanding need for such purposes as recreation and open space, but declining needs for cropland.

Many studies show that the efficiency of agricultural water use might be greatly improved, yet trends of the last decade indicate that little progress has been made. Research is needed on changes in institutional arrangements to encourage the application of known technology and of technology that may be developed.

Much of the future forest production will need to come from small private forest holdings. Research is needed on the reasons why owners of these holdings do not follow recommended practices so that suitable incentives to good management may be found.

If the family farm is to survive, research needs to find ways of adapting the most advanced agricultural technology to this type of unit. In addition, credit, taxation, and other arrangements may be devised to encourage the family farm.

There is need for improved methods of predicting quickly the probable results of alternative land and water policies.

There is general belief that resource development contributes to economic growth, but suitable methods and empirical evidence are needed to show these relationships.

15

Organization and Administration for Effective Research in Land Economics

by Joseph Ackerman and Marshall Harris*

The discussion of the organizational and administrative structure for land economics research appropriately comes last. For adequate consideration of organization and administration for research requires prior knowledge of the scope and content of the research field, the objectives and purposes of the research, the principles and theories that guide the activity, the methods and techniques of analysis, the kinds of projects needed, and the use to be made of the findings. These matters have been adequately discussed in the preceding chapters.

This chapter will, first, set forth some principles that should serve as guides in developing an effective organizational structure for facilitating research. It will next review briefly the present organization and administration of land economics research. Then it will consider successively the role in research of land-grant colleges and universities, the U. S. Department of Agriculture, private research agencies, and organized regional research groups. The concluding parts of the chapter will be concerned with problems that stem from weaknesses in the present organization and administration.

*JOSEPH ACKERMAN is managing director of Farm Foundation, located in Chicago. Born in Illinois in 1904, he received his B.S., M.S., and Ph.D. degrees from the University of Illinois. He also had a year of graduate study at Harvard. After several years of agricultural extension experience at the University of Illinois, he joined the Farm Foundation in 1939, first as associate managing director, and since 1954 in his present position. In this role, he has worked with regional committees and other groups of agricultural economists in this country and abroad. The Farm Foundation under his leadership has played a major role in making possible regional and other joint committee activities.

MARSHALL HARRIS is Agricultural Economist, Farm Economics Division, Economic Research Service, United States Department of Agriculture. (See biographical sketch, chapter 13.)

This paper expresses the personal views of the writers on the questions considered.

Authors' Note: This paper has benefited from constructive criticism from Allan Schmid and Robert Young.

GUIDING PRINCIPLES

Research is a systematic search for new information to establish fundamental relationships and to reveal basic truths. Its purpose is to extend the frontiers of knowledge. It involves collecting, organizing, and interpreting data, making deductions and drawing conclusions, and testing the findings to determine their validity. Research is a prolonged, exhaustive investigative process. If it is to be effective, it must meet several fundamental requirements.

Integrity. A researcher must be completely objective and intellectually honest to obtain reliable results. Research demands dedication to the obtaining of complete and accurate facts and a willingness to face the findings, whatever they may be. The researcher can take nothing for granted. He must weigh every variable regardless of how insignificant it may seem. He must accept the results, even if they conflict with his original hypotheses. The process of research may call for substantial revision of hypotheses until they conform to actual relationships found in real life. The researcher must be aware always of the natural inclination toward preconceived notions and biases. He must assiduously guard against any distortion of the truth.

Continuity. A number of unrelated research projects do not constitute a research program. Successive studies in a particular subject-matter area must follow in an unbroken sequence. They must be thoroughly integrated to maximize the results. Each study should build upon earlier findings. Each investigative effort should take place at a higher level. The frontiers of knowledge are rolled back by adding new truths to the existing store of information. Research is not merely a searching for what has been discovered already. It must increase the sum total of human knowledge.

Continuity is important from another viewpoint. The research process should continue to its logical conclusion without disruption. After endless hours of studying the myriad intricate details of a problem, a researcher may find tentative solutions only to discover either that another approach would produce more conclusive results or that he was working on the fringe of a much bigger problem. The loss may be serious if he terminates his investigation at this point because of lack of funds, pressure of other work, or completion of the original project. Once the research is interrupted, it may never be resumed. If it is resumed later, some of the most fruitful ideas may be lost. Research is interrupted more than occasionally, at substantial loss.

Flexibility. A research program must be adaptable, that is, subject to adjustment and change without complete disruption. A nice balance must be reached between continuity and flexibility. For example, ordinarily the researcher is required to submit project plans, including the research procedures that will be followed. The established project system may be too rigid to meet the requirements of new lines of research. Or the researcher may be unable to formulate the problem and the process with the precision necessary to obtain funds. Or the project statement may be so rigid that subsequent adjustments are difficult or impossible.

Responsiveness to Changing Needs. Research must be forward looking. It must anticipate problems before they arise, or at least before they become acute. Research is sometimes such a long process that unless the study is started as soon as the problem emerges, the problem may change before the research is completed. Research at its best provides the answer before the problem becomes widespread and difficult to solve. Land economics problems in this regard are in sharp contrast with problems in the physical and biological sciences. The former are not exactly the same from one geographic area to another or from one time period to another. The latter are more constant over time and from place to place. The ever-changing nature of land problems demands foresight in problem selection and dispatch in execution of the research.

Freedom. The researcher should have considerable freedom in the selection of both the problem on which he will work and the processes he will follow in seeking the solution. Only if he has such freedom can he think imaginatively and work enthusiastically. Complete freedom is not suggested, for that would not permit the following of other guiding principles. "Responsible freedom" might be a better term than "freedom." In the exercise of his freedom, the researcher should be conscious of his responsibility to the organization for which he works and to his fellow workers. Freedom to employ new techniques and untried processes seems essential. Freedom in problem selection and methodology is likely to be greater than freedom in the publication of the findings. But even at this crucial juncture considerable freedom should be accorded the researcher.

Efficiency. Constant efforts should be made, on the one hand, to use the most competent personnel available for each task and, on the other hand, to avoid having personnel perform services at a level below their maximum ability. Too frequently, researchers make field interviews, do typing, or perform clerical and numerous other tasks for which equally qualified persons could be employed with a lower outlay of scarce research funds. So much of the budget can easily be used for regular, full-time personnel that little is left for the numerous services that might contribute most to the efficiency of the over-all operation.

Attention to Basic Research. The pressure is usually to devote effort to the solution of practical problems -- to carry out applied research. Yet in recent years, some research agencies are placing more emphasis on adequate theory, general principles, and improvement of the thought processes. Such emphasis on basic research is needed to provide for scientific growth and proficiency in the scientific process.

Research administrators may create favorable conditions for effective research if they will, first, develop a staff of researchers of the highest integrity, and then, among other things, facilitate continuity of study to permit building upon past successes, provide for flexibility to permit changes in content and processes, encourage study of problems before they become acute, allow sufficient freedom to foster imaginative searching for fundamental truths, strive for maximum efficiency in the use of personnel and funds, and give sufficient emphasis to basic research. The administrative-organizational structure for research should always be a means, never an end -- a means by which qualified personnel are brought together, adequate funds are provided, and an appropriate atmosphere is created for scholars to work unhampered by too many rules.

OVERVIEW OF PRESENT ORGANIZATIONAL STRUCTURE

Some sort of organizational-administrative structure is necessary to provide essential personal services and other resources with which to conduct land economics research. The research organization also provides the setting and atmosphere, whether favorable or unfavorable, in which intellectual explorations are made. The setting should be conducive to scholarly inquiry and critical thinking. Sufficient funds should be made available to permit long-time planning -- an annual or short-term budget frequently prevents adequate planning. Also, the research agency needs to be relatively stable and permanent if the researcher is to benefit from past experience and accumulated knowledge. Even in a permanent organization like the U. S. Department of Agriculture, a particular line of research may be subject to frequent reorganization and threat of discontinuance.

Land economics research had its origin and major growth in the land-grant colleges and universities and the U. S. Department of Agriculture, individually and co-operatively. More recently, other agencies of the federal, state, and local governments have undertaken research directed toward solving land use and tenure problems. For example, the Bureau of Public Roads and numerous municipalities conduct research on these problems. Private foundations have also participated in research on land problems. Recreational groups are becoming increasingly interested.

Attention will be focused on problems resulting from present weaknesses in the organizational structure and administrative procedures. The weaknesses must be understood before solutions can be found. Various types of questions need to be considered. For example, can a particular type of research be conducted best by an individual or a group? By one institution or several co-operatively? By public or private agencies? By institutions of higher education or by industry?

The organizational-administrative structure should be made as effective as possible at all levels to meet future problems as they arise. As population increases and urbanization continues, greater attention will undoubtedly be given to land economics research in urban areas. More research will need to be directed to recreational uses of land, to the encroachment of growing cities upon the agricultural countryside, and to the taking of agricultural land for highways and other public uses.

Numerous groups now conduct research on various types of land economics problems. This situation adds to the need for improving organization and administration. When a multiplicity of interested groups -- urban and rural, public and private, federal and state, local and regional -- are involved, the organizational and administrative problems are much more complex than when only two or three agencies are working on a small area.

Great progress has been made during the last decade in co-operative regional research among the several states and the U. S. Department of Agriculture. A beginning has been made in integration and co-ordination of research among the several regions working on the same problem. Some progress has been made also in co-operative research in land economics between and among nations, particularly on land reform. Much of the progress has been made in spite of the present organizational administrative structure, rather than because of it. The regional research processes, for example, should be studied to determine how to resolve administrative problems that exist or that may arise in the foreseeable future. Perhaps a new organizational structure is needed if maximum effectiveness is to be attained. Those who become involved in international co-operative research should try to obtain the most effective administrative organization possible.

Land economics research may call for an organizational structure that will encourage interdisciplinary, interdepartmental, and interinstitutional research. Recent trends are toward increasing co-operation, yet the old organizational structure continues and sometimes impedes such co-operative research. An illustration may be drawn from legal-economic interdisciplinary research in land economics. At the national level, an economic research agency finds it difficult to employ legally trained personnel. Although conditions vary at the state level, professional personnel in the two disciplines are usually housed in different buildings on widely separated parts of the campus. Or they may be on different campuses. Intellectual interchange is more difficult when personnel are widely separated. Again, an organization established for research purposes may well be quite different from an organization established chiefly for teaching. The organizational difficulties may be solved by employing technically qualified personnel of one of the disciplines to work in the other's organization. Or interdisciplinary co-operation may be sought through memoranda of understanding that call for cooperative research. Attention to the administrative-organizational structure would seem to be desirable wherever interdisciplinary research is called for, whether between departments or colleges or institutions.

One characteristic of land economics research that complicates administration is that the research is often concerned with controversial problems and policy issues. The difficulty arises from two sources: First, the problem and the research procedures are not as easy to state in the project outline as on less controversial and policy-ladened research. Second, the researcher who deals in such matters is more vulnerable to attack by vested interests than one who studies less explosive subject matter. This does not mean that the research should not be undertaken. It means only that the unique requirements of such research should be understood and that the organizational structure of the agency should be designed to afford the researcher maximum protection.

Land economics research may be so completely submerged in an organization that effective research is practically impossible. Frequently it is a minor segment of a large organization. Experience has proved time after time the difficulty of building an effective program of research under such circumstances. Neither administrative attention nor resources are apt to be concentrated on a minor segment of a large agency. Individual drive, personal commitment, and stability of personnel are related to the general atmosphere in which the research takes place. One way to attain an effective working situation for land economics research is to set it up in its own administrative unit, as are comparable disciplines, but precautions should be taken to prevent the development of vested interests. In fact, except for the development of vested interests in other disciplines, a separate administrative structure for land economics would neither be necessary nor advisable.

From another viewpoint, the individual researcher is an organization for research purposes. After all, the work is actually organized around an individual and carried out by him. Looking to the future, the organization needs to encourage the development of the individual by providing for continual investment in him. Researchers should be encouraged to obtain the maximum training commensurate with their capacity. This may be accomplished in several ways. Some researchers should be financed while they return to graduate school to obtain additional academic training. Those who have completed their graduate training could be encouraged to continue their education in other ways -- sabbatical leave, participation in research workshops and symposia, and attendance at specialized short courses. A question may well be raised about the adequacy of the conventional sabbatical type of leave. Would a study of present sabbatical leave provisions indicate major weaknesses and point the way toward improved leave arrangements? Private foundations could contribute effectively to such training through the creation of scholarships and fellowships and the financing of travel and special study.

The new and emerging land economics problems will make different demands on research workers. Emphasis could well be placed on training programs to meet these needs. The older researchers need specialized, on-the-job training to make them proficient in applying new technologies of research to new problems. Those who will branch out into new areas of research, for example recreational and international, may need a period of intensive study to equip them for the tasks ahead. Such training could be more effective if provided through formal courses, seminars, and symposia than if left to the researcher alone while he is trying to establish his research. The younger researchers who do not have advanced degrees might be provided with funds to return to school for additional formal training. The organizational-budgetary setup in many agencies does not adequately encourage such training. Careful study may reveal weakness that could be remedied.

Consideration should be given to organizational-administrative obstacles to mobility of researchers. Two are quite obvious: First, automatic increases in salary, accumulated sick leave, and retirement benefits, under present arrangements, may prevent researchers from moving to new research opportunities. Second, the desire to maintain a well-qualified staff and the devices used to do so may prevent the movement of personnel from one administrative unit to another. Since the researcher is such an important factor of production in research, the research system should facilitate movement to permit employment of researchers best suited for each job. Some administrative reorganization possibly could facilitate freer movement. Provisions might be made for complete interchange of leave and retirement benefits. Any procedure that tends to freeze personnel on the job should be examined carefully.

RESEARCH IN THE LAND-GRANT INSTITUTIONS

The basic organizational structure for land economics research is built around land-grant colleges and universities. The increase in research in the U. S. Department of Agriculture, in other governmental units, in private foundations, and in industry has not changed the center of focus in the state institutions. Also, much of the research of governmental and private agencies is conducted in close association with the land-grant institutions. One of the reasons for this situation is that qualified personnel are available in the state schools. In addition, association with an educational institution or a particular faculty member sometimes lends prestige to the research and helps in getting it accepted by the administration and later by the public.

Part of the strength of the land economics work in the state institutions is due to the interrelationship between research and teaching. The land-grant schools have a dual responsibility for increasing the store of knowledge while at the same time imparting that knowledge to all whom they serve. The two responsibilities tend to complement and supplement each other. Men who are seeking answers through research are likely to have a deeper understanding of the subject matter as well as more stimulating new ideas. The researcher who also teaches is in a position to check his research findings in the classroom and in seminars. The present organizational structure of most land-grant institutions permits a satisfactory blending of research and teaching. Possibly a larger proportion of the teachers could be brought into the research stream. However, so long as a person is responsible for both teaching and research, he is apt to give an inordinate proportion of his total time to teaching. A better division of the time between research and teaching might permit some personnel to concentrate entirely on teaching for a time and then shift entirely to research.

The land-grant institutions are in a unique position to train future research workers. They can influence future researchers at the most strategic time -- when they are preparing to take their place in the world. The university, including both teachers and researchers, has an opportunity and a responsibility to help the student to establish habits of clear and critical thinking, to develop creative imagination, and to appreciate the value of careful and methodical inquiry. The type of training provided by the university is an important factor in determining the caliber of the scholars whose new findings will spell future progress.

The teacher-researcher combination is ideal for giving the prospective researcher first-hand and practical experience in research. Perhaps a larger proportion of the work for the master's and doctor's degrees could serve this purpose. Graduate requirements might be designed so that the resulting dissertation could be published as a finished piece of research. This is an area where administrative arrangements might facilitate both the student's learning and the completion of first-class research. Graduate school, might be consulted to obtain relaxation of some of the rules and regulations regarding the form in which a thesis or dissertation is to be prepared. For example, some dissertations have been mimeographed rather than typed, to permit wider distribution. Patient negotiation may be required to obtain relaxation of the "typing" requirement.

The land-grant institutions are a natural place for research and the training of researchers. They are dedicated to seeking the truth through research. Their libraries make knowledge easily accessible to the researcher. Men of learning gravitate to their staffs. And the close association of scholars stimulates creativity. More research on land economics problems could be encouraged:

1. By allowing staff members more time for research: (a) by adjusting the teaching load of selected staff members; and (b) by providing sufficient clerical and secretarial personnel and mechanical services.
2. By paying salaries that will attract and hold capable men.
3. By obtaining funds for research from independent organizations and foundations.
4. By adding research budgets to some professorships and expanding them for others.

5. By encouraging and aiding faculty members to attend professional meetings.
6. By expanding library facilities used by researchers.
7. By providing surroundings and an atmosphere conducive to more and better research.
8. By facilitating the publication of research findings through better reproduction processes and providing more copies for wider distribution.

RESEARCH IN THE U. S. DEPARTMENT OF AGRICULTURE

The U. S. Department of Agriculture has been engaged in land economics research for over half a century. Throughout this period it has co-operated actively with the land-grant institutions in the development of a joint research program. The working relationship has been close and effective. The Department would seem to be a logical agency for obtaining some co-ordination of the over-all research program. Even more important is its role in maintaining a balanced nation-wide attack on the land problems of importance to agriculture.

The land-grant colleges and the Department of Agriculture have grown up together and worked in double harness for so long that co-operative research with other agencies does not come easily. More attention might well be given to working with other public agencies -- the general farm organizations, recreational groups, urban agencies including municipal and local units of government, and various agencies of the federal government. Co-operation with these groups would be particularly helpful in determining the objectives and scope of research on land problems. Such formal contacts would help to assure continued adjustment to changing needs.

The Department of Agriculture should be concerned with problems of broad regional, national, and international significance. The research on some of these problems can be conducted in co-operation with state and local groups. The regional research committees are an important means for effecting such co-operation. Other types of co-operation, such as multilateral studies of the Department and selected states and organized groups within the states, should be used more freely. Such co-operation might well include groups interested in nonagricultural uses of land.

The contention has been made that research by the Department of Agriculture frequently is subject to bias. Research on land problems by the Department, however, is less likely to be biased than, for example, either research on ways and means of balancing supply and demand in agriculture or research on the effectiveness of established programs of the Department. Even so, the Department's researchers need to be ever mindful of the possible loss of objectivity resulting from awareness that some of their research affects directly the policies and programs of the Department.

The research-organizational structure of the Department should protect its researchers in this regard. Some provision might be made for separation of personnel between policy-programming research and the regular research activities. The best minds of the Department, of course, need to be used in the policy-programming activities of the Department. But the regular land economics research program should not be disrupted seriously by having the same personnel work on both types of research activities. One possibility would be to transfer the researcher temporarily from his research agency to an over-all planning group when his services are needed in policy-programming research. The assignment might be for a short term or for a long term, but he would return to his own agency upon completion of the policy-programming assignment. Keeping separate these two research functions is in part an organizational and in part an administrative matter. Both aspects must be watched carefully to maintain the desired degree of objectivity and to protect the research agency against pressure inherent in policy formulation and in program planning and analysis.

Land economics research in the Department of Agriculture has been subject to four other handicaps: a widely fluctuating budget from year to year, threat of discontinuance of the work, frequent changes in the program, and rapid turnover in staff. An effective research program cannot be built on an annual budget that varies widely from year to year and that is subject to pressures for adjustment from time to time during the year. Neither can an effective research program be developed when discontinuance of the agency is periodically subject to widespread discussion. Also, the best research, particularly on long-time basic problems, is impossible under a program of research that often changes significantly. Likewise, effective research is seldom accomplished by a staff that is unstable and insecure. In the interest of efficient research the organizational-administrative structure should provide a desirable working situation with respect to these four items.

ROLE OF PRIVATE AGENCIES IN RESEARCH

Private agencies, including foundations, should be encouraged to engage in land economics research. They can complement and supplement the work of public agencies. They can play several unique roles for which they may be better equipped than publicly supported research agencies.

First, they seem to be in a better position to take the lead in basic, long-range research than are public groups. Too frequently the resources available to public research agencies must be used in solving immediate short-run problems. Second, private agencies are in a good position to deal with problems that have policy implications, for they are relatively immune to public pressures. Third, they are in a superior situation to deal with program or agency appraisal and evaluation. A public agency is not in a favorable position to evaluate its own program. Neither is one public agency in a good position to appraise and evaluate the accomplishments of another public agency, particularly within the same Department. However, most operational procedures of an agency can be appraised best by the agency itself.

Private agencies and foundations are in a unique position to render another important service to land economics research. They can sponsor research workshops, seminars, institutes, and symposia for improvement of the content and nature of the research and for the development of better research methods and techniques. Two good examples will document this point. The Farm Foundation has sponsored many land tenure and land economics research workshops and institutes. Resources for the Future and the Farm Foundation supplied the out-of-pocket financing for the symposium which resulted in this volume. These activities for the improvement of land economics research probably would not have been undertaken except for the assistance of these two private foundations.

More effective co-operation in land economics research probably does not call for reorganization of either public agencies or private groups. The co-operation needed is largely an administrative matter. Although the problems of co-ordination are many, the work can be accomplished effectively within the present organizational structure through administrative action. Both public and private agencies should explore carefully opportunities for working together. Frequently, co-operative action can be much more effective than individual action.

ROLE OF REGIONAL GROUPS IN RESEARCH

During the last two decades, regional research has emerged and developed rapidly. Perhaps the three oldest regional groups interested in research are the New England Research Council and the Southwest and North Central Land Tenure Research Committees. The experience of these three regional groups served as a basis for projecting the regional research program sponsored by the U. S. Department of Agriculture and co-operating states. The New England Council was organized by the parties involved, while the Land Tenure Committees were brought together by the Farm Foundation.

The need for regional co-operation had been felt for some time. The felt need grew out of obvious duplication of effort. All states in a region do not need to conduct research on the same problem, for neither the nature of some problems nor their solution are related to state lines or other civil subdivisions. Regional co-operation also grew out of the nature of the research activity. Many researchers felt the need of discussing phases of their research with their colleagues across state lines. They were concerned with questions such as: What are the crucial problems? How can the problem best be stated? What theory is relevant? What analytical tools are likely to be most effective?

Research by regional groups is growing very rapidly. Its chief advantage is the division of labor among a number of people with different training. It enables experts on different phases of the research to work together, and it results in better research than most of them could do individually. It is particularly useful for that type of research which requires much fact gathering. The pooling of resources is a major advantage of regional research.

The effectiveness of regional research depends in large part upon the efficiency with which the details of co-ordination are handled. Individual and group roles have to be clearly defined. All personnel must understand the implications of working together. Sometimes several meetings are necessary before the group builds up mutual confidence, tolerance, and understanding.

The will to co-operate must be fortified strongly by an organizational

268

mechanism to facilitate such co-operation. The organizational structure
and administrative machinery for regional research can be cumbersome
and stifling. All regional projects have to fit into the same mold.
Formulation of project statements demands an inordinate amount of
time; and frequent revisions are necessary. Numerous reports are
required. Money is made available on an annual basis, which is much too
short a period for effective planning. The project leader or the executive
group frequently does not have sufficient time to administer the study
properly. The experience with regional research is sufficiently long and
varied to permit a forthright analysis of the entire process to point up
aspects that need strengthening.

Some of the benefits that have resulted from regional research are
elimination of unnecessary duplication, development of improved techniques and procedures, integration of small studies into larger, more
meaningful undertakings, and professional stimulation and growth among
the co-operators.

RESEARCH GAPS AND ORGANIZATIONAL STRUCTURE

An over-all review of land economics research reveals certain gaps
or unresearched areas. Consideration should be given to whether the
organization of research has tended to cause and to maintain such gaps.
Does the organizational structure tend to overemphasize research in one
area to the neglect of other equally important subject matter? Does it
put so much stress on immediate results for practical application that
progress is inhibited in areas where basic research is sorely needed and
is the key requirement? Does the structure of the educational system
provide better trained researchers in some other areas than in land
economics? Does the organizational structure provide any systematic
means of pointing out areas needing research? Any impediments that
prevent the closing of gaps should be identified and removed.

One aspect of the organizational structure and of the administrative
procedure that undoubtedly needs improvement is communication. We
have made much progress in communicating the results of research to
potential users, but we have given little attention to communication among
research workers. Sometimes administration seems to have hampered
communication among scholars. Better means need to be established for
communication among the land-grant colleges and universities, government agencies at all levels, and private organizations including industry.
Such interchange will result in fuller use of available knowledge and
better evaluation of new methods and techniques. The aim should be to
achieve higher standards of performance and more effective use of available research resources. Communication is particularly important when
new research is being planned.

A relatively recent development for communication in land economics
research is the Interregional Land Tenure Research Committee, formed
by the four regional land tenure research committees sponsored by the
Farm Foundation. The interregional group is composed of one representative from each of the four regional committees, representatives of the
U. S. Department of Agriculture, and officials of the Farm Foundation.
Its chief function is to co-ordinate the activities of the four committees

through facilitating communication. For example, it prepared a report in 1955 reappraising the scope and nature of land tenure research and outlining areas of needed research. This report has provided guidance and direction for research in the four regions during the past seven years. Currently the report is being revised to bring the reappraisal up to date.

A gap in research that needs attention is the place of the family farm in American agriculture. The economic and social problems with which it must deal are becoming more complex each year. These extend beyond the borders of the individual farm; they are interwoven with the life of the entire community. The family farm is likely to be neglected because it is of national concern, not just local, state, or regional. Also, its problems and possible lines of remedial action are not only economic; they are social, psychological, and political. Is it possible that the way research is organized causes researchers to overlook or to shy away from such important matters?

Another characteristic of the present research organizational-administrative situation that may cause serious gaps in land economics research is the tendency toward specialization. On the one hand, it has become increasingly necessary to concentrate on a limited area to accomplish stated objectives and to attain recognition. On the other hand, it has become increasingly important to look at agricultural problems in their broadest context. Because the subject matter of economics has been divided and subdivided to attain the desired specialization, it is tending to lose its essential integration.

An endeavor has been made to bridge existing gaps through co-operation within disciplines, between disciplines, and across disciplinary lines. Interdisciplinary research is often necessary to study problems in their larger setting. This is particularly true of land economics problems because of their inherent characteristics. For example, problems of the ownership and control of land have economic, sociological, management, legal, and policy implications. Such problems cannot be adequately solved without the advice and counsel of experts in disciplines outside land economics The attainment of such interdisciplinary integration is partially a matter of organization and partially a matter of administration.

In recent years legal-economic interdisciplinary research has been developed in several states. Such interdisciplinary co-operation has been formalized, for example, in the Agricultural Law Center at the State University of Iowa. This Center, in co-operation with the North Central Land Tenure Research Committee, has given impetus to interdisciplinary research throughout the North Central region. Interdisciplinary, inter-institutional, and interstate research has been conducted particularly on installment land contracts and water rights. This experience may point the way to new organizational structure and administrative changes that may well be adapted to regional and even national research. Accomplishment along this line may be as significant as the earlier contributions to regional research that flowed from the experience of the original New England Council and the early Southwest and North Central Committees.

SOME CONCLUDING REMARKS

Organizational structures and administrative procedures develop and become established in much the same manner as do research methods and techniques. Land economics researchers have held many workshops, symposia, and institutes to improve the content and methods of their research. They have given little attention, however, to organizational-administrative matters. In fact, this is probably the first endeavor to deal with organization and administration as they relate to land economics. Thus, if this treatment seems somewhat sketchy, it is due to lack of experience in dealing with the subject matter. But it will serve as a start, and possibly many minds working over a period of time will produce the desired adjustments.

Co-operation between those who administer research and those who perform the job should be strengthened. This can be done through daily contact. But frequently such contact becomes personalized and ineffectual. More satisfying results might well be attained if a major symposium were organized on the subject. In any event, the parties concerned should study the organizational-administrative problem to the end that the entire structure may meet more adequately the needs of the researcher.

Looking to the future, land economics research will play an increasingly important role in the control and use of our land and water resources. Conventional emphasis upon the strictly agricultural aspects will go by the board, for rural and urban land problems are becoming more closely interrelated and integrated, as is our entire economy. Some of the old lines of demarcation will disappear, others will become blurred. Land economics researchers of the future will need an even more favorable climate in which to work than in the past. Attention will need to be focused on how the research structure is organized and how the work is administered as surely as it will on the content of research and its analytical procedures. The demands of the future will command our best effort on both fronts.